SUPER
FAMILY
VACATIONS

SUPER FAMILY VACATIONS

THIRD EDITION

MARTHA SHIRK AND NANCY KLEPPER

HarperPerennial

A Division of HarperCollins*Publishers*

HarperCollins books may be purchased for educational, business, or sales promotional use. For information, please call or write: Special Markets Department, HarperCollins Publishers, Inc., 10 East 53rd Street, New York, NY 10022.

FIRST HARPERPERENNIAL EDITION

DESIGNED BY NANCY SINGER

Library of Congress Cataloging-in-Publication Data

Shirk, Martha

Super family vacations : resort and adventure guide / Martha Shirk and Nancy Klepper. — 3rd ed.

p. cm.

Includes index.

ISBN 0-06-273330-3

1. North America—Guidebooks. 2. Family recreation—North America—Guidebooks. 3. Resorts—North America—Guidebooks. 4. United States—Guidebooks. 5. Family recreation—United States—Guidebooks. 6. Resorts—United States—Guidebooks. 7. Caribbean Area—Guidebooks. 8. Family recreation—Caribbean Area—Guidebooks. 9. Resorts—Caribbean Area—Guidebooks. I. Klepper, Nancy. II. Title.

E41.S48 1995
917.04'539—dc20

98 ❖/RRD 10 9 8

To my favorite traveling companions—William, Tom, Bennett, and Peter Woo

M.S.

To my parents, who instilled in me a curiosity about the larger world, and to my lifelong traveling companions, Bob and Adam Klepper

N.K.

CONTENTS

RESORTS

SOUTHEAST

MIDWEST

WEST COAST AND HAWAII

SKI AREAS

NORTHEAST

SOUTHWEST AND MOUNTAIN STATES

HISTORY PLACES

ADVENTURE TRIPS

NORTHEAST

SOUTHEAST

NATURE PLACES

ACKNOWLEDGMENTS

Our deepest debt is to our families, whose zest for travel inspired the book and whose support enabled us to complete it. William, Tom, Bennett and Peter Woo and Bob and Adam Klepper cheerfully accompanied us on most of our trips and helped us to experience travel under the same circumstances that our readers will.

The book also would not have been possible without the competent assistance of our researchers: Cindy Bechtel, Joan Bray, Barbara Buchholz, Abby Cohn, Patricia Corrigan, Robert Duffy, Linda Eardley, Margaret Wolf Freivogel, Terry Ganey, Jody Gaylin, Lori Kesler, Mary Ellen Noonan Koenig, Martha Kohl, Seena Kohl, Phyllis Brasch Librach, Joan Little, Michael Lloyd, Marjorie Mandel, Jo Mannies, Geoffrey O'Gara, Jan Paul, Miriam Pepper, Deborah Peterson, Alice Powers, Gail Ruwe, Kem Knapp Sawyer, Meg Selig, Dale Singer, Tom Stites, Richard Weiss, and David Wilson. Among them they have 71 children. Michael Crawley cheerfully helped out with computer problems.

SUPER
FAMILY
VACATIONS

SUCCESSFUL FAMILY VACATIONS

ARE THEY REALLY POSSIBLE?

We've all had them—family vacations that were more work than fun, outings that were a disaster from start to finish, grand trips that proved that there's such a thing as too much togetherness. When you wake up one morning in the middle of an expensive vacation and realize that you'd rather be at home, you know that sor ething's wrong with the way you planned your family's vacation.

It doesn't have to be that way.

We know from experience. Both of us became parents long after we had developed strong vacation preferences. Suddenly, with children on the scene, our tried-and-true vacation formulas no longer worked. No more romantic weekends at country inns bursting with antiques. No more exhilarating treks into the Himalayas. No more exciting big-city vacations. No more relaxing weeks at hideaways on Caribbean islands where disposable diapers are unheard of. The prospect of undertaking one of these trips with a child in tow was daunting.

But we didn't want to stay at home. We realized that vacationing successfully with children would necessarily be different from traveling alone or as a twosome, but we were sure that it was not impossible. However, when we began looking for travel books that would guide us to appropriate places, we found none that met our needs. So we decided to write one—a book by families and for families, one that could serve as a guide for new parents, experienced parents, grandparents, and single parents.

We believe that the key to successful family vacations is planning—and that means choosing a destination that's right for every member of your family. We think that the best places for families to vacation are those that offer something for everyone—for instance, tennis and golf for Mom and Dad, if they're so inclined; counselors and organized activities for the kids, with plenty of other kids around; and a selection of activities that the whole family can enjoy together. Most of the places and vacation ideas that we feature in this book meet all these criteria. Some are strong on organized activities; some leave you alone to enjoy yourself at your own pace. Some are on the edge of big, bustling cities, with plenty of sightseeing opportunities; others are isolated. Some emphasize relaxation, others adventure. All are places where families, including our own, regularly have good times.

HOW THIS BOOK IS ORGANIZED

In this third edition of Super Family Vacations, you'll find vacation ideas ranging from a few grand old resorts—the famous places that your great-grandparents may have visited—to modern beachside or mountain hideaways, guest ranches, cruise ships, and ski areas. There are "history places" that give children a glimpse into their ancestors' lives, adventure trips that provide thrills in the beautiful outdoors, and special nature-oriented places, where vacations are learning experiences. In this edition, we concentrated on finding some great new family-oriented vacation destinations that are little-known—and some unusual and little-publicized activities to take part in at places that are well known, like the greatest national parks in the United States. We offer destinations in every region of the continental United States, as well as Alaska, Hawaii, Canada, Bermuda, Mexico and the Caribbean. There's probably a place just two hours from your home—and many farther away.

All of the places we feature have actually been visited by one of us or one of our researchers, almost always with children along. In fact, we visited many more places than we feature here. Those that weren't appropriate for families—or that were on the margin—aren't included.

We've had a lot of fun researching this book. We've learned a lot about how to travel with kids—and how not to. Our children are now seasoned travelers, conversant in the advantages of one organized children's program over another, on friendly terms with Mother Nature, at ease on the ski slopes, on a sailboat, or on a horse. The experience has broadened their horizons, and ours. For why travel with children unless you're going to take some time to see the world as they do? It's certainly easier to leave them at home. But if they weren't with you, you might not notice the shooting stars in the western sky, the multicolored stones at the bottom of the river you're rafting, the parrot in the hotel lobby, the buttons on the shoes of the woman who's making apple butter in the pioneer village.

For ease of use, we have divided our recommendations into seven different categories: destination resorts, guest ranches, ski areas, history places, cruise ships, adventure trips, and nature places. Within each category except cruise ships, we have grouped destinations by region, usually beginning on the East Coast and moving across the country.

RESORTS

Resort vacations are just about the easiest family vacations imaginable. It's for good reasons that the term "destination resorts" entered the travel industry's vocabulary in the mid-1970s. This type of resort—44 of which are featured—has become a destination in itself. Many people choose a resort without caring about what city it's near.

At a well-run full-service resort, you are likely to find every activity imaginable, comfortable accommodations, conveniently situated facilities, a choice of eating spots, impeccable service, and an atmosphere that is conducive to having a good time.

At most of the resorts we feature, you will also find well-supervised children's programs. The ready-made playmates a children's program provides guarantees that your children will have a good time on vacation and that you will have some time to yourself to enjoy adult activities. Even if you regard your family vacation as the one time you have all year to devote to each other, you'll appreciate the availability of a stimulating program in which you can place your children for just a few hours a day. For there's little point in going to a resort with a world-class golf course or round-the-clock tennis facilities if there's no one to take care of your young children so that you can play.

The nation's grand old resorts pioneered the concept of children's programs, and in recent years such programs have become a fixture at most new full-service resorts as well. The programs range from an hour or two of supervised play daily to full-fledged day camps. Some offer supervised children's dinners (followed by cartoons or games) so that parents can have a night out by themselves. Some are free to guests, and others charge a fee that can easily equal the cost of quality day care at home. Some allow drop-ins, and others require advance reservations when you book your room.

Most of the resorts also offer a variety of activities that the whole family can enjoy together, from cookouts to guided nature walks to rental bikes (in all sizes) to organized games.

Our recommendations include resorts where everything is included in the price you pay before you go, and resorts where everything is extra; resorts that are isolated, and others that are on the edge of exciting cities; resorts that are sedate and refined, and a few that are on the wild side. At one you fly on a trapeze, at others take a balloon ride, at some others play golf on five courses.

Probably the most important thing to consider when you select a resort for a family destination is whether it will feel right for your family. If you like to show up for dinner in shorts and sandals, then one of the sedate grand old resorts is probably not for you.

How much you want to be pampered should also be a consideration. If your idea of a vacation is no cooking, then you might consider one where meals are included in the room rate. If, on the other hand, you like to make breakfast and lunch yourselves and splurge on dinner, then look for a resort whose accommodations are equipped with kitchens (the room rate may be higher, but you'll save on food).

Many of the resorts we feature are truly national in appeal.

Around the pool, you'll find guests from nearly every state, and even some foreign countries. But some are strictly regional in their draw, for reasons either of remoteness or strong regional flavor.

We have also tried to include resorts in every price range; obviously, the less expensive ones won't have the range of amenities and the quality of facilities that the more expensive ones have, but all provide a quality family vacation experience. And even if your vacation budget is modest, it is possible to vacation at some of the more expensive resorts if you go in the off-season or aggressively seek information from management about cost-saving packages. The Caribbean resorts, for instance, are real bargains in the summer months, when the beaches are just as beautiful and the atmosphere just as exotic as in the higher-priced winter season.

GUEST RANCHES

Your wake-up call is likely to be the sound of 200 hooves pounding a hard-packed dirt trail as the horses make their way from their overnight pasture to their corral. Your days will be filled with opportunities to appreciate the joys of nature—on horseback, or on foot, or from a lounge chair by the swimming pool. Your meals will be hearty, the coffee as good as any you've ever tasted. And when you crawl wearily into a bunk bed made from lodge-pole pines, every muscle aching from the strain of your first horseback ride, you'll wonder why you never took a ranch vacation before.

If you've put off going to a guest ranch because you have no interest in horses, reconsider. Today's guest ranches offer far more than riding. All of the ranches we feature offer other activities, ranging from naturalist-guided walks to tennis, golf, fishing, swimming, panning for gold, hayrides, trap shooting, white-water rafting, back-country jeep expeditions, aerobics classes, and side trips to such nearby attractions as Yellowstone or Rocky Mountain national parks. For children, there are overnight camp-outs, nature-oriented arts and crafts, well-designed play areas, pizza-making parties (with cast-iron stoves), animal spotting, and pony rides. Besides all the planned activities, there are plenty of opportunities for serendipitous happenings—like sighting a moose or a shooting star.

And, of course, there's the riding. Even if you've never been on a horse before, all of the ranches we recommend will do their best to make an accomplished and enthusiastic rider out of you. Don't let your fears keep you from a great experience. The back of a horse offers one of the best vantage points for viewing the splendors of the West, where most guest ranches are located.

A week at a western guest ranch will give your children a glimpse into the past. They'll get a sense, maybe for the first time, of the rigors the pioneers experienced as they crossed rugged mountains and sprawling plains to reach their goal. And few children finish a week at a guest ranch without a new appreciation for nature, since it seems so much more accessible than at home. There must be shooting stars in the night sky in urban areas, but you're not as likely to notice them as when you're sitting around a camp fire.

Many of the families we encountered at the 11 ranches we include had been going there for years. That is typical of families who get bitten by the ranch bug: once they find one they like, they return year after year. They're treated by their hosts as family. And they, in turn, welcome new guests into the family. Many ranch guests make arrangements even before their vacation ends to return during the same week the next year to repeat their experience.

Tips to Make Your Trip More Enjoyable

- Your child's ranch experience will be enriched if you first read a few books about the West together.
- Some children may be disappointed at first by the absence of television, radios, and video games. If you explain that you're going to experience life as it was "in the olden days," most young children will be charmed. They will soon find the horses and other animals in residence at the ranch a more-than-adequate substitute.

• Before you arrive, most ranches will send you a letter advising you about what to bring. Take the advice about warm clothes seriously, since it can be quite chilly in the mountains at night. At almost every ranch, blue jeans and a few flannel shirts are all you'll need to be dressed appropriately. Some have one dress-up night a week, but all that need mean is that you put on a fresh pair of jeans. Rain gear is important.

• Riding boots are strongly recommended for vacationers who plan to ride horses. It's possible to ride a horse wearing sneakers or Topsiders, but it's much more difficult and not as safe. Buy boots early enough to break them in. And sturdy walking shoes are advised if you plan to do any serious hiking.

• If you have an infant or toddler, choose your ranch destination carefully. Unless the ranch offers child care, you'll find yourself tied down by a child who's under 6. Some ranches are better than others at arranging baby-sitting for very young children. Talk to the ranch management about how welcome young children really are. Some will allow you to bring a baby-sitter for free.

• The weekly rates at ranches are high. But before you reject a ranch vacation as too expensive, consider all that the weekly rate includes. By figuring out what your family is likely to spend at a resort on à la carte meals, a room, and sports activities, you may find that your total expenses are no more at a ranch.

• Be sure to budget money for tips to ranchhands. Rather than levy a service charge, most ranches maintain a tip pool that is divided among ranch staffers at the end of the season. Ranch managers say that most guests tip 12 to 15 percent of their total bills.

SKI AREAS

No matter how great a thrill you get from schussing down an expert slope by yourself, it can't equal the joy that comes from watching your toddler make his or her first complete run down a beginner's slope, even if the skis are in a rigid wedge shape and the poles akimbo. Or the special kinship you'll feel when your 10-year-old says, "Hey, Mom, how about a run down with me?" Or that burst of pride that will overcome you as you watch your teenager conquering slopes that you wouldn't dare set ski on.

Skiing with children is one of the all-time great winter pastimes. It provides one of the few opportunities for extended outdoor activity during the winter months—amidst scenery that is inevitably majestic. And child development specialists agree that it's a terrific way for children to build self-esteem. Because it's an individual sport, there's no competition, except with one's fears and misgivings. It's a rare child who doesn't make steady progress on the slopes and take great pride in a successful run. And fortunately for once- or twice-a-year skiers, skiing is something like riding a bicycle; once you've mastered the basics, you'll never forget.

Luckily for parents, ski areas have focused their marketing incentives on families in recent years out of sheer necessity: the population on which they have traditionally counted for business, singles and childless couples between 18 and 34, is diminishing in size. Families are their best hope for future growth, and that realization is to your benefit. Today, families will find plenty of family-oriented restaurants, full nursery and child-care facilities, and excellent children's ski instruction programs at scores of ski areas throughout the nation.

For the non-skiers in the family, a full array of indoor activities is usually available, from sitting by a cozy fire and watching the activity on the slopes, to taking classes in cooking or pottery, to spending the day at a spa or health club, to playing in well-equipped playrooms with one's peers. Most full-service Alpine ski areas today offer groomed cross-country trails as well.

How to choose from among the 600-odd ski areas in 39 states? Obviously, proximity is a compelling factor. If you live in western Kansas, you're not likely to head to New England to ski; Colorado is all too close, and attractive besides. If you live in the Northeast, that's going to be the least expensive place to ski. Plan your family ski vacation for midweek if possible. The ski area that is packed to the tree line on weekends is likely to be gloriously deserted in midweek.

We feature 28 ski resorts that hold special appeal for families. We've included a few in Canada that, besides providing great skiing, offer Americans the experience of a family vacation in a foreign country.

All the successful ski areas today offer families a range of accommodations, from cozy rustic lodges, where meals are included in the rate, to budget-priced motel rooms, to modern condominiums, with all the comforts of home.

Lodges usually provide a congenial après-ski experience, with communal meals (no cooking chores for Mom or Dad), game rooms or TV lounges for the kids, and plenty of opportunities to gather around a fireplace with like-minded people and trade stories about successful runs. Motels provide attractive rates, but the benefits may be lost at the cash registers in the restaurants you'll have to frequent. Condominiums provide spaciousness—and their kitchens promise freedom from trying scenes with small children in restaurants. There are advantages and disadvantages to each option.

Distance from the slopes is a factor you'll want to consider before deciding where to stay. While ski-in-ski-out accommodations are great for expert skiers, they won't be worth the added cost if you've got an 11-month-old you've first got to deposit in the nursery or a 5-year-old who doesn't have the strength to manage the shuffle to the ski school. Most ski areas these days operate shuttle buses that enable you to leave your car in the condominium parking lot.

A Note About Equipment and Clothing

Whether to buy your children's equipment or rent it is another choice you'll have to make. Most experts believe that children should have their own equipment if they are going to ski regularly. But if your family is going to ski together only once or twice a year, the cost of buying equipment is prohibitive. Most ski areas today have large stocks of children's ski equipment and can be expected to outfit your child appropriately and comfortably. Indeed, for a child who is growing, rented equipment may fit better than personally owned equipment that he or she is in the process of outgrowing.

What you wear may be the single most important decision you make during your entire ski holiday, for a cold skier is an unhappy skier. Forget style and dwell instead on comfort. Warmth and ease of movement should be the watchwords for your family's wardrobe. Layering is the way to easily achieve both warmth and comfort, since thin layers trap warm air and can easily be shed as the day warms up. Bib pants are an excellent choice for children, complemented with a water-repellent ski jacket. A wool hat is de rigueur, as are good warm mittens, preferably with nylon outer covers and insulation. And a turtleneck shirt will prove more useful than a scarf in warming a child's neck (there are no loose ends to get caught in chair-lift bars or on trees).

What About Ski Schools?

Experts, without exception, recommend professional lessons for both children and adults—and not just because they're trying to keep their classes full. Remember trying to teach your 4-year-old the Australian crawl? Remember the first time you got in a car with your 16-year-old behind the wheel? Remember the frustration and awkwardness you yourself felt when you first put on skis? Eliminate an inevitably stressful situation by enrolling your child, whatever his or her age, in ski school.

Professional ski instruction is offered beginning at age 3 at most ski areas, although for the very youngest in that age group the instruction can best be characterized as snow play on skis. Many experts believe that age 5 is the best time to start children on skis. Most 5-year-olds have sufficient agility, self-confidence, and a sense of daring to enjoy the challenge. After a ski week at a well-run resort, many 5-year-olds will be ready to ski an intermediate slope.

Ski Areas in the Summer?

Ski areas make marvelous summer destinations. Many operate as four-season resorts, and offer attractive price structures and a full array of recreational activities to attract summer guests. They've already got the scenery going for them. That mountain you skied down last winter looks entirely different when covered with wildflowers in the summer. Consider visiting your favorite ski resort in the summer and take advantage of the extremely low rates. (But make sure first that it has something to offer besides cheap accommodations. There's nothing more depressing than a ski area in the summer if you're the only guests and there is nothing special to do.)

HISTORY PLACES

Children have a natural curiosity about the past. And creative parents constantly encourage it when they talk with their children about their own childhoods and the childhoods of their grandparents.

Whole new types of history museums have developed in recent years that can be the focus of an enriching family vacation. Visitors to some simply observe the past; in others, whole families can role play and pretend they are living 100 years ago. It's history in the first person, and it's a marvelous family vacation idea.

We have included 13 wonderful history places around the country (and Mexico) that really bring history to life for family visitors. Each does a wonderful job of explaining what life was really like in the past and of telling us about values, beliefs, attitudes, and the way people really lived. What was school like? How did parents treat their children? What did children do for entertainment before TV?

History places re-create or restore a real place where real people once lived; they do away with museum buildings and put visitors on a farm as it would have appeared a century or two ago, or in the streets of an authentic period town. Interpreters dress in period clothing to demonstrate crafts and describe how people lived. The emphasis is on the mechanics of producing necessities such as food, brooms, cloth, and pottery, often by hand. Watching a person handle a plow behind a team of oxen—or better yet, struggling with the plow yourself—gives real meaning to the nature of farm work 100 or more years ago. Try spinning yarn to put a shopping spree at the local mall in perspective.

Tips to Make Your Trip More Enjoyable

- Children must have a sense of history before they can relate well to history place experiences. They normally develop this capability at about 8 years of age. History places are not appropriate for younger children, who will lose interest rapidly, particularly if they are required to be observers and not participants.
- Be sure to prepare your family a little before you go. Do some reading. Talk about what life might have been like in the past and what you might expect to see and do at the museum.

CRUISES

Cruises make wonderful family vacations. They offer families a complete break from routine and an escape into a fantasyland that has appeal to adults and children alike. Special children's rates—and the all-inclusive policies of most cruise lines—make taking a cruise comparable in price to staying at a 4-star resort.

According to the Cruise Lines International Association, most of its 35-member lines now offer organized children's programs, under the supervision of trained youth counselors, to lure families. These vary from an hour of organized children's games daily to a breakfast-to-bedtime snack program that can occupy all of your child's waking hours. The facilities used for children's activities can vary from a corner of an underutilized nightclub to a fully equipped children's playroom and nursery.

Among the attractions for children on the most family-oriented ships are special "nightclubs" for teenagers, wading pools for toddlers, libraries stocked with children's books and magazines, trained nannies, special shore excursions for children, cinemas that show cartoons and first-run family films, computer learning centers, video arcades, and collections of toys that rival those of the best-equipped day-care centers. Some lines bring along special kids' entertainers, such as magicians, puppeteers, and adults who dress as Mickey Mouse and Donald Duck. The kind of supervised events you can expect include scavenger hunts, limbo contests, aerobics and dance classes, visits to the captain's bridge, costume parties, ice-cream sundae and pizza-making parties, and sports competitions. And for preschool-aged children, group baby-sitting is usually offers. Private baby-sitting by off-duty social staff members can sometimes be arranged.

Then there are the inherent attractions of the cruise experience itself. What 5-year-old wouldn't be intrigued by all the nooks and crannies in a typical stateroom, small though it is? What 8-year-old wouldn't be captivated by a visit to the captain's bridge, with an opportunity to steer a massive ocean liner? What 10-year-old wouldn't revel in the freedom to explore the ship's public rooms in the company of some new chums? What teenager wouldn't swoon over the opportunity to stay up later than usual and dance to a live band with some new friends of the opposite sex?

A cruise can literally broaden your family's horizons, for the world looks entirely different from the deck of a ship than from land. Your seventh-grader might finally understand why Columbus shocked the world with his notion that the world was round, because it truly looks flat at sea. As you watch dolphins or even whales follow your ship's path across the sea, your children will get a deeper understanding of the separate world beneath the surface. And the scene in the harbor, with tugboats guiding your ship to its berth and local residents waving from the shore, is one so chock-full of excitement that only the most jaded child could remain unexcited.

In our section on cruises, we describe five cruise lines, with a total of 32 ships, that will appeal to offer families with children of all ages. Before you book passage, grill your travel agent about how appropriate a particular ship is for families with children the age of yours. Ask for a sample schedule of children's activities (that will give you an idea of how comprehensive the children's program is). And reserve special equipment, such as a crib, high chair, or refrigerator, in advance.

Ports of Call

One of the least attractive aspects of cruising is the vision of hundreds of ship passengers being disgorged all at once on the dock in a Caribbean harbor before they head off to the duty-free section of town, ignoring any evidence of local culture or tropical flora along the way. Small wonder that some residents of these ports treat cruise passengers as though they were merely walking opportunities to make some money. For many cruise passengers, the ports of call seem almost incidental; some don't even disembark, and many who do simply wander from one shop to another, inspecting the same duty-free merchandise that they've looked at in previous ports.

But with some advance planning, you can make the ports of call an adventure for your family. Make your way to the local office of the port's tourist information service (better still, write for information in advance) and find out what easily accessible attractions will appeal to children—a nice stretch of beach with gentle waves, a history museum, a local cultural center, a zoo.

But don't delude yourself that you're going to learn much about the country you're visiting. Few ships stay in a particular port longer than 12 hours, which is barely enough time for a visitor to get his or her bearings in the harbor area. This doesn't seem to bother many cruise passengers, for whom one country's straw basket is as good as another. But if you have a genuine interest in foreign cultures, you're bound to be disappointed with how little you get to experience them. Look at your port outings, instead, as an opportunity to try a small sample of the local culture—and if it appeals to you, vow to come back for more.

Tips to Make Your Trip More Enjoyable

- Although many families avoid cruises because of fear of a mishap at sea, it is virtually impossible for someone to fall off a ship's deck inadvertently. After warning him about the hazards of climbing on the deck's fence or going into forbidden areas, you can give a mature 8-year-old the run of any ship without too much worry. Just make sure he knows where to find you—and that you always have an agreed-upon time and place to meet.

- Most ships have two seatings for meals. The earlier one is the best bet for families because at the later one the crowd tends to be older, and dressier clothes are expected. You'll find the servers on the ships we describe friendly to children and eager to accommodate your special needs. Ask to be seated alone or at a table with another family whose children are similar in age.

- A short cruise, three or four days in length, is the best bet for families with preschool-aged children, and a good way for any family to sample cruise life and find out whether it's appealing. Some people bring babies on cruises, but we don't advise it. We've seen too many bedraggled parents walking the narrow corridors of ships in the wee hours of the night with their unhappy babies.

- Talk to your pediatrician in advance about whether to give your children medication to prevent motion sickness. Seasickness is a real possibility for children, who seem less able to tolerate a ship's motion than adults.

- Don't hesitate to ask your cabin steward to do whatever he can to make life easier for you. He'll be happy to provide endless supplies of ice for cooling children's juices, fresh fruit for toddlers, extra pillows and blankets, and anything else you need.

- Take the cruise line's tipping suggestions seriously. On most lines, cabin stewards, waiters, and busboys are paid abysmally poor wages, and really do rely on tips to earn a living wage. Don't try to save money on your vacation by shortchanging them.

ADVENTURE TRIPS

Family adventure trips can provide some of the most satisfying vacation experiences—closely shared family activities in settings of beauty and grandeur, the joy of living close to nature, the self-satisfaction that comes with learning a new skill. But it is important to understand what makes family adventure vacations work.

Nature is equally fascinating for adults and children, but the participation goes on at different levels. Parents see majestic mountains; young children see colorful rocks and interesting insects. Young children just don't see what we see. And we are often blind to their perceptions until we stop, observe, understand, and share them. If the stops on a gravel bar are frequent and long, your young child will not enjoy the raft trip, no matter how beautiful the scenery. Your indifferent teenager may not lift an eye to the canyon walls, but come alive only when the raft drops into a hole in the rapid and snowmelt water floods the boat.

Outdoor adventures are great family trips when family members can participate at their own levels and, at the same time, share the experience. The only mistake you can make in choosing an outdoor trip is to fail to adequately consider the needs and interests of every family member.

This book describes 11 outdoor adventure trips that will please many families—canoeing, hiking, rafting, camping, sailing, and even exploring the famed Galapagos Islands by yacht.

Outdoor adventures are a lot more enjoyable when other families and children are in the group. Ask the outfitter if other families are joining the trip you are considering.

NATURE PLACES

If your family wants an outdoors-oriented vacation, several considerations might steer you toward a nature place rather than an adventure trip. One is comfort. A family that wants to enjoy nature but still enjoy creature comforts will choose a nature place over an adventure trip for an outdoor family vacation. Nature places allow families to be out in nature by day and "home" in their snug rooms by night.

The lower physical demands and greater creature comforts of nature places make them a better choice than adventure trips for families with young children. For the same reasons, nature places might be ideal for an intergenerational family get-together where grandparents, parents, and children unite for some time together in a wonderful natural setting.

The organized learning component is a second compelling reason for choosing a nature place. Most of the 19 nature places we describe have professional naturalists and ecologists on staff. Their program offerings usually vary in intensity, allowing you to choose casual introductions to nature or more serious experiences. Several offer the opportunity to earn college credit in special study programs during your stay.

Tips to Make Your Trip More Enjoyable

- Preparation is important, not only for your children but also for you. Anticipating how other family members will react helps you react (or refrain from reacting) when the moment of truth—the first rapid, or the first 45-degree hillside, or the first swarm of yellowjackets—arrives.
- If a bit of hiking is involved and your young children have never been on a hike, take them to the local park and try it out. Discover how fast they move when left to set their own pace. How do they react to being pushed along a bit? What interests them? Consider the skills that would enhance the experience for family members.
- If your child will have the opportunity to snorkel on a tropical reef for the first time, get a mask and snorkel and experiment in the bathtub and in the local swimming pool before leaving home.
- Go to your library or a bookstore and find some books that relate to the upcoming adventure trip. Read to your younger children about the cultural and natural history of the area you will visit. Read about the skills you will use to paddle the canoe or guide a horse.

• Nothing contributes more to comfort in the out-of-doors than appropriate clothing and equipment. Heed recommendations from the outfitter or nature place staff, and don't cut corners. If the outfitter says bring a warm sleeping bag, you run a significant chance of suffering through long, cold nights if you bring that light summer bag that you already have stashed in the attic.

ABOUT RATES

Rates at vacation spots can change overnight, and the trend is usually upward. They do go down sometimes, if, for instance, there's a glut of hotel rooms in a particular area, or political unrest has scared off potential visitors, or a destination has suddenly and inexplicably become unfashionable. But the reality at most destination resorts and ranches is a 5 to 10 percent increase each year in both off-season and high-season rates.

Rather than list specific rates for each destination we discuss and risk being almost immediately out of date, we have instead created categories and assigned each place we discuss to a category, and to more than one if there's a wide range of rates. This will give you a rough idea of the cost for two adults and two children for a room without meals. Call the facility for current rates.

Here are the categories to which we have assigned the vacation destinations:

$ Inexpensive: Under $100 a day
$$ Moderate: $100 to $125 a day
$$$ Expensive: $125 to $185 a day
$$$$ Very expensive: Over $185 a day

Published rates are not always directly comparable, because some are all-inclusive, covering all meals and all activities, along with a room, and others are either American Plan (three meals), Modified American Plan (breakfast and dinner), or European Plan (no meals). For purposes of comparability, for ranches, cruiseships and American Plan resorts we have subtracted $50 a day per adult from their published daily rates to arrive at a basic room rate, even if a room-only rate is not available. In instances in which two meals a day are included, we have subtracted $35 per adult to arrive at a basic room rate.

For resorts, ranches, and cruise ships where many otherwise expensive recreational activities are covered by the basic rate (such as horseback riding, scuba diving, or greens fees), we have also subtracted an "activities allowance" of $25 a day per adult to arrive at a basic room rate.

Before you dismiss the cost of a cruise or a ranch vacation, for instance, as too high, consider their comparability to what seems on the surface to be a less expensive vacation—a week-long stay at a beachfront hotel, for instance. Consider all the amenities, services, and recreational opportunities that the basic rate for the cruiseship, ranch, or all-inclusive rate covers, and what it would cost you to pay for such extras at the hotel.

At some places, where there is a range of charges for accommodations, you will find a destination assigned to two categories, such as Moderate and Very Expensive. You can count on reduced rates during the low season at almost all destinations, but you might not find such amenities as organized children's activities then. When you inquire about current rates, be sure to ask about package plans and weekend rates that might provide more advantageous rates than the published nightly rate.

Happy Traveling!

RESORTS

NEW SEABURY CAPE COD
New Seabury, Massachusetts

No matter what you want from a vacation—a cozy villa with an ocean view, challenging and top-rated golf or tennis facilities, fine dining, quaint and historic attractions less than an hour away, or an enriching children's program—you can find it at New Seabury Cape Cod.

On the south shore of the Cape, between Falmouth and Hyannis, the sprawling 2,000-acre resort allows you to do as much, or as little, as you want.

The steady stream of traffic toward Cape Cod on summer weekends proves vacationers are attracted to the area like bargain hunters to Filene's Basement in Boston. The mixture of quaint New England charm and the seashore is irresistible.

As one admittedly biased employee of the resort put it, "Once you're here, there's no reason to leave if you don't want to." But if you do, all the attractions of the Cape Cod peninsula beckon.

ACCOMMODATIONS: $$$ The New Seabury complex, which celebrated its 25th anniversary in 1987, comprises 165 villas scattered around several "villages." Guests live in the comfort and convenience of homey surroundings with separate sleeping and living rooms, but they still receive the convenience of housekeeping services.

Maushop Village offers units that typify what the rest of the world thinks of as Cape Cod living. Right on Popponesset Beach, they were designed to recall 19th-century Nantucket cottages, with white picket fences and narrow, winding lanes. Maushop Village units are not air-conditioned, depending instead on ocean breezes for natural cooling. Contemporary California-style patio homes are available at another village, known as The Mews, where some units even have their own private swimming pools. Tidewatch Village, another waterfront area, is located between the greens of the complex's golf courses and the water of Nantucket Sound.

All villas have balconies or decks and fully- equipped kitchens, including utensils and table settings for 6. Many units include washers and dryers.

New Seabury is open from April through October. Rates are highest in summer, with bargains available in early June.

DINING: Only The Seabury restaurant is open year-round. In the summer, breakfast and lunch are available under the outdoor gazebo at the Marketplace Café (either eat-in or take-out). Several beachfront cafés serve soups and sandwiches so you never have to leave the waterfront area.

On summer evenings, families searching for a casual meal can eat at the Marketplace Café or in the lounge at Popponesset Inn. More elegant dining is available in the summer either at the Country Club or at the dining room at Popponesset Inn, featuring New England seafood, of course. Men are asked to wear jackets in the evening at the more formal restaurants.

The general store in the Popponesset Marketplace has basic supplies so that you can cook in your villa.

ACTIVITIES

 Sixteen courts; pro shop, instruction.

 Two challenging 18-hole golf courses. The Blue Championship course, surrounded by water in a spectacular setting, has been ranked as one of the top 100 in the nation by Golf Digest. The Green Challenger course is less demanding.

 In the Atlantic Ocean from three miles of pristine beach or in several attractive pools.

 Sailboat rentals, instruction.

 Rental bicycles (summer only) in a shop in the Popponesset Marketplace.

Hundreds of acres have been preserved in their natural state for wildlife refuges and hiking.

Room with Nautilus equipment, aerobics and aquatic exercise classes.

 New Seabury serves as the home for Summer Concerts by the Sea, a series of several concerts featuring conservatory bands, guitar duos, wind quartets, and soloists.

FOR CHILDREN: The Farley Outdoor Education Center, a private, not-for-profit organization owned by the Cape Cod 4-H Camp Corp., operates Camp New Seabury on the resort premises in July and August. Children must be signed up for a week; half-day or full day rates are available. The full day runs from 9 A.M. to 5 P.M.; the half day is from 9 A.M. to 12:30 P.M.

Four through 12-year-olds are divided into four groups for activities including arts and crafts, soccer, basketball, nature study, swimming lessons, biking, archery, canoeing, fishing, theater arts, dancing, tennis, rocketry and woodworking. Older children are sometimes taken to Camp Nan-Ke-Rafe, in nearby Brewster, to challenge themselves on a low ropes course.

Besides recreation, the aims of Camp New Seabury include helping children acquire problem-solving, communication, decision-making, coping and leadership skills.

Camp New Seabury is popular among children who live full-time in New Seabury or spend much of their summers there, so early reservations are advisable. Call (508) 477-0181.

Baby-sitting can be arranged through the resort office.

NICETIES: Some units have a guest book to sign, and reading the comments of others who have stayed there before you gives a nice sense of community that other, less personal resorts cannot match.

A "video tour" of New Seabury is offered daily in the executive offices to acquaint guests with all the resort has to offer.

OF INTEREST NEARBY: Cruises to Nantucket and Martha's Vineyard leave from both Falmouth and Hyannis, each about 10 to 15 miles away, and automobile ferry service is available from Woods Hole. Since the boat rides are about four hours round-trip, set aside a full day for each of the excursions. Advance reservations are advised.

The island of Martha's Vineyard is known as a paradise for

artists and photographers. There are tiny fishing villages to discover, old colonial homes in Edgartown, gingerbread cottages in Oak Bluffs, and breathtaking views, such as the colored clay cliffs of Gay Head. Wildlife refuges offer a pristine look at the island, including the state lobster hatchery at Oak Bluffs. Many special events take place on the island in the summer. Sightseeing is best done either by tour bus or by rental bicycles.

Nantucket Island is a former whaling port, complete with cobblestone streets and historic landmarks. Art galleries, restaurants, and shops are located in many of the old mansions on the island. You can tour Nantucket by bus, by bicycle, or on foot. Fishing, public beaches, and two public golf courses round out the activities.

Back on the Cape, less than an hour away by car, is Sandwich, on the northern coast. Children will enjoy the Yesteryears Doll and Miniature Museum, filled with historic dolls and dollhouses. The Sandwich Glass Museum displays exquisite examples of the area's glass artistry, and the Heritage Plantation is a 76-acre site featuring various crafts, a military museum, and restored automobiles, as well as gardens, nature trails, and a working mill. The plantation is open from 10 A.M. to 5 P.M. daily from mid-May to mid-October.

Whale-watching trips can be taken from Provincetown.

FOR MORE INFORMATION: Write New Seabury Cape Cod, Box 549, New Seabury, MA 02649, or call (800) 999-9033.

THE BALSAMS GRAND RESORT HOTEL
Dixville Notch, New Hampshire

At least once every four years, tiny Dixville Notch makes the news. Its 30 permanent residents are the first in the nation to vote in the presidential election. For the rest of the time, Dixville Notch is content to be known simply as home to one of New England's most prestigious resorts.

The Balsams has been a summer resort since 1866. It began with a clapboard inn and grew dramatically with a 1916 stucco addition. It is the addition, with its red tile roof, that gives the inn its European flavor. Add Lake Gloriette in the foreground and the towering White Mountains in the background, plus 15,000 acres of virtually undeveloped land, and it is obvious why The Balsams has the well-deserved nickname "The Switzerland of America."

Like most grand resort hotels, The Balsams had its heyday in the early part of this century, when guests came for the entire summer. Warren G. Harding, Franklin Roosevelt, and Will Rogers enjoyed the healthful New Hampshire air, golf, and leisurely formal dinners.

Today the hotel operates from late May through mid-October and mid-December through March at near capacity. Its historic buildings are being slowly and splendidly renovated and restored to their turn-of-the-century grandeur.

But it is more than excellent facilities that constitutes the secret of The Balsams' success. Their emphasis on service is obvious from the bottle of New Hampshire maple syrup that welcomes back each returning guest to the beautifully mani-cured garden with 30,000 flowers. As one of the owners notes, "We do not sell land, space, or time...The Balsams is one of the last hotels of this scale being run as a hotel catering solely to overnight guests."

ACCOMMODATIONS: $$$ to $$$$ The 232 rooms and suites at the Balsams are comfortable, clean, and cozy. They are New England simple, with painted Ethan Allen furniture, wall-to-wall carpeting, and beautiful views of either the lake or the moun-tains. Generous walk-in closets are a vestige of the time when most guests came for "the season." Even today, 40 percent of the guests come for 10 days or more.

Many of the rooms have fireplaces. Guest rooms don't have television sets. For diehard watchers, a large-screen television set is located off the main lobby.

The Balsams has four categories of rooms, ranging from stan-dard to deluxe. Children are charged $6 times their age per night, with a minimum charge of $24. Rates include all meals and activities.

DINING: The Balsams provides its guests with three meals daily. Every meal is an event. Cuisine is largely continental, with many New England specialities. Special dietary requirements can be accommodated.

Breakfast may be ordered from the menu or selected from a sumptuous buffet. The Balsams' luncheon buffet is renowned. Guests may choose from 10 hot dishes, 20 cold dishes, salads, cold cuts, fruits, breads, and 20 desserts arrayed on tables that stretch 100 feet across the dining room.

Dinner is the most formal meal of the day; jackets are required for men and dresses or fancy pants for women. Dinner offers a choice of eight entrées. Two or three special children's entrees are always offered.

For dinner, some parents order room service for their children (there's a nominal service charge) and enjoy a leisurely dinner alone.

ACTIVITIES

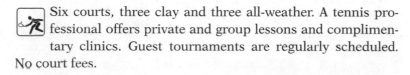 Six courts, three clay and three all-weather. A tennis professional offers private and group lessons and complimentary clinics. Guest tournaments are regularly scheduled. No court fees.

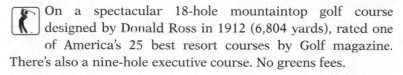 On a spectacular 18-hole mountaintop golf course designed by Donald Ross in 1912 (6,804 yards), rated one of America's 25 best resort courses by Golf magazine. There's also a nine-hole executive course. No greens fees.

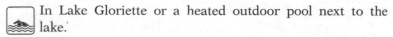 In Lake Gloriette or a heated outdoor pool next to the lake.

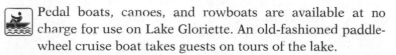 Pedal boats, canoes, and rowboats are available at no charge for use on Lake Gloriette. An old-fashioned paddlewheel cruise boat takes guests on tours of the lake.

In the lake. The hotel's kitchen will clean and cook your catch.

Hiking is a challenge in the White Mountains surrounding The Balsams; a naturalist guides walks. Guests have reported seeing moose, bear, and fox just a short distance from the hotel.

Shuffleboard and horseshoes; a game room with video games and a Ping-Pong table. The Balsams offers a lecture series to guests with topics ranging from "A Naked Eye Supernova in Our Lifetime" to "Yankee Humor." At night there are first-run movies and cabaret shows, dancing in the Switzerland of America Ballroom, a late-night piano bar in the Patio Garden Lounge, and a lively combo in the Wilderness Lounge.

Ice skating, snowshoeing. (Dixville Notch gets an average of 250 inches of snow a year).

 The Balsams Wilderness Ski Area, with 12 trails, bustles during the Balsams' four-month ski season; rentals available. For Nordic skiers, The Balsams has 70 kilometers of groomed trails; rental equipment available.

FOR CHILDREN: From July 4 through Labor Day, The Balsams operates a free comprehensive children's program called "Camp Wind Whistle." The program is staffed by three counselors, and usually serves 15 to 25 children, ages 5 to 13, daily.

The counselors meet the children at 9:30 at the children's playroom, 7 days a week, and organize a busy day of hiking, games, arts and crafts, swimming, and boating. The afternoon program ends at 4 P.M., but resumes at dinnertime, with activities available until about 9 P.M. Parents who want sitters can make arrangements through the front desk.

Every recreation area at The Balsams is extremely well supervised. Parents can feel confident letting their older children swim at the pool or the lake, under the watchful eye of lifeguards, or play on the playground.

For teenagers The Balsams offers "The Minor's Cave," off the main lobby. It's open Wednesday and Saturday nights and features rock videos, movies, music and refreshments.

During ski season, The Balsams has a nursery at the base lodge for children through age 6. Hours are 9 A.M. to noon and 1 P.M. to 4 P.M. Parents must care for their children over lunch. Older children can participate in the Wind Whistle Ski School free of charge.

NICETIES: The Balsams has a small library stocked with best-sellers. There's always a jigsaw puzzle in progress.

Several shops are located on the first floor of Hampshire House. The Balsams Gift Shop also carries magazines, books, and film. Several boutiques sell clothing and supplies for golf, tennis, and swimming. Every summer, New Hampshire artisans demonstrate their crafts and sell their wares.

FOR MORE INFORMATION: Write The Balsams, Dixville Notch, NH 03576, or call (800) 255-0800 from New Hampshire or (800)

255-0600 from elsewhere in the U.S. and Canada. A video brochure is available.

MOHONK MOUNTAIN HOUSE
New Paltz, New York

No travel literature can adequately prepare you for your first glimpse of Mohonk Mountain House. About two miles past a simple gatehouse on a country road in New York's Shawangunk Mountains, it looms ahead: a magnificent red-roofed Victorian castle, a relic from another century. Because of its splendor and rich history, the Mountain House and its surrounding land were declared a National Historic Landmark in 1986, rewarding the owners for more than a century of extraordinary stewardship. Mohonk is owned by the Smiley family, descendants of twin brothers Albert and Alfred Smiley, who purchased the spectacular site in 1869 after Alfred discovered it on a hike.

The hotel sits at one end of a half-mile-long, 60-foot-deep natural mountain lake about two hours northwest of New York City. Rugged glacial outcroppings rise dramatically from the water. Surrounding the Mohonk property is a 22,000-acre natural area comprising state parks and private preserves.

It is as much the so-called Mohonk experience as the beautiful setting that draws guests back generation after generation. That "experience" reflects Mohonk's heritage. The Smiley twins were schoolteachers and devout Quakers, who built their grand hotel on the site of a rowdy tavern where overly-rambunctious guests were chained to trees. The Smileys banned liquor, card-playing, and dancing in favor of nature walks and daily prayer services. Even today, there is no bar or cocktail lounge, although you can get a drink with lunch and dinner or order a bottle to drink discreetly in your room. There is no smoking in the dining room or parlor, jackets are required at dinner, and a prayer service is offered every morning during the busy summer season.

This is a hiker's paradise. The views of the lake, the Mountain House, and the surrounding valleys are truly spectacular. Walk or jog a mile away from the lodge and you're as likely to see a family of deer as a family of fellow guests. Or hike up to Sky Top, a stone tower that marks the highest point on the property, and look out at six states.

Mohonk is renowned for its 40 special weekends, with themes like Cooking, Mystery, Tennis, Star-gazing, Fitness, or Tower of Babble (foreign-language instruction).

ACCOMMODATIONS: $$$ Mohonk Mountain House has 277 rooms, about half with working fireplaces and two-thirds with balconies. Most have good views of the lake (even-numbered rooms) or the mountains (odd-numbered rooms). Some adjoining rooms share a bathroom, which makes them perfect for a family with small children.

All rates, except for these adjoining rooms, are per room, per night, for two persons, and include three meals per person and afternoon tea. Peak season is May through October. Weekly rates are available. For families, the double occupancy rate applies to the first two occupants of double-bedded rooms, with a children's rate available for children sharing the room. In adjoining rooms, the first three occupants are charged the full rate regardless of age, and each additional occupant age 2 to 12 is charged a children's rate. Children under 4 stay free.

DINING: All meals are taken in either the Main Dining Room or a smaller dining room. Food at Mohonk is abundant.

Early-morning coffee is available from 7 to 8 A.M. Breakfast, served from 8 to 9:30 A.M., is a bountiful buffet. Continental breakfast is served from 9:30 to 11 A.M.

A luncheon buffet is served from 12:30 to 2 P.M. During the summer, a barbecue lunch is also offered outdoors. The evening meal is served from 6:30 to 8 P.M. and offers selections from a menu.

Guests have the same waiter—and the same table—for all their meals. Make your reservations early to ensure a seat in the Main Dining Room, which has an incredible view.

ACTIVITIES

 Four red clay and two Har-Tru courts, two lighted platform tennis courts; pro shop, lessons, rental equipment, tournaments, partner matchup.

 Nine-hole, Scottish design, par 35 course, open from April through October; 18-hole putting green.

 In Mohonk Lake; inner tubes and beach chairs provided.

Mohonk Lake. Rental boats available.

 Mohonk Lake. Rental equipment available.

 The 5,000-acre Mohonk Preserve protects the area's natural beauty and encourages visitors to appreciate it. Educational and interpretive nature programs are offered year-round. Maps of trails through the preserve are provided.

 Guided English or Western-style trail rides four times a day from April through October; carriage rides.

Indoor Fitness Center with a Universal weight machine, exercise bicycles, ballet barre, saunas, and showers. Classes are offered regularly; massage available.

The energetic activities staff organizes guest tournaments in putting, croquet, lawn bowling, Ping-Pong, shuffleboard, softball, volleyball, and platform tennis, as well as hayrides, skating parties, snow-tubing outings, guided jogs and rock scrambles, prayer services, and afternoon tea. Lots of special activities are offered for families, including cookouts, barn museum tours, forging demonstrations, softball and volleyball games, and outdoor movies.

 Ice-skating and ice fishing is available.

 Cross-country skiing is on groomed and double-tracked trails; equipment rentals.

FOR CHILDREN: There's a well-organized children's program, whose underlying philosophy is "Let kids be kids." It emphasizes outdoor activities and nature appreciation. The program is available daily except Monday during the summer and on weekends and holidays the rest of the year.

"Mohonk Tykes," for 2- to 4-year-olds, meets from 9:30 A.M. to 12:30 P.M. in a facility equipped with a wide selection of toys, including a play tunnel, rocking horses, blocks, puzzles, and lots of art materials and books. Parents are welcome to drop in whenever they like. The Tykes play mostly indoors, but are also taken out for walks, games, and pony rides.

Three separate programs for older children meet from 9:30 A.M.

to 12:30 P.M., recess for lunch with parents, and resume from 2 to 5 P.M.

Children aged 5 and 6 are called "Explorers" and engage in such activities as peanut hunts, croquet, swimming, field games, ice cream making, and frog hunts.

Children aged 7 and 8 are called "Scramblers." They go on hikes and scavenger hunts, swim, take pony rides, run an obstacle course, make arts and crafts projects.

The "Adventurers" are the 9- to 12-year-olds, who go rock scrambling, swim, play putt-putt golf, hike, fish, play field games, and make kites.

Each evening there are either activities for children only (5- to 12-year-olds) or entertainment for the whole family.

There are no special activities for teenagers or for children under 2. Baby-sitting can be arranged.

NICETIES: On Friday nights, late arrivals may order a late supper between 8 and 10 P.M.

The Mountain House is accessible to wheelchairs, and Guest Services can provide a special chair with pneumatic tires for outdoor use.

There's a laundry in the basement of the Mountain House.

If you run out of diapers or other essentials during your stay, the staff will purchase them for you in a nearby town for a small service charge.

OF INTEREST NEARBY: If you're driving from New York City, budget some time to explore the small towns along the way, which are dotted with antiques shops and interesting restaurants.

Newburgh, about 15 miles from New Paltz, was George Washington's headquarters for more than a year during the Revolutionary War, and later was a center of the whaling industry. Washington's headquarters, at Liberty and Washington streets, is now a state historic site. Local sightseeing maps and brochures are available at the Chamber of Commerce, 72 Broadway.

At Rhinebeck you'll find the Old Rhinebeck Aerodrome, a collection of antique airplanes built between 1908 and 1937. Barnstorming rides may be available in an open cockpit biplane. Call (914) 758-8610 for hours.

Hyde Park, about 45 minutes from Mohonk across the

Hudson River, is the home of the Franklin D. Roosevelt Library and Museum, and Roosevelt's home. The museum is excellent, and the home, through which tours are available, provides you with an intimate glimpse into the Roosevelts' family life. Call (914) 229-8114 for hours. The Eleanor Roosevelt National Historic Site, the First Lady's private retreat, is nearby. Call (914) 229-9115 for hours.

FOR MORE INFORMATION: Write Mohonk Mountain House, New Paltz, NY 12561, or call (800) 772-6646 or (914) 255- 1000.

THE SAGAMORE, AN OMNI CLASSIC RESORT
Bolton Landing, New York

For most of a century, the Sagamore has been a luxurious resort with an exclusive clientele. Built in 1883 on Green Island near "Millionaire Row," the Sagamore quickly became the center of Lake George's glittering social life. America's wealthiest families spent leisurely summers boating on the lake and enjoying sumptuous meals in the Sagamore's dining room.

After World War II, the hotel went into gentle decline and closed in 1981. It was completely rehabilitated and reopened in 1984 under the management of the Omni chain. In its newest incarnation, the Sagamore is "An Omni Classic Resort and Conference Center."

The Sagamore retains its old-fashioned charm. Guests can still enjoy morning coffee or cocktails in the Sagamore's magnificent portico with its stunning view of the lake and the Adirondack Mountains, just as their predecessors did a hundred years ago. But it's very much a modern resort.

ACCOMMODATIONS: $$$ to $$$$ The Sagamore has 350 rooms and suites divided between the Victorian Landmark-style main building, new lodges adjacent to the original hotel, and the Hermitage, an executive retreat. All of the rooms in the main building have been renovated recently.

Summer rates in the main building are offered under the Modified American Plan (MAP). Children 3 to 18 pay reduced rates; children under 3 stay and eat free.

Best suited to families are the new lodges. Each lodge suite has its own kitchen, small patio, dining area, living area (with sleep sofas), private baths, and one or two bedrooms. Color television sets are in the living rooms and bedrooms. MAP rates are also offered here, and are somewhat lower than in the old building. Ask about the Family Fling package, which includes some special amenities.

DINING: Breakfast, served in the Sagamore dining room, is an experience not to be missed. In addition to a buffet of hot and cold entrées, a trio of chefs makes omelettes to order.

The Sagamore has many options for dinner. The most elegant is the Trillium Room. The Sagamore Dining Room serves American regional cuisine. The Club Grill, two miles from the hotel on the golf course, has a 1920s style and is a treat for adults and older children. Least intimidating to children for lunch and dinner is Mr. Brown's, serving informal meals in a casual, clublike atmosphere.

In the summer, the hotel organizes special event meals at the Pool Terrace. This casual dining is perfect for families. One of the most popular events is a clambake with unlimited portions of clams, lobster, and seafood salad.

All of the restaurants have children's menus, and low-fat specialties are available at all meals.

ACTIVITIES

 Two indoor and four outdoor courts.

Eighteen-hole Scottish-style course designed by Donald Ross. Located two miles from the main hotel, it can be reached by a regular shuttle bus. Golf professional Tom Smack is arranges clinics and tournaments.

Heated indoor pool and whirlpool at the hotel. In Lake George from a sandy beach (be aware that even in the middle of the summer the water is frigid). Parents should bring life jackets or "floaties" for young children, since there is no children's pool or shallow pool area.

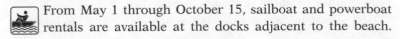 From May 1 through October 15, sailboat and powerboat rentals are available at the docks adjacent to the beach.

Three cruises a day are offered on the Morgan, a 72-foot replica of a turn-of-the-century touring vessel.

 Lake George abounds with lake and rainbow trout, salmon, perch, pike, and bass. Charters and equipment available.

 The Sagamore Spa is a luxurious European-style health spa with exercise equipment, a loofah room, saunas, steam and massage rooms, whirlpools, and hot and cold plunge pools. Facials and complete massages are available.

 In the evenings during the summer, the Sagamore offers movies or its dinner theater revue.

 Cross-country skiing on groomed trails across the golf course.

 Downhill skiing is available at the West Mountain Ski Center, in nearby Glens Falls, with six chair lifts and 19 trails (some lighted for night skiing). Half an hour from the Sagamore is Gore Mountain, with 41 trails; complimentary shuttle.

 Ice-skating on the flooded tennis courts. Hardy guests may want to participate in the Lake George Winter Carnival in January and February. Events include polar bear swimming, ice fishing, and outhouse racing.

 One of the first impressions you get of the Sagamore is of multicolored parachutes high above Lake George. The sport is parasailing, and instead of dropping from planes, the participants are pulled by motor boats. Also available are sunrise hot-air balloon flights. Both activities are expensive.

FOR CHILDREN: The Sagamore's children's program, the Teepee Club, operates daily in the summer season and on holidays and selected weekends in the winter, for children 3 to 13. Activities are offered from 8 A.M. through 4 P.M., and again from 4 to 9 P.M. Supervised children's lunches and dinners are offered.

The program is supervised by adult counselors. The toddler group, ages 3 to young 5s, listens to stories, swims, does art projects, and plays games at the resort's inventive playground. Older children (mature 5- to 13-year-olds) swim, participate in golf and

tennis clinics, go on scavenger hunts, play kickball and volleyball, and attend movies. Theme parties are held daily for both
groups.

There's a charge for the program, but the rate is discounted
for the second and third child within a family.

Baby-sitters can be arranged.

NICETIES: In mid-afternoon guests may enjoy a complimentary
tea or lemonade with chamber music at the Lakeside Pavilion,
or they may opt for high tea in the Veranda, with its 180-degree
view of the lake.

Parked on the Sagamore's gracious circular driveway during
the summer is a surrey with a horse and driver for complimentary tours of the grounds. In the winter, horse-drawn sleigh rides
are given over the snow-covered golf course.

OF INTEREST NEARBY: Lake George is a paradise for history
buffs. Half an hour north of Bolton Landing is Fort Ticonderoga,
a pre-Revolutionary War fort, which has a military museum. In
Lake George Village, 10 miles south, Fort William Henry was the
site of the last battle of the French and Indian War.

Children find Lake George Village a wonderland of amusement and theme parks, including The Great Escape, with its
Desperado Plunge flume ride, and Gaslight Village.

Saratoga Springs, about half an hour from Lake George, is
well known for both its racetrack and its performing arts center.
The track is the oldest in America, and races are held in August.
The Performing Arts Center, an open-air theater, draws the
Philadelphia Orchestra, the New York City Ballet, and many top
theater and show business performers.

FOR MORE INFORMATION: Write The Sagamore, P.O. Box 450,
Bolton Landing, NY 12814, or call (800) 358-3585.

FOUR SEASONS INN ON THE PARK
Toronto, Ontario, Canada

Only 20 minutes from the hustle and bustle of downtown
Toronto, the Four Seasons Inn on the Park has the ambience of
a country resort. Families can spend a busy morning soaking up
culture and adventure in one of North America's most interest-

ing and family-friendly cities and then repair to the hotel pool for an afternoon of relaxation.

Located next to the beautiful 600-acre Wilket Creek Park, the Four Seasons Inn on the Park provides recreational opportunities unthinkable at most urban hotels—tobogganing and cross-country skiing in the winter and swimming, tennis, bicycle riding, horseback-riding and hiking in the summer. Because of the excellent children's program, parents who need to be in Toronto on business often bring their children along, contributing to a family atmosphere amid the elegance of the hotel.

This AAA five-diamond hotel manages to serve both business travelers and family vacationers well. Set amidst lovely gardens in a courtyard are a playhouse and excellent playground equipment. And the concierge staff is as willing to help visiting parents find a baby-sitter as to fax business documents for a conference attendee. The Four Seasons group has built its fine reputation on attention to detail—from complimentary overnight shoeshining right down to the colorful bumper pads in the cribs!

ACCOMMODATIONS: $$$ The 568 guestrooms, including 26 suites, are located either in the main building or in the Tower Suites. The rooms are spacious and beautifully furnished, with sitting areas. Each room has a mini-bar and remote-control color television, and some have balconies. Parents of small children can request a first-floor room that opens onto the courtyard and its playgrounds. Children under 16 stay free of charge.

DINING: There are two restaurants, a poolside snack bar, and two cocktail lounges. Seasons is the hotel's premier restaurant; it features continental and nouvelle American cuisine in an elegant atmosphere. The Harvest Room is a cheerful and friendly family-style restaurant; children will enjoy coloring their special menu. Lunch and afternoon snacks are served at the outdoor Cabana Café. Room service is available around the clock.

ACTIVITIES

 Three tennis courts (bubbled for winter play), five squash courts, and five racquetball courts at the Parkview Racquet & Fitness Club on the premises; court fees.

 Guests have privileges at the nine-hole Flemingdon Golf Course, five minutes away, and the beautiful and exclusive 18-hole Parkview Golf & Country Club, 30 minutes away.

A heated indoor pool with adjacent whirlpool, 25-meter outdoor pool, and separate diving pool. During the summer, a portable splash pool is provided for toddlers.

 Complimentary bicycles are available for riding on miles of trails in adjacent 600-acre Wilket Creek Park, which is also a jogger's paradise.

 There are shuffleboard and badminton courts in the courtyard and a gymnasium and indoor track at the Racquet Club; massage available.

 Late-night dancing and entertainment in the Copper and Terrace lounges. Special social activities are offered during holiday periods for families.

 Complimentary cross-country skiing equipment available for use on 16 miles of groomed trails through Wilket Creek Park.

 Complimentary toboggans for use in the park.

FOR CHILDREN: Daily during the summer and on every weekend during the rest of the year, the Inn offers "InnKids" a free supervised children's program for children between 5 and 12; children under 5 may participate if accompanied by a parent or baby-sitter. The program is supervised by a full-time staff member with a background in childhood development; a ratio of one adult to eight children is maintained. The program attracts about 20 children a day.

The children gather at 9:30 A.M. in the V.I.K. (Very Important Kid) Room next to the indoor pool. The day typically begins with swimming and games in the indoor pool, followed by lunch. In the afternoon, children enjoy arts and crafts, outdoor games, storytelling (in the "hideaway hut"), and more swimming. The program ends at 4 P.M.

The courtyard contains terrific playground equipment and plenty of run-around room for young children, as well as a pond filled with fish and frequented by ducks. There's a video game room next to the V.I.K. Room.

NICETIES: The pool attendant will lend your child water toys, water wings, or a lifejacket.

The housekeeping department can lend you a stroller. It also can supply diapers, wipes, thermometers, pain relievers, bottles, and pacifiers.

Among the offerings from room service: milk and cookies at bedtime and popcorn and pizza for snacks.

OF INTEREST NEARBY: On weekends, pack a picnic lunch and join the locals on their family outings by ferry to the Toronto Islands, especially Centre Island, which has an excellent amusement park called Centreville, miles of biking trails, formal gardens, fishing ponds, playgrounds, beaches, and a free tram.

The Ontario Science Centre, less than a mile from the hotel (ask for directions to the path through the park), is one of the best of its kind, with hundreds of hands-on exhibits in a striking building.

The Metro Toronto Zoo has more than 4,000 animals displayed in naturalistic settings scattered across its 710 acres. Locals like to ski around the zoo in the winter!

The Royal Ontario Museum has mummies, dinosaurs, and suits of armor, as well as a Ming tomb, an Islamic home, and a Buddhist temple. Adjacent McLaughlin Planetarium has an excellent theater with laser light shows and special shows for children.

The Art Gallery of Ontario, a few blocks away, has the world's largest collection of sculptures by Henry Moore, as well as his seashell and bone collection.

Families can ride a glass-walled elevator to the top of the CN Tower, the world's tallest free-standing structure, for a panoramic view of Toronto and Lake Ontario.

Ontario Place is a futuristic lakefront theme park featuring a terrific Children's Village amusement area, a Waterplay Area with a 370-foot waterslide, restaurants and shops, a three-dimensional movie theater, boat rides, and the Canadian Baseball Hall of Fame and Museum.

Black Creek Pioneer Village, on the outskirts of town, is an excellent living-history museum that evokes the feel of life in Canada in the 19th century.

FOR MORE INFORMATION: Write the Inn at 1100 Eglinton Avenue East, Toronto, Ontario, Canada M3C 1H8, or call (416) 444-2561.

HOTEL HERSHEY
HERSHEY LODGE
Hershey, Pennsylvania

Amid the rolling green hills of southern Pennsylvania, the choco-holic will find his dream and the hapless dieter his nightmare: "Chocolate Town, U.S.A", otherwise known as Hershey, Pa. While strolling among the rose beds of Hershey Gardens or bowling on the lawn at the Hotel Hershey, you'll occasionally detect a cocoa-like smell emanating from the massive chocolate factory.

The biggest drawing card in Hershey for most families is Hersheypark, an 90-acre theme park. But reasons to stay more than one day in the area will be easily found at the Hotel Hershey or the Hershey Lodge.

The palatial Hotel Hershey, the flagship property of Hershey Resorts, sits high on a hilltop, looking over the roses of Hershey Gardens and the attractions surrounding the amusement park. Founder Milton Hershey built it in the 1930s to provide jobs for the Depression-threatened townspeople. From the Mediterranean-inspired lobby with its tiled fountain to the beautiful Circular Dining Room overlooking the formal gardens, the hotel combines elegance with hospitality.

Hershey Lodge is in a lush valley several miles away, closer to the Hersheypark entrance. The lodge, set on 30 landscaped acres, is less formal than the hotel, and is considered one of Pennsylvania's premier family resorts. Like the hotel, it offers a full assortment of resort activities and amenities.

ACCOMMODATIONS: $$$ to $$$$ Hotel Hershey has 241 guest rooms and 17 suites, most with beautiful views overlooking either the formal gardens or the front veranda. The west wing has several rooms that open directly to the indoor pool. Set in a pine grove on the hotel grounds, a guest house offers families privacy, still close to the hotel's amenities. The guest house, more rustic than elegant, has a fireplace, kitchenette, and sleeping loft.

Rates vary depending on the season and meal plan. Children are charged graduated rates according to their ages. The hotel offers a variety of packages plans that include greens fees or amusement park admission.

Hershey Lodge has 457 beautifully decorated rooms in several two-story buildings that look out over a rolling green lawn and a small lake. Rates are lower than at the hotel. Numerous package plans are available.

Hershey also operates its own well-shaded campground, 55-acre Hershey Highmeadow Camp. For reservations there, call (717) 566-0902.

DINING: Guests on a package plan at the Hotel Hershey take their meals in the Circular Dining Room. With its stained-glass windows overlooking the hotel's gardens, the dining room is a beautiful setting in which to enjoy any meal.

Breakfast is a splendid buffet featuring made-to-order omelets. Lunch is also a buffet, and the Sunday brunch attracts day trippers from throughout Pennsylvania. Dinner is more formal and requires dress-up clothes, but the menu includes several children's plates.

The more casual Fountain Cafe serves lunch and dinner. In the summer, you can dine on the adjacent veranda. The menu features fresh seafood, poultry, gourmet pizzas, and freshly made pasta.

The Club House Cafe, overlooking the first tee and the pool at the Executive Nine Golf Course, serves sandwiches, salads, hamburgers, hot dogs and desserts throughout the day.

Cocktails and after-dinner entertainment are served up at the Iberian Lounge, which is located off the lobby.

Hershey Lodge offers three dining choices with varying price ranges. The Copper Kettle serves three meals a day in a relaxed, family environment. The Hearth is a medium-priced restaurant which also serves three meals a day and features Pennsylvania Dutch cooking. The Tack Room, the Lodge's fine dining restaurant, serves lunch, Sunday brunch, and dinner, and specializes in steaks and seafood.

ACTIVITIES

 Four lighted courts at the hotel, two lighted courts and two platform courts at the lodge.

 Hershey is known as the "Golf Capital of Pennsylvania," with 72 holes available for visitors. The Hershey Country Club has two 18-hole courses (the 6,860-yard, par 73 West

Course, designed by Maurice McCarthy, and the 7,061-yard, par 71 East Course designed by George Fazio). The Hershey Parkview Golf Course is an 18-hole, 6,146 yard, par 70 public course, also designed by Maurice McCarthy.

Spring Creek Golf Course is a nine-hole, 2,318-yard, par 33 course that was originally designed specifically for children; it's now open to all. Hotel Hershey has a nine-hole 2,680-yard, par 33 course that winds through a pine forest on the hotel grounds. The lodge has a par 3 chip and putt course that wraps around a lake on the front lawn.

 Indoor and outdoor pools at both the hotel and lodge.

 Rental bicycles at both hotels.

 Exercise rooms, whirlpools, saunas at both facilities.

 Tobogganing and sledding.

 Cross country skiing. More than 500,000 festive lights adorn Hersheypark's Christmas Candyland over the winter holidays.

 Lawn bowling on the manicured grass of the hotel, shuffleboard and croquet. First-run movie theater at the lodge; game rooms at both facilities.

FOR CHILDREN: In the summer, the hotel and lodge both offer daily activities for the whole family, including scavenger hunts, bike rides, and chocolate chases (hunting for Hershey Kisses). Penny dives in the pool, coloring contests, and relay races are some of the other events in which your kids will want to participate. Younger children must be accompanied by parents.

Babysitting is available through the Concierge.

NICETIES: At check-in, everyone in the family gets a Hershey bar.

Carriage rides are available at the hotel. The 15-minute ride circles the hotel grounds.

During the summer, free shuttle buses run from both the hotel and the lodge to the main attractions in Hershey.

OF INTEREST NEARBY: Hersheypark provides thrill seekers plenty of action with several huge roller coasters and water rides. Tidal Force, new in 1994, is the world's tallest and wettest splashdown ride. You're guaranteed to get wet after you plunge 100 feet into a pool! There are also plenty of kiddie rides for younger children. The park also offers six hours of live entertainment daily, including a dolphin and sea lion show and several other variety shows featuring rock 'n' roll, country, and Broadway numbers. The park is open from the middle of May early October. Children 3 and under are free.

Included in the Hersheypark admission price is a visit to ZooAmerica. Set on 11 acres next to Hersheypark, the zoo features over 200 animals in exhibits that showcase their natural habitats. Separate admission is available for those wishing to visit just ZooAmerica.

Just outside the amusement park gates is another popular stop: Chocolate World, an automated tour showing how chocolate is made. Kids love the large swirling chairs that transport them through the display. The Chocolate World tour is free and is offered daily from 9 A.M. to 6:45 P.M.

Close to the Hersheypark entrance is the Hershey Museum, which features displays on Native Americans and early pioneer settlers and hands-on activities for children. The museum is open daily from 10 A.M. to 6 P.M.

The Middletown & Hummelstown Railroad, just outside Hershey, offers 11-mile rides along Swatara Creek from Middletown to the Indian Echo Caverns, where you can take a 45-minute guided tour.

Pennsylvania Dutch Country is 30 miles southeast of Hershey. There you can drive by working Amish farms, shop at farmers' markets and factory outlets, tour a pretzel factory, and go antiquing. Call (800) 735-2629 for tourist information.

FOR MORE INFORMATION: For hotel availability and rates, call Hershey Hotels at (800) 533-3131.

For general information about Hershey, call (800) HERSHEY.

SKYTOP LODGE
Skytop, Pennsylvania

"Secluded in the Poconos," the mood-setting advertising slogan used by Skytop Lodge in Pennsylvania's glorious Pocono Mountains, is an understatement. Amidst the garish billboards for the Poconos' other famous resorts, it's hard to find a single directional sign for Skytop.

Seclusion is what attracts visitors to Skytop—that and a wide array of seasonal outdoor activities, a genteel, old-fashioned atmosphere, impeccable personal service, and endless opportunities to just relax. Staying at Skytop, one has the feeling of belonging to a private club, and for good reason—it was a private club until the late 1970s.

Constructed of granite and topped with a slate roof, the main building sits in an imposing setting on a plateau ringed by gentle hills, looking much like the administration building of a 200-year-old college. It was founded in 1928 by rich New Yorkers as a golf retreat, and remained a haven for members only until the increasing age of its members and the skyrocketing costs of running a full-service resort forced it to open its doors to "those who will be congenial at the Club."

Today, the resort is overrun with families, many from Philadelphia and New York City, each a two and a half hour drive. On a typical weekend, toddlers waddle the length of the long, old-fashioned Pine Room, which functions as the resort's living room. On the lower level, teenagers play exuberant games of Ping-Pong or billiards, gorge themselves on old-fashioned ice-cream sundaes, watch a wide-screen television set, or waste a month's allowance on video games. And at any hour of the day, the heated indoor pool is likely to be the venue for a game of water tag.

Skytop still reflects the manner and customs of a bygone era. The Pine Room, with its overstuffed chairs, flowered draperies, and grandfather's clock, is your great- grandmother's parlor writ large. To its rear, the library provides a quiet, smoke-free environment for letter writing and reading. Game rooms recall the era in which families gathered to play table games rather than watch TV. A covered porch furnished with Adirondack lawn chairs overlooks gardens and manicured lawns in the foreground, with the Delaware Water Gap, one of the East's outstanding natural attractions, in the background 20 miles away.

ACCOMMODATIONS: **$$$ to $$$$** Skytop has 166 rooms, most in the main lodge. They are various sizes; all have full bathrooms and have been redecorated since 1991. Under the family plan, children 17 and under stay and eat free if they share their parents' room. There are nine cottages with four bedrooms each.

Three full meals a day are included in the room rates. A service charge is added to the bill.

DINING: Mealtime is an event at Skytop, and guests are encouraged to dress for dinner, though sportswear is appropriate for breakfast and lunch.

Breakfast, served from 7:30 to 9 A.M., includes such regional favorites as Philadelphia scrapple and steamed finnan haddie. Lunch, served from noon to 1 P.M., includes a choice of four appetizers, relishes and crudités, two soups, and entrées ranging from Maryland crab cakes to braised Swiss steak. Vegetables, served family-style, and a choice of three salads and six desserts round out the meal.

Dinner, served from 7 to 8 P.M., allows the chef to show off. There's usually a choice of five entrées.

Cocktails, wine, and beer may be purchased in the dining room or enjoyed before dinner in the Tap Room, a cocktail lounge on the lower level. If hunger pangs strike anytime during the day, a lower-level tea room serves light snacks and ice-cream sundaes.

ACTIVITIES

 Five Har-Tru tennis courts and two all-weather courts; instruction, pro shop.

 Eighteen-hole golf course, rated among the finest in the country, with only an 84-foot variation in grade over the entire course; three putting greens and a practice hole, pro shop, instruction.

 Heated indoor pool, large outdoor pool (new in 1989), kiddie pool; swimming in small lower lake.

 Rental rowboats and canoes at the Boat House on the 74-acre Upper Lake (small privately owned sailboats also are welcomed). Daylong or half-day-long canoe trips can be arranged on the Delaware River, about 20 miles away, through Kittatinny Canoes, Inc.

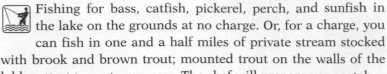 Fishing for bass, catfish, pickerel, perch, and sunfish in the lake on the grounds at no charge. Or, for a charge, you can fish in one and a half miles of private stream stocked with brook and brown trout; mounted trout on the walls of the lobby attest to past successes. The chef will prepare your catch.

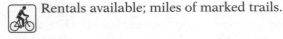 Rentals available; miles of marked trails.

 Nine miles of marked trails crisscross the resort's 5,500 acres. Topographical map supplied to each guest, interpretive walks led by the staff naturalist in July and August.

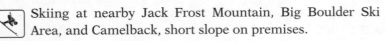 Off premises at Carson's Riding Academy near Mt. Pocono.

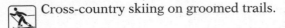 Fitness center with whirpool and sauna; lawn games such as lawn bowling, horseshoes, croquet, archery, badminton, miniature golf, and shuffleboard.

Barbecues along the lake on Saturdays in the summer; movie showings scheduled throughout the week; hayrides in summer and fall. Piano concerts most Friday evenings in the Pine Room; Saturday night dances; periodic night walks and stargazings.

Skiing at nearby Jack Frost Mountain, Big Boulder Ski Area, and Camelback, short slope on premises.

Cross-country skiing on groomed trails.

Ice-skating on 6,000-square-foot-rink; sledding on resort's hills and tobogganing on 350-foot slide onto Skytop Lake (equipment provided).

FOR CHILDREN: Skytop's children's program, called the "Camp in the Clouds," operates five and a half hours a day, daily except Sunday, in July and August. The program is geared toward children from 3 to 12. Each day's activities are adjusted to take into account the ages and abilities of the children present. A daily fee is charged.

A converted conference room on the shore of the lower lake serves as the playroom and activity center. From 9:30 A.M. to noon, children participate in activities ranging from arts and crafts to storytelling, or take group instruction in swimming, golf, tennis, archery, badminton, croquet, boating, and fishing. One morning a week, the group goes by van to the Pocono Playhouse in nearby Mountainhome, Pa., for a children's play. On another morning, the staff naturalist leads a nature walk.

After a break for lunch with their families, camp resumes at 2 P.M., with swimming the primary afternoon activity. The camp director, who has teacher training, is assisted by two college students.

In the off-season, many scheduled activities are suitable for school-age children.

NICETIES: Continental breakfast is served in the Pine Room for early risers, along with a selection of local and national newspapers.

The library is stocked with several thousand volumes, including children's books. Board games are available in the game rooms on the main level.

Flowers can be ordered to grace your table during your visit.

FOR MORE INFORMATION: Write the Skytop Lodge, One Skytop, Skytop, PA 18357, or telephone (717) 595-7401 or (800) 345-7759. Write the Pocono Mountain Vacation Bureau at 1004 Main St., Stroudsburg, PA 18360, or call (717) 421-5791.

THE TYLER PLACE
Highgate Springs, Vermont

From its opening in 1945, The Tyler Place has been managed by the Tyler family. Frances Tyler and her late husband set out to create the kind of place their own family would like to vacation, with just the right mix of togetherness and time apart. During its 50 years of operation, The Tyler Place has turned catering to family vacationers into a fine art.

Among the ingredients in the Tyler formula: comfortable and nicely decorated cottages and suites, memorable meals, an atmosphere of overwhelming friendliness, probably the best children's programs anywhere, and a little bit of magic. When almost 90 percent of the guests are returnees, it tells you something about a place.

The resort occupies 165 acres and a mile of lakefront on unspoiled Lake Champlain, just a few miles from the Canadian border. It's on the outskirts of a village consisting of a few houses, a small, picture-perfect New England-style church and Martin's General Store, which endeared itself to our children with its selection of penny candy.

"Mrs. T," as Frances Tyler likes to be called, turned 90 in 1994, but still plays a very active role in running the place. Her daughter, Pixley Hill, and son, Ted Tyler, have taken over many of the day-to-day responsibilities, and Ted's daughter, Tasney, works at the front desk. But Mrs. T is still quite likely to get on the phone with prospective first-time guests to make sure that The Tyler Place is the right place for their families.

ACCOMMODATIONS: $$$ to $$$$ The 27 cottages at The Tyler Place, decorated with Waverly fabrics, have a quaint charm, and are comfortable enough to earn a three-star rating from the Mobil travel guide. Every cottage has a fireplace and from one to four bedrooms, including an air-conditioned master bedroom. Although all meals are served at the Inn, each cottage has a small kitchen.

In addition to the cottages, there are suites in the Inn, more modern than the cottages but not as charming. The suites are air-conditioned and feature separate children's rooms. The Inn is the social hub of The Tyler Place. It houses the dining facilities, the fireside and porch cocktail lounges, recreation rooms, and the only public telephone at the resort. There are no telephones or television sets in the rooms or cottages.

The Tyler Place operates on the American Plan, with all meals, sports, activities and children's programs included in the rate. The cottages are priced according to their proximity to the lake or the Inn. For most of the summer, registration and departure are on Saturdays; guests must stay for a week. During spring, early summer, and early fall, a two-night minimum stay is required. Special rates in May, June and September are available at a 15 to 30 percent savings, with the same services and meals. A 10 percent service charge is added to each bill.

DINING: In general, children and adults dine separately, but a family breakfast room and family picnic lunches are available. In addition, a family lunch room operates from May to July 2 and again in September. Older children and adults choose from similar menus; the food is filling and wholesome, and Vermont products are often served. Young children have their own dining room, their own chef, and, of course, a special menu.

All meals are served semi-buffet style, and guests usually have three entrees to choose from. Dinner is served from 6:30 to 8 P.M., preceded by a 5:30 P.M. cocktail hour. Dress at all meals is informal.

ACTIVITIES

 Six outdoor courts. Round-robin doubles, singles tournaments. Privileges at nearby indoor facility. Aerobics classes, weights room, and archery course.

 Privileges at three country clubs, 15 to 45 minutes away.

 In the indoor and outdoor heated pools, each with a separate children's wading pool, or in Lake Champlain.

 Sailing, sailboarding, kayaking, canoeing, powerboating, and water-skiing on Lake Champlain. Canoe trips on Rock River.

 Fish are plentiful in the lake (a license is required for adults, available in nearby Swanton). Motorboats can be rented.

 Six dozen complimentary one-speed bikes (adults' and children's sizes) for touring on country roads; babyseats and helmets available. Forty mountain bikes available for rental; complimentary on guided bike rides.

 You can hike a section of Vermont's famed Long Trail from an access point about a hour from The Tyler Place.

 Exercise Facilities: Lifecycle, NordicTrak, weights, jacuzzi.

 Basketball, softball, soccer, tennis, and badminton competitions; nature hikes; visits to a local farm; ice cream socials; champagne cruises on a pontoon boat. On some evenings, there's a DJ, square-dance caller, or Vermont storyteller. Parlor Game Night features spirited games of charades and Pictionary; Monte Carlo Night features bingo, horse racing and roulette.

FOR CHILDREN: The resort's seven separate children's programs are so extensive that descriptions of them fill an eight-page brochure! They are well-supervised, highly structured, and lots of fun. The programs operate mornings through lunch. Children spend afternoons with their parents, and then return to their programs for an early supper and evening activities while adults are having a candlelight dinner together.

The age-segregated programs are as follows: "Pre-Midgets," (ages 18 months to 2 1/2 years); "Junior Midgets" (2 1/2 to 3 1/2); "Senior Midgets" (3 1/2 to 5 1/2); "Juniors" (5 1/2 to 7); "Pre-Teens" (8- to 10- year-olds); "Junior Teens" (11 to 13), and "Senior Teens" (14- to 16-year-olds).

Each group has its own recreation center and, except for the Pre-Midgets, participates in sports, lake activities, swimming, talent shows, hayrides, and other activities. (The Pre-Midgets stick pretty close to the Midget House.) At night, the teens have dances, go water-skiing or bumper riding, or have karaoke contests. All groups are well-supervised by enthusiastic and creative college students, with training in CPR and first aid.

Babies and toddlers are welcome, particularly from opening day thrugh mid-June, and from late August through mid September, when there aren't as many school-age children in residence. Infant and toddler care is provided from 8:30 A.M. to 1:30 P.M. daily in the Infant/Toddler Activities Center, well-equipped with developmental toys. There's also a large, fenced-in playground, and a fleet of red wagons and strollers. A nurse or emergency medical technician is always on duty, and breakfast, snacks and lunch are provided. Alternatively, you can hire a "parents' helper" and have her take your infant or toddler to the "Morning Play Group," in the Midget House. In the evening, "parent helpers" provide infant and toddler care at the Carriage House while parents dine. These are the only children's programs for which extra fees are charged.

Afternoon and evening babysitting is easy to arrange. You can also bring your own babysitter, for a very nominal charge. He or she is expected to eat in your cottage.

NICETIES: Each week, The Tyler Place publishes a list of its guests, the names of their children, and their home addresses.

Not surprisingly, many children become winter pen pals. At the end of the week each camper gets a picture of his or her group.

A professional photographer is available for family photos.

It's easy to find partners for bridge, tennis, or other sports.

OF INTEREST NEARBY: Highgate Springs is equidistant from three interesting tourist areas: Montreal, Stowe, and the Shelburne Museum.

The Tyler Place provides literature about points of interest in Montreal. Most guests who have made a trip there feel that it is a city better appreciated by adults than by children.

However, the Shelburne Museum, about an hour away, is a perfect family jaunt. Shelburne has been called "a collection of collections." Most of its buildings have been brought from other places and reconstructed at Shelburne. Children love the Ticonderoga, a luxury side-wheeler that used to cruise Lake Champlain. Not to be missed are the antique doll collection and the hand-carved miniature circus parade, so long that it is displayed in its own semicircular building.

Stowe is well known as the home of the von Trapp family, of Sound of Music fame. It is also a tourist area in the summer, with many quaint craft shops.

FOR MORE INFORMATION: Write The Tyler Place on Lake Champlain, Box 419, Highgate Springs, VT 05460, or call (802) 868-3301.

AMELIA ISLAND PLANTATION
Amelia Island, Florida

In the midst of the environmental devastation that developers have created through much of Florida, a few resorts stand out as models of thoughtful, ecology-minded development. Amelia Island Plantation, a 1,250-acre complex on Florida's northern-most barrier island, 29 miles northeast of downtown Jacksonville, has been cited in numerous competitions for its environmentally-sound master plan. The resort opened in 1974 and has been expanded substantially since then. The developers have successfully integrated a full-service, four-star resort into a beautiful stretch of oceanfront property.

Where else can you wander on a marked trail around the perimeter of a 900-year-old Indian burial mound between playing a round of golf and swimming in the Atlantic Ocean? Where else can your child climb a ladder into a treetop hideaway and pretend he's Robinson Crusoe? At how many other resorts can you go out for a morning beach walk and encounter members of Greenpeace trying frantically to save a beached loggerhead turtle?

Amelia Island's villa-type accommodations are scattered throughout a spacious property covered with moss-draped live oak, palmetto, magnolia, and palm trees and bordered by a wide, four-mile-long beach. More than 230 species of birds have been sighted there.

ACCOMMODATIONS: **$$** to **$$$$** Amelia Island has daily, weekly, monthly, and long- term rentals available in both hotel rooms and 517 one- to three-bedroom villas with complete kitchen facilities. The villa units are all individually owned and decorated to the owner's taste. Each cluster of villas has a slightly different character.

Prices depend on the size of the unit and whether there's a

view of the ocean. High season runs from mid-March to the end of April. Rates are much lower in the winter and during some parts of the summer.

DINING: Amelia Island's six restaurants vary greatly in atmosphere, price and type of food.

The Amelia Inn has a spectacular view of the ocean and serves fresh seafood, steaks and poultry with a continental flair. Every Sunday, there's a fabulous brunch at which Amelia's chefs present an array of fresh seafood, carved roasted meats, crisp salads, and delectable desserts.

The Verandah, at Racquet Park, serves fresh, locally caught seafood for dinner. The Beach Club Sports Bar, adjacent to the main swimming pool, serves casual lunches and dinners in a fun-filled atmosphere. The kids can enjoy video games, pool tables, darts, and electronic basketball, football and golf while their food is prepared.

The Golf Shop Restaurant, within the pro shop, serves breakfast and lunch, with a late-afternoon menu available. The Long Point Putter Club serves continental breakfast and lunch.

The Coop, in the cluster of shops near the main entrance, is the perfect place for young children. It serves made-to-order fast food at breakfast and lunch.

Groceries can be purchased at the large supermarkets in Fernandina Beach or a small market next to the Reception Center. Amelia Island Plantation also offers room service from 7 A.M. to 10 P.M. Roberto's Pizza, made on premises, delivers from 11 A.M. to midnight.

ACTIVITIES

 Two Deco Turf II, 19 Fast-Dry and four Omni-Turf courts, three lighted; professional instruction; pro shop.

 Twenty-seven holes designed by Pete Dye and 18 holes designed by Tom Fazio. The golf courses are among the most picturesque anywhere, with sweeping views of the Atlantic Ocean on the Oceanside Nine. The Oakmarsh and Oysterbay nines feature twisting fairways, marsh views, and lush greenery.

Twenty-four pools and the Atlantic Ocean (the best pool for families is at the Beach Club, which has a wading pool for toddlers, and an adjoining wooden playground).

 Asphalt and wooden bike trails; rentals available, including childseat-equipped adult bikes and junior-size bikes.
Wooden trails wind through miles of "sunken forest," the valley between the primary and secondary dune lines. Descriptive signs identify flora. Boardwalks on the edge of the marshlands at Drummond Park provide a perfect vantage point for bird watching or taking in the sunset.

 At nearby Seahorse Stables.

 At the health and fitness center at Racquet Park (sauna, whirlpool, Nautilus, Universal equipment, racquetball courts, indoor/outdoor lap pool, organized classes). The Baker International Wellness Clinic has a sports medicine program here.

 Freshwater and saltwater, charters available through Amelia Angler at the Beach Club.

 The recreation staff publishes a monthly calendar of events. On a typical Saturday in June, for instance, the schedule includes high-energy exercise, beginners' racquetball, a golf clinic, beach volleyball, poolside bingo, ocean seining, and a mixed doubles tennis round robin.

In the evenings, adults may dance or enjoy live music and cocktails in the Amelia Inn Lounge; family movies are shown two or three times a week. Dances and barbecues are sometimes scheduled at Walker's Landing, a lovely spot on the marsh.

FOR CHILDREN: Amelia Island has a delight for children around virtually every corner. It has the best collection of playgrounds of any resort we've seen, from the climbing structures right outside the reception center (perfect for stretching travel-weary legs), to the elaborate wooden structures overlooking the ocean next to the Beach Club pool, to the replica of a tall-masted schooner on Aury Island, to the Robinson Crusoe-type treetop structure at Drummond Park.

Aury Island has a special fishing pier just for kids; the recreation staff can provide tackle and bait. Kids also will enjoy fishing from the walkway behind the Coop.

The organized children's program, for which there's a fee, is called "Kids Campelia," and an energetic staff of counselors works hard to make it attractive to children. The program runs during Thanksgiving week, the five or six weeks surrounding the Easter holidays, and from Memorial Day to just after Labor Day.

Preschoolers between 3 and 5 can join the program from 8:30 A.M. to 1 P.M. Monday through Saturday. Lunch, usually with known child-pleasers like peanut butter and jelly or hot dogs, costs extra. Activities include safety tips, exercises, fishing, shell collecting and crafts, feeding goldfish, and pool games.

Children from 6 to 8 can take part in half-day or full-day programs (they're cheaper if paid for by the week). A typical day includes beach soccer, a swim in the ocean, fishing at the Coop, beach games, a walk through the dunes and discussion of the dune's ecosystem, a kickball game, arts and crafts, relay races in the pool, and a scavenger hunt. Lunch is optional and costs extra.

Children between 9 and 12 have their own half- and full-day programs. They take field trips to nearby factories, the Jacksonville Zoo, the Jacksonville Airport, a Waterslide, nearby state parks, and local restaurants. Nature education is emphasized.

The program is run by the plantation's full-time youth program director and is staffed by between 12 and 14 senior college students working toward degrees in recreation. A lengthy list of local baby-sitters also is available at the front desk.

NICETIES: Ten complimentary trams ply the roads within the complex so that you can forget about driving while you're there.

A 900-year-old 60-foot-high burial mound for the Timucuan Indians has been excavated and carefully restored at Walker's Landing. It is one of Florida's finest and largest Indian burial mounds. Descriptive markers explain the Timucuans' lifestyle.

OF INTEREST NEARBY: Fernandina Beach, a 15-minute drive from the resort, is a charming town. Fernandina Beach was once the busiest shrimping port in the nation. A 30-block downtown area dotted with Victorian homes has been listed in the National Register of Historic Places. It is perfect for long, leisurely walks followed by lunch in one of numerous good restaurants.

The Fort Clinch State Park at the northern tip of Amelia

Island has a pre-Civil War fort that kids love to explore. Costumed interpreters help bring the past alive.

FOR MORE INFORMATION: Write Amelia Island Plantation, Highway A1A South, Amelia Island, FL 32034, or call (800) 874-6878.

CHEECA LODGE
Islamorada, Florida

You don't have to go all the way to the Caribbean to find azure seas, live coral reefs, lush tropical flora, rare birds, freshly caught seafood, and balmy breezes. The Florida Keys can provide all that, as well as a family-oriented resort that rivals any in the United States for attention to detail.

Cheeca Lodge, on a spit of land between the Atlantic Ocean and the Gulf of Mexico, is a compact, self-contained vacation destination that offers boundless opportunities for activity in an atmosphere that is also irresistably conducive to relaxation.

Although its facilities are unparalleled in the Keys, Cheeca Lodge's strongest card is its commitment to preserving the area's rare beauty and special charms. In 1990, the resort won the Gold Key Environmental Achievement Award from the American Hotel & Motel Association for its unique environmental education programs for guests.

ACCOMMODATIONS: $$ to $$$$ Cheeca Lodge's 203 accommodations include beautifully furnished ocean-view and gulf-view rooms in the main lodge and 64 one- and two-bedroom villas, each equipped with a living room and kitchen, in about two dozen low-rise buildings scattered around the property. All units are air-conditioned, with ceiling fans and mini-bars. Most include private screened-in balconies.

Special packages are available. There's no charge for children under 17 who share their parents' rooms (limit two children per room).

DINING: Breakfast, lunch and dinner are served in the Ocean Terrace Grill, a casual open-air dining room and terrace next to the main pool.

The Light Tackle Lounge overlooking the Atlantic Ocean serves a variety of fresh Keys seafood.

Dinner is special at the Atlantic's Edge Dining Room, a lovely semi-circular room with sweeping views of the ocean. The chef specializes in freshly caught local seafood and the Sunday brunch is the culinary highlight of the week. Children's menus are available, although children who wish to order off the regular menu receive a 50 percent discount.

Many other restaurants located within a few miles of the lodge.

ACTIVITIES

 Six lighted, Laykold courts; instruction available. Court fees.

 On a par-three, nine-hole executive course.

 Three pools; two freshwater and one saltwater. Swimming in the Gulf of Mexico from the lodge's 1,100-foot stretch of beach.

 Rental windsurfers, Hobie cats, glass-bottom paddle boats, and rafts. Parasailing can be arranged.

 Half-day and full-day excursions for tarpon, grouper, wahoo, mackerel, barracuda, and sailfish as well as guided expeditions on the shallow flats of Florida Bay for bonefish, snapper, and redfish. Rental equipment available at the Beach Hut for fishing from the 525-foot lighted pier.

 Cheeca Divers offers day and night skin- and scuba-diving trips; instruction and equipment rental available.

 Five hot tubs, resident masseur.

FOR CHILDREN:"Camp Cheeca" is Cheeca Lodge's award-winning program for children from ages 6 to 12. The program's goal is for children to have fun while learning about the fragile ecology of the Florida Keys.

Camp Cheeca operates every Friday, Saturday, and Sunday through the year and nearly daily between Memorial Day and Labor Day. Full-day and half-day rates are available. The morning session runs from 9 A.M. to noon and the afternoon session from 1 P.M. to 4 P.M., with a supervised lunch at the Camp Cheeca cottage for an extra charge.

On a typical day, participants play getting acquainted games, followed by hands-on instruction in marine life identification. Then they'll take a walk along the resort's own nature trail or along the beach, trying out their newfound powers of plant and animal identification, before heading to the pool for some water games.

After lunch, there's more learning about sea creatures during a "Fashion a Fish" session in which the children create their own fish and discuss its attributes. That's often followed by the resort's most popular activity for children: catch-and-release fishing from the pier with a hand line.

Periodic field trips are scheduled to John Pennekamp Coral Reef State Park, the Dolphin Research Center, and the Theater of the Sea. The tennis pro offers individual and group lessons for children.

NICETIES: There's always a pile of sand toys available under one of the thatched-roof huts on the beach.

Each unit includes a VCR (be sure to bring your kids' favorite tapes) and a hair dryer.

OF INTEREST NEARBY: Theater of the Sea, on Windley Key, just north of Islamorada, offers glass-bottom boat rides and a performing dolphin show.

John Pennekamp Coral Reef State Park, the only underwater state park in the continental United States, is just 20 minutes away. Snorkeling, diving, and sightseeing trips are offered to the reef.

The state of Florida offers boat rides and guided walking tours to Lignum Vitae and Indian Keys. Lignum Vitae, on Islamorada's gulf side, is home to many rare trees that are over 10,000 years old, as well as other rich plant life. Indian Key, on the Atlantic side, was Dade County's first county seat and is a state historic site.

Key West, a colorful community of artists, writers, shopkeepers, treasure-hunters, and great chefs, is just 82 miles south.

FOR MORE INFORMATION: Write Cheeca Lodge, P.O. Box 527, Islamorada, FL 33036 or call (800) 327-2888.

SANDESTIN
Destin, Florida

At this sprawling resort on Florida's "Emerald Coast" (formerly known, more prosaically, as Florida's "Panhandle"), you're never far from the water. On the south, there's the emerald Gulf of Mexico with miles of pristine sugar-white beach. On the north, there's scenic Choctawhatchee Bay, home to bald eagles and osprey. In between, there are 2,400 acres of rolling golf courses and impeccably landscaped gardens—and recreational facilities that rival those at any Florida resort.

Built on the old hunting and ceremonial grounds of the Creek Indians, Sandestin has become a favorite destination for families from throughout the Southeast and Midwest. They're attracted mainly to its beautiful beaches and its moderate weather. The climate here permits outdoor recreation year-round (well, maybe not swimming). The average daytime temperature ranges from 61 degrees in January to 89 degrees in August.

ACCOMMODATIONS: $$$ to $$$$ Guests can stay in one to three-bedroom units in the high-rise Beachside Towers, directly on the gulf; one to four-bedroom villas and cottages bordering the fairways and lakes; the bayside townhomes, or in the recently renovated 175-room Bayside Inn. The resort has a total of 550 rental units, making it the largest resort in northeastern Florida.

Each of the villas has a fully equipped kitchen, a washer and dryer, and cable television.

A free shuttle service links all the facilities on the property. The Inn is handicapped-accessible and features kitchenettes in every room.

Golf and tennis packages are available.

DINING: The attractive Elephant Walk is Sandestin's poshest restaurant. Built into the dunes overlooking the gulf, its menu features innovatively prepared fresh seafood and sinful desserts, such as Barbados banana rum cheesecake and key lime pie. The three-course "Governor's Choice Dinner" is a good bargain. For a special treat, take your children for one of the restaurant's exotic ice cream drinks.

Sunset Bay Cafe, in the Bayside Conference Center, is the

resort's family restaurant. It's got a Caribbean atmosphere, and serves 9 different burgers and 9 different grilled chicken sandwiches, as well as steaks, seafood, jambalaya, and smoked baby back ribs. For a new taste treat, try "Hot Rock" cooking, in which you prepare shrimp, beef or chicken yourselves over fiery volcanic rock. The Saturday night prime rib special is a good bargain.

In the summer, there's live entertainment every weekend on Taylor's Tiki Deck, overlooking the bay.

Chan's Market Cafe, in the Market at Sandestin, is a deli and bakery offering fresh Gulf seafood, chargrilled burgers, and fresh-baked breads.

Leonardo's Pizza delivers pizza to guest units.

ACTIVITIES

14 courts, 5 clay, 6 hard-surface, and 3 grass, all lighted, plus the largest tennis shop in northwest Florida. Round robins, matches, daily clinics, private lessons. Sandestin hosts the Professional Grass Court Tournament every June, drawing competitors preparing for the Wimbledon championships.

Sixty-three holes, two full-service pro shops, practice facilities and a driving range. The resort's newest course, the 18-hole Burnt Pine Course, stretches along beautiful Choctawhatchee Bay. It was designed by Rees Jones (7,000 yards, par 72). The Baytowne Golf Club includes the Dunes nine, the Harbor nine, and the Troon nine. The course winds through pine forests, offering views of the gulf. The 18-hole Links course (6,700 yards, par 72) features bass-filled lagoons and large contoured greens. Daily clinics, private lessons.

Two outdoor pools, the Bayside Pool, next to the Sunset Bay Cafe (adjacent infant pool) and the Elephant Walk Pool; towels provided. Swimming from 7 1/2 miles of beach; rental chairs, umbrellas, sailboats, waverunners, kayaks, sea cycles, and boogie boards. Snorkeling and scuba-diving outings through local outfitters.

The Baytowne Marina can accommodate guests' boats up to 100 feet; rental powerboats and waverunners available.

Deep-sea and freshwater charters and party boats; billfish, cobia, snapper, grouper, mackerel, blue and white marlin are among the catch. Bass and bream fishing in the resort's stocked lakes.

Adult and child-size coaster bikes; hourly, half-day, daily and weekly rates, helmets, baskets, child seats and locks. Bike-trails throughout property.

A resort employee leads two-hour nature walks once a week. The Osprey offers 3 1/2-hour cruises from the Baytowne Marine through the Cypress Wilderness Area, in the easternmost reaches of Choctawhatchee Bay. Here you can see nesting bald eagles, osprey, and herons. Call (904) 837-7245.

The Sports Spa features Nautilus equipment, free weights, Stairmasters, stationary bikes, treadmills; exercise classes, massage, facials and body treatments. Three volleyball courts on the beach.

Poolside bingo, water relays, volleyball games, family movies (with free popcorn and drinks), basketball shootouts, arts and crafts, bike hikes, scavenger hunts, holiday activities.

FOR CHILDREN: The Sandestin Youth Program offers supervised activities for 4 through 12-year-olds daily between Memorial Day and Labor Day. (Some children's activities are also offered during holiday periods.) The summer program runs from 9 A.M. to noon for 4- to 6-year-olds and from 9 A.M. to 3 P.M. for 7- through 12-year-olds, Mondays through Saturdays. There's a daily fee, which includes a souvenir t-shirt.

Activities for 4 to 6-year-olds include supervised swimming, pool games, arts and crafts, storytelling, treasure hunts and parachute play.

Activities for 7- to 12-year-olds include scavenger hunts, field games, bike riding, wacky Olympics, and supervised aquatic games.

For teens, there are complimentary afternoon and evening events scheduled throughout the summer, including frisbee golf, sports clinics, and movies. Junior golf and tennis clinics are offered during the summer.

On Mondays, Wednesday, Friday and Saturday nights during

the summer, there's a supervised pizza dinner in the Bayside Recreation Room from 6 to 9 P.M. for 4- through 12-year-olds. Games and a movie follow. On Friday nights, children of guests dining at the resort's restaurants get a discounted rate.

Niceties: The Market at Sandestin, near the resort entrance, offers 28 specialty shops.

Arriving guests get a free drink at Taylor's Tiki Hut at the Bayside Pool.

Non-smoking rooms are available.

OF INTEREST NEARBY: Eight miles down the road, in Destin, you'll find all the recreational diversions your children could want: bumper boats, miniature golf courses, bungee jumps, race-car tracks, and fast-food restaurants.

The Naval Air Museum in Pensacola is a good destination for a rainy day. Children will enjoy seeing the aircraft on display there.

FOR MORE INFORMATION: Call (800) 277-0800 or (904) 267-8000.

SONESTA BEACH RESORT KEY BISCAYNE
Key Biscayne, Florida

It is just after dawn as you take a cup of coffee out to your balcony overlooking the Atlantic Ocean. A luxury cruise ship is silhouetted against the sun, a red orb inching up over the Atlantic. In a few minutes, pool attendants begin rearranging the deck chairs, and a tractor is driven out to rake the sand. A father and son make their way to the beachside playground, while an early-morning sailor pushes a catamaran out to the turquoise sea. In the foreground, palm trees sway gracefully in the breeze, and sea gulls and pelicans begin their day-long search for sustenance.

A new day has begun at the Sonesta Beach Resort Key Biscayne.

This luxury hotel stands like a Mayan temple on a beautiful 500-foot stretch of beach on Key Biscayne, a palm-fringed island with a semi-tropical air just a short ride from downtown Miami. The island is just close enough to Miami for its vices and virtues to be within easy reach, and just far enough away so that none of the hubbub intrudes. The resort, opened in 1969, was the third constructed on the island, which is mainly residential, with large pockets of land reserved for public use. It was totally remodeled after being heavily damaged by a hurricane in 1992.

The Sonesta Beach is a popular vacation destination for Europeans and South Americans, which gives it an international air. It also has the feel of a small hotel, despite its nearly 300 rooms and extensive group meeting facilities.

ACCOMMODATIONS: $ to $$$$ The 293 guest rooms in the hotel are tastefully furnished and decorated in light, airy colors. Half have balconies overlooking the ocean (the ocean view is worth the extra cost); the other half have balconies overlooking the island and bay. The rooms come with either a king-size bed or two double beds and stocked mini-bars.

Package plans at a lower cost than the published rates are frequently available. Rates plummet in the summer.

DINING: The Two Dragons Restaurant features Chinese (Cantonese, Mandarin, or Szechuan) food at dinner only. The Purple Dolphin features Florida and Caribbean cuisine at breakfast, lunch and dinner. The Greenhouse Café serves inexpensive breakfasts, lunches, and dinners, and will pack its items for eating on the beach or in your room.

The Snackerrie, built to blend in with the sea grape trees on the beach, serves casual food. Since the playground is a stone's throw away, you can enjoy a quick snack while your children cavort in the sand. Drinks are served at the Seabreeze pool bar, Seagrape Beach bar, Desires, and the Bar of the Two Dragons.

There are numerous restaurants elsewhere on Key Biscayne.

ACTIVITIES

 Nine Laykold tennis courts; pro shop, rental equipment, lessons.

 Privileges at the 18-hole Key Biscayne Golf Course, three minutes away.

 Atlantic Ocean and beachfront swimming pool. Snorkeling and scuba-diving trips can be arranged.

Catamarans, kayaks, aquabikes rentals at the beach.

 Deep-sea fishing charters at nearby Key Biscayne Marina or the Miami Marina.

 Rentals available, including bikes with child seats, children's bicycles, and quadricycles.

 Fitness center on the hotel's lower level, with whirlpool, sauna, steam room, exercise room, and massage room; daily exercise classes. Sports Court has exchangeable surfaces for volleyball, basketball and skating.

 Jewelry-making workshops, limbo contests, card and board games, volleyball, tug-of-war on the beach, and organized excursions to nearby shopping centers, museums, and attractions.

FOR CHILDREN: The complimentary "Just Us Kids" children's program runs year-round. The program entertains children between 5 and 13 from 10 A.M. until 10 P.M., with a break between 5 and 6 P.M. Children can participate for any amount of time you choose. The children's program's counselors are college students, and in the periods when the program is most utilized, there may be 15 on the staff. Many are bilingual.

Each morning, the program features sightseeing expeditions to such popular attractions as Metrozoo, the Seaquarium, the Monkey Jungle and the Parrot Jungle. The children return to the hotel for lunch together, usually at the Snackerrie on the beach, and then begin an afternoon of beach and pool activities and games.

Many of the afternoon activities take place at the wooden playground on the beach; you can easily see what's going on from your chaise lounge at the pool.

At 6:30 P.M., the children can have dinner with their counselors at one of the hotel's restaurants, where they can choose from special children's menus. The evenings feature movies, crafts classes, or games in the game room.

The headquarters for the program is the video game room on the hotel's lower level. The counselors keep a closet full of kids' games and crafts materials to pull out on rainy days.

Baby-sitting for younger children can be arranged through the hotel's housekeeping service.

NICETIES: Participants in the Just Us Kids program receive T-shirts.

The hotel's literature is printed in both English and Spanish.

OF INTEREST NEARBY: The Bill Baggs Cape Florida State Recreation Area occupies over 900 acres on the southern tip of Key Biscayne, an easy bike ride from the hotel. It has a historic lighthouse and museum and a reconstructed keeper's home and office, as well as lovely picnic facilities and beaches.

Miami Seaquarium, on the causeway linking Key Biscayne to the mainland, is a 60-acre park with marine life displayed in four show areas (including Flipper, America's most beloved dolphin, and an orca whale). It also has aquarium exhibits and a refuge for shore birds.

Parrot Jungle and Gardens is a marvelous private park with hundreds of beautiful birds on display. You can converse with them and watch several amusing shows.

The Venetian Pool in nearby Coral Gables is a unique free-form swimming pool fed by underground artesian wells. There are small grottoes to swim into and waterfalls to swim under.

Biscayne National Park, about an hour's drive south of Key Biscayne, provides unparalleled snorkeling and diving opportunities on a pristine reef. Call (305) 247-2400 for information about glass-bottom boat trips, canoe rentals, and snorkeling expeditions.

FOR MORE INFORMATION: Write the Sonesta Beach Resort Key Biscayne, 350 Ocean Drive, Key Biscayne, FL 33149, or call (305) 361-2021 or (800) SONESTA.

SOUTH SEAS PLANTATION
Captiva Island, Florida

Legend has it that the island of Captiva was used in the 1800s to sequester the female captives of pillaging pirates. Today, it is the site of one of the most comfortable, yet unimposing, seaside resorts in North America, South Seas Plantation.

Sprawling across the entire northern half of a barrier reef island off the western coast of Florida near Fort Myers, South Seas Plantation has two and a half miles of the best shelling beach in North America, a wildlife refuge that harbors thousands of migratory birds, and some of the most beautiful flora this side of Tahiti. Interspersed among the mangrove swamps and coconut palm groves are all the recreational facilities and amenities you'd expect at a full-service resort.

The atmosphere at South Seas is quiet and low key. You can spend all your time lying on a virtually deserted beach or take part in one of the most ambitious social programs in southern Florida. You can grab a bite to eat at Cap'n Al's Pub or dress up for the resort's elegant continental restaurant, the King's Crown.

Captiva and its sister island Sanibel are among the most attractive resort areas in Florida. Development has been guided by a concern for the ecology of the area and its natural beauty.

ACCOMMODATIONS: $$ to $$$$ South Seas offers a wide range of accommodations, from hotel rooms to four-bedroom beach houses. Most of the 600 guest quarters have full kitchens. The accommodations are all tastefully furnished; cable TV (with HBO) is provided. All units have screened-in porches or balconies with lovely views.

The accommodations are clustered in small villages, each with its own character and ambience. Like to watch the comings and goings of 100-foot yachts? Then stay at the Marina Villas, overlooking the resort's small, but busy, yacht harbor. Is tennis your top priority? Then the Tennis Villas, right next to the courts, may be for you. Do you like hearing the roar of the surf all night long? Then rent a beach house or cottage.

DINING: The resort offers a range of eating options, from casual to elegant, as well as two small grocery stores that stock everything you'll need to cook. Room service is available from 7 A.M. to 11 P.M.

The most informal restaurant—and the most fun for kids—is Cap'n Al's at the marina. It serves traditional breakfasts (you can sit outside and watch the early-rising yacht crews swab their decks) and reasonably-priced lunches. At night, Cap'n Al's features all-you-can-eat barbecues and buffets.

Chadwick's, near the resort's entrance gates, specializes in local seafood and serves breakfast, lunch, and dinner.

The lovely King's Crown Restaurant, in a converted key lime warehouse on the island's northern tip, is the resort's formal restaurant.

If you venture off premises for a meal, have it at the Bubble Room, just a short drive down Sanibel-Captiva Road. This special restaurant will appeal to the child in every adult, and every child will adore it. It is decorated with antique toys and 1940s memorabilia; an electric train whizzes along a track mounted over the bar and meanders on through one of the dining rooms.

Another fun place to eat is the Mucky Duck on the Captiva Beach, which features pub food. Parents can dine at picnic tables while their children play in the sand.

ACTIVITIES

 Twenty-one Laykold courts, many lighted; pro shop, rental equipment, instruction, game-arranging service.

 Nine holes bordered on three sides by the Gulf of Mexico, 2,946 yards, par 36; pro shop, rental equipment, instruction.

 Gulf of Mexico and 18 freshwater swimming pools; half a dozen hot tubs.

 Rental sailboats, powerboats and sea kayaks available on site. Steve and Doris Colgate's Offshore Sailing School is based here, offering instruction for both beginners and accomplished sailors. Sports Illustrated has called it the best sailing instruction program anywhere. Banana boat rides, shelling excursions, nature cruises, sunset and dinner cruises. Waterskiing, waverunners, jet skiing, parasailing.

 Pier fishing; charters available at the marina for tarpon, grouper, snook, and redfish fishing.

 Exercise Facilities: Fitness center with Keiser fitness equipment; aquasize, step aerobics classes; personal training, nutritional/fitness counseling.

 Rentals available, including bikes with child seats. Bike path runs the length of Captiva and Sanibel.

 Guided nature hikes, manatee and sea turtle awareness programs, beach walks, canoe excursions and seining expeditions for the whole family.

 Volleyball, shuffleboard, croquet, Ping-Pong equipment.

Well-rounded social program, with many of activities suitable for the whole family (water volleyball, beach walks, ice-cream socials, shell craft instruction, canoe outings). The bar in Chadwick's features live entertainment and dancing on weekends.

FOR CHILDREN: South Seas Plantation offers a year-round children's program staffed by full-time employees, all with college degrees in recreation. They are supplemented by interns, each in his or her last semester of college. Activities generally run from 9 A.M. to 1 P.M. and 5:30 to 8:30 P.M., daily except Sunday.

Children are separated by age into three groups: "Turtle Tots," for 3- through 5-year-olds; "Dolphins," for 6- through 8-year-olds, and "Manatees," for 9- through 11-year-olds. The daily fee varies, depending on the activity.

Each day's activities are organized around a different theme: sports Olympics, ecology, the beach, the Wild West, cartoons, and "messy mania." In the evenings, there are carnivals, circus activities, pizza parties, and music video parties.

A teen coordinator organizes special activities for teens, including beach bonfires, volleyball games, junior golf clinics, pizza parties, scavenger hunts, and beach parties.

The recreation staff also schedules special events for the whole family, such as bingo games, family fishing expeditions, hermit crab races, and arts and crafts classes.

Pirate's Cove, a video game room, is open from 9 A.M. to 11 P.M. Children can borrow games, books, and sports equipment from the activities office. An attractive playground outside Pirate's Cove also provides hours of fun.

The children's counselors will baby-sit during their free time.

NICETIES: Propane-powered trolleys travel the resort's roads continuously, discharging and picking up guests along the way.

OF INTEREST NEARBY: One of the main reasons to spend your vacation on Captiva is the proximity of the J. N. "Ding" Darling National Wildlife Refuge. Hundreds of species of birds winter here. Serious bird-watchers set up their tripods along the dirt road through the refuge, hoping for a glimpse of an osprey or a roseate spoonbill. Your children will delight in the almost sure sighting of an alligator. A small museum at the refuge's entrance explains the significant role the refuge plays in the island's ecology.

One of the most pleasant outings on the island is a canoe ride along the Commodore Creek Canoe Trail through the refuge. Canoes can be rented at the Tarpon Bay Marina. The water is shallow, so children 4 and over can accompany you safely. But for a truly tranquil morning, leave the children behind.

Excursion boat rides to Cabbage or Useppa cays make nice outings. The biggest thrill comes from seeing dolphins play in the boat's wake.

FOR MORE INFORMATION: Write South Seas Plantation, P.O. Box 194, Captiva Island, FL 33924, or call (800) 237-3102.

CALLAWAY GARDENS
Pine Mountain, Georgia

The gambit around the swimming pool here is not "Where are you from?" but, rather, "How many years have you been coming here?" It is a rare guest who is here for the first time, and a rare first-timer who ends a week's stay not intending to come back. What contributes to guests' intense loyalty is a gorgeous physical property, an exhausting schedule of planned activities, an indefatigably friendly and helpful staff, an atmosphere of southern hospitality, and one of the best children's programs anywhere.

Callaway Gardens is located on an idyllic site in the foothills of the Appalachians about 70 miles south of Atlanta. It is among the very few American resorts operated by a nonprofit foundation, in this case the Ida Cason Callaway Foundation, whose stated purpose is "to provide a garden of natural beauty where people may find relaxation, inspiration and a better understanding of the living world." The foundation's intent was to restore the land to its previous beauty and diversity and to preserve the native plant life of the southeastern region

The resort's facilities (rated four-star by Mobil) are dispersed throughout a 2,500-acre botanical garden that draws tens of thousands of day-trippers each year. The gardens include miles of azalea trails featuring over 700 varieties, holly trails with over 450 varieties, and a model vegetable garden that serves as the backdrop for a nationally televised garden advice show. A state-of-the- art greenhouse and garden complex, the John A. Sibley Horticultural Center, features spectacular flower displays. A restored pioneer log cabin set in a woods is interesting to visit, as is the Ida Cason Callaway Memorial Chapel, a charming stone retreat used for meditation, weddings, and organ concerts.

Many recreational activities center on Robin Lake, which is said to have the longest inland man-made beach in the country. Water-skiers crisscross each others' wakes off in the distance, while children frolic in the guarded, roped- off areas close to shore. The *Robin E. Lee* Riverboat toots as it passes by with another load of sightseers. A miniature golf course and volleyball, badminton, tennis, and shuffleboard courts provide more diversion, while a playground provides an outlet for toddlers' climbing instincts. And for those who just want to relax, there are comfortable cane-backed rockers to sit in and observe the passing sideshow.

Just a stone's throw from all this is the Big Top, where the "Flying High" circus from Florida State University performs all summer long. Once or twice a day, the 50-member circus puts on a per-formance of near-professional quality, complete with high-wire acts, trapeze artists, jugglers, and clowns (but no animals). In between shows, the performers serve as counselors in the children's program.

ACCOMMODATIONS: $$ to $$$$ Callaway Gardens has a range of accommodations, from 350 rooms at the Callaway Gardens Inn to 49 Mountain Creek Villas, to 155 two-bedroom cottages. From June through August, cottages are rented for one or two-week periods as part of the resort's Summer Recreation Program.

The cedar cottages, scattered throughout a fragrant pine forest, have all been built since 1985. Each has a fully equipped kitchen with dishwasher, beautifully furnished dining and living room with fireplace, two bedrooms with two double beds each, two baths, screened porch with barbecue grill, and a deck.

DINING: Families in the Summer Recreation Program tend to eat most of their meals in their cottages; groceries are available in nearby Pine Mountain. A snack bar called the Flower Mill offers breakfast, lunch, and dinner at moderate prices; teenagers like to gather here at night. Hearty meals with a country flavor are available at the Country Store, a restaurant and specialty shop about two miles from the cottages.

In the inn, the Plantation Room offers extravagant breakfast, luncheon, and dinner buffets, and the fancier Georgia Room serves continental cuisine. To our minds, the loveliest restaurant on the property is the Veranda, a continental- style restaurant that overlooks the serene Mountain Creek Lake. On the floor above the Veranda is The Gardens, a less formal restaurant with nightly entertainment. Children are welcome at all the restaurants.

ACTIVITIES

 Nineteen lighted tennis courts (eight Har-Tru and 11 Plexi-Pave); two racquetball courts; instruction available. Pro shop.

 Three 18-hole courses and a nine-hole executive course; instruction, two pro shops.

 A beautiful pool and hot-tub complex, with a limited snack bar, located in the cottage area; smaller pool at the Inn; guarded swimming area in Robin Lake.

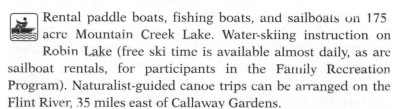 Rental paddle boats, fishing boats, and sailboats on 175 acre Mountain Creek Lake. Water-skiing instruction on Robin Lake (free ski time is available almost daily, as are sailboat rentals, for participants in the Family Recreation Program). Naturalist-guided canoe trips can be arranged on the Flint River, 35 miles east of Callaway Gardens.

 Bass and bream fishing in Mountain Creek Lake (fee, license required). Orvis-endorsed fly fishing program and fly shop.

 Adult bicycles (with child seats) and children's bicycles can be rented by the hour, day, or week. Helmets available.

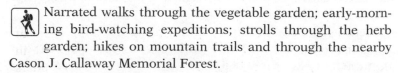 Narrated walks through the vegetable garden; early-morning bird-watching expeditions; strolls through the herb garden; hikes on mountain trails and through the nearby Cason J. Callaway Memorial Forest.

 At nearby stables.

The range of group activities here will leave you breath-less. Many are free to persons staying in the family cottages; for others, there are nominal fees. A typical day offers the option of participating in a bus tour of the gardens, attending an organ concert in the chapel, touring the Sibley Center, watching the circus, or going to a movie.

That's not all. You can run in an early-morning 5,000-meter fun run, take part in an arts-and-crafts session, go on a guided walk through Mr. Cason's vegetable garden, attend golf or tennis clinics, and learn to juggle or to walk a tightrope.

In the evenings, guests can enjoy entertainment in the Vineyard Green Lounge, twice-weekly family cookouts, and thrice-weekly family movies.

FOR CHILDREN: Callaway Gardens is proud of its summer children's program (entirely free to cottage guests), and with good reason. For 1- and 2-year-olds, care by mature staff members is available from 9 A.M. to 3 P.M. Mondays through Fridays: the Toddler Center maintains a ratio of 1 adult to 4 children.

Organized activities are available from 9 A.M. to 3 P.M. for children between 3 and 6 at the Early Childhood Center near Robin Lake. Children are separated by age for a morning of art, free play, storytelling, and circus activities. Lunch is served (there's a small charge), and afterwards the children are taken to swim in a shallow, roped-off area of the lake. The counselors are generally elementary school teachers or college seniors.

Children between 7 and 12 can attend a day camp under the Big Top. They are divided into three age groups, and activities include games, swimming, arts and crafts, sports, water-skiing, tennis, bike hikes, and acting workshops. Their program also runs from 9 A.M. to 3 P.M. and includes lunch (extra charge).

Teenagers between 13 and 16 have a program that begins at 9 A.M. and ends at 4 P.M. and includes lunch (extra charge). They take part in some of the nature programs, as well as water-skiing, beach activities, golf instruction, arts and crafts, tennis, and sailing (only for teens 15 and over).

Teenagers 16 and over (the hardest group to please) hang out at a game room near the Flower Mill. The room is equipped with electronic games, Ping-Pong, and board games. A disc jockey provides the music for a dance once a week.

Children's movies are shown Tuesday and Thursday evenings at 7 P.M. at Laurel Hall.

A special children's fishing program is offered from 6:30 to 8 A.M. Monday through Friday. Poles, bait, and transportation to a fishing lake are provided for a small charge.

Baby-sitting can be arranged.

NICETIES: Each week, members of the management staff of Callaway Gardens meet guests for continental breakfast (the resort's treat) at Robin Lake Beach. They take all questions and complaints; not infrequently, the exchange results in changes in the program the following year.

Tram service is provided on the resort grounds from 9 A.M. to 5 P.M. daily.

A coin laundry across from the pool makes it possible to do your laundry in between dips in the pool.

OF INTEREST NEARBY: Georgia operates Franklin Delano Roosevelt's old retreat at nearby Warm Springs, the Little White House, as a state historic site. The home is much as it was when he died; another home nearby has been converted into a museum, with presidential memorabilia. The springs where Roosevelt underwent rehabilitation for polio are being refurbished

FOR MORE INFORMATION: Call (800) 282-8181 or (404) 663-2281 or write Callaway Gardens, P.O. Box 2000, Pine Mountain, GA 31822-2000.

THE CLOISTER
Sea Island, Georgia

There are a few resorts in the nation to which a visit is like a voyage back in time. The legendary Cloister, on Sea Island, just off Georgia's southern coast, is one of them. Visiting Sea Island is like stepping back into another era, into bygone days when ladies and gentlemen—and even their offspring—dressed for dinner and tea was an event, not just a drink. Television was introduced here only in the mid-1980s—and only after prolonged debate. The compromise between opposing factions of management was to hide each television set in an armoire so that its presence wouldn't intrude into guests' lives unless they invited it.

But The Cloister is more than just a historic relic. It's a place where you can sample southern cuisine (peanut soup on ice is standard fare), ride on a jeep train to a "plantation supper," play a spirited game of bingo, dance to either reggae or waltz music, or go for a horseback breakfast ride. Above all, it's a place for families to enjoy each other.

The main hotel has intense romantic appeal, with its terracotta roof, vaulted windows, and grand piano in the Spanish Lounge. The Spanish moss for which Georgia is famous, the palm trees, the abundance of spring-blooming azaleas, and five miles of impeccably groomed beach are all part of The Cloister's lush surroundings.

What makes a vacation here so inviting is the special combination of great natural beauty (10,000 acres of unspoiled forest and marshes) and attractive structures (there are no high rises or strip shopping centers to be seen). It's probably no accident that it was on Sea Island that Eugene O'Neill, perhaps America's greatest playwright, wrote his only happy play, Ah, Wilderness!

ACCOMMODATIONS: $$ to $$$$ You may choose from small rooms with a double bed, larger rooms with a sitting alcove and wet bar, large beachfront rooms, guest house suites or ocean-front parlor suites. You will find them more than comfortable; many of the 263 rooms are quite elegant with lovely views. Many of the 500 privately owned luxury homes in the Sea Island cottage colony also can be rented through Sea Island Properties.

Rates include three full meals daily. Special spa, tennis and golf packages are available. Children who share a room with their parents are charged only for meals on a scale that rises with age (there's no charge for children 2 and under). The high season is spring through fall.

During the Family Festival, from mid June through early September, there is no charge for children's meals (that's true also during the Christmas and New Year's holidays).

DINING: Eating is an experience at Sea Island, with extravagant meals offered in the Cloister Dining Room or, as an alternative, at the Sea Island Beach Club, a short walk away, the Sea Island Golf Club, or the St. Simons Island Club (the latter two are a short drive). At every meal, fresh flowers decorate tables set with crisp linen tablecloths.

Breakfasts are sumptuous, and the buffet lunches are formidable (the Beach Club is a nice venue for this meal). Dinners are elegant and delectable seven-course affairs.

Men must wear jackets for dinner in the Cloister Dining Room, and collared shirts for breakfast and lunch (dress at the Beach Club is more casual). Women are expected to dress up too. On Wednesday and Saturday nights, it is customary for guests to wear gowns or dinner jackets with black ties, but many of the younger guests forgo that tradition.

Children may dine with their parents or eat dinner together in the children's dining room during the summer and at Christmas and Easter. Supervision is provided from 6 to 9 P.M. daily, except Sunday, for 4- through 11-year-olds.

ACTIVITIES

 Eighteen fast-dry clay composition tennis courts, with professional instruction available. Clinics and guest round robins scheduled each week. No court or greens fees for players under 19.

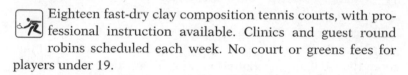 Five golf courses with a total of 54 holes, many of which have beautiful views of the Atlantic Ocean; state-of-the-art Golf Learning Center. The greens are interrupted by lovely groupings of azaleas and huge live oaks. Four nine-hole courses designed by Colt and Alison: Seaside, 3,384 yards, par 36; Plantation, 3,516 yards, par 36; Retreat, 3,326 yards, par 36; Marshside, 3,192 yards, par 36. Eighteen-hole course at St. Simons Club, 6,308 yards, par 72, designed by Joseph Lee. Driving ranges, putting greens, instruction, pro shop.

 Two large pools and a wading pool that overlook the ocean and The Cloister's five-mile-long strip of beach. Pool chairs and towels available without charge.

 Rentals of inland boats and oceangoing sailboats available; one and a half hour sightseeing cruises.

 Nearby waters abound with trout, bass, drum, flounder, whiting, croaker, and sheepshead.

 Rental fleet numbers 550—including tandems, bikes with children's seats, and children's bikes.

Regularly scheduled nature walks.

The Long family has managed the stables since 1948, and it's a favorite hangout for little girls, who are allowed to help groom and pamper their mounts. The Longs care for more than 40 horses and offer lessons in the ring or on a trail, and rides through the marsh and on the beach.

 Three skeet courses; instruction, rental equipment.

 Full service spa. Services include facials, massage, Swiss shower, hydrotherapy, and other aesthetic treatments.
Exercise/cardiovascular equipment, classes, and personal assessments.

Movies, lectures on the history of the area and the resort's founding, bridge tournaments, and guided walks; croquet, badminton, and other lawn games.

Bingo is one of Sea Island's big evening attractions for families; the games on Tuesdays and Thursdays frequently attract more than 100 guests. Plan to join in the line dancing when the game is over. If you've never done the bunny hop or the alley cat, you'll learn quickly. Another Sea Island highlight is the Friday evening Plantation Supper, outdoors at the torch-lit Ocean Grove by the beach. Nightly dancing (except Sunday) is popular with adults; you'll hear everything from beach music to reggae to waltzes.

Special themed winter programs focus on bridge, food and wine, wildlife, personal financial planning, and gardening.

FOR CHILDREN: The Cloister offers a free supervised children's program from June through early September and during the Thanksgiving, Christmas, and Easter school breaks.

Junior staffers (college students) will keep 3- to 11-year-olds occupied during most of each day, every day except Sunday. The list of activities reads like a summer camp brochure—shuffleboard, lawn games, scavenger hunts, pony rides, sand-sculpture contests, nature walks, kite flying, croquet, jeep rides, and morning and afternoon swims. The junior staffers are all warm, friendly, and energetic.

Children under 3 may participate in these activities if accompanied by a parent or sitter.

Older children will enjoy the many sports and social activities, from bicycling to bingo. Children over 11 seem happy to spend time on their own at the Beach Club, where they swim and play shuffleboard or Ping-Pong.

On rainy days, the resort schedules movie parties, magic shows, and arts and crafts classes. Sometimes there are cooking classes and classes on "modern manners."

The holidays offer excuses for other activities—a dance for teenagers on New Year's Eve, an Easter sunrise service and egg hunt, fireworks and dancing on the Fourth of July, and a Thanksgiving harvest celebration.

Baby-sitters are easy to come by.

NICETIES: During the cooler months, afternoon tea is served in the Spanish Lounge. In late evening, you'll find a tray set out with milk and cookies.

For early risers, continental breakfast is available.

OF INTEREST NEARBY: Sea Island is one of Georgia's Golden Isles. St. Simons, adjacent to Sea Island, has many older homes as well as one of the nation's oldest continuously working lighthouses.

Jekyll Island, to the south, was once a vacation destination for the Rockefellers, Morgans, and Vanderbilts, and is now a state park. You can tour the historic district (called Millionaires' Village) or enjoy the wildlife refuge, beaches, and picnic sites. Like Sea Island, Jekyll Island and St. Simons are accessible by car.

Cumberland Island, farther south, is a national seashore on which cars are not permitted. The island may be reached by boat from the mainland. It offers wonderful opportunities for nature study and solitude.

FOR MORE INFORMATION: Write The Cloister, Sea Island, GA 31561, or call (800) 732-4752.

THE GROVE PARK RESORT
Asheville, North Carolina

Built into the western slope of Sunset Mountain and overlooking the city of Asheville, the Grove Park Resort has a spectacular setting. The hotel was built in 1913 from enormous boulders brought from local quarries. "Built not for the present alone, but for ages to come, and the admiration of generations yet unborn"—that was the motto of its founder, Edwin Wiley Grove, a pharmaceutical firm owner from St. Louis.

In its 80-plus-year history, the hotel has hosted such illustrious guests as inventor Thomas Edison, President Franklin D. Roosevelt, and industrialists Harvey Firestone and Henry Ford. F. Scott Fitzgerald did much of his writing in the 1930s from his own special room here.

Like many of the nation's grand hotels, it was taken over by the State Department during World War II and used first as an internment center for Axis diplomats and later as a rest center for Navy personnel. Returned to recreational use in 1945, it underwent a number of management changes and expansions. In 1984, it was updated with a new heating system and additional facilities and became a year-round resort. It is listed in the National Register of Historic Places.

With a country club, a large sports facility, playground, and children's program, the Inn offers plenty of activities to keep you on the grounds. But with the Smoky and Blue Ridge mountains within easy reach for hiking and sightseeing, there's also plenty to do beyond.

ACCOMMODATIONS: $$$ The Main Inn offers rooms decorated with antique light fixtures and authentic mission oak furnishings; the rooms open in toward one of the country's first hotel atriums and have views looking either over the gardens and hillside or toward the distant mountains. The Sammons Wing and the Vanderbilt Wing (opened in 1988) are modern additions, designed to complement the Inn's original architecture. In all, there are 510 rooms.

Low season is from January through March. Various package plans are available that include meals, golf or tennis fees, or admission to sights such as the Biltmore House. Children under 16 are free.

DINING: The Grove Park Resort features several fine restaurants, each with its unique atmosphere and cuisine. The Sunset Terrace offers a spectacular setting along with a traditional American-continental menu; open only in warm weather, the terrace looks toward the Blue Ridge Mountains and is a lovely place to linger over lunch.

The Blue Ridge Dining Room and Terrace serves breakfast, lunch, and dinner in a lovely setting in the Inn's new Vanderbilt wing. The Horizons Restaurant, specializing in innovative versions of classical dishes, is open for dinner only. Horizons requires reservations and jackets for men. Most suited to family dining with younger children is the Carolina Café, which serves casual food.

At the Country Club is the Pool Cabana, which serves hamburgers and hot dogs for lunch.

ACTIVITIES

 Six Laykold courts outdoors, three Plexi-Pave courts indoors; squash and racquetball courts also available.

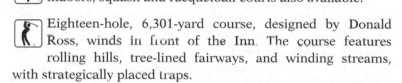 Eighteen-hole, 6,301-yard course, designed by Donald Ross, winds in front of the Inn. The course features rolling hills, tree-lined fairways, and winding streams, with strategically placed traps.

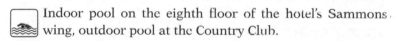 Indoor pool on the eighth floor of the hotel's Sammons wing, outdoor pool at the Country Club.

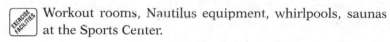 Workout rooms, Nautilus equipment, whirlpools, saunas at the Sports Center.

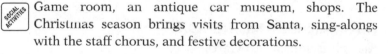 Game room, an antique car museum, shops. The Christmas season brings visits from Santa, sing-alongs with the staff chorus, and festive decorations.

FOR CHILDREN: The Inn runs two supervised activity programs for children, ages 3 to 5 and 6 to 11, from 9:30 A.M. to 4:30 P.M. every day except Sunday from late May through Labor Day, and on weekends the rest of the year. The activities include nature hikes, crafts, swimming, and low-key instruction in tennis, racquetball, and badminton. The fee includes meals.

A "parents' night out" program is offered from 6 to 10:30 P.M. on Friday and Saturday nights throughout the year at the activity room at the indoor pool. The charge includes movies, pizza, and soft drinks.

Next to the Sports Center there's a playground for children, equipped with a climbing center, corkscrew slide, swing, and horizontal ladder.

NICETIES: Rows of rocking chairs await you near the landscaped front entrance.

A shuttle bus runs frequently between the Inn and the Country Club.

OF INTEREST NEARBY: Asheville's major tourist attraction is the Biltmore House. You'll probably want to allow at least a half day to tour this immense mansion and its beautiful gardens and winery. While children under 11 are admitted free, this might be better enjoyed when the kids are in the children's program.

The Western North Carolina Nature Center is a small zoo and mini-farm with both indoor and outdoor exhibits. The nocturnal hall, with its collection of owls and opossums, will delight your children, as will the small petting area. A picnic area on the Nature Center grounds borders the Swannanoa River and makes a good spot for a lunchtime romp.

FOR MORE INFORMATION: Write to The Grove Park Resort, 290 Macon Avenue, Asheville, NC 28804. Or call (704) 252-2711 or (800) 438-5800 for reservations.

KIAWAH ISLAND RESORT
Kiawah Island, South Carolina

As you enter Kiawah Island Resort's sprawling grounds for the first time, you're likely to encounter a white-tailed deer leaping across the road, an alligator languishing on the shore of a lagoon, or an egret fishing in a water trap on the golf course. Their presence is concrete evidence of the environmental sensitivity that's governed the development of this resort.

Built in 1976 on an undeveloped beach 21 miles south of

Charleston, the resort occupies about half of a 10,000-acre barrier island. Several miles of beachfront remain undeveloped, reputedly the longest stretch of privately owned and undeveloped beach on the East Coast. Even in the developed area, you still feel as though you're in the midst of a maritime forest, for each grouping of villas has been designed to blend into the surrounding forest of palmetto, live oak, loblolly pine, and magnolia.

Unless you stay at the Kiawah Inn, your villa is likely to be at the end of a long and winding road. No overhead lights shine on the roads at night, and even the Inn lighting is dim, because light would disturb the loggerhead turtles that nest on the beach. The island is home to over 150 species of birds, 18 species of mammals, and 30 species of reptiles and amphibians.

The resort is divided into two parts—West Beach, which includes the Inn, a golf course and a tennis complex, and East Beach, which includes the 21-acre Night Heron Park, the conference center, and another golf course and tennis complex. Each section has its own amenities.

Kiawah is a year-round resort, though business drops off considerably in winter, when temperatures dip into the 50s and can be as low as the 30s. The climate permits year-round golfing, tennis, and other land sports, but swimming isn't possible in the winter.

ACCOMMODATIONS: $$$ to $$$$ Choose accommodations closest to the activity you are likely to spend the most time at. Ocean lovers would do well to take a room at Kiawah Island Inn or a beachside villa. Inn rooms have mini-bars, but no kitchen facilities; however, the one- to four-bedroom villas have fully equipped kitchens, as well as washers and dryers.

Non-beachside accommodations are clustered near the tennis centers, the golf courses, the park, or the pools, almost all overlooking a beautiful lagoon. Families with small children should one of the two villa complexes near a pool—Turtle Point or Night Heron Park. Prices for non-beachside accommodations are lower. All beachside villas have balconies, and all landside villas have screened-in porches.

Special golf, tennis, and family packages feature lower-than-daily rates. There are 150 inn rooms and 310 villas. Rates fall considerably during the winter months.

DINING: Kiawah's flagship restaurant, the Jasmine Porch, is the only restaurant that serves breakfast, lunch, and dinner. The fare is delicious and the atmosphere pleasant. It's at the inn.

In East Beach, the Indigo House serves lunch and dinner daily, featuring fresh seafood, pastas and salads. The Sundancer is a poolside bar and grille with a casual island atmosphere and an ocean view. The Ocean Course Restaurant, accessible by shuttle, offers views of the ocean and the golf course on which the 1991 Ryder Cup Matches were held.

Snacks and drinks are also available at various activity centers around the resort, including the Inn pool area and the golf and tennis areas.

Families with villa accommodations can buy groceries at the General Store, a convenience food shop on site, or at a supermarket about four miles toward Charleston along a scenic two-lane road.

ACTIVITIES

 Twenty-three Har-Tru courts and five hard courts, two lighted. Pro shop, daily clinics for adults and children. Court fees.

The 6,223-yard, par 71 Marsh Point course, designed by Gary Player, challenges golfers with 13 water-hazard holes and undulating greens. The Jack Nicklaus-designed course at Turtle Point (6,889 yards, par 72) offers long, narrow fairways and three scenic oceanside holes. Tom Fazio was the architect of a third course, Osprey Point (6,840 yards, par 72). Pete Dye built the Ocean Course, with every offering dramatic views of the Atlantic. The Ocean Course hosted the 1991 Ryder Cup matches. All courses have clubhouses, pro shops, driving ranges, and putting greens.

In the Atlantic Ocean from a south-facing beach; low rolling surf, water temperature in the 80s in the summer. The three pool complexes—at Night Heron Park, Turtle Point, and the Inn—are popular gathering places. The Inn has an upper-level pool for adults only and a lower-level pool for families. All have baby pools.

Sailboat and windsurfer rentals are available through Kiawah Island Inn. At the beach, you can rent windsurfers, sailboats, rafts and boogie boards.

 Charter fishing excursions from nearby Bohicket Marina.

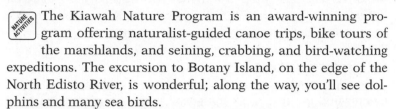 The Kiawah Nature Program is an award-winning program offering naturalist-guided canoe trips, bike tours of the marshlands, and seining, crabbing, and bird-watching expeditions. The excursion to Botany Island, on the edge of the North Edisto River, is wonderful; along the way, you'll see dolphins and many sea birds.

Half-day, daily or weekly rentals with child seats and helmets; tandems, tow carts, three-wheelers available. Fourteen miles of paved trails.

 Fitness center with state-of-the-art equipment; Jazzercize and water aerobics classes.

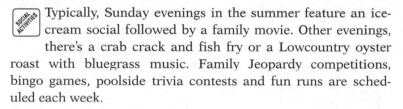 Typically, Sunday evenings in the summer feature an ice-cream social followed by a family movie. Other evenings, there's a crab crack and fish fry or a Lowcountry oyster roast with bluegrass music. Family Jeopardy competitions, bingo games, poolside trivia contests and fun runs are scheduled each week.

FOR CHILDREN: Kamp Kiawah provides supervised activities for children during the summer, from 9 A.M. to 4:30 P.M. The program is offered for 3- to 12-year-olds, Monday through Friday; half-day and full day rates are available. Among the activities offered are water games, face-painting, spin art, tye dying, and beach activities.

"Kiawah Nature Club' offers 8 to 14-year-olds the chance to explore the fun side of nature with a staff biologist. Participants learn about pond life, comb the beach for sea shells, sponges and crabs, and learn about the island's abundant bird population.

Night Heron Park has a small playground with a variety of equipment on a sand base. For the 4- to 6-year-old group, a "tiny tot" tennis program is offered from 8:30 to 9 A.M., Monday through Friday in the summer, for a nominal charge.

Activities for teenagers are scheduled daily, including volley-ball, pizza parties, dances, 3 on 3 basketball tournaments, music trivia contests and pool parties.

Baby-sitting can be arranged.

NICETIES: The tennis pro will match you with partners of equal ability in case you're not traveling with one. Round robin tennis tournaments are arranged for parents and children.

OF INTEREST NEARBY: Tours to Charleston can easily be arranged through the Inn's guest services coordinator, or you can go off by yourself to tour the historic district at the tip of the peninsula. Charleston's historic homes, gardens, museums, forts, wharves, and shops make this a worthwhile trip. A cruise of the harbor or to Fort Sumter, where the Civil War began, are fun and educational diversions for children and adults.

FOR MORE INFORMATION: Call (800) 654-2924 or write Kiawah Island Resort, P.O. Box 12357, Charleston, SC 29422-2357.

SEA PINES PLANTATION
Hilton Head, South Carolina

Our kids had figured out the truth about Hilton Head before we even arrived at our rental villa.

"There aren't any bumper boats here," said one.

"Where are the video arcades?" asked another.

"It's all nature stuff," said the third.

Right. That's why we were vacationing here.

In contrast to many other beach resorts, Hilton Head, South Carolina, is refreshingly unspoiled. It has many of the amenities that kids seem to expect from a beach resort—numerous minia-ture golf courses, and a water park, for instance. For the most part, though, they are hidden away or so tastefully landscaped that they don't scream out at you as you pass by, "Spend money here."

Hilton Head is a barrier island in the Atlantic Ocean off the coast of South Carolina. The nearest city is Savannah, Ga., 45 miles away. From the air, the island looks like a big foot. Sea Pines Plantation is located on the foot's toes.

Sea Pines was the island's first resort development, and it's still the largest. Its construction in 1957 by visionary developer Charles Fraser turned Hilton Head into a major tourist destination. Fraser designed Sea Pines with the idea of setting a new standard for beach communities. His resort was to blend into the environment, rather than obliterate it. And so it does.

Sea Pines sprawls across 5,000 acres on the southwest part of the island. Within the complex are three distinct areas in which you can rent villas or houses: Harbour Town, with a cluster of outdoor cafes, a great playground, the tennis complex and a bustling marina; Fairways and Lagoons, private homes scattered around the golf courses, and South Beach, with New England-style architecture, a small marina, a dozen restaurants and shops, and a nice pool.

ACCOMMODATIONS: $$ to $$$$ Sea Pines manages 450 rental villas and homes, ranging from one to six bedrooms in size. All are fully furnished and include washers and dryers. You can find everything from an moderately priced villa without a water view to a beachfront home with its own swimming pool.

DINING: About 200 restaurants are scattered around the island's 42 square miles. Almost all have children's menus; the offerings range from Mexican to Italian to Mediterranean to seafood, seafood and more seafood.

In South Beach, Salty Dog Cafe is a fun place for lunch or a casual dinner.

The most authentic local restaurant is Abe's Native Shrimp House. Family-owned and operated, with three generations of family members helping out at any given time, it features such regional specialties as lowcountry shrimp boil, gumbo, black-eyed peas, hush puppies, shrimp and okra, and stewed oysters.

ACTIVITIES

 Five miles of beach; numerous pools within walking distance of each rental unit.

The Sea Pines Racquet Club, in the Harbour Town area, has 24 Har-Tru courts and 4 hard-surface courts, all lighted. An extensive instruction program includes several daily clinics; private lessons available. Monday mornings, there's a free guest mixer and pro evaluation session. Monday evenings, the pros put on an exhibition, with free refreshments for the audience. Round robins, mixers throughout the week. No court fees for guests.

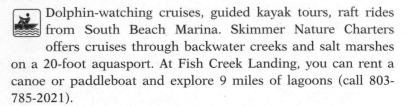 Three public courses. Harbour Town Golf Links', the resort's most famous course, was designed by Pete Dye (6,912 yards, par 71). *Sports Illustrated* has called it "nothing short of a work of art." The Ocean Course (6,614 yards, par 72) was designed by George Cobb. It's the oldest golf course on the island and features great views of the ocean. The Sea Marsh Course (6,515 yards, par 72), is another of George Cobb's designs; it winds through island forests and natural salt marshes and past scenic lagoons (watch out for alligators!)

The 24 pros on the staff of the Sea Pines Academy of Golf offer lessons and stroke evaluations; beginners are their specialty. Reduced course fees and preferred tee times for resort guests.

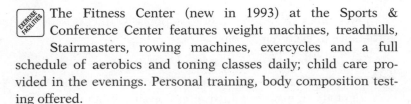 Dolphin-watching cruises, guided kayak tours, raft rides from South Beach Marina. Skimmer Nature Charters offers cruises through backwater creeks and salt marshes on a 20-foot aquasport. At Fish Creek Landing, you can rent a canoe or paddleboat and explore 9 miles of lagoons (call 803-785-2021).

 Parasailing, windsurfing opportunities at South Beach Marina and Harbour Town.

 Crabbing from docks and roadways. Shrimping expeditions on the *Tammy Jane*. Deep-sea and in-shore party boats, shore fishing.

 Fifteen miles of shaded paved paths running parallel to the roads; hourly, daily weekly rentals; tandems, baby seats and trailers, helmets.

The Fitness Center (new in 1993) at the Sports & Conference Center features weight machines, treadmills, Stairmasters, rowing machines, exercycles and a full schedule of aerobics and toning classes daily; child care provided in the evenings. Personal training, body composition testing offered.

The Forest Preserve is a 605-acre natural area within Sea Pines that includes nature trails, several lakes and an ancient Indian shell ring. At the Stoney Baynard ruins, a former cotton plantation within Sea Pines, you can discover how 18th-century residents built walls out of a material called "tabby," made from crushed oyster shells, water and sand. Naturalists from the Museum of Hilton Head Island lead walks through Pinckney Island National Wildlife Refuge on Wednesdays; visitors can also go out with museum volunteers on their nightly sea turtle patrols.

 Lawton Stables (803-671-2586) offers guided rides and horsedrawn carriage tours through the Sea Pines Forest Preserve.

Bingo and pool games, guided hayrides, ice cream socials, beachside kite-flying, crabbing lessons, tie-dyeing work-shops, cookouts, and group games. Guided day trips to Savannah. Free activities nearly every summer night somewhere on the island. Singer and storyteller Gregg Russell has been a fixture under the Liberty Oak in Harbour Town for more than 20 years; he performs from 8 P.M. to 10 P.M. nightly, except Sunday, in the summer.

FOR CHILDREN: Sea Pines' "Fun for Kids" program offers super-vised activities daily in the summer for 4 through 12-year-olds. Full-day (9 A.M. to 3 P.M.) and half-day (9 A.M. to noon) rates are available; there's a discount if you enroll your child for a whole week.

Children meet at the Sports and Conference Center in the morning and then go off with their age groups for swimming, tennis and golf lessons and such activities as arts and crafts, horseback riding, dolphin-watching, crabbing, pool games, miniature golf, nature study, soccer or basketball. Every week, there are field trips to the island's Fun Center (complete with batting cages and video games), to the Waterfun Park Wet & Wild, and the local fire station. Swimming is on the schedule daily.

The program employs teachers and college interns, all trained in CPR; a 1 to 6 ratio is maintained for preschoolers, and a 1 to 8 ratio for school-age children.

On Tuesday and Thursday nights during the summer, the "Children's Dinner Club" meets for three hours. The fee includes dinner and an activity: a hayride, a trip to the waterslides, pool games, or a boat cruise.

Tennis classes are offered for children 4 and over; the Junior Stan Smith Tennis Academy provides 2 1/2 hours of intensive instruction daily for serious teen and pre-teen players.

Commander Zodiac, a concessioner at South Beach Marina, offers children-only raft rides and a "Kids' Water Fun" program, which provides a morning of beach games, sailboat or power-boat rides, crabbing and scavenger hunts. Call (803) 671-3344.

The Gypsy offers special two-hours Kid's Cruises at 9:30 A.M. Tuesdays through Thursdays; call (803) 363-2900.

NICETIES: Room service is available between 7 A.M. and 11 P.M.

Sea Pines has a fulltime concierge to help smooth out problems and arrange activities.

OF INTEREST NEARBY: From Harbour Town Marina, you can take a boat trip on the *Vagabond* across Calibogue Sound to Daufuskie Island, a barrier island still inhabited by descendents of the slaves who once worked the island's cotton plantations. Call (803) 842-4155.

FOR MORE INFORMATION: Call Sea Pines Plantation at (800) 845-6131. For general tourist information about Hilton Head, call the Chamber of Commerce at (800) 523-3373.

THE TIDES INN
Irvington, Virginia

The setting of the Tides Inn could not be more exquisite. This small, special resort is located on a dot of land surrounded by water on three sides, creating a quiet haven. You'll enjoy the natural beauty of Carter's Creek and find it provides a sheltered spot for sailing and canoeing.

Water is definitely the controlling element here. The Inn is located eight miles up the Rappahannock River from the western shore of the Chesapeake Bay, enabling guests to arrive by yacht.

The Tides Inn is both comfortable and unpretentious. It is family run, and every effort is made to make guests feel at home. This was the tradition started by E. A. Stephens and his wife, Ann Lee Stephens, who opened The Tides Inn in 1947. When the Stephenses first bought the point, it was overgrown with honeysuckle, briers, and vines. They cleared the land and built the inn using native wood. The cypress you see today in the View Room and the Dining Room came from a swamp 20 miles from the Inn.

The Stephenses' son, Bob Lee, and his wife, Suzy, took over when Bob Lee's father retired in 1963. Bob Lee started working here in 1947 as an elevator boy. He and his wife share the same commitment to understated luxury and "quiet quality." And now their oldest and youngest sons, Lee and Randy, have begun to take over. Family is, indeed, fundamental at the Tides Inn!

ACCOMMODATIONS: $$$ to $$$$ When the Tides Inn first opened in 1947, there were 47 rooms. Now there are 110 in the Main Building, the East Wing, the Garden House, the Lancaster House, and the Windsor House. Many rooms have balconies or patios. Family suites are also available. All of the rooms are light and airy. E. A. Stephens had planned for every guest to enjoy the view. "So few places I stay are built the way I like them," he said. "I'm building this one my own way." So most of the rooms have windows 13 feet wide and almost five feet tall, set so low you can lie in bed and look out.

Rates include three meals daily. There is no charge for children under 12, except for a modest daily service charge. Children 12 through 15 pay a reduced daily rate for meals, and children 16 and over pay the regular daily third person rate.

DINING: The Tides Inn is known far and wide for its excellent southern cooking. You'll find an abundance of Chesapeake Bay specialties as well. The dining-room employees all wear name tags showing how many years they've been on staff.

Guests will delight in breakfast (E. A. Stephens' favorite meal). The main breakfast is served from 8 to 9:30 A.M. A continental break-fast is also available, from 7:30 to 8 A.M. and again from 9:30 to 11 A.M.

If you take an early-afternoon cruise on *Miss Ann*, you'll have lunch aboard. You may also choose to eat in the Dining Room or walk down to the Summer House next to the saltwater pool and enjoy a casual buffet luncheon, served between 12:30 and 2:30 P.M.

Or you may wish to explore the Tides Lodge for lunch. This facility is located just across Carter's Creek and is operated by Mr. Stephens' brother.

Soft-shell crabs are a delicacy you'll find on the menu every evening. Other entrées will vary, but you'll find a wonderful selection—everything from roast goose with fennel to baked ocean grouper with crabmeat. The Sunday night Seafood Buffet is also a real treat.

For a change of scenery, dine at Cap'n B's, located at the Golden Eagle Gallery Club House, two miles away. (There's a courtesy van service.) Cap'n B's offers an interesting history, with a building modeled after a house in New Orleans, and Cajun food.

ACTIVITIES

 Four outdoor courts, two clay, two all-weather. No court fees.

Three courses in beautiful settings. They are the 18-hole Golden Eagle Course (6,943 yards, par 72), the 18-hole Tartan Course at the Lodge (6,500 yards, par 72), and the nine-hole Executive Course (par 3). Pro shop, instruction. Reduced greens fees in March and December.

Saltwater pool next to a beach looking out on the creek, shallow end for children.

The High Tide and the recently refurbished *Miss Ann* departs once or twice daily on cruises—a cove cruise on Carter's Creek, a bay shore picnic, or a luncheon cruise. Sailboats, canoes, and paddleboats are also available without charge.

Ponds on the golf course are well stocked for freshwater anglers. The dockmaster can also arrange saltwater fishing. Local captains will take guests fishing for spot, croaker, or bluefish.

Complimentary, including tandems and bikes with child seats.

Play pavilion with pool, Ping Pong, croquet, and shuffle-board. Dancing several nights a week, movies, slide shows, shipboard-style horse racing, bingo, or a golf clinic. If you're planning a trip in the fall or spring, ask about the theme weekends, such as watermen's weekend, country weekend, and history weekend.

FOR CHILDREN: A free supervised program for children ages 4 to 12 is offered daily from Memorial Day through Labor Day. Several college-age counselors supervise the program from 10 A.M. to 5 P.M. (with a noon starting time on Sundays). Two nights a week they supervise a children's dinner.

Children meet in the playroom for games and crafts. They usually have lunch at the Summer House by the pool. Afternoon activities include swimming, paddleboating, beach trips, excursions to the local history museum, guided nature walks or a movie. The children may also visit a local crab house, where they'll get an insider's view of the seafood industry.

The children's favorite activity is crabbing in Carter's Creek. Their bait is chicken wings tied to strings.

Children are free to participate in the program as much or as little as they please.

Teenagers will find plenty to do—canoeing, sailing, tennis. The pool is a particular magnet; it's open 24 hours a day.

Baby-sitters are available.

NICETIES: You'll find a retractable clothesline in the bathroom, as well as a coffee and tea maker and hair dryer in the room.

Small pets (under 50 pounds) are welcome to stay with guests in the soundproof Garden House wing.

OF INTEREST NEARBY: Stratford Hall, the plantation home and birthplace of Robert E. Lee, is one of Virginia's most beautiful historic homes and only an hour's drive from the Tides Inn. The views of the Potomac are spectacular.

About half an hour's drive from the Tides Inn you'll find the Yorktown Battlefield. The film "The Siege of Yorktown," shown at the Visitors Center, is well worth seeing. While you're at the Visitors Center, take a look at the military tents used by George Washington during the Yorktown campaign. Also ask for the map outlining two self-guiding auto tours through the battlefield. The Yorktown Victory Center also shows a movie, called "The Road to Yorktown."

Williamsburg is an hour's drive from The Tides Inn.

FOR MORE INFORMATION: Write The Tides Inn, P.O. Box 480, Irvington, VA 22480, or call (800) TIDES INN.

WINTERGREEN RESORT
Wintergreen, Virginia

Wintergreen was founded as a ski resort, but after several snowless winters, its operators learned that winter resort economics aren't built on variable weather. Since the mid '80s, Wintergreen has worked hard to become a four season resort. As a result, there's no time of year that a visit here isn't rewarding.

Wintergreen's greatest asset is its size—10,800 acres in the Blue Ridge Mountains, with one half of the acreage set aside for preservation, research and education. Much of the acreage is forested with oak and hickory trees that turn brilliant hues of gold and orange in the fall. Springtime is special here because of the huge population of wildflowers. Summer permits a full range of recreational opportunities, and snowmaking equipment has now made downhill skiing a staple of winter recreation.

Wintergreen's homes and condominiums are scattered throughout its expansive acreage. Visitors have the choice of a lakeside condo or "farmhouse" amid rolling farmland, a townhouse or single-family home perched on a mountain glade, or an apartment on one of the two golf courses.

The focal point of most of Wintergreen's social activity is the Mountain Inn, perched on one of the resort's highest ridges. The Mountain Inn's wide patio is an excellent vantage point for Wintergreen's most pleasurable pastime—watching the changing face of the dramatic Blue Ridge Mountains.

ACCOMMODATIONS: $$ to $$$$ Wintergreen has 350 rental homes and condominiums ranging in size from studios to seven bedrooms. Each tastefully furnished unit has a a fully equipped kitchen, washer and dryer, cable TV, central air conditioning, and a patio or balcony. Most units have fireplaces.

Special themed week-end packages are offered throughout the year.

DINING: Several types of dining experiences are available at the resort's five year-round and two seasonal restaurants.

Light fare—soup, salad, pizza, pasta and sandwiches—is offered at Cooper's Vantage, with live entertainment some evenings. Adjacent to the Mountain Inn is the Coper Mine, with a continental menu and an atmosphere dubbed "casually elegant." The Garden Terrace is a quiet spot with a view of both the valley and the indoor spa (kids eat free at breakfast time daily and from 5:30 to 6:30 P.M. Wednesdays through Sundays). In the valley, The Verandah, at the Stoney Creek Golf Clubhouse, offers lunch and dinner.

Families will enjoy the Rodes Farm Inn. It's worth the 10-mile trip to the valley for genuine Southern cooking, served family style. The long pine tables at the restored 19th century farmhouse are piled high with homemade biscuits, apple butter, Southern fried chicken, country ham, and peach cobbler. After a meal, parents can relax in the garden while their children play on the nearby swings and jungle gym.

The Devils Knob Golf Clubhouse serves casual food from spring through fall. During ski season, Wimmydiddles Cafeteria serves hamburgers, hot dogs and chili.

During the winter ski season, kids 12 and under eat free at some of the resort's restaurants.

ACTIVITIES

Sixteen composition clay and 3 all-weather hard-surface courts at the Devils Knob Tennis Center; 4 composition clay and 2 hard-surface courts at Stoney Creek. The resort's Tennis Academy offers private instruction, stroke of the day and junior clinics, and round robins, and guarantees you a partner upon request. Court fees.

Eighteen-hole Devils Knob Golf Course (6,576 yards, par 70) built on a mountaintop plateau at an elevation of 3,851 feet, making it the highest course in Virginia; it was designed by Ellis Maples. The Stoney Creek Golf Course (7,080 yard, par 72) is located in the valley; it was designed by Rees

Jones, son of Robert Trent Jones. Pro shops, golf academy, greens fees.

 Large indoor pool at the Wintergarden Spa and four outdoor pools. For thrills, try Paul's Creek Water Slide, a natural water slide and swimming hole.

 Rental boats and canoes for use on several manmade lakes. The nearby James River offers white water rafting and canoeing in the spring and fall.

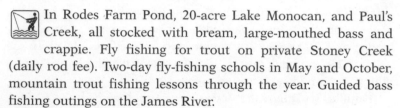 In Rodes Farm Pond, 20-acre Lake Monocan, and Paul's Creek, all stocked with bream, large-mouthed bass and crappie. Fly fishing for trout on private Stoney Creek (daily rod fee). Two-day fly-fishing schools in May and October, mountain trout fishing lessons through the year. Guided bass fishing outings on the James River.

 Mountain bike rentals for use on beginning and intermediate single-track trails; guided rides.

Thirty miles of trails crisscross Wintergreen, and a section of the Appalachian Trail is easily accessed. Wintergreen offers an excellent packet of trail guides in a waterproof packet.

Equestrian Center and stables at Rodes Farm in the valley. From April through October, the center teaches "vaulting"—gymnastic exercises on horseback. Weekly horsemanship clinics through the summer; private lessons daily except Wednesdays. Private trail rides and hacks for English riders; pony rides.

Doug Coleman, the resident naturalist, offers at least five nature-oriented field trips weekly through the spring, summer and fall, with a focus on wildflowers, butterflies, geology, archaeology, birding, fossil hunting, landscaping with native species, or lake, pond and stream ecology. Each September, Wintergreen hosts a week-end retreat on Virginia's natural history, including lectures and field studies.

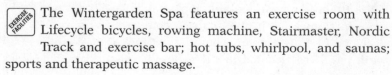 The Wintergarden Spa features an exercise room with Lifecycle bicycles, rowing machine, Stairmaster, Nordic Track and exercise bar; hot tubs, whirlpool, and saunas; sports and therapeutic massage.

Wintergreen is one of only five resorts south of New York that offer a 1,000-foot vertical drop and runs up to 4,450 feet. Its 17 runs crisscross over 82 acres, and are served by one double and four triple chairlifts. Slopes are geared for every level, from beginning to advanced, and 10 are lighted for night skiing. Backup snowmaking equipment covers all runs, guaranteeing skiing from early December through late March. Skiers get a free lesson when they rent skis here. Lift tickets are free for children 5 and under.

 Easter week-end is special, with egg basket and egg-dying workshops and an egg hunt. Memorial Day week-end features a kite-making workshop, country and western dancing, stargazing, and a paper airplane show. The Fourth of July at Wintergreen is a real family affair with hayrides, ice cream making and a spectacular fireworkes display. Mountain Heritage Weekend in October features historical encampments, crafts workshops, and a clogging demonstration. Halloween brings a chairlift "ghost express", haunted house, costume-making workshop, magic show, pumpkin carving workshop, costume contest and part. Christmas is made extra-special with old-fashioned carol sings, carriage rides, ornament and craft workshops, and lots of organized snow play.

FOR CHILDREN: Wintergreen offers an ambitious selection of children's programs.

"Kids in Action" operates daily during the summer and winter ski season for children 2 1/2 to 5 and 6 through 12, and on week-ends through the spring and fall; half-day and full day rates are available. Kids meet at the 2,500 square foot Treehouse, which includes playrooms, a playground, and "sport courts" for basketball and volleyball. They fan out from there for water rodeos, hayrides, fishing contests, nature scavenger hunts, horseback or pony riding, swimming, craft workshops, and a special "Kids in the Kitchen" program hosted by a chef.

On Friday and Saturdays night from the July 4th though Labor Day week-ends, children 4 to 12 can take part in "Kids Night Out at the Treehouse" from 7 to 11 P.M. Activities include night hikes, swimming, watching movies, arts and crafts and scavenger hunts.

Every July, "Kids Nature Camp" introduces children 6 to 12 to Wintergreen's natural treasures through a three-night overnight camping experience. Hands-on experience is provided in a variety of natural sciences. Kids also go canoeing and swimming and learn Indian lore. At the Equestrian Center, two day camps are offered each summer. One focuses on vaulting and the other on riding.

Teen Outdoor Adventure Camp is scheduled the last week of July for teens in grades 8 through 12. It challenges teens through a variety of outdoor sports, including a ropes course, whitewater canoeing, rapelling, mountain biking and backpacking.

On July and August week-ends, regular teen activities include scavenger hunts, murder mystery parties, cookouts, riding, tennis lessons, golf competitions, and fly fishing instruction.

During the ski season, "Ski Cats" provides three hours a day of on-slope instruction for ages 4 through 12, plus lunch and playtime. "Mountain Explorers" is aimed at more skilled 5- through 12-year-olds, and offers 4 1/2 hours of lessons, plus lunch. The "Ski Buddy" program for ages 4 through 12 is just what it sounds like; a private instructor will ski with your child all day. Private lessons are available for ages 3 and up and group lessons for ages 4 and up.

Babysitting can be arranged with 24 hours notice.

NICETIES: An indoor shopping mall at the Mountain Inn has everything from sports clothes to home furnishings. In addition, a small grocery store and gas station are nearby.

OF INTEREST NEARBY: Wintergreen is near some of Virginia's most famous historical and scenic attractions. Its entrance is just minutes from the Blue Ridge Parkway/Skyline Drive, which is maintained by the National Park Service and provides hiking and picnicking opportunities. Numerous roadside overlooks allow motorists to safely enjoy the breath-taking panoramas.

Just off the parkway is the Natural Bridge in Lexington, dubbed one of the seven natural wonders of the world, Natural Chimneys Regional Park in Mt. Solon, and Crabtree Falls, said to be the highest waterfall east of the Mississippi.

History buffs will want to visit Charlottesville, only 30 minutes from Wintergreen, and site of Thomas Jefferson's masterpiece, the University of Virginia. The Charlottesville area has homes owned by three of our Presidents: Jefferson's Monticello, James Monroe's Ash Lawn, and James Madison's Montpelier.

Civil War enthusiasts will want to explore Lexington, the site of Stonewall Jackson's house, his grave and his beloved Virginia Military Institute. Close by is New Market battlefield, the Shenandoah Valley, and the Appomatax Courthouse where Lee surrendered to Grant.

For More Information: Write Wintergreen, Wintergreen, Virginia, 22958, or call (800) 325-2200.

OGLEBAY RESORT
Wheeling, West Virginia

Surrounded by the breathtaking splendor of the West Virginia hills, Oglebay Resort is a 1,500-acre four-seasons resort. Formerly the summer estate of industrialist Earl W. Oglebay, it was willed to the city of Wheeling for "public recreation". Today, Oglebay serves as a nationwide model for self-sustaining public parks.

This exceptional resort offers a myriad of recreational opportunities for all ages. Seasonal activities include tennis, downhill and cross-country skiing, championship golf, gardening classes, fishing, boating, horseback roading and swimming. The only children's zoo in West Virginia is located here, and features animal petting areas, displays of endangered species, a science theater, room-sized o-gauge railroad display and a miniature train ride.

Waddington Gardens, recreated as they were early in this century, offers three seasons of floral beauty along neatly laid red brick walks. The newest attraction is the Craftsmen Center, where glassmaking and decorating can be observed close up. The Carriage House Glass Building also houses Oglebay Institute's Glass Museum, with its priceless collection of Wheeling glass and china.

Oglebay offers numerous seasonal and weekend packages that are great for family visits, including the Festival of Lights from November through January, Farm Days weekend in June, the West Virginia Glass Festival, the All-classes Car Show in August and Oglebayfest in October.

ACCOMMODATIONS: $$ Wilson Lodge offers 204 attractively decorated rooms, most with balconies or patios. Suites with spacious living rooms and one or more connecting bedrooms and freestanding chalets are perfect for families.

Oglebay also has 47 cabins in natural woodland settings. These deluxe cabins feature open stone fireplaces, central heating, completely equipped kitchens, and cable television. All have living rooms, two to six double bedrooms, and one to three baths; they sleep up to 14 people. They are rented by the week in the summer and by the day or week-end at other times.

Rates are lowest in winter.

DINING: The multi-level Ihlenfeld Restaurant in Wilson Lodge offers daily family specials and a varied children's menu for those under 14. The Sunday brunch is a favorite tradition with locals.

There are several other places to eat at the resort: Hamm Clubhouse Grill at the Speidel golf course, offering a sandwich menu during golfing season; Par III Clubhouse; Carriage House Glass; Schenk Lake Boat House; Good Zoo, and the Pine Room.

ACTIVITIES

Eleven Har-Tru lighted courts, open from April through October, and two paddle tennis courts. Nearby Wheeling Park has six additional outdoor Har-Tru courts and four rubberized courts in an air dome that extends the tennis season through the winter months.

Three 18-hole courses. The Speidel course, designed by Robert Trent Jones, features multiple tee placements and has been the home of the West Virginia Ladies' Professional Golf Association Classic for 11 years. Clubhouse with grill room, locker room facilities, pro shop; instruction available. The Crispin Center course is a beautifully landscaped year-round facility that traverses the West Virginia hills. Par III Course is short, but with a very hilly lie; a 30-tee lighted driving range adjoins it. Miniature golf course in the Children's Center near Schenk Lake.

A large outdoor pool complex with a separate toddlers' pool at Crispin Center. Youth and adult lessons are available. Wilson Lodge has an indoor aquatic complex with a pool, two hot tubs and a whirlpool set among natural vegetation and waterfalls.

Exercise Facilities: Exercise room with state-of-the-art equipment.

 Paddleboat rentals on Schenk Lake.

 Trout, bass and catfish fishing at Schenk Lake. Fee for fishing; no license required.

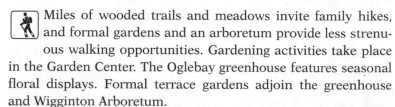 Miles of wooded trails and meadows invite family hikes, and formal gardens and an arboretum provide less strenuous walking opportunities. Gardening activities take place in the Garden Center. The Oglebay greenhouse features seasonal floral displays. Formal terrace gardens adjoin the greenhouse and Wigginton Arboretum.

 Horseback riding lessons in indoor and outdoor rings at Oglebay's riding academy. Horse shows held regularly.

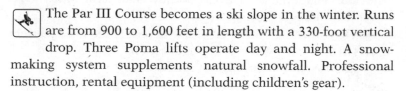 The Par III Course becomes a ski slope in the winter. Runs are from 900 to 1,600 feet in length with a 330-foot vertical drop. Three Poma lifts operate day and night. A snowmaking system supplements natural snowfall. Professional instruction, rental equipment (including children's gear).

 Cross-country skiing and sledding on the rolling hills of the resort; ice-skating in a covered rink at nearby Wheeling Park.

 Glassworks Lounge features dance floor and occasional entertainment.

FOR CHILDREN: Specialized camps for youngsters are held at the Children's Center, which encompasses the Brooks Nature Center, the Miniature Golf Park, a playground, picnic sites, Schenk Lake, and the Good Zoo.

During the summer months, Zoocamp provide children ages 4 through 12 a marvelous adventure, with lots of animal handling, games, arts and crafts, and movies (advance reservations are advised). The Brooks Nature Center also holds special camps for children, as well as guided nature walks and storytelling sessions. Special tennis and golf camps are also scheduled.

The Good Children's Zoo is a 65-acre haven for animals and families. The zoo's collection includes bison, deer, bear, otter, goats, sheep, a camel, and a llama. Children can feed and pet deer and goats. Within the accredited zoo, visitors can visit a reproduction of a late-19th-century West Virginia farming, logging, and mining community, complete with model-train exhibit.

The curvy slide in the walk-through Red Barn is an enticing play area. A miniature train, modeled on the 1863 vintage C. P. Huntington, takes visitors on a one and a half mile circuit through the bison range and over a waterfall.

The astronomy offerings include slide presentations on an 180-degree curved screen in the Benedum Science Theater and star-gazing through a refractor telescope in the Nature Center Observatory.

OF INTEREST NEARBY: Wheeling Park features an Olympic-sized pool with a 350-foot water slide (open from mid May until September), a playground, paddleboats, miniature golf and a nine-hole golf course. There's hockey and ice-skating from November through February.

Oglebay Institute's Stifel Fine Arts Center is the headquarters of arts and crafts for the valley. Exhibitions, festivals, and arts programs are offered throughout the year.

Oglebay Institute's Mansion Museum is in Earl Oglebay's former summer home. The museum depicts upper-class life in the Ohio valley in the 19th century.

Exhibits and a craft shop are part of historic West Virginia Independence Hall, at Sixteenth and Market streets in Wheeling.

Jamboree U.S.A. Capitol Music Hall is the site of a famous country music show.

FOR MORE INFORMATION: Call (800) 624-6988 or write Wilson Lodge, Wheeling, West Virginia 26003.

EAGLE RIDGE INN AND RESORT
Galena, Illinois

Eagle Ridge Inn and Resort is located in the rolling hill country of northwestern Illinois, six miles from the quaint town of Galena. Although reminiscent of New England, Eagle Ridge is solidly Midwestern in its informality and its relaxed way of life. The resort offers an outstanding array of year-round recreational activities on its spacious 6,800 acres, surrounding lovely 220-acre Lake Galena.

A fire in January 1992 destroyed the original inn. It has since been rebuilt and tastefully expanded.

Galena was once the largest Mississippi River port north of St. Louis. Its economy was built on streamboating, lead mining, and the Blackhawk Indian War. Today, it has one of the highest concentrations of preserved mid-19th century buildings in the Midwest. Ninety percent of Galena's buildings are listed in the National Register of Historic Places, including one of the homes of Ulysses S. Grant. Many preservationists believe that Galena has the finest collection of period architecture in the Midwest.

The resort is a favorite vacation escape for Chicagoans; the Loop is just 153 miles away.

ACCOMMODATIONS: $$ to $$$$ The 80-room Inn overlooking Lake Galena offers four types of rooms, including some with fireplaces and four-poster beds. Children under 18 stay free in their parents' room.

An alternative to the Inn are the 285 resort homes overlooking the lake or nestled deep in the woods or along the fairways. These are condominiums, cottages, and townhouses with one to four bedrooms. All are fully furnished, with well-equipped kitchens, fireplaces, washers and dryers, and daily maid service.

Twenty-five special packages are offered throughout the year, including golf, family, romance, and riverboat gambling package.

DINING: Woodlands Restaurant is the resort's formal restaurant, with great views of rolling hills and the lake. Shooters Sports Bar & Grill offers families an informal dining atmosphere. Children will delight in the old-fashioned ice-cream parlor offerings at Scoops Ice Cream Parlor.

Food and beverages are available poolside and in the pro shops. The General Store has a deli and bakery, gourmet items, beverages, and all the essentials to prepare your own meals.

ACT.IVITIES

 Four outdoor latex courts, court fees. Instruction.

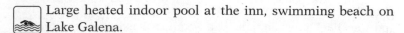 On two 18-hole championship courses—the 6,836-yard North Course and the 6,762 South Course, both par 72— designed by Roger Packard. There's also a 2,648 yard, 9-hole East Course (par 34). Driving range, putting green, three pro shops, club and cart rentals. An indoor golf center operates between November and March.

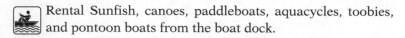 Large heated indoor pool at the inn, swimming beach on Lake Galena.

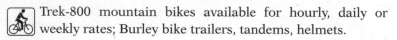 Rental Sunfish, canoes, paddleboats, aquacycles, toobies, and pontoon boats from the boat dock.

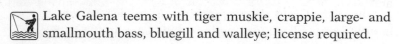 Lake Galena teems with tiger muskie, crappie, large- and smallmouth bass, bluegill and walleye; license required.

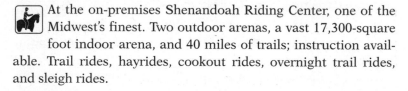 Trek-800 mountain bikes available for hourly, daily or weekly rates; Burley bike trailers, tandems, helmets.

At the on-premises Shenandoah Riding Center, one of the Midwest's finest. Two outdoor arenas, a vast 17,300-square foot indoor arena, and 40 miles of trails; instruction available. Trail rides, hayrides, cookout rides, overnight trail rides, and sleigh rides.

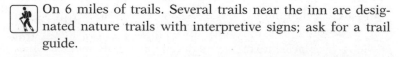 On 6 miles of trails. Several trails near the inn are designated nature trails with interpretive signs; ask for a trail guide.

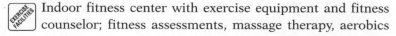 Indoor fitness center with exercise equipment and fitness counselor; fitness assessments, massage therapy, aerobics

and swimnastics classes. Outdoor fitness trail with 21 exercise stations. Two lighted sand volleyball courts.

 Mississippi River cruises, parachute games, scavenger hunts, health talks, family Olympics, riverboat gambling excursions, tours of historic Galena, poolside bingo, squirt-gun tag, pontoon tours of the lake, adult crafts, family movies, canoe races, and seasonal holiday events.

 Cross-country skiing on 36 miles of groomed trails.

 Ice-skating rink and sledding hill; instruction, rental equipment.

 Nearby Chestnut Mountain Resort offers downhill skiing on 16 runs served by two triple lifts, one quad-chair lift, and six rope tows. Slopes lighted for night skiing. Rental shop, Ski Wee program for 4- to 10-year-olds.

FOR CHILDREN: The "I Am an Eagle Ridge Kid" youth program runs every day but Sunday between Memorial Day and Labor Day and welcomes 3- to 12-year-olds. Trained counselors lead children in games, swimming, arts and crafts, boating, and special field trips. Half-day and full day rates are available.

The program also operates on Saturdays throughout the year and daily over the December holidays and Thanksgiving and Presidents' weekends.

Organized teen activities include volleyball, alpine slide outings, casino nights, swimming and movie parties, and pizza parties.

Kid's Night Out programs are held Saturday nights from 7 to 10 P.M. and are centered around themes like carnival, beach party, and pirate's night (there's a fee). On Friday and Saturday nights, the Kids Night Klub provides group baby-sitting, for an hourly fee, from 5 to 11 P.M. in the Kids Night Klub. The room is equipped with toys, TV, board games and sleeping mats.

Baby-sitting is available with 24-hour notice.

NICETIES: The grocery delivery service will stock a resort home with the foods of your choice before your arrival or at any time during your stay.

Each resort home has a VCR, and the resort has an ample supply of rental tapes.

OF INTEREST NEARBY: The main street of historic Galena has an abundance of shops, and restaurants, and historic homes. The Galena/Jo Daviess County History Museum presents a 15-minute film on Galena's history and has permanent exhibits on the town's past. The Old General Store Museum is an excellent reproduction of a 19th century general store.

The Ulysses S. Grant Home State Historic Site preserves a home given to Grant, a native son, by grateful citizens after the Civil War.

Galena's Kandy Kitchen is owned and operated by the third generation of a candy-making family whose patriarch was the creator of "Chuckles." Tours include tastings.

Riverboat cruises are offered regularly on the Mississippi River near Galena.

FOR MORE INFORMATION: Write Eagle Ridge Inn and Resort, U.S. Route 20, Box 777, Galena, IL 61036 or call (800) 892-2269 or (815) 777-2444. For general tourist information, call the Galena/Jo Daviess County Convention and Visitors Bureau at (800) 747-9377.

RUTTGER'S BAY LAKE LODGE
Deerwood, Minnesota

Before the fur traders arrived in Minnesota, the Brainerd Lakes region was Sioux territory. The Sioux navigated the region's rivers, built permanent sod homes on the shores of local lakes, and turned Mille Lacs Lake into an urban center. Two hundred years ago, their cousins from farther north, the Ojibwes, drove them out of the area. The decisive battle took place on what is now the site of Ruttger's Bay Lake Lodge, one of the longest operating, family-run lodges in the great northwoods.

At Ruttger's today, you'll find a a respectful admiration for the earliest inhabitants, plus an array of recreational facilities as modern as any in Minnesota. Joseph and Josephine Ruttger started the lodge as a fishing camp in 1898, and Chris Ruttger, their great grandson, has managed it since 1991. The tradition of family ownership, plus a magnificent setting, is what keeps vacationing families coming back year after year.

Located two hours north of Minneapolis and 18 miles from

Brainerd, the nearest big town, Ruttger's is known far and wide for its gardens, which feature about 40,000 annuals, plus many rose bushes, perennials and flowering shrubs. On Bay Lake, which stretches for 2,400 acres in front of the lodge, you're likely to see some of the water fowl for which Minnesota is famous: ducks of many kinds, loons, osprey and eagles. Its 75-foot deep waters shelter game fish that attract pursuers from all over the Midwest.

Ruttger's is open from April through October.

ACCOMMODATIONS: $$ to $$$$ Guests stay in 165 units with one to three bedrooms. The units include cottages, condos, and villas, in either the standard or deluxe category. Most of the condos have private balconies or patios. The cottages don't have TVs, and the lower deluxe condominiums are the only units with fireplaces. All deluxe condominiums come with fully equipped kitchens. Specially designed units are available for guests who are deaf or use wheelchairs.

Rates including no meals and no golf, some meals and golf, or all meals and golf are available. Special golf packages are offered in May and June.

DINING: Meals are served and in the lodge's original hand-hewn log dining room, complete with open beams and big game trophies, and in the elegant Colonial Room. From the Log Dining Room, diners can look out over Bay Lake. Chef Terry Dox presides over Ruttger's kitchen, and every winter, while the resort is closed, he spends time developing new recipes. Among his specialties are Minnesota wild rice soup, barbecued pork loin ribs, chicken parmerosa and rhubarb pie.

Lunch is often served on the patio. If you're going off on an outing, the kitchen will pack you a picnic lunch with a few hours' notice. Room service is available from June 3 through Labor Day week-end.

A bar operates from noon to midnight during the summer, with reduced hours in the spring and fall. Among its specialities are six varieties of Rhine wine imported from the Ruttger family winery in Neuleiningen, Germany.

Ice cream is available at The Porch, next to the Country Store.

ACTIVITIES

 Two hard courts and two Omni surface courts by Lodge Nine; one laykold court at Battle Point. Lessons, clinics, rentals available.

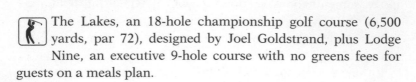 The Lakes, an 18-hole championship golf course (6,500 yards, par 72), designed by Joel Goldstrand, plus Lodge Nine, an executive 9-hole course with no greens fees for guests on a meals plan.

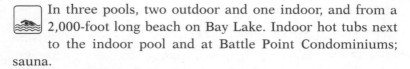 In three pools, two outdoor and one indoor, and from a 2,000-foot long beach on Bay Lake. Indoor hot tubs next to the indoor pool and at Battle Point Condominiums; sauna.

 Rentals at motor house.

 Topnotch fishing for largemouth bass, sunfish, northern pike and crappie in Bay Lake; walleye fishing down the road in Mille Lacs Lake, trout fishing nearby in a series of flooded iron ore pits along the Cuyuna Range. Fishing licenses can be purchased at the front desk; guide service available.

 Two volleyball courts; shuffleboard courts on the east deck, horseshoe pits near the golf course condos and at Battle Point. Water aerobics classes.

 Horseback riding can be arranged through MB's Riding Stables.

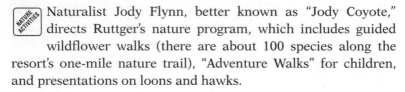 Naturalist Jody Flynn, better known as "Jody Coyote," directs Ruttger's nature program, which includes guided wildflower walks (there are about 100 species along the resort's one-mile nature trail), "Adventure Walks" for children, and presentations on loons and hawks.

Golf clinics, tennis clinics and mixers, pontoon rides, arts and crafts, bingo, windsurfing clinics, bonfires, line-dancing, and karaoke parties.

FOR CHILDREN: "Kids Kamps" is the resort's supervised children's program for 4- through 12-year-olds. It's free to children whose families are on the Modified American or Full American plans; there's a moderate daily fee for children staying on the European plan.

Children are divided into two groups, the "Juniors" and the "Seniors," for age-appropriate activities supervised by a half-dozen counselors of college age. The Juniors start out the morning with free play on the resort's well-equipped playground, complete with a wooden fort, followed by puppet making, games, nature activities, or a hike. After lunch, they go swimming, build sand castles, or make arts and crafts. They end the afternoon's activities on the playground.

The older group goes orienteering, windsurfing, canoeing, and waterskiing; plays tennis; takes part in putting, driving, and pontoon clinics, and swims.

Between June 10 and Sept. 1, the program operates from 9 A.M. to 2 P.M. daily, except Sundays. Four evenings a week in the summer—Tuesdays, Wednesdays, Fridays and Saturdays—the children eat dinner together, and then watch a movie, go fishing, go for a boat ride, or play games.

The program is also offered on Saturdays on "Kids Stay Free" week-ends in the spring and fall, and on Saturdays and Sundays of the Memorial and Labor Day week-ends.

Babysitting can be arranged through the front desk.

NICETIES: The staff will clean and store your fish until you're ready to go home. Alternatively, the chef will prepare it for you.

OF INTEREST NEARBY: Within a 30-minute drive are the Ojibwe Indian Reservation, with its historical museum, Brainerd International Raceway, and Kathio State Park, which offers hiking and naturalist-led activities.

In Brainerd, kids love the Paul Bunyan amusement park featuring the famous talking giant. (Paul calls out a personal greeting to each child as they climb up his giant shoes.) The park is manageable in size; a visit of just a few hours is adequate.

Farther away, but worth the drive, is Itasca State Park, home of the headwaters of the Mississippi River, which you can walk across.

FOR MORE INFORMATION: Write P.O. Box 400, Deerwood, MN 56444 or call (800) 950-7244 or (800) 450-4545 (from Minnesota).

THE LODGE OF FOUR SEASONS
Lake Ozark, Missouri

Built in 1964, The Lodge of Four Seasons was envisioned as a resort that would blend in with the wooded beauty of the shoreline of the manmade Lake of the Ozarks, the largest privately owned inland lake in the United States. Its total shoreline is 1,375 miles, more than the Pacific coast of California!

The lodge's late founder, Harold Koplar, bought 3,200 acres for his dream retreat—but built the 31-unit resort only on about 10 percent of the property. Much of the rest of the land was left in its natural state, serving as a wooded backdrop for the resort and for Koplar's unobtrusive developments of custom houses and condominiums nearby.

Thus, the Lodge of the Four Seasons is a resort complex that is generous in scope, yet compact in size. There's no need to walk long distances, because most of the resort's many amenities are within a few steps. In fact, most of the resort's indoor action is under one roof. But resort vans are available for transportation elsewhere on the resort grounds.

The main lodge is perched atop a hill overlooking the lake. The building houses 31 function rooms, two ballrooms, multiple restaurants, a night club, bowling alley, cinema, and an indoor pool surrounded by a complete health spa. Most of the buildings that house guest rooms are connected to the main lodge.

Nestled into nooks and crannies throughout the complex are four outdoor swimming pools, eight tennis courts, a sandy beach and numerous rock gardens and waterfalls. Flowers are everywhere; the resort has its own greenhouse and grows all its flowers from seed. The Lodge features waterfalls indoors and out. Many large windows offer spectacular views of the grounds and lake.

ACCOMMODATIONS: $ to $$$$ There are 311 guest rooms, 13 suites, and seven parlors, most with lovely views and some with fireplaces. Some have white wicker furniture and watercolor paintings, while others have a dark, Mediterranean look.

Most of the rooms and all of the luxury suites are in the Main Lodge or in a connected addition called the Atrium. Next to the Main Lodge, and overlooking the main terrace pool, are two one-story buildings that house the Lanai rooms, which are great for families with small children.

Nestled into a bluff next to the Main Lodge are the Lakeside accommodations—three multi-story buildings that house rooms with the best views of the lake. A short walkway connects the buildings to each other and to the Main Lodge. The Lakeside units have their own outdoor pool.

At the nearby Four Seasons Racquet & Country Club, Water's Edge, Treetop Village and Charleston condominium complexes, 100 two- and three-bedroom condominiums can be rented.

The Lodge offers numerous package deals for multi-night stays or over holiday weekends.

DINING: Each of the restaurants in the Main Lodge has a different atmosphere. Children's menus are available.

The Lodge's main dining room is Toledo's, with white table clothes, elegantly dressed waiters, and gourmet food. During the summer, there's jazz music. Toledo's also offers a spectacular Sunday brunch.

SeaChase Seafood Restaurant flies in fresh seafood daily and offers a great view of the lake. Roseberry's Café serves breakfast and lunch in a casual atmosphere. The Atrium Cafe prepares fresh-baked pastries and muffins, while the Country Deli, next to the bowling alley, serves a variety of sandwiches and snacks.

Across State Road HH is HK's Steak House and the Sandtrap Lounge, overlooking the golf course. HK's (for Harold Koplar) features a custom-designed elevated charcoal grill on which chefs prepare only certified Angus beef.

Within driving distance are a number of other eating places, ranging from fast-food outlets to sit-down restaurants.

ACTIVITIES

Four indoor, 10 outdoor hard-surface courts, and three clay courts at the Racquet Club; six outdoor courts at The Lodge. The resort is the Midwest home of the Dennis Van der Meer Tennis University; year-round clinics and instruction, court fees.

The Robert Trent Jones Sr. Championship Golf Course is considered one of his classics, with rolling fairways, large greens and spectacular par 3s. Nearby Seasons Ridge (6,416 yards, par 72) is considered Missouri's top public course; it was designed by Ken Kavanough. A 9-hole executive course, par 30, is another alternative. Greens fees include golfcart.

In the lake, four outdoor pools at the Lodge, 10 outdoor pools and an indoor pool with a shallow baby section at the Racquet Club; several pools at the condominium complexes.

The lodge's 200-slip marina is one of the largest on the lake. Rental ski boats, runabouts, and pontoon boats; the 43-foot Bluewater Yacht can be chartered, complete with captain.

Parasailing available. Visitors can take a one-hour sighseeing cruise on the Seasons Queen.

The lake is ranked among the nation's best for bass fishing. Guides, equipment available; license required.

Two-mile guided trail rides from the resort's own Equestrian Center. Young children may ride on their parent's horse.

Trap shooting available.

Extensive trails for walking and jogging.

The Health & Fitness Conditioning Center has an aerobics room, exercise machines, weightlifting equipment, racquetball court, sauna and whirpool; water exercise, aerobics classes. On-site trainer, health evaluations, massages.

Numerous theme parties and holiday celebrations, poolside bingo, water volleyball games, casino night, relays, crafts classes, basketball and volleyball games; cinema, bowling alley, murder mystery dinner theater. During the summer, the nightclub features live entertainment.

FOR CHILDREN: From Memorial Day to Labor Day, and over some school holidays, The Lodge operates the Wild Adventure Club, a supervised activities program for children 4 to 12. Hours are 10 A.M. to 4 P.M.; the fee includes lunch. The program operates out of a little white building on the grounds and is staffed by 25 college interns working towards degrees in recreation. The program rarely has more than 12 children at a time, so they get plenty of individual attention.

On Tuesday, Friday and Saturday nights during the summer, and over some holiday week-ends, the counselors run "Big Bear Bunch" from 6 to 10 P.M. Children enjoy snacks, movies, arts and crafts and games while their parents dine alone.

The resort has a small playground uphill from The Lodge.

In-room babysitting is available.

NICETIES: A prize-winning Japanese garden surrounds the Main Lodge. It was created by former Hollywood set designer Buffy Murai.

Koplar was a movie buff, and the memorabilia he collected is displayed throughout the resort.

OF INTEREST NEARBY: Bagnall Dam, created in 1931 to produce hydropower, is worth a visit. Tours are conducted daily.

Ha Ha Tonka State Park preserves some of the most beautiful scenery on the lake, as well as the picturesque ruins of an old castle.

Lake of the Ozarks is famous for its outlet shopping malls, antiques and crafts shops, and video arcades.

FOR MORE INFORMATION: Call (800) THE LAKE or write The Lodge of Four Seasons, P.O. Box 215, Lake Ozark, MO 65049.

PORT LUDLOW GOLF & MEETING RETREAT
Port Ludlow, Washington

Getting to Port Ludlow can be an adventure in itself. Visitors can get there via seaplane, roads, or ferries, but the truly adventuresome will want to charter a boat in the Seattle harbor and fish during the two- to three-hour trip across Puget Sound.

No matter how the journey is made, a vacation at Port Ludlow rewards the traveler. This is a wonderful vacation place, with magnificent views of the Olympic Mountains to the southeast and the islands and waters of Puget Sound at your doorstep.

A lumber mill once stood at the site of Port Ludlow. It folded in the Great Depression, but its owners, the Pope and Talbot Company, retained the land and eventually developed the present-day resort. A few traces of the old mill can still be seen in the concrete foundation for a huge furnace, now a picnic area, and at the tip of Burner Point and a small lagoon, now enjoyed by boaters, which once impounded logs awaiting processing at the mill.

The accommodations are first rate, with a wide choice of luxurious condominium units. The food is memorable. And the possibilities for recreation are boundless, with a good marina and one of the nation's most scenic golf courses heading the list.

All this and family activities too. Good facilities and services for children are built into the recreation program.

ACCOMMODATIONS: **$$** to **$$$** Beautiful native wood siding, wood-shingled roofs, and exposed interior beams link the buildings, with 180 units, including 50 suites, to their forested surroundings. Guests can choose from individual bedrooms or full condominium units with a loft bedroom, living and dining area, completely equipped kitchen, a private balcony or deck, and a fireplace.

The peak season is May through October; winter rates are lowest. There is no charge for children under 12.

DINING: The Harbormaster Restaurant is a short walk from the accommodations at Port Ludlow and serves three meals a day. The food is delicious, with the salmon, halibut, crab, and oysters of the Pacific Northwest heading the menu. A children's menu is also available.

Niblicks serves lunch at the pro shop.

Other seafood restaurants of note are an easy drive from Port Ludlow. You might guess that the 3 Crabs Restaurant in Dungeness, 40 minutes away, serves crab, and it does, along with wonderful other seafood. Port Townsend, with its main street of beautifully restored Victorian buildings, also has several good seafood restaurants.

Guests who want to prepare some of their own meals can buy provisions in the resort's general store. More substantial shopping is available in Hadlock, 20 minutes north of the Resort.

ACTIVITIES

 Seven Plexi-Pave courts, no fees. Equipment rentals.

 Championship 6,800-yard golf course designed by Robert Muir Graves: the American Society of Golf Course Architects rates it among the top one percent of the best-designed courses in the nation. Pro shop, snack bar, putting green, driving range, instruction.

Heated pool shielded from the wind by glass walls.

The Marina at Port Ludlow, with 300 slips, is one of the largest on Puget Sound. Several charter companies will equip you with dinghies, 21-foot Victory day sailers, 27-foot Ericson sailers, or even larger boats. On sailing trips of one or more days you can explore Mats Bay, Port Townsend, the city of Victoria in Canada, or the San Juan Islands. Skippered sight-seeing cruises and moonlight champagne cruises can be arranged. Complete instruction.

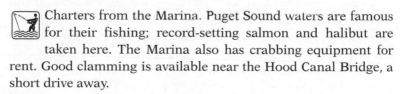 Charters from the Marina. Puget Sound waters are famous for their fishing; record-setting salmon and halibut are taken here. The Marina also has crabbing equipment for rent. Good clamming is available near the Hood Canal Bridge, a short drive away.

Rentals, including children's bicycles, available. The resort provides maps with cycling, jogging, and walking routes.

 The Beach Club complex houses a squash court, exercise equipment, and saunas; rental equipment.

FOR CHILDREN: Organized children's activities are scheduled during the summer months for children 5 and older. Many of these fall on weekends, when the children of Port Ludlow homeowners join in. Activities include games, a t-ball competition, nature hikes, a treasure hunt, an aqua scout race, or beachcombing. At spring vacation time and on summer holiday weekends, the schedule steps up to three or four organized children's activities a day.

The Recreation Office lends equipment for volleyball, badminton, croquet, lawn bowling, softball, Frisbee, football, tetherball, basketball, fishing, lawn darts, snorkeling, horseshoes, and t-ball.

NICETIES: Rental cars are available on site.

OF INTEREST NEARBY: The Olympic Peninsula is a natural treasure. Olympic National Park and Olympic National Forest offer snow-capped mountains, rain forests, hot springs, and unparalleled views. U.S. 101 rings the Olympics with access roads radiating from 101 into the mountains. The drive to Hurricane Ridge is particularly rewarding, with its views of the Olympic Mountains, the Strait of Juan de Fuca and the San Juan Islands.

In Port Angeles, visit the Arthur D. Feiro Marine Laboratory just east of the Ferry Terminal. Its tanks contain a fine collection of Puget Sound marine specimens. Watch the crabs and starfish feed, and handle the marine life in the touch tank.

The Dungeness Spit is the nation's longest sand spit and the center of a network of bays and estuaries that teem with birds, marine life, and seals. Take a picnic lunch and enjoy a walk along this seven-mile stretch of sand.

A trainer of animals for Hollywood movies established the Olympic Game Farm near Sequim, not far from Port Ludlow. A wide variety of North American and some African animals are displayed here. Self-guided driving tours are available.

Pope and Talbot, the developers of The Resort at Port Ludlow, began their Northwest logging operations at Port Gamble, across the Hood Canal Bridge, a short drive from the resort. The sawmill at Port Gamble has been in operation since 1853, and the original New England-style buildings of this company town have been beautifully restored. There's a museum in the basement of the general store.

FOR MORE INFORMATION: Call (800) 732-1239 or (206) 437-2222.

SUNRIVER RESORT
Sunriver, Oregon

Sunriver Resort is a place for family rest and recreation in all seasons of the year. Located in the Oregon high-desert country in the shadow of the Cascade Mountains, Sunriver boasts a wonderful summer climate and easy access to Cascade Mountain skiing in the winter. From March through October, opportunities for warm-weather outdoor activities abound. Lovers of golf, tennis, cycling, canoeing, white-river rafting, swimming, and fishing are in their element here. From November through late spring, Sunriver is a short distance from excellent downhill and cross-country skiing.

Sunriver is a resort built to harmonize with its surroundings. An investor from Portland who came to the Bend, Oregon, area in the 1960s with the intention of building a simple fishing cabin recognized the potential of the site. Determined to preserve the natural beauty of the location, he carefully developed this 3,300-acre tract of ponderosa pine forest and meadows bordering the Deschutes River. Despite the fact that the Sunriver development has 1,500 homes, over 650 condominiums, and 1,400 year-round residents, the natural beauty has been preserved.

ACCOMMODATIONS: $$ to $$$ The lodge building houses the front desk, guest services, recreation management offices, shops, and restaurants. Accommodations are in nearby condominium-style units or in lodge bedroom units. Lodge suites have fully equipped kitchenettes and a loft bedroom. All units have magnificent stone fireplaces and decks, with tasteful furnishings. Lodge suites comfortably accommodate an additional child or two on a Murphy bed.

It is also possible to rent one of more than 100 vacation homes or condominiums in the Sunriver development through the Sunriver Lodge rental program.

Rates are highest in the peak summer months and over the December holidays. Spring and fall golf and recreation packages are available, as are two- to seven-day winter ski packages.

DINING: Two restaurants are located in the main lodge building. Both overlook the Deschutes River with the high Cascades as a backdrop.

The Provision Company, open for breakfast, lunch, and dinner, is a very comfortable place for families. The Meadows Restaurant is the resort's gourmet eatery for dinner. With outdoor dining and a breathtaking view of the Cascade Mountains, this dining experience is hard to surpass. The menu features classic Northwest cuisine, including Pacific salmon and local trout.

A few hundred yards from the lodge is Sunriver Village Country Mall, with restaurants and a supermarket. You'll find Chinese, Mexican, and Italian food, as well as delis and sandwich shops. The supermarket sells everything you need to prepare meals in your own kitchenette.

ACTIVITIES

Twenty-eight outdoor Plexi-Pave courts; three indoor courts and five racquetball courts at the Sunriver Racquet Club. Pro shop, instruction, tournaments, rental equipment, summer tennis camps.

Three 18-hole courses. The North Course (6,880 yards, par 72) was designed by Robert Trent Jones Jr. and is considered one of his best. The South Course (6,960 yards, par 72) was designed by Fred Federspiel. The third course, new in 1995, was designed by Robert E. Cupp. All play through beautiful mountain scenery. Pro shops, instruction, clinics.

Two heated swimming pools. The Olympic-size South Pool is closest to the lodge. It has a separate wading pool with a maximum depth of one and a half feet, two spas, saunas, and changing rooms. Lessons in swimming, scuba diving, water polo, water basketball, water volleyball, and water aerobics.

 Canoes can be rented at the marina for use on placid stretches of the Deschutes. Vans leave the marina daily for half-day and full-day white-water raft trips.

 In the Deschutes River at Sunriver's front door. A guide service can provide half-day and full-day fishing trips on other nearby rivers.

 More than 25 miles of paved bike paths snake through the Sunriver development. The Lodge Bike Shop rents more than 175 bikes ranging from a monster five-seater to tandem bikes and 10-speed, three-speed, and single-speed cruisers, some with child seats. Children's bicycles, some with training wheels, are also available.

 From its large and attractive building near the marina, the Nature Center's professional staff mounts excellent exhibits on the natural history of the Cascades and high desert, and offers hands-on activities for children. Snakes, lizards, birds of prey, and scorpions are on display. The center offers an impressive schedule of classes and guided hikes.

Sunriver Stables has guided horseback rides throughout the summer and on winter weekends. Trails wander over the Deschutes River meadows and into the pine forests. Longer rides afford wonderful views of the Cascade Mountains. Day trips, wagon ride cookouts, and riding lessons are available.

An indoor lap pool, a spa, saunas, and an exercise room with a full range of equipment at the Sunriver Racquet Club; daily aerobics classes.

In August, the Music Festival brings professional musicians to Sunriver for a series of classical music concerts. Bus tours to the nearby High Desert Museum and to Mt. Bachelor for a chairlift ride leave the lodge five days a week.

Sunriver is only 18 miles from the Mt. Bachelor ski area. The ski season extends from mid-November until mid-spring. The lodge operates a shuttle to the slopes.

The Sunriver ice-skating rink operates during the winter, and sleigh rides are offered over snow-covered lanes.

 Ten miles of groomed cross-country trails on the golf course; equipment rentals and lessons.

FOR CHILDREN: Between 9 A.M. and noon on summer and holiday season mornings, the "Kid's Klub" is in session for children 6 through 12. Kid's Klub activities include field trips to places like Benham Falls or a fish hatchery, canoeing and swimming, arts and crafts, and games. Lunch is included in the fee.

Organized activities for teenagers include inner-tube floats, trivia contests, Frisbee, golf, bicycle rodeos, video game competitions, and dances.

Sunriver also has a fully licensed day-care center, "The Playroom," for children 3 months through 10 years of age.

Near the lodge is a fine children's playground with great equipment, including a wonderful log stockade and fort.

NICETIES: The Sunriver Village Country Mall has a wide variety of shops where you will find the clothing you forgot to bring or the perfect gift for that person back home. You can even drop in on a stockbroker to check on your investments.

OF INTEREST NEARBY: The Oregon High Desert Museum, 8 miles from Sunriver, has excellent exhibits on the natural and social history of the region. Lectures on birds of prey and feedings of the Museum's two otters, Bert and Ernie, are scheduled daily.

Lava River Cave is three miles from Sunriver. Bring flashlights, or rent a lantern at the cave, and tour a mile-long lava tube formed thousands of years ago.

The Lava Cast Forest, nine miles up a good dirt road off Highway 97, provides an opportunity to walk over a lava flow on good paths and view the largest collection of lava cast trees in the world. Picnic tables and potable water are available.

Drive to the top of a volcanic cinder cone at Lava Butte, which is skirted by Highway 97 between Sunriver and Bend, Oregon. The Lava Lands Visitors Center is at the foot of the cinder cone.

FOR MORE INFORMATION: Write Sunriver Resort, Sunriver, OR 97707, or call (800) 547-3922.

DANA POINT RESORT
Dana Point, California

On a bluff overlooking the Pacific Ocean, midway between Los Angeles and San Diego, this luxury resort manages to evoke both the charm of Cape Cod and the casual ambience of southern California. Surrounded by 42 acres of brilliant, emerald green public park, the Dana Point Resort promises guests that "the view follows you everywhere," and it never disappoints.

Dana Point Harbor was discovered in 1835 and has long provided shelter to yachtsmen, but it only became a destination for tourists traveling overland when the hotel opened in 1987. The area below the hotel now draws day-trippers from all over southern California who are attracted by a 2,500-slip harbor with two separate marinas, a fine public beach and park, an interpretive center, and a three-themed shopping area: The Pavilion, Mariner's Village, and Dana Wharf.

The Dana Point Resort is perfectly situated to provide easy access to the tourist attractions of both Los Angeles and San Diego. But at the same time, it provides a soothing refuge from the congestion and fast pace of southern California. You need never leave the premises to have a good time.

ACCOMMODATIONS: $ to $$$ Dana Point's 350 rooms and suites are beautifully decorated in colors that evoke the seaside setting—blues, grays, and sands. Most rooms have private terraces; all have remote-control TVs, clock radios, two phones, and lounging robes.

The concierge level accommodations offers such added amenities as twice-daily maid service and complimentary continental breakfast, cocktails, and desserts. For budget-minded travelers, the Cape Cod rooms on the top floor are the least expensive. Special promotions during slow periods (just before and after Christmas, for instance) can make a stay here inexpensive.

DINING: Breakfast, lunch, and dinner are served in Watercolors Restaurant, which has gorgeous harbor views. The chef specializes in contemporary American cuisine, with an emphasis on inventively prepared fresh vegetables and seafood. The Sunday Champagne Brunch draws diners from as far away as Los Angeles. An elegant afternoon tea is served Wednesdays through Sundays in Lantern Bay Lounge.

The children's menus are printed on coloring books, which they may take home. Room service is available from 6 A.M. until 2 A.M. Poolside service is available from 10 A.M. to 6 P.M.

There are numerous other restaurants in Dana Point and nearby Laguna Beach.

ACTIVITIES

 Three lighted cement courts; rental equipment, court fees.

 Privileges at five nearby courses, ranging from classic Scottish links to short executive courses.

 Two heated pools with ocean views, adjacent hot tubs. Swimming in the Pacific Ocean from the beach at Doheny State Beach.

 Charters, rental sailboats available at Dana Point Yacht Harbor, just below the hotel.

 Parasailing, wind-surfing equipment available.

 Deep-sea fishing expeditions available from Dana Wharf Sportfishing; half-day, twilight, and three-quarter-day excursions.

 Rental bicycles available for use on nearby streets and paved biking trails; biking maps available.

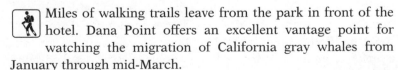 Miles of walking trails leave from the park in front of the hotel. Dana Point offers an excellent vantage point for watching the migration of California gray whales from January through mid-March.

Health club with sauna, steam rooms, Jacuzzi, workout equipment, massage therapists. Outdoor basketball court, Ping-Pong tables, horseshoe pits. Fitness parcourse in neighboring park.

Piano music most nights in Lantern Bay Lounge; live music and dancing on weekends in Burton's. Poolside orchestral concerts are held monthly between May and September.

FOR CHILDREN: "Club Cowabunga," the resort's children's program for 5- to 12-year-olds, operates from 10 A.M. to 4 P.M. and 6:30 P.M. to 9:30 P.M. every day during the summer and on weekends the rest of the year. There's a fee.

A typical day starts with a special coded message with the day's activities slipped under your door. Participants gather in the club's playroom or at the tennis courts for such activities as kite-making and flying, t-shirt art, walks, group tennis lessons, pool games, and arts and crafts. Field trips go to the nearby Orange County Marine Institute, Doheny Beach State Park Interpretive Center, and the *Pilgrim*, a replica of Henry Dana's tall ship.

In the evenings, children can eat dinner together, make origami or jewelry, play video games, watch movies, and go on a moonlit hike to the state park's amphitheater, where counselors will regale them with stories, point out constellations, and toast marshmallows.

Baby-sitting can be arranged for younger children.

NICETIES: Complimentary coffee is served each morning in the lobby. The concierge keeps a selection of board games, basketballs, volleyballs, kites, and croquet sets for use by guests.

There's a terrific playground and basketball court just down the hill from the resort in a public park.

OF INTEREST NEARBY: Doheny State Beach, Lantern Bay Park, and the Dana Point Marina, all adjacent to the resort grounds, offer plenty of activities for families. The Orange County Marine Institute has aquariums featuring local specimens and offers opportunities for hands-on learning experiences. Excursions are offered on the Pilgrim, which is moored at the Institute. You can also spend hours exploring the tidepools nearby or just watching the windsurfers.

The Mission at San Juan Capistrano is just a few minutes away.

Laguna Beach, just north of Dana Point, has scores of unique shops and fun restaurants along its scenic streets.

Disneyland and Knotts Berry Farm are each about an hour from the resort.

FOR MORE INFORMATION: Call (800) 533-9748 or write 25135 Park Lantern, Dana Point, CA 92629

HOTEL DEL CORONADO
Coronado, California

A handful of hotels in America are so architecturally distinctive that they are repeatedly used as the backdrops for movies and television shows. Hotel Del Coronado is one of them. It was the main setting for "Some Like It Hot," and in recent years has been featured in "The Stunt Man" and "K-9 Cop." It also served as the inspriration for the movie, "Somewhere in Time," and is said to have been the basis for the design of Emerald City in "The Wizard of Oz." More recently, it was the backdrop for episodes of "Hart to Hart," "Simon & Simon," and "Lifestyles of the Rich & Famous."

What attracts Hollywood producers to this national historic landmark is the same thing that charms vacationers: its quirky Victorian design (some observers have likened it to a gigantic red-iced wedding cake) and its spectacular beachfront setting. With 33 acres of snow white beach and beautifully landscaped gardens, it's the largest beach resort on the Pacific Coast between Alaska and Acapulco.

"The Del," as regulars call it, was the first hotel west of the Mississippi to install electric lights (Thomas Edison himself supervised the first lighting of an outdoor Christmas tree in 1904). But it's not just a place to go to appreciate history. Its recreational facilities are among the best in southern California. And the moderate San Diego climate makes outdoor recreation possible year-round.

ACCOMMODATIONS: $$ to $$$$ The 700 guest rooms are divided among the original five-story hotel, called the Victorian building, and two modern, motel-like annexes: the seven-story Ocean Towers, with 214 rooms, and the Poolside annex, with 97 rooms. The Victorian building rooms are one-of-a-kind, decorated in period furnishings. They range from rather small rooms with limited views, to ocean-view suites. The rooms in the annex are, in general, more expensive, and range from standard-size motel rooms to two-bedroom apartments. There's no additional charge for children 15 and under when sharing their parents' room.

DINING: The Del has four restaurants, each with a distinctive personality. The Crown Room, just off the main lobby, is something to behold, with its damask-covered chairs and hand-rubbed sugar pine paneling, which rises skyward to create a 33-foot ceiling. The restaurant serves breakfast, lunch and dinner, and a memorable Sunday brunch.

The Prince of Wales, named after one of the hotel's most famous visitors, provides a blend of traditional and modern cuisine in an elegant atmosphere. It serves dinner only. Men must wear jackets.

The Ocean Terrace is a casual setting for breakfast, lunch and dinner, with a California flair. Its outdoor tables overlook the tennis courts and the ocean beyond.

The Del Deli, in the lower lobby, was carved out of the hotel's old concrete rainwater storage cistern, giving it the feel of a rathskeller. It's a good place to grab a bagel for breakfast or pick up a picnic lunch for the beach.

Continental breakfast and late-afternoon and evening pastries and coffee are served in the Palm Court, in the main lobby.

ACTIVITIES

 Six lighted hard-surface courts. Ben Press has been the resident pro for more than 20 years. Round robin tournament on Wednesday nights; "stroke and strategy" clinics.

 18-hole Coronado Municipal Golf Course nearby. Fifty other courses in the San Diego area.

 Olympic-size pool on terrace overlooking the ocean, smaller pool at Ocean Towers. Scuba-diving classes. Gorgeous beach, with gentle surf.

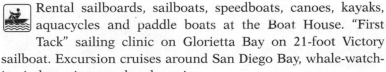 Rental sailboards, sailboats, speedboats, canoes, kayaks, aquacycles and paddle boats at the Boat House. "First Tack" sailing clinic on Glorietta Bay on 21-foot Victory sailboat. Excursion cruises around San Diego Bay, whale-watching in late winter and early spring.

Rental bikes available for use on 15 miles of bike paths on Coronado Island; daily guided bike tours.

 Daily "power" walks, aquaerobics and "tennisize" classes. Adult lap swim daily from 8 to 9 A.M. Croquet course, volleyball court. Poolside massage service, including 15-minute back and foot rubs.

 One-hour guided tours of the hotel's grounds and the beach, Thursdays, Fridays and Saturdays in July and August.

 In the summer, family activities include marshmallow roasts, bingo, croquet playoffs, ice cream float parties, beach volleyball, cooking demonstrations by the resort's chefs, walking tours of the hotel. Entertainment and dancing nightly in the Ocean Terrace Lounge; nightly piano music in the Palm Court Bar.

FOR CHILDREN: The Del operates supervised activities programs for children from 1 to 4 P.M . daily, beginning late June and ending around Labor Day. There's a fee.

"Camp Oz" is for 4- to 6-year-olds, and features games, sandcastle building, scavenger hunts, songs, swimming, arts and crafts and snacks. "Camp Breaker," for 7- to 12-year-olds, includes paddle boating, sailing excursions, games, crafts, nature walks, swimming and crafts.

"Wind Riders," for 13- to 17-year-olds, provides surfing and sailing classes on Glorietta Bay from 9:30 A.M. to 11:30 A.M. daily in the summer.

In the Youth Tennis Program, expert tennis instruction is offered to children 6- to 15 from 10 to 11 A.M. daily, beginning in late June. "Teeny Tennis" is offered to 3- to 6-year-olds from 9 to 9:30 A.M. Wednesdays and Saturdays during the summer.

Four evenings a week during the summer, and over some holiday periods, "Kids Jamboree" provides three hours of supervised activities for 6- to 12-year-olds so parents can have dinner alone (there's a modest fee).

Every summer week, there's a drawing contest for kids. And between 11:30 A.M. and 12:30 P.M. on Tuesdays, Thursdays and Saturdays during the summer, there's an arts and crafts class for children (fee charged for materials). Children under 7 must be accompanied by an adult.

NICETIES: The hotel's "History Gallery" on the lower level displays hotel furnishings and equipment from 100 years ago, including the original electric lamps that Thomas Edison helped install. The old photos and architectural drawings are fascinating.

The shops on the hotel's lower level feature everything from Australian opals to European coats of arms to children's playclothes to books.

Every night from 6 P.M. to midnight, The Del shows classic movies on its private television channel. All of the movies were shot at The Del, or inspired by it.

OF INTEREST NEARBY: Coronado makes a good base from which to explore the treasures of San Diego. Balboa Park, just minutes from The Del, is San Diego's cultural center, with galleries, gardens, and museums.

San Diego Zoo is renowned for its natural habitats. The zoo's separate Wild Animal Park is farther west in San Diego County. It features bird and animal shows, a hiking trail, and a 50-minute monorail ride that gets you close to the hundreds of animals that roam freely within the park.

Mission Bay Park is San Diego's recreational "heart," with miles of beach. It's main tourist attraction is Sea World, a 100-acre marine park. The shows are fun, and there's even a marvelous children's playground, Cap'n Kids World.

La Jolla makes a lovely destination for a day-long outing. Its coves and beaches are fun to explore, and its shopping, restaurants and galleries are unsurpassed in the area. There's also a contemporary art museum and a children's museum. And Scipps Institute of Oceanography has a small aquarium and an outdoor tidal pool.

Tijuana is only 10 miles away, and is reachable by car or trolley. It's a fun day trip.

FOR MORE INFORMATION: Write Hotel del Coronado, 1500 Orange Avenue, Coronado, California 92118, or call (800) HOTEL DEL.

HILTON HAWAIIAN VILLAGE
Honolulu, Oahu, Hawaii

Just a few generations ago, Waikiki was an untidy collection of taro patches. Today, its beach has become an icon of international tourism and the most visited vacation destination in the whole Pacific.

If you want to be where the action is on Waikiki, there is no better place than Hilton Hawaiian Village, a resort with something for everyone. Recent renovations have given the Hilton a decidedly Hawaiian ambiance with acres of lush tropical gardens, displays of live native wildlife, beds of tropical plants, and a 10,000-square foot, two-tier swimming pool complete with lava waterfalls.

Hilton Hawaiian Village is also a shopper's paradise, with scores of shops and boutiques on the premises, plus the many shops in the Waikiki neighborhood, only a short walk away.

ACCOMMODATIONS: $$$ to $$$$ With more than 2,500 rooms in four towers—Rainbow, Tapa, Diamond Head, and Ali'i—the hotel is the largest resort on Oahu. A whole floor of each tower is given over to non-smoking rooms. The rooms are spacious and beautifully decorated. Many have a view of Waikiki Beach.

The concierge-served Ali'i Tower provides the most deluxe accommodations, with many special services included—preferential seating in hotel restaurants and nightclubs, a concierge, and its own health club, sauna, and swimming pool.

There is no charge for children when they occupy their parents' room. Be aware that state law limits room occupancy to four.

DINING: The Hilton Hawaiian Village has 22 restaurants and lounges. Bali by the Sea is the award-winning headline restaurant, offering elegant continental cuisine. The Golden Dragon serves up magnificent Chinese cuisine, including Imperial Beggar's Chicken and Peking Duck.

Other restaurants offer more casual dining. The Rainbow Lanai Restaurant features nouvelle Hawaiian and Pacific cuisine and has many menu items that are low in sodium, cholesterol, and calories. The Village Steak and Seafood Restaurant offers a daunting seafood buffet every Friday and Sunday.

Children's menus are available in all restaurants and from room service.

ACTIVITIES

  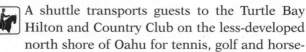 A shuttle transports guests to the Turtle Bay Hilton and Country Club on the less-developed north shore of Oahu for tennis, golf and horse-back riding.

 The huge "Super Pool" is a magnet for hotel guests, and Waikiki Beach is only a few steps away. The small, quiet Hilton lagoon is a perfect place to swim.

 Surfboard and sailboat rentals at the beach. The Hilton Rainbow I catamaran sails on champagne breakfast cruises, a sunset cruise that includes dinner and dancing, and tours of Pearl Harbor. Excursions are also available in Atlantis submarines.

 Guided walking tours of Waikiki and the crater of Diamond Head (take a flashlight).

 Lei making, hula lessons, and instruction in such ancient Hawaiian games as stone rolling and spear sliding. Each evening, there's a Polynesian review in the Dome Showroom. And every Saturday afternoon the Polynesian Cultural Center brings Polynesian dancers, musicians, and artisans to the Hilton's Village Green for a demonstration of one of the rich Polynesian cultures.

Since 1990, the Hilton Hawaiian Village has presented a musical and dance tribute to King David Kalalaua, the "Merrie Monarch," on Friday evenings on the Super Pool terrace, climaxed by a fireworks show over Waikiki Beach. On other evenings, terrace entertainment includes a torchlighting ceremony and hula dancing by Hawaiian children.

FOR CHILDREN: An activity-packed children's program is available daily throughout the year for children 3 to 12. A cruise on the hotel catamaran, tropical bird shows, Hawaiian storytelling and games, treasure hunts, cooking demonstrations, a children's "olympics" and a wildlife tour are among the hotel-based activities. The program also includes excursions to the Honolulu Zoo,

Waikiki Aquarium, Dole Pineapple Cannery, Maritime Museum, and the Children's Museum, and a hike up Diamond Head. Lunch and snacks are included in the fee.

NICETIES: The Disney channel and three other cable channels are free in rooms.

The staff of the Hilton makes genuine efforts to impart some of Hawaii's rich culture to guests.

OF INTEREST NEARBY: Pearl Harbor, site of the Arizona Memorial, is the most visited tourist site in Honolulu.

Other excursions popular with families include the Honolulu Zoo and Aquarium, the Sea Life Park at Makapuu Point, the Dole Pineapple plant, the Polynesian Cultural Center, and the Bishop Museum, with its world-famous collection of Hawaiian and Polynesian art and artifacts.

FOR MORE INFORMATION: Write Hilton Hawaiian Village, 2005 Kalia Road, Honolulu, HI 96815-1999 or call (800) HILTONS.

KONA VILLAGE RESORT
Kailua-Kona, The Big Island, Hawaii

The drive from the Kona Airport to Kona Village Resort, on Hawaii's Big Island, crosses ancient lava fields; no people inhabit this lunar landscape. But tucked away in a pocket of land the lava flows missed lies Kona Village Resort. It is a true hideaway, with no other resorts and no human settlements in the vicinity.

Kona Village Resort is on the ocean at the site of the ancient Hawaiian village of Manuahi. Today, the historic remains of this site are integrated into the resort, making this a place of archaeological significance as well as one of natural beauty. The ancient village people thrived by fishing and trading; the modern resort is built around pools of water that were the fish ponds of Hawaiian kings. Petroglyphs are found over more than 15 acres of Kona Village; guided walks help visitors explore these historic sites.

Families have the option of being busy every moment of the day or of relaxing in the hammock outside their hale (guest house) and enjoying the tropical beauty of this world-class resort. Fifty percent of the guests each year are return visitors. Few would think of challenging the resort's claim that it's "the most dreamed about place on earth."

ACCOMMODATIONS: $$$ to $$$$ Kona Village Resort is built around the ancient stone platforms of the historic Hawaiian village. Guests stay in one of 125 hales scattered throughout the 82-acre village site. Some perch on the side of ponds, others face the beach, and still others are in lush tropical vegetation or in lava gardens.

Hale architecture was inspired by traditional Micronesian and Melanesian housing; the influence is reflected in the shape of each unit, in the thatched roofs, and in details like rope lashing on moldings and door frames. Some hales have the shape and roof line of Fijian or Samoan traditional houses; others mimic Tahitian, New Hebridian, or Maori housing styles.

Hale interiors are smashing. Bedspreads and pillowcases are silk-screened or hand painted by local artists. Much of the furniture and accessories are the works of Hawaiian and Pacific island craftsmen. Hales vary from two-person units to two-bedroom suites for up to five people. Many hales have lanais, or screened-in porches. Ceiling fans and trade winds do the cooling. All hales are equipped with mini refrigerators and coffee makers.

In keeping with Kona Village Resort's get-away-from-it-all philosophy, there are no phones, television sets, or locks on the doors (each room has a small in-room safe).

The resort operates on the American Plan. Children's rates are available and rise with age. There is a minimum stay requirement in the Christmas season.

DINING: Meals are usually taken in the Hale Samoa or Hale Moane, a dining room inspired by New Hebrides longhouse architecture. Rare 19th-century murals depicting Hawaiian life hang in the dining room. Breakfast is served from 7:15 to 9:45 A.M. Lunch is served buffet style on The Terrace adjacent to the dining room. Buffet tables are laden with fresh seafood and salads. Box lunches can be arranged.

Dinner menus feature local fresh seafood, veal, roast beef, and steaks. Successful fishermen can have their catch prepared for their evening meal. A keiki's, or children's, menu is available, with fish, chicken, and, of course, hamburgers.

Guests book for one of three seatings at dinner. The 6 P.M. seating is recommended for families with children.

Some evening meals feature themes, such as Luau Night, with a roast pig as the centerpiece of a traditional South Pacific feast, and the Western Paniolo Steak Fry. At least once during your stay you'll want to eat dinner at the Hale Samoa, which features exquisite cuisine in a grownups-only setting (a surcharge may apply).

If you desire a dinner that will provide memories for years to come, consider the dinner cruise aboard the 54-foot luxury sailing yacht *Makani Kai* (there's an extra charge).

The Kona Village Resort dress code absolutely forbids jackets, ties, or fancy dress at any meal.

ACTIVITIES

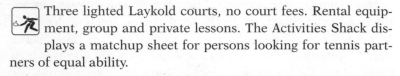

Three lighted Laykold courts, no court fees. Rental equipment, group and private lessons. The Activities Shack displays a matchup sheet for persons looking for tennis partners of equal ability.

Privileges at several outstanding golf courses nearby on the Kona Coast.

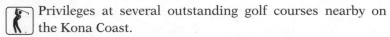

Two freshwater pools, each with its own whirlpool. The sandy beach adjacent to the Activities Shack is the best place for ocean swimming. There are six additional beaches, each with its own character. Snorkeling gear is available in children's as well as adult sizes. The Shipwreck Bar at the main pool is the converted hull of the *New Moon*, a 42-foot schooner owned by Johnno Jackson, the founder of Kona Village.

Sunfish, kayaks and outrigger canoes are available at no charge. There are daily cruises on a glass-bottom boat, *Hooloko*, and a daily sail and snorkeling cruise goes out on a 38-foot catamaran; the half-day trip visits a secluded beach and the world-class coral reefs off the Kona Coast. Quality snorkeling gear, snorkeling instruction, a marine life lecture, and refreshments are included in the cruise fee. The sailing fleet includes a 38-foot catamaran.

Fishing: Deep sea fishing charters.

 Horseback Riding: On the world-famous Parker Ranch.

 Programs on Hawaiian weaving, Hawaiian toys, origami, sand art, feather crafts, seed and shell work, and Hawaiian quilting; pictograph tours; hula or ukulele lessons; guided walks; imu ceremony; poi pounding; Hawaiian games; fishing contests. Ping-Pong, volleyball, and shuffleboard equipment available at the Activities Shack. In the evening cocktails are served at The Bora Bora, which is also the scene of nightly music for entertainment and dancing.

 Kona Coast waters are superb for scuba diving. Daily charters are available, and night dives are made once each week. A range of scuba instruction is offered, from a single introductory dive to full NAUI open-water II certification (seven-day minimum). Special family instruction rates are available.

FOR CHILDREN: Some families, or 'ohana, have been coming to Kona Village Resort for three generations, attracted here by the truly authentic Hawaiian experience. It's more than simple arts and crafts; it is Hawaiian people sharing their history and culture through activities that are entertaining and enjoyable. Staff members like Auntie Eleanor have been showing children how to play Hawaiian games and string leis for years.

Activities offered year-round include paddling outrigger canoes and exploring petroglyphs. For children under 5, accompanied by an adult or baby-sitter, the activities are numerous and range from hula lessons to fishing contests to coconut husking. Those 6 to 12 engage in tidal pool exploration, ukulele lessons, star-gazing, kite flying, and a host of other activities. For teenagers, there's snorkeling, volleyball, sailing, scuba diving, tennis, and swimming—and much more.

A supervised children's dinner is offered at 5:30 P.M. daily, followed by social activities until 8 P.M.

Baby-sitting arrangements can be made on 24 hours' notice.

NICETIES: You are welcomed in Hawaiian style with a lei and tropical drink. Registration includes an orientation to the resort.

Throughout your stay, you are pampered in many small ways, such as fresh Kona coffee beans and coffee-making equipment in your room.

Families will appreciate the washers and dryers on the premises.

The Island Copra Trading Company stocks film, swim and resort wear, beverages, sundries, and gifts.

OF INTEREST NEARBY: Deep-sea fishing, circle island tours, and volcano tours can be arranged through the concierge. Rental cars can be arranged at the resort for day trips around the Big Island.

FOR MORE INFORMATION: Write Kona Village, P.O. Box 1299, Kai'lua-Kona, HI 96745, or phone (800) 367-5290 or (808) 325-5555.

BERMUDA

SONESTA BEACH HOTEL & SPA BERMUDA
Southampton, Bermuda

In the fiercely competitive Bermuda hotel world, each of the major family resorts has a claim to fame. At the Sonesta, it's the three pink sandy beaches, one of them just right outside the guest rooms of the Bay Wing (no time-consuming shuttle required here to get your kids to the beach.) And if you're lucky enough to have a room with a lanai, your children can build sandcastles as you enjoy a room-service breakfast and the ocean view!

There are plenty of other reasons families flock to this resort: its free, well-run children's program; its fine restaurants; its family-pleasing social activities; its athletic facilities; its casual atmosphere, and its seclusion. Though this full-service resort has 400 rooms, it imparts the feel of a small resort.

The Sonesta occupies one of the most beautiful stretches of coastline in Bermuda. From Honeymoon Point, on a rocky bluff overlooking the ocean, there's a wooden staircase leading down to a secluded beach. There, you can watch the waves crash into the coral outcroppings and pretend you're in paradise.

ACCOMMODATIONS: $$$ to $$$$ The Sonesta's 400 rooms include regular hotel rooms, one-bedroom suites, mini suites and presidential suites. Most are in the six-floor main buildng, while others are in the four-floor Bay Wing, which provides the easiest access to a beach. Every room has a balcony or lanai, radio, and remote control color TV. Bermuda law limits room occupancy to four.

A fixed gratuity is charged daily to cover services by bellmen, doormen, dining room and housekeeping staff.

The Sonesta's family package, available from early April through mid November, is a good value. Kids stay free and eat free at the resort's restaurants, when their parents are on a meal plan. And kids get free ice cream, any time they want it!

DINING: The hotel has five restaurants. On the lower level, Lillian's, open only for dinner, features northern Italian cuisine. La Sirena is the place for continental breakfast and a huge breakfast buffet.

Just off the main lobby, the Boat Bay Club offers casual bistro-style lunches and dinners; children feel very welcome here. In the summer, grilled delicacies are served at lunchtime and dinnertime at the Sea Grape Terrace, outdoors overlooking Boat Bay.

The Cafe, in the hotel's shopping arcade, serves light lunches and snacks, as well as ice cream and frozen yogurt.

If you're staying under the hotel's "Dine-Around Program," you can also eat dinner at Henry VIII's, an independently owned English-style pub and grill, at the top of the Sonesta's driveway.

Room service is available from 7 A.M. to 12:45 A.M.

ACTIVITIES

 Six laykold courts, two lighted for night play. Pro shop, clinics, private lessons. No court fees.

 The Sonesta is 10 minutes from Port Royal Golf Club, whose course was designed by Robert Trent Jones (6,565 yards, par 71). The course includes some of Bermuda's most beautiful oceanside terrain. Bermuda has seven other golf courses. The concierge can arrange a game at most of them.

 Two heated pools, one enclosed in a glass dome to ensure year-round swimming. Three beaches; complimentary chaise lounges and towels.

 Scuba, snorkel and windsurfing shop on premises; instruction, rental equipment.

 From shore or rock outcroppings.

 Bermuda's old railroad bed has been turned into a foot-path. It's a short, but uphill, walk from the hotel.

 Moped rentals on premises.

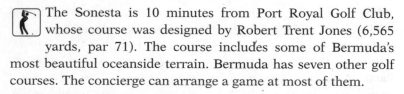 State-of-the-art exercise equipment, whirlpool, sauna. European-type spa offering daily stretch and aerobics

classes, specialized face and body treatments, massage. Special spa packages.

Volleyball, shuffleboard, putting green, croquet, and video game room. Complimentary family movies, afternoon tea, bingo games, special holiday activities. Regular entertainment at night in the Palm Court Club; late-night karaoke and dancing.

FOR CHILDREN: The complimentary "Just Us Kids" program for 5- through 13-year-olds operates between June 15 and Labor Day and over some holidays. The counselors are local teachers or college students on their summer breaks. In the summer, the program operates from 9 A.M. to 5 P.M. seven days a week.

Children gather in the "Kids' Korner," the play room near La Sirena. Mornings are filled with sandcastle-building, pool games, outdoor sports, and hikes to Gibbs Hill Lighthouse. Children can eat lunch with their counselors, or join up with their parents. In the afternoons, there are more indoor or outdoor games, fishing off the rocks (with a prize for the biggest catch!), and beach activities. Each week, there's a field trip to the Bermuda Aquarium and a ferryboat ride..

The "Tiny Tots" program offers supervised activities from 10 A.M. to 2 P.M. for 2- through 4-year-olds seven days a week. Participants in both programs get a free t-shirt. The "Tiny Tots" spend their time on the playground or in the play room, painting, playing with toys, and watching videos.

Monday nights, there's a "birthday" party for "Myrtle the Turtle," the hotel's mascot, from 5:30 to 6:30. Thursday nights, there's a family dinner at the Sea Grape Terrace, followed by a magic show. Friday nights, kids have a pizza and movie party, allowing their parents a dinner by themselves. Saturday nights, there's a family marshmallow roast and singalong at Cross Bay.

There's a small playground on the property.

Babysitting can be arranged.

NICETIES: Eleven of the island's major shops have branches in the hotel's shopping gallery.

There's a shuttle bus to take guests to South Road, where they can catch a public bus, and to Cross Bay Beach, the resort's most remote beach.

OF INTEREST NEARBY: The Bermuda Aquarium, Museum and Zoo is charming, with a nice collection of local marine life.

The hotel is within walking distance of Gibbs Hill Lighthouse. You can climb 185 steps to the top for a panoramic view of the islands.

The Royal Naval Dockyard, a bus or taxi ride away, makes an interesting day trip.

FOR MORE INFORMATION: Write P.O. Box 1070, Hamilton, Bermuda HMEX or call (800) SONESTA.

SOUTHAMPTON PRINCESS
Southampton, Bermuda

Soon after we arrived in Bermuda, our children devised a game: to keep a list of everything they saw that was pink. Only an hour into the game, our 8-year-old passed us a note: *"Everything's pink!"* he wrote.

He wasn't far off. From the sand to the paint on many homes to the police cars, it sometimes seems as though everything in Bermuda *is* pink. And the pinkest building of all is the Southampton Princess, the island's most luxurious, yet family-friendly, resort.

The nine-story pink and white hotel is perched on the island's highest hill, guaranteeing every room a view of either the Atlantic Ocean or Hamilton Harbor. The 100 acres of grounds are a blaze of color year-round, with oleander, hibiscus, bougainvillea, and royal poinciana creating a tropical atmos-phere against the backdrop of a turquoise sea.

With its truly unique combination of British and island cus-toms, Bermuda makes a wonderful (though fairly expensive) family vacation destination. You won't find friendlier people anywhere.

ACCOMMODATIONS: $$$$ The 600 rooms and suites are excep-tionally spacious. Each has a private balcony, two double beds or a king-size bed, a bath/shower combination, radio and cable TV, and includes such amenities as bathrobes and a hairdryer. The walk-in closets are big enough to accommodate a crib. Bermuda law limits room occupancy to four people.

Children 16 and under stay and eat for free (breakfast and dinner) from April through November if their parents are on the Modified American Plan. Mandatory gratuities are charged for each room occupant, including children.

DINING: Except at the Princess Beach Cabana, where you can eat a hamburger, hot dog, or light snack, eating is on the formal side here. Many guests come on the Royal Dine Around Plan, which allows them to have dinner in any of the four hotel restaurants, and, for a surcharge, at two others. Dinner reservations are required at all the restaurants.

For nearly any meal, the best bet for young children is Wickets Brasserie, which serves a buffet breakfast daily and sandwiches, light entrees and children's favorites at lunchtime and early evenings. Windows on the Sound serves a more elaborate breakfast buffet, and continental cuisine, with"silver service," in the British tradition, in the evening (jackets and ties required for men).

The Rib Room, at the Golf Club House, is very English, and specializes in prime rib, ribs and chops. The Whaler Inn, on a cliff overlooking the ocean, specializes in local seafood. The Waterlot Inn, in a 320-year-old cedar-beamed building, offers an eclectic menu of European, island and American dishes, served formally (jacket and tie required) and with a surcharge.

The Newport Room (another surcharge) is where island residents like to come for a special occasion. With mahogany, teak and brass dominating the decor, it has the feel of the grand salon of an ocean-going yacht. If you go to either the Waterlot Inn or the Newport Room, leave the children behind.

For guests on the European plan, downtown Hamilton offers many less expensive dining choices than the hotel restaurants.

ACTIVITIES

 11 all-weather courts, three lighted.

The hotel's 18-hole course (2,684 yards, par 3) is among the island's most famous because of its lofty views and scenic setting. Crazy Joe's Mini-Golf, the island's only miniature golf course, is a short bus ride away at the Belmont Hotel.

In heated indoor and outdoor freshwater pools, or in the Atlantic Ocean at the hotel's private beach club (accessible by shuttle bus).

 Parasailing and sea kayaking at the beach club; snorkeling and scuba diving can be arranged.

 Deep-sea fishing can be arranged.

 Rental mopeds and scooters on premises.

 The 18-mile-long Bermuda Railway Trail skirts the hotel property.

 The hotel's Body Tech Heallth Club operates a fitness center (daily or weekly fees) with Stairmasters, treadmills, exercise bicycles, weight machines. Massages, beauty treatments, fitness evaluations, and aerobics and water exercise classes.

 Afternoon tea, guided walks, cash bingo, clay pigeon shoots, island orientation talks, kitchen tours and cooking demonstrations, winetastings, lectures on Bermuda's marine life and history. The Neptune Lounge offers dancing nightly except Mondays. During holiday periods, special activities, such as Easter egg hunts and kite-flying festivals, are offered.

FOR CHILDREN: The Southampton Princess offers a free well-planned children's program, Camp Minor Manor, from mid-June through Labor Day. Supervised activities are offered for children 5 to 11 and 12 to 16.

Complimentary group babysitting is provided for children ages 2 to 4 from 9 A.M. through 2 P.M. Mondays, Wednesdays and Saturdays. Babysitting for younger children can be arranged for a fee.

The hangout for kids of all ages is Lenny's Loft, a recently refurbished suite of rooms on the hotel's lower level, which stays open from 8:30 A.M. to 11 P.M. The room is named after Lenny, the hotel's mascot (a sea turtle). It includes a large general-use playroom, a separate playroom for toddlers, a snack bar, a juke-box and video arcade.

Among the daily activities are cricket lessons, lizard catching contests (the lizards are later set free), arts and crafts, guided hikes, and beach games. Each day, children have a "Mocktail Hour" from 4 to 5 P.M., with free drinks, popcorn and pizza. Several times a week, the groups take field trips to some of the island's most child-oriented attractions (fees charged).

Evening activities include movies, games, and karaoke contests. A supervised dinner is offered twice a week. On Friday nights, children can "dress to impress" and dine as a group at Windows on the Sound (extra charge).

NICETIES: Each floor has its own soft drink machines.

The hotel operates its own ferry to downtown Hamilton four times daily (fee charged).

OF INTEREST NEARBY: The Bermuda Aquarium, Museum and Zoo is a charming facility that gives visitors a good introduction to the island's native species.

Children will enjoy exploring the buildings at the Royal Naval Dockyard. Among the exhibits at the Maritime Museum are treasures taken from shipwrecks as far back as the 16th Century and relics from the *Sea Venture*, the wrecked ship that brought Bermuda's first colonizers.

In St. George's, it's interesting to explore a replica of the *Sea Venture* and walk around the narrow byways of the island's oldest settlement.

FOR MORE INFORMATION: CALL (800) 223-1818, FAX (809) 238-8245, or write Southampton Princess, P.O. Box HM 1379, Hamilton 5, Bermuda, HM FX.

CASA DE CAMPO
La Romana, Dominican Republic

This sprawling 7,000-acre resort on the southeastern coast of the Dominican Republic calls itself "the most complete resort in the Caribbean," and, for once, an advertising claim may not be pure hype. This resort seems to have it all.

In Spanish, Casa de Campo means "a house in the country." Gulf & Western built the resort in 1974 on the site of an old sugar plantation. It is still surrounded by 240,000 acres of sugar cane, comprising the largest privately held sugar plantation in the world. The resort was bought from Gulf & Western in 1984 by the Fanjul family of West Palm Beach, Florida, along with the surrounding sugar cane acreage. It's now operated as part of the Premier Resorts & Hotels group.

The Dominican Republic is the third most visited destination in the Caribbean, after Puerto Rico and Jamaica. It offers easy connections to major cities in the United States, a balmy tropical climate, lush greenery, a rich history, and friendly people who make visitors feel welcome. Although the Spanish language is spoken here, many Dominicans speak English, which makes it an easy country in which to get around, and a rewarding one to explore. As on many Caribbean islands, though, you will notice extremes in the living standards of the local residents, which your children may find upsetting.

Casa de Campo, with a capacity of about 1,500 guests, attracts an interesting mixture of North Americans, South Americans, and Europeans. In the summer and during the Christmas holidays, it attracts a great number of families.

ACCOMMODATIONS: $$$ to $$$$ Casa de Campo has 300 hotel rooms, called casitas, in low-rise groupings. The casitas are roomy enough for a family and feature two double beds, a balcony or terrace, walk-in closet and dressing area, and cable TV. The second-floor units have high ceilings, which adds to a sense of spaciousness.

Another option for families is a rental villa. The 150 rental villas range from one to four bedrooms in size and come with a full-time maid (for an extra charge, you can also have a butler or nanny). The exquisitely decorated villas offer the ultimate in luxury; many have private swimming pools. The maid will cook breakfast (provisions come from a central commissary).

The cost of a small villa is comparable to a casita. Rates are considerably lower in the summer than in the winter. Numerous package plans are offered.

DINING: There are nine restaurants on the property or at nearby Altos de Chavon. Café el Patio serves casual breakfasts, lunches, and dinners (it's the best bet for families). The Lago Grill is a casual place for breakfast and lunch. At the beach, guests can grab lunch or a light snack at Las Minitas, the beachside restaurant.

In the main hotel, Tropicana is a dinner-only restaurant that frequently features a massive seafood buffet and at other times specializes in Oriental food. Many guests eat lunch at the snack bar by the main pool.

Several of the resort's restaurants are tucked away in the scenic splendor of Altos de Chavon, the replica of a colonial village that is just a short shuttle bus ride from most accommodations. Café del Sol is a quiet spot that features brick oven-baked pizzas, sandwiches, salads, and local specialties for lunch and dinner. For casual dining at night, there's El Sombrero, which serves Mexican food. Fine gourmet cuisine is offered nightly at Casa del Río, high on a cliff over-hanging the Río Chavon. La Piazzetta is a lively trattoria featuring Italian cuisine and strolling musicians.

A 10 percent service charge and 8 percent government tax are added to all restaurant bills. All of the resort restaurants offer high chairs and children's menus.

ACTIVITIES

 Thirteen courts, many lighted for night play, in a country club complete with pro shop and outdoor dining facilities.

Two distinctive golf courses designed by Pete Dye. The oceanfront Teeth of the Dog course has been called the best golf course at any resort in the world by Golf magazine. The Links, Dye's inland course, has one of the longest and broadest driving ranges anywhere. Golf country club, pro shop, restaurant, and elevated observation lounge.

 Fourteen pools. The main swimming pool complex, with its tables shielded by thatched roofs, is always a center of activity; there's a separate shallow pool for children, as well as a separate lap pool. Minitas Beach, the resort's man-made beach on the Caribbean, is an active spot during the day, with hundreds of sunbathers (and seabathers), wind surfers, and small-boat sailors. Be sures to take a day trip over to Catalina Island, with its beautiful beach and snorkeling trail over a coral reef.

Deep-sea or snook fishing in the scenic Río Chavon.

A stable of horses is available for one to three-hour trail rides. During the polo season—November through May— three polo games are played weekly at the Equestrian Center. Polo instruction is also available. In between games, it's fun to visit the stables and watch the horses being cared for.

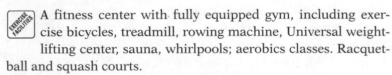 A fitness center with fully equipped gym, including exercise bicycles, treadmill, rowing machine, Universal weight-lifting center, sauna, whirlpools; aerobics classes. Racquetball and squash courts.

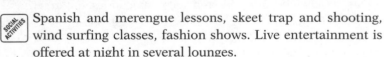 Spanish and merengue lessons, skeet trap and shooting, wind surfing classes, fashion shows. Live entertainment is offered at night in several lounges.

FOR CHILDREN: Casa de Campo operates one of the few full-fledged children's programs in the Caribbean. Aimed at 5- to 13-year-olds, it operates year-round. Part-day, full-day and weekly fees are available. Many Americans who reside year-round in the area use the program as a summer day camp for their children.

The program runs from 9 A.M. to 5 P.M., Monday through Saturday, with lunch provided for full-day attendees. Children are separated into two or three age groups. Among the activities featured daily are swimming, beach games, rides on a horse-drawn cart, pony and horse rides, a sailboat excursion, golf and tennis lessons, treasure hunts and arts and crafts. Artisans from Altos de Chavon give weaving and pottery instruction.

Occasional activities are scheduled for teenagers.

For younger children, there's a staff of 50 nannies available for hire on an hourly, daily, or weekly basis. Playgrounds are located near the golf club and at the beach.

NICETIES: A shuttle system links all of the resort's facilities and eliminates the need for a rental car. But four-passenger rental golf carts are very popular with families for use on the resort's extensive grounds.

Volleyball, dominoes, checkers, chess, Scrabble, bingo, and backgammon equipment is available from the concierge.

Bottled water is provided in all the rooms.

OF INTEREST NEARBY: Altos de Chavon, the resort's $30 million replica of a 16th-century colonial village, is a site to behold. Built on the top of a cliff overlooking a gorge created by the Río Chavon, the village looks like a movie set. It draws tourists from all corners of the country with its boutiques, art galleries, restaurants, Taino Indian museum, and small stone church. International stars such as Frank Sinatra, Sergio Mendes, Gloria Estefan, and Julio Iglesias have performed in its 5,000-seat Grecian-style amphitheater. Professional artists are in residence for months at a time, as well as 200 boarding students at the junior college operated there by the Parsons School of Design, the Caribbean's only college-level training school in the arts.

Excursions to Santo Domingo can be arranged through a tour operator at the hotel or taken on your own. Old Santo Domingo is a treasure trove for history buffs. Many of the original 16th-century buildings have been restored and others lovingly re-created. There are also numerous museums that document the Caribbean's early Indian and European history.

FOR MORE INFORMATION: Call the Miami sales office at (800) 877-3643 or write Premier World Marketing, 2600 S.W. Third Avenue, Miami, FL 33129. The hotel's direct phone number is (809) 523-3333.

CLUB MED FAMILY VILLAGES
Eleuthera, The Bahamas
Punta Cana, Dominican Republic
Huatulco, Mexico
Ixtapa, Mexico
St. Lucia, West Indies

If the name Club Med conjures up visions of nubile 22-year-olds in string bikinis and muscle-bound Lotharios, consider some of the visitors to Club Med Punta Cana the same week we were there: 70 children, six obviously pregnant women, and at least five sets of grandparents. Oh, the nubile 22-year-olds and the Lotharios were there, but the atmosphere was distinctly wholesome and the appeal to families strong.

The Club Med organization operates five family-oriented villages among its 15 villages in the Caribbean, Mexico and the Bahamas: in 1993, 58,000 children vacationed at them, which tells you something about their appeal to families. Elsewhere in Club Med's global network, there are 28 other villages with special children's programs.

We visited Club Med Punta Cana, on the remote southeastern tip of the Dominican Republic. Here, the beach is breathtakingly lovely, banked on one side by a grove of coconut palms and on the other by the azure waters of the Caribbean Sea. A coral reef several hundred yards from shore serves as a brake on the action of the waves, so swimming is safe and relaxing. The sand is the perfect texture for castle building, and there are plenty of chaise lounges for adults.

An integral part of the Club Med concept is quality control. Little differs from one village to another. The buffets can always be counted on to be lavish and well prepared, with a few locally inspired dishes thrown in for atmosphere. Sports are varied and active, and participation encouraged. The GOs (short for *gentils organisateurs*, the French term for "congenial hosts") are all attractive and fit. Even the music which ends the nightly shows is the same at each village (you can buy a tape of it to take home).

Club Med's repeat rate among GMs (*gentils membres*, its term for guests) is high. Families who want a foreign vacation in a sheltered setting know they can count on Club Med to provide the same quality vacation year after year, at whatever village they choose.

ACCOMMODATIONS: $$ to $$$$ At Punta Cana, the rooms were small, but adequate, with two or three single platform beds and a small, built-in vanity. A short corridor leading to the doorway contained two closets with built-in shelves, a bathroom with a shower stall and sink, and a separate toilet area. Although the window would open, it was unscreened. Walls were white-washed concrete block, and the floors red tile. Room safes were provided.

At each resort, there are a few adjoining rooms. Families of five or more are lodged in two or more rooms.

At every Club Med village, all meals and most activities are included in the rates. During certain months of the year, children under 5 are free at the family-oriented Club Med villages.

DINING: At Punta Cana, food is prepared by both French and Dominican chefs, and the influence of both cuisines is obvious. All meals are served buffet-style in a large open-air dining room with a circuslike atmosphere; one guest said it reminded him of his college's cafeteria. Guests are seated as they arrive at tables for eight, so unless you arrive at the same time as newly made friends, you're likely to be seated with someone else.

A breakfast buffet is served from 7:30 to 9 A.M. Late-risers can eat in the cocktail lounge until 11:30 A.M.

Lunch, served from 12:30 to 2 P.M., features eight to 10 buffet tables. Dinner is served from 7:30 to 9 P.M. On perhaps five of the seven nights of the week, there's a particular theme, such as Asian Night, Italian Night, or Seafood Night. There's always a selection of wonderful appetizers (carpaccio one night, raw tuna in garlic sauce another) and several seafood, meat, chicken, and pasta entrées. Complimentary Dominican wine and beer are served.

Children can either take their meals with their parents or eat together as a group in a special area equipped with child-size furniture. Parents must accompany children under 4 to this area at dinnertime (the children's dinner is at 6:30 P.M.).

For a special treat at Punta Cana, guests can reserve a table at the beachside annex restaurant, La Hispaniola. There, you'll be served by waiters and enjoy French specialties in a more relaxed atmosphere. Reservations are taken at 12:30 P.M. daily, and fill within five minutes. A second specialty restaurant, La Cana, serves late lunches and Italian specialties for dinner.

ACTIVITIES

 Tennis courts at all family villages. Instruction, weekly tournaments.

 At Huatulco, guests can play golf at an 18-hole, par 72 course, minutes from the village.

 Large pool at each resort; separate pools for children. Ocean swimming.

 Daily instruction in water-skiing, wind surfing, kayaking, snorkeling, and sailing, plus free time to enjoy these sports.

 Available at Punta Cana from an off-premise concessioner.

 Before-breakfast stretch exercises, before-lunch water exercises, and aerobics classes. Many guests also take advantage of the instruction available in such circus activities as juggling and high-trapeze artistry. Volleyball, basketball, and archery equipment.

 Periodically through the week, special activities such as a wind-surfing regatta (with free sangria and barbecue) or a free happy hour are offered.

The GOs stage nightly entertainment. A highlight of the week is the circus performance in which both adults and children show off their newly learned skills. The bars and disco stay open until the last guest leaves.

FOR CHILDREN: At each "Family Village," the Club offers three separate programs for children, generally from 9 A.M. to 9 P.M. daily: the "Petit Club," for 2 and 3-year-olds; the "Mini- Club," for children 4 through 7; and the "Kids' Club," for children 8 through 11. When there are large numbers of teenagers present, special activities are offered. All of the family-oriented villages offer scuba experiences for children, starting at age 4.

The Petit Club features such activities as sand-castle building, jumping on a trampoline, splashing about the pool, free play, and arts and crafts. Children may be left in the program from 9 A.M. to 5 P.M., and brought back from 7:30 P.M. to 9 P.M., but few children of this age do well for such a long time away from their parents. There are designated hours during the day when children can be brought to the program, but they can be taken away at any time.

The Mini-Club is a more active program, featuring circus activities, pool games, swimming instruction, beach activities, arts and crafts, and performances in one or two evening shows.

The best of the children's programs is the Kids' Club. There, your 8- to 11-year-old children can learn archery, water-skiing, snorkeling, sailing, tennis, and circus skills.

The villages at Ixtapa and Eleuthera each has a Baby Club, where babies 12 months and older are cared for between 8:30 A.M. and 6 P.M. daily. A special baby food chef prepares food from fresh ingredients. Cribs, strollers and potties can be borrowed at no charge, and a "convenience room" with a refrigerator is open around-the-clock so that parents can safely store juice, formula and baby food. Eleuthera's Baby Club operates only in the summer.

The children's programs are staffed by special children's GOs, all of whom have college degrees and experience in child care. Each serves a six-month to one-year stint at a village before moving on to another village. When we visited Punta Cana, most were outgoing, energetic, and enthusiastic. Most speak both French and English.

Each village in North America has some special features. At Punta Cana, three fairly new buildings near the perimeter of the property house all the children's activities. In addition, there's a special shallow pool for kids, which is guarded during swimming times. Scuba diving lessons are offered for 4- to-12-year-olds.

At Huatulco, the newest Family Village, children 4 through 11 stay for free between late April and early December.

The village at Ixtapa has a brand-new Baby Club, a remodeled Mini Club with a private dining room for children, a Big Top circus tent, and a separate kids' bar stocked with healthy drinks and snacks. Ixtapa also offers an intensive tennis program for children between 8 and 14.

The village at St. Lucia offers go-kart and pony rides and horseback riding.

At some of the villages, in-room baby-sitting is difficult to arrange.

NICETIES: There's a physician on call at each village, as well as nurses in residence. There's no charge for children's visits, and only a nominal charge for adults. Commonly needed drugs are kept on hand.

At Punta Cana, the hostess had a supply of old paperback books and games such as checkers, backgammon, and Scrabble for guests' use.

FOR MORE INFORMATION: Call (800) CLUB-MED, or write Club Med Sales, Inc., 40 West 57th Street, New York, NY 10019.

BOSCOBEL BEACH RESORT
Ocho Rios, Jamaica

Until the mid-1980s, Jamaica was a tourist destination catering mostly to couples and singles. With resorts with names such as Hedonism II and Couples, what family would even consider Jamaica as a destination for a family vacation? Then, in 1987, came Boscobel Beach Resort, on the site of the refurbished Playboy Club on a lovely cove about 15 minutes from downtown Ocho Rios. Where Playboy bunnies once entertained, children now play.

This glistening beachside resort on Jamaica's north coast resembles a permanently moored cruise ship. There's an activity every hour of the day, including the wee hours of the morning, and plenty of deck chairs and chaise lounges in which to relax. There are lavish buffets and elegantly prepared dinners—and free drinks. There's a host of social directors—and a select group of Super Nannies to care for your children. And then there's the Caribbean Sea—a mosaic of turquoise, royal blue, and aquamarine that beckons constantly.

Although the main buildings have been in place for more than two decades, the resort has an all-new feel since it was extensively refurbished after Hurricane Gilbert in 1988. Most of the guest rooms are grouped in two three-story buildings that look out over tropical gardens, the pool, and the sea beyond.

ACCOMMODATIONS: $$ to $$$$ Boscobel Beach has 207 guest rooms, most with ocean views. Most are "junior suites"—exceptionally spacious rooms with separate sleeping and sitting areas; 14 have two bedrooms. The rooms are beautifully decorated and equipped with ceiling fans, air-conditioners, refrigerators, telephones, radios, and cable TV. The tubs are tiled and sunken, and the balconies are large, with plenty of chairs. Roll-away beds and cribs are available.

Rates are lowest in the late spring, summer, and fall. Up to two children under 14 are free in each room, and children over 14 who are sharing their parents' room are charged $50 per night. The rate covers all meals, including drinks; all activities; transfers to and from the airport at Montego Bay, and three off-premises excursions. In the summer, a single parent traveling with two children pays no supplement. No tipping is permitted.

DINING: The chef here uses many local vegetables and fruits in the cuisine, which provides you with an opportunity to taste such exotic offerings as ackee (a scrambled-egg-like vegetable), cho-cho (similar to squash), and curried goat. In addition, there is no better coffee in the world than Jamaican Blue Mountain, and you'll get to drink bottomless cups of it at every meal (served, in the British style, with evaporated milk).

A breakfast buffet is served daily from 7:30 to 10 A.M. on the Jippi Jappa Terrace overlooking the swimming pool and the sea beyond. Alternatively, you can ask for a continental breakfast to be served on your balcony.

Lunch is served buffet-style on the Terrace and generally features five entrées, including one sure child-pleaser, and an extensive array of salads. The dessert table is irresistible. A separate snack bar at the beach serves hamburgers, hot dogs, and french fries to those who don't want to leave their beach chairs.

A children's dinner is served from 6 to 7 P.M. on the Terrace. The regular dinner is served from 7 to 10 P.M. in the open-air dining rooms upstairs and in an Italian restaurant in the luxury wing (new in 1990). Families can, of course, eat together.

ACTIVITIES

 Four Laykold courts.

 Privileges at Superclubs' golf courses in Runaway Bay; no greens fees. Professional instruction available.

 Two large pools, daily scuba-diving and snorkeling lessons and thrice-daily excursions to the reef (free use of all equipment).

A half dozen sailboats and windsurfers and a powerboat for water-skiing are available to guests. The staff will even provide sailing, water-skiing, and wind-surfing lessons, or take you out for a spin (child-size life preservers are available). A glass-bottom boat makes several trips daily to the reef for coral and fish viewing.

 Aerobics and dance exercise classes on the Terrace; beach-front gym with weights, exercise equipment, Ping-Pong, Jacuzzis.

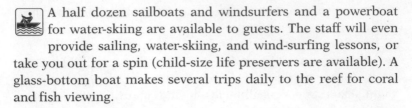 Instruction in hat-making, Jamaican culture, bicycle tours, arts and crafts, sand-sculpting, basket-weaving, a reggae dance class, and tennis and table tennis tournaments.

At night, the Terrace comes alive with the sounds of a steel band or a reggae group. One night each week, a local cultural group performs. The disco opens at 11 P.M. The piano bar offers a romantic site for a drink.

FOR CHILDREN: Boscobel operates one of the most ambitious children's activity programs in the Caribbean. The kids' center is a circular, mostly glass-walled building just outside the lobby. It is open daily from 9 A.M. to 10 P.M. and accepts children between 6 weeks of age and 12 years, although most children over 9 seem to find other things to do.

The center is staffed by local women whom the resort calls "Super Nannies." Separate activities are offered for 3- to 5-year-olds, and 6- to 11-year-olds. Among the activities are "Mousercise," swimming lessons, pool games, shell hunts, arts and crafts, nature walks, donkey rides, reggae dance classes, glass-bottom boat rides, computer play, treasure hunts, movies, and patois classes.

The facility is equipped with about a half dozen computers, which are a big hit with the over-6 set. Cribs are made up for napping babies, and cushions and quilts are spread on the floor in front of a giant-screen TV for toddlers who don't want to miss some of their favorite cartoons. Snacks are served, and the staff will feed your child lunch if you wish.

Old McDonald's Farm, just behind one of the hotel wings, is home to several dozen exotic birds and small farm animals, which children love to visit. There also are several swing sets and an expansive grassy play area.

Sitters can be hired for the evening. Children under 6 must be accompanied by a sitter if they are in the kids' center after 6 P.M.

NICETIES: There's a lot to be said for staying at an all-inclusive resort, where you never need to dig into your pockets to pay for a thing. Children can easily get accustomed to walking up to a bartender and asking for "a strawberry daiquiri—without the rum, please."

The resort is largely accessible to wheelchairs (there's an elevator to the beach). Several families were accompanied by children in wheelchairs when we visited and had no trouble getting around.

Fresh beach towels are delivered to your room each evening so that you'll be ready for an early-morning swim. In addition, there are supplies at the beach and pool.

OF INTEREST NEARBY: Dunn's River Falls is one of Jamaica's premier tourist attractions, and the resort schedules a daily trip there. The falls cascade 600 feet down a series of steplike rock outcroppings into the sea. No visitor is either too young or too old to enjoy playing in the many ice-cold pools along the way. But to really experience it, you have to climb the falls, which is done with the help of a local guide.

The resort also offers daily tours to nearby Prospect Plantation, which offers a tram ride past fields of bananas, pineapples, sugar cane, coffee, limes, and pimento—and samples along the way. The plantation also is the site of the scenic White River Gorge.

Ocho Rios is a 20-minute drive from the hotel, and most guests make at least one foray into the town by tourist van to shop the many straw and souvenir markets. Be aware that the peddlers are very aggressive.

FOR MORE INFORMATION: Write Boscobel Beach at P.O. Box 63, Ocho Rios, Jamaica, or call (800) 859-7873 (305-925-0925 from Florida) or (809) 975-7087.

For general tourist information, write the Jamaica Tourist Board, 866 Second Avenue, New York, NY 10017, or call (212) 688-7650.

THE HYATT REGENCY CERROMAR BEACH HYATT DORADO BEACH
Dorado, Puerto Rico

Imagine taking a vacation to an exotic island paradise where you don't need a passport, don't have to change your money, and don't need to brush up on your French or Spanish because most of the natives speak English. The place is Puerto Rico, where a rich broth of culture has been simmering for eons, as Indian natives mingled with settlers from Spain, England, France and the Netherlands and slaves from West Africa. The island is a protectorate of the United States.

The Hyatt resorts in Dorado, a beautiful area on the north shore about 22 miles west of the San Juan airport, are truly world-class. Originally, the ground on which the two Hyatt resorts now stand was a coconut and grapefruit plantation. It later became a private playground for Laurance Rockefeller, who opened the Dorado Beach resort to the public in December 1958. Cerromar Beach, the sister resort, opened in 1971, two miles down the road.

In 1985, the Hyatt Hotel chain bought both resorts for $40 million and lavished time and attention—and another $75 million—on renovation. It has been money well spent; the hotels are beautiful. And with a mean year-round temperature of 76 degrees, outdoor sports are possible anytime.

The hotels' grounds are heaven on earth for the serious horticulturalist—and the weekend gardener. The 1,000-acre properties are verdant with nearly 600 species of tropical plants. The resort's own beehives produce honey for its kitchens, and the numerous coconut palms are the source of meat and milk for tropical drinks.

ACCOMMODATIONS: $$$ to $$$$ The Dorado Beach is made up of low-rise buildings with a total of 300 rooms. The upper level rooms have terra-cotta tile floors and bamboo frames around king-size beds and are awash with the tropical colors associated with Caribbean island hideaways. Deluxe rooms and beachfront casitas, in small clusters but with private patios, cost more than standard hotel rooms. From just before Christmas until late April, rates include breakfast and dinner.

The Cerromar Beach has 504 rooms, including 19 suites, in a

seven-story building; most rooms have a view of the sea, and many have private balconies. The rooms are spacious, with marble baths, tile floors, and tropical furnishings.

Rates at both hotels drop considerably—as much as 60 percent—after the high season, which generally lasts from mid-December to late April. A Modified American Plan package can be purchased for an additional charge at the Cerromar Beach. At both hotels, children 15 and under stay for free in their parents' room (limit two children per room).

DINING: Most dining at the resorts is done in spacious, windowed rooms with spectacular views of the ocean. The favorite of many guests is the Su Casa Restaurant. The restaurant is in a colonial mansion that was the home of the plantation's original owner and features gourmet Caribbean and Spanish specialties, which rely largely on fresh seafood and unusual spicing.

At the Cerromar, Medici's, the main restaurant, features Northern Italian and Caribbean cuisines and fresh seafood. The outdoor Swan Café, open for breakfast and lunch, is a triple-level restaurant next to the river pool. The Sunday brunch here is hard to beat, with its extensive array of fresh seafood, Caribbean specialties, and made-to-order omelets.

The main restaurant at the Hyatt Dorado Beach is the Surf Room, which serves international food in a formal atmosphere overlooking the ocean. The more casual, open-air Ocean Terrace, which is open from morning through dinner, is a delightful spot to sip coffee, eat from the breakfast buffet, and watch the ocean. It has nightly theme parties. This is also a good place to dine with children.

All the restaurants offer children's menus with entrees under $3; children can also choose from the regular menu at a 50-percent discount.

ACTIVITIES

 Twenty-one Decoralt-surface courts, some lighted. Private and group lessons, pro shop; court fees.

Four 18-hole courses designed by Robert Trent Jones. The two courses at the Dorado Beach are regarded as among the great seaside links of the world; they wind through tropical forests and citrus groves, out along the Atlantic Ocean, and past a chain of lakes and a man-made lagoon.

 The Cerromar claims the longest swimming pool in the world—1,776 feet long, or 526 feet longer than the Empire State Building is high. It takes 15 minutes to float from one end to the other. The pool, which cost more than $3 million, is actually five free-form pools connected with 14 waterfalls and four slides. The beautifully landscaped pool features a 187-foot spiral water slide, a swim-up bar, and a lounge with underwater seats, a subterranean Jacuzzi, water volleyball and aerobics courts, and a kiddie area. The Dorado Beach has three swimming pools. And of course, there's the Atlantic Ocean.

 Deep-sea fishing and scuba diving trips can be arranged. Water sports offered at the Lisa Penfield Windsurfing School and Watersports Center.

 Rentals available, including adult-sized tricycles.

 Spa Caribe, new in 1988, offers computerized body composition analyses and exercise and diet recommendations, talking Powercise exercise machines, Dynacourt warm-up equipment, aerobics classes, massages, and skin and body care programs. Miles of jogging trails; in-line skating at Dorado Beach.

 Spanish lessons, gourmet cooking classes, sightseeing tips, art expositions, carriage rides, scuba shows, ice-carving exhibitions, movies, snorkeling tours, and garden walks. At the Cerromar Beach, a large open-air bar and cocktail lounge called the Flamingo Bar offers live entertainment nightly. The Lobby Bar at Dorado Beach, overlooking the Atlantic Ocean, also offers nightly entertainment. Both hotels have casinos, which means they're quite lively at night.

FOR CHILDREN: "Camp Hyatt," a supervised children's activities program for youngsters from 3 through 12, operates daily at Cerromar Beach, and also welcomes children staying at the Dorado Beach. The hours are from 9 A.M. to 4 P.M. daily and again from 6 to 10 P.M. A fee is charged.

A typical day in the children's program starts with registration, followed by outdoor games, such as jump rope, hopscotch, soccer, castle building, or kite flying. Then come pool games, such as swimming relays, raft relays, pool volleyball, and treasure hunts. At 11:30, lunch preparation begins, after which there are indoor activities such as bingo, coloring, arts and crafts, Spanish lessons, board games, movies, and cartoons, followed by outdoor games and more pool games. The evening schedule starts with a get-acquainted session between 6 and 6:30, followed by dinner in the main dining room, movies, cartoons, quiet games, or clown and mime shows.

Children's facilities include a good playground at Cerromar Beach, which is equipped with climbers, tunnels, and swings. Bilingual babysitters can be obtained for in-room child care.

NICETIES: A San Francisco-style cable car (on wheels) shuttles guests betweeen the resorts.

Recipes of some of the resort's most popular Caribbean-style dishes are gladly provided to guests.

OF INTEREST NEARBY: Don't miss Old San Juan. It is a maze of little streets with street vendors, fancy department stores, galleries and charming cafés that offer heady concoctions of coffee and who-knows-what-else, as well as tropical drinks. Old San Juan is also an interesting architectural study, with many well-maintained colonial-era buildings painted in pastel colors. Also of interest is the old walled city, with its parapets, lookout towers, and cannons. It offers spectacular views of the ocean and city.

The Caribbean National Forest, commonly called El Yunque, has 28,000 acres of rain-forest vegetation and is the only tropical forest in the U.S. National Forest System. The forest, about 50 miles southeast of San Juan, offers great hiking trails. It's the home of the very endangered Puerto Rican parrot.

FOR MORE INFORMATION: Write the Hyatt Regency Cerromar Beach or the Hyatt Dorado Beach, Dorado, Puerto Rico 00646, or call Hyatt Resorts Puerto Rico at (809) 796-1234. For reservations call (800) 233-1234; in Nebraska, call (800) 228-9001; in Alaska and Hawaii, call (800) 228-9005.

BITTER END YACHT CLUB
Virgin Gorda, British Virgin Islands

The British and American Virgins are located in one of the best sailing areas of the world. They promise sailors warm air and water temperatures year-round, steady trade winds, sheltered anchorages, and unspoiled beauty. The easternmost of these mountainous islands form a rough ellipse that defines a great cruising basin. The popularity of sailing in this region is apparent even as you fly into Virgin Gorda—the water below is dotted with sails. Boats anchored off the white sand beaches cast shadows on the sandy bottom below. Coral reefs are everywhere.

Sparsely populated Virgin Gorda itself has an up-and-down profile of green mountains. Leaving the airport, the taxi climbs to the top of Mount Gorda and descends the other side to Gun Creek on North Sound. There, a launch waits to ferry you to the Bitter End Yacht Club. Bitter End is one of the great sailing resorts of the Caribbean. It welcomes families and offers a wide variety of sailing and water-based recreational activities.

At Bitter End, steep hillsides covered with flowering bougainvillea and hibiscus fall to white sand beaches that ring a secluded sound. "Paradise" is an over-used word, but paradise this is.

ACCOMMODATIONS: $$$$ Rates vary with the season, with stays around Christmas and Easter the most expensive. Rates are lowest in the summer. Bitter End has 100 accommodations in several categories. Chalets, the most luxurious accommodations, perch high on the hillside with great views of North Sound and the yacht harbor. They have over 600 square feet of space, air-conditioning and ceiling fans, balconies, two queen-size beds, marble baths, and garden-view showers. Hillside Villas are open and spacious with private decks overlooking the sea, twin beds, ceiling fans, two-sink bathrooms, and enormous showers with private views of a garden or the sea. Beachfront Villas are slightly older and smaller. Villas are arranged in groups of two (larger families could rent both and have two bedrooms and two baths). Each room has a coffee maker and small stocked refrigerator. Maid service is twice daily.

Another option is to sleep on a Freedom-30 sailboat moored at the Bitter End dock. The Freedoms sleep up to six and have hookups for electric lights and running water. Daily maid service is included.

Rates include all meals, and for stays of seven nights or more, unlimited day sailing, daily snorkeling trips, participation in Sunday regattas, and a manager's cocktail party.

A variety of packages is available. The summer family package is a great enticement to a summer vacation here. From the beginning of May to the beginning of November, Bitter End charges two adult family members the lower summer rate, throws in a second room and bath for two or more children, and charges only a flat daily rate for each child.

DINING: You are a captive diner at Bitter End, since there are no other restaurants for miles around. But oh, to be at the mercy of these chefs more often! The food in both restaurants is marvelous.

The English Carvery is located in a striking open-air pavilion surrounded by tropical gardens. The menu features roast meats and poultry served in an elegant, candlelit atmostphere.

The Clubhouse Steak and Seafood Grille is at the harbor and docks. Fresh fish and Caribbean lobster head the menu. Dinner in The Grille is by early and late sittings. Each day, the staff will seat you at a different table. In the process, you'll meet a widening circle of other guests at adjacent tables.

Breakfasts and lunches at The Grille are healthy, ample buffets. The breakfast juice bar includes a bottle of chilled champagne, and rum punch is one of the luncheon drink options.

The poolside bar offers sandwiches. Families can obtain box lunches for boating excursions.

ACTIVITIES

 There's a freshwater swimming pool that's four-foot deep throughout. Each day, the *Ponce de Leon* pontoon boat takes snorkelers out to Eustatia Reef, a short distance from Bitter End. Life belts and flippers in all sizes are available. Bring your own mask and snorkel or purchase them in the resort's shop.

Guests have unlimited use of most of the resort's sailboats, which include windsurfers, Sunfish, Lasers, Rhode 19s, and J-24s; sailing and wind-surfing lessons available for an extra charge. Boston Whalers are always available for exploring within North Sound. Paranda, the Bitter End's 48-foot catamaran, takes guests on sunset cocktail sails and makes at least one trip each week to Dog Island for swimming and snorkeling.

 Trails crisscross Virgin Gorda.

 The Bitter End's Vita Course 2000 has a 1/8-mile jogging track with a low-impact surface in a tropical park setting and 16 exercise stations that provide isometric, weight resistance and stretching exercises; lighted for evening workouts.

 Scuba diving on Virgin Island reefs with the Kilbride family is one of the adventures of a lifetime. Bert Kilbride was made "Keeper of the Wrecks" that litter Anegada and other Virgin Island reefs by Queen Elizabeth II. No one knows these waters better. The Kilbrides offer daily scuba trips and beginning instruction. They furnish tanks, weights, and backpacks. You can bring your own regulator, fins, mask, and snorkel or rent them.

FOR CHILDREN: Bitter End Yacht Club does not encourage stays of families with children younger than 7, but the staff has great patience with older children and welcomes them in all the activities. This is a good place for your older child to learn to snorkel, sail, or wind-surf.

During the summer, Bitter End offers a complimentary half-day sailing instruction program daily to children between 7 and 16 whose families are there on the family plan.

Children return again and again to the large fish tank at the harbor dock, which is lighted at night. It holds a fascinating collection of sea turtles, tarpon, sharks, blowfish, remora, and other tropical species. Lobster boats call occasionally and replenish the restaurant's supply, which is stored in the adjacent lobster tanks.

The Sand Palace Theater plays several movies a day on its large video screen. Those scheduled early in the evening are generally suitable for children.

The Flipper, one of only two dozen "aquascopes" made in France some years ago, takes children and their parents on a one-hour tour of Eustatia reef. Passengers ride in a submerged compartment of Plexiglas with unobstructed views of the coral and marine life on the reef on both sides. The tour includes views of the cannon and anchors from a Spanish galleon.

NICETIES: When you arrive at your room, you'll find fresh flowers and a complimentary bottle of Virgin Islands rum. The flowers are replaced every day.

Bitter End Yacht Club stretches for nearly a mile along the shore of North Sound. You can reach any point in a few minutes at a leisurely pace, but a pontoon boat provides a free taxi service along the waterfront.

OF INTEREST NEARBY: The 50-foot excursion boat *Prince of Wales* makes day trips several times a week. Visit the Baths, where huge boulders on the beach form grottoes and pools, or Anegada, the only coral atoll in the Virgin Islands, and the site of over 300 shipwrecks. Pirates used to light false beacons on Anegada to lure ships onto the rocks.

A sightseeing and shopping trip to Road Town on the nearby island of Tortola is another option.

FOR MORE INFORMATION: Write the reservation office, Bitter End Yacht Club, 875 N. Michigan Ave., #3707, Chicago, IL 60611, or call (800) 872-2392.

HYATT REGENCY GRAND CAYMAN
George Town, Grand Cayman Island

Ask any serious scuba diver or snorkeler for a list of the world's great diving spots, and the Cayman Islands are certain to be on it. The coral reef just off North Sound on Grand Cayman offers some of the most accessible snorkeling and diving in the Caribbean in water so clear that visibility is often 150 feet. The awesome sponges, magnificent corals, and colorful fish that you'll see here will make diving experiences elsewhere pale in comparison.

This British colony occupies three tiny islands in the Caribbean, equidistant from Cuba and Jamaica. Grand Cayman, the largest of the three, is the main tourist destination. Visitors are drawn to its unique combination of British politeness and Caribbean mellowness. People also come for the climate (the lowest recorded temperature ever was 68 degrees), the breath-taking aquamarine water, and the low-key ambience.

The Hyatt Regency Grand Cayman, which opened in 1986, is the most complete family resort in the Caymans.

ACCOMMODATIONS: $$$$ Most guests stay in the 236 luxury hotel rooms in seven low-rise buildings. Connecting rooms and a few suites are available. All rooms have ceiling fans and air conditioning, mini-bars, and room safes (there's a charge). The rooms are decorated in soothing pastels, with bleached ash, rattan, wicker, and teak furnishings. Either a king-size bed or two doubles should be specified when reservations are made.

About two dozen individually owned villas bordering the golf course can also be rented. These have full kitchens, washers and dryers, a patio or balcony, and one to three bedrooms.

DINING: Guests eat breakfast in the Garden Loggia, an airy room opening on to a garden, which offers a buffet with cooked-to-order eggs. The restaurant, with both indoor and outdoor seating, is also open for dinner from May through December. The Loggia Lounge serves snacks outdoors until midnight. On Friday evenings, there's a prime rib carvery and lavish seafood buffet. Children can choose from an assortment of inexpensive items on the children's menu or eat for half-price from the regular menu.

Hemingway's, at Hyatt's Beach Club, serves lovely lunches and dinners both inside and outside, with gorgeous views of the Caribbean. The menu features some Caribbean specialties, as well as classic continental offerings. Also at the Beach Club, the Pool Grille serves sandwiches throughout the day.

The Brittania Grille at the golf course serves sandwiches, salads, and light meals. For villa guests, Foster's Food Fare, two blocks away, offers all the necessary groceries.

ACTIVITIES

 Four Plexi-paved lighted courts, no fees; rental equipment available. Adults' and children's clinics, private lessons.

Brittania, the island's only golf course, is on the resort grounds. Designed by Jack Nicklaus, the 3,202-yard course can be played three different ways: as a nine-hole regulation course, an 18-hole executive course, or an 18-hole "Cayman ball" course. The Cayman ball has pimples instead of dimples and is half the weight of a regular ball.

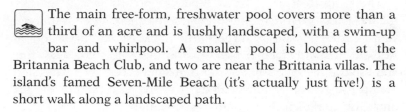 The main free-form, freshwater pool covers more than a third of an acre and is lushly landscaped, with a swim-up bar and whirlpool. A smaller pool is located at the Britannia Beach Club, and two are near the Brittania villas. The island's famed Seven-Mile Beach (it's actually just five!) is a short walk along a landscaped path.

Instruction and rental pedal boats, aqua trikes, wind-surfers, sailboats, and jet skis at the Beach Club. For a novel experience, rent the inflated Banana Boat, which is towed by a powerboat.

 Sunset, dinner, and star-gazing cruises are offered on *The Spirit of Ppalu*, an excursion catamaran. Snorkeling or scuba-diving instructions and expeditions are offered daily on *The Spirit of Ppalu*, and on two Red Sail Sports dive boats. The excursion to Sting Ray City is a must.

 Marlin tuna, dolphin, and wahoo expeditions on charter boats that depart from the hotel's small marina.

Rental bikes and mopeds at the Beach Club.

A health club with Stairmasters Nordic Track, free weights, Lifecycles, treadmills and Liferower; no fees. Water aerobics classes daily in the main pool, as well as land-based stretching sessions. Croquet, organized water volley-ball games.

 The manager holds a cocktail reception every Tuesday night.

FOR CHILDREN: Camp Hyatt welcomes children between 3 and 12 for daily activities during the summer and over school holi-days and on weekends the rest of the year. The program, for which an hourly or daily fee is charged, features snorkeling expeditions, t-shirt painting, visits to the Cayman Island's trea-sury and history museum, movies, beach activities, tennis lessons, and pier fishing. It usually operates from 10 A.M. to 4 P.M., and 6 to 8 P.M. Participants receive a Camp Hyatt cap and magic slate.

NICETIES: An impressive collection of both modern and ancient sculpture is scattered around the property.

OF INTEREST NEARBY: Grand Cayman is short on conventional tourist attractions. The Turtle Farm is the island's main tourist draw. It's the only facility in the world that raises green sea turtles for commercial use. Several thousand green sea turtles and Kemp Ridleys, an endangered species, are released into the sea each year to replenish the natural population.

Hell, a patch of eerie dead coral formations, is of primary interest to visitors who want an unusual postmark on their postcards. The Cayman Islands National Museum, which opened in 1991 in an old courts building on the waterfront at Hog Sty Bay, has exhibits on the islands' natural and cultural history.

Dave Miller, a Caymaner whose family has lived on the island since 1655, leads excellent personalized tours around the island. He knows the best snorkeling places and can even satisfy a personal interest in Cayman beekeeping techniques. Call 70643 or 71047 to make arrangements.

FOR MORE INFORMATION: Call (809) 949-1234; FAX (809) 949-8528. For reservations, call (800) 229-9001 from Nebraska, (800) 233-1234 from elsewhere in the continental U.S. and Canada, and (800) 228-9005 from Alaska or Hawaii.

GUEST
RANCHES

RANCHO DE LOS CABALLEROS
Wickenburg, Arizona

Imagine a country inn set in the middle of country club grounds with a 60-horse stable and rugged desert mountain ranges on three sides. That's Rancho de los Caballeros. The fact that 65 percent of its guests are repeat visitors testifies to its success as a family vacation destination. Some families have been coming for 40 years; their children now bring children of their own.

Rancho de los Caballeros was founded in 1947 when Wickenburg could lay claim to being the "dude ranch capital of the world." Its founders, Dallas and Edie Gant, set out to create a somewhat smaller version of Bishop's Lodge near Santa Fe, where Dallas Gant had been manager. The Spanish name they chose for their ranch means "Ranch of the Gentlemen on Horseback." It truly is a ranch as well as a resort. The Gants run cattle on the surrounding 20,000 acres.

The Gants built the original buildings on a mesa with a 360-degree view of the surrounding mountains: the Weaver Mountains to the north, the Hieroglyphic Mountains to the east, and the Vulture Mountains, with distinctive Vulture Peak, to the south. That view, seen best from the back of a horse on the top of a nearby foothill, is still breathtaking.

The ranch's public rooms are cozy and welcoming. The copper-hooded fireplace in the living room has been warming guests since the ranch first opened. Many a poker game has been played on one of the leather-covered tables in the gameroom/library, as well as Chinese checkers and bridge. There's a lovely view from the library's wall of windows of the jade-green putting green in the foreground and knob-shaped Vulture Peak in the background. Cactus gardens dominated by the magnificent saguaro meander through the grounds near the ranch buildings.

The founders' son, Dallas "Rusty" Gant Jr. runs the ranch

today. Because of the summer heat, the ranch is open only from October to mid-May.

ACCOMMODATIONS: $$$$ The ranch can accommodate 150 guests in 74 rooms and suites, ranging from several older units with traditional hand-painted furnishings to the 21 luxurious Bradshaw Mountain Rooms, which feature elegant Southwestern furnishings and fireplaces. The best bet for large families are the 11 two-bedroom suites, which have two bedrooms and a livingroom, three bathrooms and three patios. Adjoining double rooms also can be arranged.

The Bradshaw units are by far the largest; each has a kitchen, one or two bedrooms with queen-size beds, and a living room with a sofa bed. Most have private patios.

A new addition in the '90s: televisions and telephones in every room.

A 14 percent service fee is added to the bill in lieu of tipping.

DINING: The ranch, which operates on the American plan, has an excellent chef. Meals are leisurely and memorable; the emphasis is not just on bounty, but also on quality. Smoking is forbidden in the dining room.

Breakfast, served at 7:30 A.M., offers a choice of table service or a vast buffet. Lunch, served at 12:30 P.M., is always a lavish buffet; many guests take their plates out to the umbrella-shaded tables around the pool. On Sundays, the brunch attracts many day-trippers from Phoenix, which is evidence of its quality.

Dinner, served at 6:30 P.M., features soup, at least four main entrees, beautifully prepared vegetables, salads and sumptuous desserts. Men must wear jackets at dinner, and children aren't permitted to wear t-shirt or shorts.

The ranch has a charming cocktail lounge decorated with Mexican tiles and furniture. It's a friendly place to trade horse tales after a day on the trail.

ACTIVITIES

Eighteen-hole golf course designed by architects Greg Nash and Jeff Hardin, (7,025 yards, par 72), rated among the top 10 in Arizona. Makes good use of the natural desert terrain, and provides spectacular views of mountains on three sides. Clubhouse with restaurant, shop and locker rooms.

Putting equipment can be borrowed for a game of mini-golf on the putting green.

 Two grass and two acrylic courts, no fees. Instruction available.

 Outdoor heated pool.

 The corral foreman visits with guests each evening at dinner to find out who to expect on the daily trail rides, held at 10 A.M. and 2:30 P.M. He assigns each guest an appropriate horse, and many are able to ride the same one throughout their visit. Riding costs extra.

Skeet and trap shooting offered Tuesday and Thursday afternoons, upon request.

Guided nature walks on the property. If you're a nature buff, visit the Nature Conservancy's Hassayampa River Preserve, three miles southeast of Wickenburg, which preserves one of the state's finest example of riparian vegetation. It's home to 230 species of birds, rare raptors, lizards, and mule deer, bobcats, ring-tailed cats and even a mountain lion.

Hay rides, golf and tennis tournaments and clinics, bingo, crazy hat contests, square dances, shopping trips and outings to the western museum, the Nature Conservancy and the petting zoo in Wickenburg. About five times each season, the ranch participates with two or three others in the area in a festive gymkhana; guests and ranchhands alike ride for fun and prizes.

FOR CHILDREN: The complimentary "Caballeros Kids' Program" entertains children between 5 and 12; special activities also are provided for teen-agers. The program is run by an adult counselor who is assisted by local teen-agers.

Children gather at 7:45 A.M. in the "Caballeros Kids Hideout" and then eat breakfast together in their own special dining room. Children 8 and over who have some trail experience can go on a daily trail ride at 9:30 A.M. (there's a fee). Children 7 and under are walked around an arena on "Shorty," a pony. (They delight in seeing horses drink from a trough in which goldfish are swimming around.) A separate ride is sometimes organized for teen-agers.

After the morning rides, children regroup for activities ranging from arts and crafts, nature walks, swimming, story-telling, putt-putt golf, game-playing, to volleyball. They eat lunch at 12:15 P.M., either in the children's dining room or on the lawn near the swimming pool. Children are returned to their parents at 1:30 so that families can enjoy activities together. But a second trail ride is offered at 2 P.M. for those who wish more riding experience.

Children meet again for dinner at 6:15 P.M.; they're also welcome to eat with their parents. Sometimes, they have their own cook-out and a singalong with the cowboys. They play games, listen to stories, or make crafts until 9 P.M., which allows enough time for their parents to have a leisurely dinner.

A special table is set up in the main dining room for teen-age guests. Babysitting can be arranged for children too young for the supervised program.

NICETIES: The basket of toiletries in each room includes sunscreen and lip balm—musts for coping with the desert sun.

Coffee and fresh-baked rolls are available in the dining room beginning at 6:30 A.M.

The living room has a large supply of games and jigsaw puzzles for family fun in the evening. There's a pile of sheet music near the grand piano, and impromptu concerts are common.

OF INTEREST NEARBY: Wickenburg is a quaint old town. There are numerous art galleries and Western shops stocked with boots, hats and other cowboy regalia.

Pick up a tour map from the Wickenburg Chamber of Commerce and spend a few hours ambling from site to site—21 points of interest in all, among them "The Jail Tree," to which outlaws used to be chained. The Desert Caballeros Western Museum is a charming little museum with exhibits on the town's history as a gold-mine boom town and stagecoach stop.

The Foothill Ostrich Farm and Zoo is just what it sounds like. Children will enjoy petting baby llamas, antelope, potbelly pigs, fainting goats, miniature donkeys and four-horned sheep.

FOR MORE INFORMATION: Write Rancho de los Caballeros, Wickenburg, Arizona 85358, or call 602-684-5484 (FAX: 602-684-2267).

TANQUE VERDE RANCH
Tucson, Arizona

The Tanque Verde Ranch has been a working cattle or horse ranch since the 1860s. Founded on a land grant from the Spaniards, it was the site of frequent Apache ambushes and a crossroads for Don Esteban Ochoa's mule trains before it was transformed into a guest ranch in the 1930s. Since 1957 it has been owned by the Cote family, which has turned it into one of the premier guest ranches in the Southwest.

Set in the foothills of the Rincon Mountains on the eastern edge of Tucson, the ranch commands a sweeping view of Tucson and the mountain ranges that ring it. The vegetation is typical of the upper Sonoran Desert, with the desert's signature cactus, the magnificent saguaro, visible at every turn. The ranch owns 640 acres, and its eastern border is the rugged 1.3-million-acre Coronado National Memorial Forest and its southern border the 63,000-acre Saguaro National Monument, so there's plenty of space to ride and roam. And it's the riding that brings guests back here time and time again—that, and the comfortable accommodations, bountiful meals, and relaxed ambience.

ACCOMMODATIONS: $$$ Up to 150 guests stay in four small "ramada" rooms or 56 larger adobe-look casitas, each attractively furnished with a mixture of antiques and southwestern-style furniture. The larger casitas have fireplaces, with a more-than-adequate supply of mesquite wood just outside the door. Each accommodation has an outdoor patio or sitting area from which you can take in the majestic views, day or night.

The rooms have no television sets, although you can rent one if your children absolutely cannot do without; there's a large-screen set in the living room in the main ranch building. Many units have refrigerators for storing snacks and drinks. A coin-operated laundry facility is available.

The ranch operates on the American plan, with all meals and most activities included in the rate.

DINING: Memorable meals are served in a large, adobe-style dining room with big windows overlooking the outdoor pool and surrounding mountains. The menu is posted daily on a bulletin board outside the main building. Most breakfast items are on a buffet, but eggs, hotcakes, French toast, and breakfast meats are cooked to order. Lunch also is usually a buffet.

Dinner offers a choice of entrées, with something to please every palate, including the calorie conscious. Beer and wine are served with meals for an additional charge. Dietary restrictions can be accommodated.

The hostess attempts to seat guests at different tables for each meal so that by the end of their stay they will have met nearly everyone there. This is helpful to new guests, since repeat guests can offer a wealth of helpful hints.

The ranch encourages children over 4 to take their meals together in the special children's dining room, but children are welcome to eat with their parents. The dining-room staff will gladly fill a baby bottle or provide you with children's snacks to take back to your room.

ACTIVITIES

Five Laykold courts, several lighted, supervised by a tennis pro between November and April. Privileges at six courses in Tucson.

Heated indoor pool; the outdoor pool serves as a popular gathering place for families after the afternoon ride. A waterfall—with cascading hot water—is both scenic and therapeutic if you place your shoulders directly in the water's path.

The Rincon Mountains foothills have numerous trails for hikers; a map is provided in each guest room. One of the unique features of the ranch is a bird-banding program, held every Thursday morning at the crack of dawn. Master bird banders licensed by the U.S. Fish and Wildlife Service capture and band wild birds in the only year-round banding operation in the state. More than 60,000 birds of 155 species have been banded. Guided nature walks are offered six times each week by a naturalist.

Tanque Verde has the largest stable of riding horses in Arizona—115—and a skilled wrangling staff that can size up your level of ability in a glance. Two or three scheduled rides are offered daily, as well as two riding lessons (all included in the room rate). Each lesson ride is divided into two groups, beginners and lopers. Rides range from one-hour jaunts on ranch property to all-day rides across the Saguaro National Monument. Breakfast rides, featuring pancakes cooked over an open fire, are especially popular.

 El Sonora Spa is a health facility equipped with a heated indoor pool, saunas, whirlpool, and exercise equipment. Equipment for lawn games and basketball at the front desk.

 Catch-and-release fishing for largemouth bass in the ranch's spring-fed Lake Gambusi; tackle provided.

 Programs are offered each evening for the entire family, including bingo, square dancing, snake demonstrations, lectures on desert ecology, and demonstrations of Indian crafts. Once or twice a week, an evening cookout is held in the Cottonwood Grove, with dancing under the stars and cowboy singing and music. Adults gather before dinner in the Dog House, a converted bunkhouse that serves as a cocktail lounge. Lockers are available to store each guest's liquor, which must be bought by the bottle at the ranch office.

FOR CHILDREN: This is the only ranch in southern Arizona with an organized children's program. It operates daily from mid-November to May 1 and serves children between 4 and 11. Baby-sitting is available for younger children.

The program is run by two counselors, but when there are large numbers of children in the program, extra staff members are added. Children are divided by age into two groups, 4- to 6-year-olds and 7- to 11-year-olds, with activities geared to each age level. While riding is the main focus, the program includes swimming, nature talks, hobo hikes, tennis, games and arts and crafts.

Activities end at 3:30 P.M., but the children meet again at 6 for dinner. Between the conclusion of dinner and 8:15 P.M., they usually go to the Tack Room for games or storytelling.

All-day rides, punctuated by a cookout lunch on the mountain, are offered occasionally for children 7 and up. Each week there is usually at least one trail ride to Cottonwood Grove, followed by a picnic lunch and a sing-along with the ranch hands. Parents may ride along on the children's trail ride; children 12 and over go on the adult rides.

If there are many teenagers staying at the ranch, a teen table is set up in the dining room, and social activities are arranged.

NICETIES: Fresh fruit, coffee, and herbal tea are available nearly around the clock in the dining room. Early risers can snack on Danish rolls and coffee beginning at 6 A.M.

Major plant specimens are labeled so you can quickly become familiar with desert plants.

The front desk maintains a stock of fruit juice in large cans, as well as soda, six-packs of beer, and bottles of liquor. A coin-operated beer and wine machine is located in the Dog House. The staff makes a supply run into town once a week and will gladly pick up necessities for you for a small charge. Guests are welcome to ride along.

OF INTEREST NEARBY: The Arizona Sonoran Desert Museum is world famous for its living exhibits featuring 200 species of animals and 300 species of plants native to the Sonoran Desert. It's an hour or more from the ranch, but worth the drive.

Sabino Canyon provides a look at another type of environment. A motorized tram takes visitors on a nine-mile ride up the canyon; you can get off at numerous points and picnic or hike. The cascading river creates many deep pools that are popular swimming holes.

Old Tucson is a former movie and TV show location, with shoot-'em-up gun fights re-enacted daily. There are rides and shops and buildings designed to suggest the flavor of Tucson in the 1860s.

Saguaro National Monument East is just outside the entrance to the ranch. A visitors center offers a slide show and lectures on the desert environment.

FOR MORE INFORMATION: Write Bob Cote, Tanque Verde Ranch, 14301 E. Speedway, Tucson, AZ 85748, or call (602) 296-6275.

For general tourist information, wrote the Metropolitan Tucson Convention and Visitors Bureau at 450 West Paseo Redondo, Tucson, AZ 85705, or call (602) 624-1817.

PEACEFUL VALLEY LODGE AND RANCH RESORT
Lyons, Colorado

Peaceful Valley Lodge and Ranch Resort is a handsome all-season ranch resort whose goal is a happy and shared family experience. Owned and operated by Mabel Boehm and her daughter and son-in-law, Debbie and Randy Eubanks, it is large enough to provide activities for all tastes and small enough to be flexible and intimate. A plaque on the wall in the dining room proclaims "He who enters is a stranger but once!" symbolizing the emphasis on informality, hospitality, and personal attention to each guest.

Located in the South St. Vrain Canyon near Rocky Mountain National Park just 60 miles from Denver, the Swiss chalet-style lodge and Alpine-type cabins seem a bit out of place until the ranch's history is understood. The current ranch's founder, Karl Boehm, was an Austrian refugee from the Nazis who trained in the Rockies when he was a member of the U.S. ski corps, the Tenth Mountain Division. On the night that Boehm and his Kentucky-born wife, Mabel, purchased the ranch in the mid-1950s, the existing ranch buildings burned, and the Boehms built from scratch incorporating architectural features from Karl's beloved Austrian Alps. (Karl died in 1993.)

The overall effect is charming. A unique feature of the ranch is its Alpine-style chapel overlooking the valley and the jagged mountains that form the Continental Divide. Services are held twice weekly during the summer.

ACCOMMODATIONS: $$$ to $$$$ There's a wide variety of accommodations in separate buildings: 21 rooms in the Main Lodge, 12 in the Edelweiss Chalet, and 11 freestanding cabins. Some of the rooms include sitting rooms; others have separate vanity and dressing areas. All the rooms are nicely decorated with attention to detail and comfort. The capacity is about 120 guests.

The cabins each has one to three bedrooms and a living room with a fireplace; some have hot tubs or Jacuzzis. Some have porches overlooking the St. Vrain River, which runs through the property. Other cabins are located in the woods.

The larger cabins are well suited for larger families. The largest separate cabin, Seven Gables, has 10 rooms grouped around a common living room. Isolated from the Main Lodge, it is perfect for large family reunions.

There are three rate categories—best, superior, and moderate—according to different appointments and room size. Week-long stays are required in the summer. Children's rates are available. Children 2 and under are free.

DINING: Meals are served family-style in a bright pine-paneled dining room, with each table set with fresh flowers. The breakfast bell rings at 8 A.M., but guests have until 10 A.M. to amble in. Lunch is served to all at 1 P.M., and dinner at 6:30 P.M. Wine and beer are available before dinner at the Edelweiss Room and can be purchased with dinner.

The food is traditional American cooking with a few European dishes thrown in (Wiener schnitzel is one of the chef's specialties). The variety of vegetables and salads at meals enables one to keep to a diet, although willpower will be required to resist the delicious pastries, desserts, and freshly baked rolls. The staff is responsive to special diet needs.

A variety of table sizes permits different seating arrangements; you can meet new people or remain within your own family group. During the summer, there are separate children's tables.

Throughout each summer week there are special dining highlights, such as a poolside barbecue, chuck-wagon breakfast on the mountain, and other cookouts. The coffee shop is open during the day for soft drinks, coffee, pie, cakes, and ice cream.

ACTIVITIES

 One outdoor hard-surface court.

 Public course in nearby Estes Park.

 In a large indoor solar-heated pool; adjacent sauna, whirlpool.

 Half- or full-day rafting trips can be arranged on the Colorado or Poudre rivers.

 In a small stocked trout pond (no license required) or in the St. Vrain River. Many mountain lakes nearby. The chef will cook your cleaned fish.

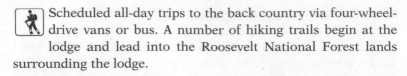 Scheduled all-day trips to the back country via four-wheel-drive vans or bus. A number of hiking trails begin at the lodge and lead into the Roosevelt National Forest lands surrounding the lodge.

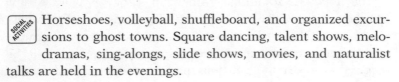 Large string of gentle horses. Trail rides are scheduled each day along a variety of routes that accommodate varying abilities; instruction offered. There are all-day rides, breakfast rides, lunch rides, and supper rides. Once a week guests take part in a gymkhana (a combination horse show and rodeo). The ranch has large indoor and outdoor arenas. For an additional fee, summer guests can take an overnight pack trip into the high country of the Indian Peaks region (highly recommended!)

 Horseshoes, volleyball, shuffleboard, and organized excursions to ghost towns. Square dancing, talent shows, melodramas, sing-alongs, slide shows, movies, and naturalist talks are held in the evenings.

 Cross-country skiing.

Telemarking, snowshoeing (equipment can be rented), sledding and sleigh rides.

FOR CHILDREN: From mid-June through late August, special full-day programs for children over 3 and teenagers include riding, swimming, crafts, fishing, games, nature lore, and hiking. Parents may take their children in and out of the program as they please.

Children under 6 do no trail riding but ride in a pony cart or in the ring. Older youngsters may ride twice a day (one trail ride, one horsemanship lesson). Well-trained counselors supervise each group. Special arrangements can be made for child care for younger children for an hourly fee.

The playground, with its wooden fort and gigantic sandbox, is the center of daily activities for the younger set; they also enjoy the petting farm, with kid goats, lambs, calves, and foals. A highlight each day is the milking of the ranch cow!

Older children gravitate to the game room next to the dance hall, where they can play foosball, pool, air hockey, Ping-Pong, or Pac Man. A counselor helps the teen group plan its own schedule of activities, including special camp-fire programs, trail rides, and hikes on which llamas carry the packs.

Family Day, an outing into the mountains, is scheduled weekly for the enjoyment of parents and children. You can climb a mountain ridge for a view of a big glacier basin or hike to a waterfall.

NICETIES: Riding or hiking boots can be rented at the Sport Shop, as well as tennis racquets, tennis shoes, and fishing equipment.

A clock-radio in each cabin and a coin-operated set of washers and dryers are useful amenities.

OF INTEREST NEARBY: Central City is a renovated gold mining town filled with a variety of shops, a museum and a 20-minute gold mine tour. The renovated Opera House holds performances Tuesday through Sunday in the summer.

Estes Park is the entrance to the Rocky Mountain National Park. From mid-May to mid-September you can ride the aerial tramway to the summit of 8,700-foot Prospect Mountain. Anywhere in the park, the hiking is wonderful.

The Estes Park Area Historical Museum has exhibits on local Indians, early settlers, and a homestead cabin.

FOR MORE INFORMATION: Write Mabel Boehm, Peaceful Valley Lodge and Ranch Resort, Box 2811, Lyons, CO 80540, or call (303) 747-2881.

TUMBLING RIVER RANCH
Grant, Colorado

The first thing you notice when you pull into Tumbling River is the friendliness that blankets the air. It's not just the staff that lays out the welcome mat, but the other guests as well. They take their cue from Jim and Mary Dale Gordon, transplanted Texans who bought the ranch in the early 1970s.

Tumbling River was established as a guest ranch in the 1940s on a secluded site 50 miles southwest of Denver (elevation 9,200 feet). It had been homesteaded in the 1890s on a tight 200 acres of wilderness wedged between mountains in Pike National

Forest. Five miles of Geneva Creek—the so-called tumbling river—cut through the ranch.

At the upper end of the ranch is the five-level main lodge, built by a 1920s-era mayor of Denver. It houses five guest rooms, each with a fireplace and bath, two lounges, and a dining room that affords a picture-postcard view of bighorn sheep on the rocky cliffs of Flag Mountain. A half dozen cabins, the Gordons' house, the Trading Post, a swimming pool, whirlpool, rec room, and corral are also clustered on the upper ranch.

Down the road is the lower ranch, or Pueblo. Louise Porter, Adolph Coors's daughter, brought Indians from the Taos Pueblo in New Mexico in the late 1920s to build the lodge of stucco, stone, and hand-carved wooden beams. On the first floor are spacious living and dining areas built around large stone fireplaces; upstairs are seven airy guest rooms.

ACCOMMODATIONS: $$$ to $$$$ Cabins and individual rooms at the upper ranch are furnished in charming antiques. Bookshelves are lined with mysteries and novels. All cabins and individual rooms have porches and fireplaces, which always have firewood laid and kerosene-soaked sawdust ready to ignite.

Guest rooms at the Pueblo are larger, more comfortable, more modern, and furnished in a southwest decor.

Children's rates are available. Discounted rates for adults and children apply through most of June and again in September. The rates cover lodging, meals, horses, the children's program, and all activities except overnight pack trips and raft trips. The ranch's capacity is about 60. Guests arrive and leave on Sundays.

DINING: A bell rings each morning, noon, and evening to signal that chow time is 15 minutes away. Guests and some staff members sit together at tables for six or eight; Pueblo guests eat in the dining room there. Food is served family style, all you can eat. The recipes have all been developed and tested on the staff by Mary Dale. Breads and desserts are all homemade.

A typical dinner includes barbecued steak, fettucini, fresh asparagus, warmed spiced apples, and banana fudge pie. Candlelight-and-wine dinners are served for adults only two nights a week. On other nights, families eat meals together.

You must supply your own liquor. The staff will be happy to pick up mixers for you in a nearby town.

ACTIVITIES

 Heated outdoor pool, adjacent whirlpool. Hot tub and cabana at the Pueblo.

 Raft trip through the Brown's Canyon section of the Arkansas River (extra charge). Children must be at least 8 years old.

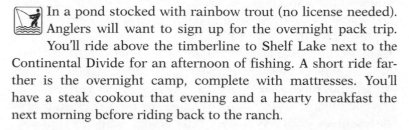 In a pond stocked with rainbow trout (no license needed). Anglers will want to sign up for the overnight pack trip. You'll ride above the timberline to Shelf Lake next to the Continental Divide for an afternoon of fishing. A short ride farther is the overnight camp, complete with mattresses. You'll have a steak cookout that evening and a hearty breakfast the next morning before riding back to the ranch.

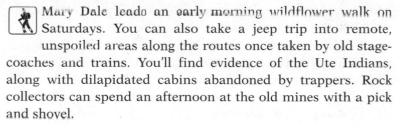 Mary Dale leads an early morning wildflower walk on Saturdays. You can also take a jeep trip into remote, unspoiled areas along the routes once taken by old stagecoaches and trains. You'll find evidence of the Ute Indians, along with dilapidated cabins abandoned by trappers. Rock collectors can spend an afternoon at the old mines with a pick and shovel.

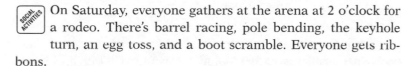 Rides of varying lengths are offered each day. There's a breakfast ride on Tuesday, a brunch ride on Tuesday, and a trail ride that winds up at a lunch cookout at Duck Creek Thursday. Wednesday's all-day ride takes guests to a point near the Continental Divide.

On Saturday, everyone gathers at the arena at 2 o'clock for a rodeo. There's barrel racing, pole bending, the keyhole turn, an egg toss, and a boot scramble. Everyone gets ribbons.

Rec hall with Ping-Pong and pool tables. There are lots of off-ranch excursions each week. Vans take guests each Tuesday over Guanella Pass to the quaint mining town of Georgetown for an afternoon of shopping and a ride on a narrow-gauge train. On Fridays, there's a van trip to South Park City Museum, a restored western town in Fairplay. Each Monday, a hay-packed pickup truck takes guests to Jack's Mine, an old mining town above the timberline. Square dancing, hootenanny, and a guest talent show are held in the evenings.

FOR CHILDREN: A children's program, geared to three separate age groups, operates from 9 A.M. to 6:30 P.M. Tuesday through Friday and up till the rodeo on Saturday. Children ride separately from their parents, but sometimes meet up with them on the trail for lunch. The program is very flexible: anytime you want to spend an afternoon fishing or swimming with your child, just let the counselor know.

Almost every morning, children aged 6 to 11 take their horses out on trails with a counselor and wrangler at the head and tail. The rest of the day offers a full menu of activities: a train ride in Georgetown, climbing on antique locomotives at South Park City Museum in Fairplay, Ping-Pong and pool, swimming, and fishing (they love to see the cooks serve that day's catch).

A counselor leads the 3- to 5-year-olds on ponies. When they're not riding, they're likely to keep busy playing games, swimming, jeeping, making pressed-flower pictures or painting horseshoes.

During Tuesday's candlelight dinner for the grown-ups, kids have their own weenie roast and play "Capture the Flag." Thursday evening is a spaghetti dinner followed by bingo and other games. And the kids never tire of tagging after the ranch pets—Daisy, Molly, and Macy (golden retrievers), Catman (a tabby cat) and numerous unnamed ducks, geese, and calves.

A special treat each week is a campout in a log fort or teepee on the night that adults and children 12 and older go on the backcountry overnight.

Teens often join the adults on the all-day rides and jeep trips or take a raft on the Arkansas River. Tuesday is a special teen day, when the most energetic youths climb a mountain and the others ride to brunch with the adults.

NICETIES: On arrival, each guest is given a concho, or leather neckpiece, with his or her name on it and the ranch's brand. Wearing the conchos helps the guests get to know each other's names quickly. The horses have them, too.

In your room, you'll find a small basket of fruit with a hand-printed welcome note. If you want, coffee will be brought to your cabin door at 7 A.M., giving you time to wake up before the breakfast bell sounds.

There's a guest laundry with commercial-size washers and dryers and free soap.

OF INTEREST NEARBY: Georgetown, known as the Silver Queen of the Rockies, is an hour's drive over a narrow dirt road that winds through Guanella Pass. Said to have been the greatest producer of silver in the world in the 1880s, the old mining town now is a motherlode of antiques and crafts shops, restaurants, old hotels, and historic buildings. It's also the home of the narrow gauge railroad, the Georgetown Loop, on which you can take an hour's ride.

Also nearby is the historic mining town of Fairplay, with its locomotives and western town of restored buildings assembled from all parts of Colorado.

FOR MORE INFORMATION: Write Tumbling River Ranch, Grant, CO 80448, or call (800) 654-8770.

VISTA VERDE GUEST AND SKI TOURING RANCH
Steamboat Springs, Colorado

Vista Verde, aptly named, is located in a small green valley in the Rocky Mountains of northwestern Colorado. There are exquisite views in all directions, and wildlife is abundant, with frequent sightings of deer, elk, beavers, eagles, marmots, and even an occasional bear. In the summer, wildflowers are everywhere, despite the elevation of 7,800 feet.

The 500-acre ranch is a working cattle and horse operation surrounded by the 1.4-million-acre Routt National Forest, with over 100 lakes and 900 miles of mountain streams, and the Mount Zirkel Wilderness Area, a 140,000-acre area restricted to foot and horseback travel. The snow-capped peaks of the Continental Divide can be seen on most days.

Vista Verde is intimate and family-oriented. The number of guests typically ranges between 25 and 35. The owners' goal is to provide a secluded wilderness experience without sacrificing the comforts of home. The staff is well-trained and includes many outdoor enthusiasts with an interest in the natural sciences. Guests are invited to experience some of the ranch work activities, including riding herd on 100 head of cattle, checking fences, and helping with wrangling and saddling.

ACCOMMODATIONS: $$$$ The eight cabins and three lodge rooms are inviting. They embody the philosophy of the ranch: comfort, attention to detail, and charm. Along with modern bathrooms, there are small touches that recall the past: lace curtains, down comforters, antiques, and dried-flower arrangements.

The cabins sleep up to six; several have lofts for children. They are made from hand-hewn logs of native pine; each has a snack bar and comfortable living room with a wood-burning stove. Each has a front deck overlooking a small stream.

Rates cover accommodations, all meals, activities and excursions. The minimum stay is one week in summer; guests arrive and leave on a Sunday. Children's rates are available. The ranch closes in spring and fall.

DINING: The food is classic American cooking with a gourmet flair, served family style in the new lodge or on picnic tables near the outdoor barbecue. Portions are large, and seconds are always available. The chef is a graduate of the Culinary Institute of America, and his training shows in the taste, variety, and attention to presentation.

Special diets can be accommodated with advance notice. Bread and pastries are home-baked, and the chef offers cooking seminars and wine tastings on the occasional rainy days. Wine may be purchased at dinner. Families eat together, except for four adult dinners weekly. Throughout each week there are scheduled breakfast cookouts, and lunch and evening barbecues. Box lunches are provided for the all-day trips.

ACTIVITIES

 Privileges at courts five miles from the ranch.

 In a lake or pond on premises or a heated pool down the road. Hot tub and sauna.

 All-day rafting trip on the upper Colorado River included in the rate.

 Trout fishing in nearby mountain streams and stocked ponds. Fly-fishing guides available for a fee.

There's an attractive log spa overlooking the valley that houses a large whirlpool, sauna, hot tubs, showers, and exercise room. A masseur comes out to the ranch on appointment.

 All-day hike in the wilderness area, sometimes on the old Wyoming Trail once used by cattle rustlers and outlaws.

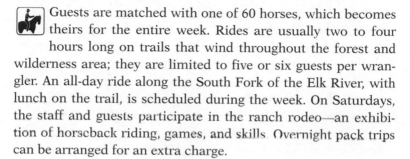 Guests are matched with one of 60 horses, which becomes theirs for the entire week. Rides are usually two to four hours long on trails that wind throughout the forest and wilderness area; they are limited to five or six guests per wrangler. An all-day ride along the South Fork of the Elk River, with lunch on the trail, is scheduled during the week. On Saturdays, the staff and guests participate in the ranch rodeo—an exhibition of horseback riding, games, and skills. Overnight pack trips can be arranged for an extra charge.

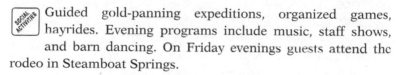 Guided gold-panning expeditions, organized games, hayrides. Evening programs include music, staff shows, and barn dancing. On Friday evenings guests attend the rodeo in Steamboat Springs.

A rock-climbing clinic is conducted once a week. Mountain bike tours of the Routt Forest are offered.

Hot-air balloon rides can be arranged.

 Cross-country skiing on 18 miles of marked and groomed trails on the ranch and countless miles of trails in the adjacent national forest lands.

 Snowshoeing, ice fishing, dogsledding, ice climbing, and sleigh rides pulled by Doc and Dillon, a team of Percheron draft horses.

 Steamboat Springs is a center of downhill skiing, including national and international ski jumping competitions.

  FOR CHILDREN: Children 6 and over can participate in the general riding program with adults, although special programs, games, and rides are also offered.

Children from 3 to 5, whom the ranch calls Buckaroos, have

their own program, with a distinct Western flavor. Activities include the care and feeding of farm animals, from ducks and chickens to goats and lambs. They learn about horses and their care with the cooperation of Jose and Tony, two miniature horses that they can saddle and halter lead or ride. The children's activities coincide with the adult rides.

Additional activities such as fishing, gold-panning, hiking, scavenger hunts, and rides in an antique fire engine keep kids happy. At dinner one night, you're likely to find that your children hand-cranked the ice cream! On the nights when adults eat by themselves, children have an early dinner and then go on a hayride, go fishing, or play games and make crafts.

There is an imaginative children's playground, Fort Smiles, with a play house, slides, and swings located within easy distance and sight of the cabins.

NICETIES: Hummingbird feeders hang from the front porch of the lodge, and there are rope hammocks hanging near the cabins so you can nap to the gurgle of the nearby stream.

Each cabin has a small refrigerator. Coffee, tea, and hot cocoa are provided, along with snacks and cookies.

A bountiful welcome baskets awaits you in your cabin, along with an informational packet that tells you almost everything you need to know about the ranch.

OF INTEREST NEARBY: The ranch is 45 minutes from Steamboat Springs, a major ski center in the winter and a popular western-flavor tourist stop in the summer. Steamboat Springs has many art galleries, shops and restaurants, as well as a large hot-springs swimming pool and giant water slide.

In the summer, the Repertory Theatre, Strings in the Mountains festival, and the Perry-Mansfield School of Dance offer public performances. The Fourth of July Rodeo is considered one of the best in the West. The ski area's gondola operates year- round.

Golf, tennis courts, boating, and sailing are available nearby.

FOR MORE INFORMATION: Write Vista Verde Guest and Ski Touring Ranch, Box 465, Steamboat Springs, CO 80477, or call (303) 879-3858 or (800) 526-RIDE.

AVERILL'S FLATHEAD LAKE LODGE AND DUDE RANCH
Bigfork, Montana

The setting is idyllic: 2,000 acres on the shoreline of Flathead Lake, North America's largest natural freshwater lake west of the Great Lakes, with the Swan River National Wildlife Refuge as a backdrop. The activities are endless: riding, boating, fishing, swimming, hiking, and tennis. The food is hearty, the staff energetic, the guests friendly, and the ambience totally conducive to relaxation.

All in all, Averill's Flathead Lake Lodge offers everything anyone could want in a western family vacation, unless your wants extend to glamorous nightlife and a fast pace. There's none of that here, and there never will be. The closest thing to nightlife you'll find is the summer stock production at the nearby Bigfork Summer Playhouse.

The Averill family has been operating this first-class dude ranch since 1945, and their formula for hospitality remains unchanged. The ranch is now in the hands of a second-generation Averill, Doug, a former rodeo rider, and his wife, Maureen, and they make their home here, as well as their livelihood. Their own children move from activity to activity and provide welcome reassurance to guests that children aren't just tolerated here.

This AAA four-diamond ranch is so popular with guests that it's frequently booked more than a year in advance. The return rate is on the order of 90 percent plus. That kind of loyalty from guests—and the 4-star rating from Mobil—prove that the Averills are doing something right.

ACCOMMODATIONS: $$$$ The 125 guests at the ranch are assigned to 22 cottages and 20 lodge rooms, depending upon the size of their families and availability. The two- to three-bedroom cottages are rustic and furnished with handmade beds.

Rates include all meals and many activities. Children's rates rise with age; infants are charged only a nominal amount. All guests arrive and leave on a Sunday. The season extends from May through September, with families accounting for most of the business in July and August.

DINING: All the cooking is done by college students, most of whom are studying for degrees in the hotel and restaurant management field. The food is hearty and the servings ample. Meals are served family style in the Main Lodge, built by the Civilian Conservation Corps in 1932 and featuring larch walls and floors, a dozen or so trophies of past hunting expeditions, and a huge stone fireplace. Old saddles line the balcony railing, and there's a piano for sing-alongs (and sheet music, too).

Breakfast, at 8 A.M., typically features a local favorite, such as huckleberry pancakes (much better than blueberry, as any bear will tell you). Lunch, at 12:30 P.M., is usually served outdoors on the terrace overlooking the lake. Dinner, at 6:30 P.M., is a one-entrée offering, ranging from prime rib to crown roast of pork to Cornish game hens. Children are served a half hour before adults, and then a staff member takes them to the game room or the swimming pool so that their parents can enjoy a leisurely meal. Families may eat together if they wish.

A highlight of each week is the Wednesday night steak fry in the mountains, which guests ride to on horses or a hay wagon.

The ranch has no liquor license, but guests may bring their own and place their bottles in the cozy Saddle Sore Saloon, which is off limits to kids. Mixers are available there.

ACTIVITIES

 Four Plexi-Pave courts.

 Privileges at an 18-hole course on the other side of Bigfork.

 Large outdoor pool.

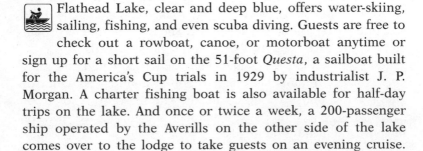 Flathead Lake, clear and deep blue, offers water-skiing, sailing, fishing, and even scuba diving. Guests are free to check out a rowboat, canoe, or motorboat anytime or sign up for a short sail on the 51-foot *Questa*, a sailboat built for the America's Cup trials in 1929 by industrialist J. P. Morgan. A charter fishing boat is also available for half-day trips on the lake. And once or twice a week, a 200-passenger ship operated by the Averills on the other side of the lake comes over to the lodge to take guests on an evening cruise. (Watch out for the powerboats that chase the boat. They're

filled with kids armed with water balloons!) The lodge's own full-time outfitter organizes several white-water rafting or tubing excursions weekly.

Several professional fishermen on the lodge's staff can serve as guides or direct guests to proven holes. Fly-fishing equipment, including waders, is available for the asking. A scenic fishing trip on a raft is offered on the upper Swan River for adults and children 6 and over (extra charge).

Several outings are planned weekly to Wildhorse Island State Park, a nature preserve accessible only by boat. Rocky Mountain sheep and wild horses roam the island. On the 20-mile boat ride there, passengers can see an old Indian site. Some rock paintings from prehistoric times are still visible.

Riding is decidedly the favored activity here. The lodge has 60 horses and schedules two rides daily, as well as special day-long, breakfast, and luncheon rides.

Barn dances with a bluegrass band, steer roping in the arena by professional ropers, or a bonfire on the lakefront in the evenings. Many guests go to the summer theater in Bigfork one evening; it's a pleasant walk there, and the lodge will arrange return transport in its 1913 white open-air limousine.

FOR CHILDREN: Separate children's rides are offered in the morning and afternoon. A high point of each week for many children is the overnight campout in the two teepees by the lake. There's also a game room that serves as a hangout for children.

Each of the activity areas on the lodge property is staffed at all times, so you need not worry about your children being unsupervised. Staff members are alert to the needs of children and keep an especially watchful eye on the waterfront.

Because of the special allure that horses hold for children, an extra effort is made to acquaint children with all aspects of their care. Those who are interested can be assigned a horse for which they are responsible for the week. They'll learn all about feeding and grooming and exercising—and cleaning out stalls.

Near the stable is a "bucking bronco" made out of a suspended barrel. Kids love sitting here and pretending that they're out on the range.

The ranch has between 30 and 35 children as guests in any

given week, most of them 8 or older. With advance notice, the management will be happy to arrange regular baby-sitting for a younger child for the entire week, or as needed.

NICETIES: The Averills will provide a portable intercom so you can keep an ear tuned to a sleeping child while sunning yourself on the lawn.

Cars are available free for local use and at a competitive rental rate for longer trips to Glacier Park or other nearby attractions.

There's a bookcase full of old classics, western novels, spy thrillers and science fiction in the main lodge.

OF INTEREST NEARBY: Glacier National Park is about an hour's drive from the lodge, and most guests schedule at least a day's outing there. For a more intimate look at the park, plan to spend a few days there after your stay at the ranch. The park offers numerous ranger-led activities for children and endless hiking opportunities. The scenery is spectacular.

FOR MORE INFORMATION: Write Averill's Flathead Lake Lodge, Box 248, Bigfork, MT 59911, or call (406) 837-4391.

LONE MOUNTAIN RANCH
Big Sky, Montana

There's a reason Montana calls itself Big Sky country, and why the community where the Lone Mountain Ranch is located is called Big Sky. The sky really does seem bigger here. The mountain peaks also seem higher, the wildflower colors more vivid, the drinking water fresher and colder, the air crisper, the whole environment more invigorating.

Lone Mountain Ranch occupies a spectacular setting on the edge of the Lee Metcalf Wilderness Area, which encompasses the rugged Spanish Peaks range. In the background towers Lone Mountain, which is often snow covered, even in August. The area surrounding the ranch is protected from development and hence offers boundless opportunities for undisturbed trail rides or hikes on which one can view elk, moose, coyote, mountain sheep, mountain goat, deer, and eagles—and sometimes even a bear. Yet it's just 75 minutes from the airport at Bozeman, Montana.

After a multi-state search for an ideal site for a guest ranch, Vivian and Bob Schaap bought the ranch in 1977 and set out to turn it into one of the West's premier guest ranches and cross-country ski-touring centers. It is one of the few ranches in the West that operates year-round.

ACCOMMODATIONS: $$$$ The ranch has about 20 log cabins that range in age from brand-new to more than 50 years old; they accommodate a total of about 60 guests. Some cabins sit by the North Fork River; others perch on a hillside, affording panoramic views. All have electric heat and modern bathrooms, as well as front porches, and most have fireplaces or wood-burning stoves (with a large stock of wood and kerosene-soaked fire starter). Much of the furniture is made from lodgepole pines, which lends the cabins a truly rustic air. The large family-size cabins typically have two bedrooms and a large living room with fireplace.

Rates are set according to the number of people in a cabin; there are discounted rates for children between 2 and 5. Children under 2 are free. Several of the larger log cabins are well-suited to sharing by two families. The rate includes all meals, an organized children's program, transportation to and from the Bozeman airport, and most regular ranch activities. The Rancher package includes riding in the rate; for guests on the other packages, it's extra.

DINING: The ranch has an excellent chef in Gerard van Mourik, who has made it his permanent home. All meals are served in a western-style dining hall, replete with cowboy and Indian art and a huge rock fireplace. The ranch management calls the cuisine "ranch cooking with a gourmet flair," which is appropriate.

Breakfast is served buffet style from 7 to 9:30 A.M.; lunch is also served buffet style, from 11:30 to 2 P.M.

Dinner is a sit-down affair, with a hostess directing guests to different tables each night to ease mingling. Dinner entrees include Montana beef and lamb, fresh bison, Pacific salmon and vegetarian dishes. With advance notice, the chef will prepare special meals that meet specific dietary requirements. Wine and beer can be purchased.

Each week, weather permitting, several meals are served outside: a steak barbecue and singalong are held one night a week by the Schaaps's house on top of a hill with glorious views.

ACTIVITIES

 White-water rafting on the nearby Gallatin and Yellowstone rivers. The ranch arranges at least one rafting excursion weekly (extra charge).

 Daily walks guided by naturalists, which provide a great way to learn about the greater Yellowstone ecosystem, local wildflowers and birds, and Indian lore. Excursions each week into Yellowstone National Park.

 Superb trout fishing on the nearby Gallatin River, a blue-ribbon trout stream, or on the Madison, Firehole, Yellowstone, Gibbon, and Henry's Fork rivers, somewhat longer drives. Lone Mountain is one of only a few resorts in the country to win the designation "Orvis Endorsed Lodge" from the Orvis Co. An Orvis shop in the ranch's main building arranges guided fishing trips and instruction. Orvis rental equipment is also available.

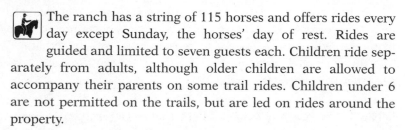 The ranch has a string of 115 horses and offers rides every day except Sunday, the horses' day of rest. Rides are guided and limited to seven guests each. Children ride separately from adults, although older children are allowed to accompany their parents on some trail rides. Children under 6 are not permitted on the trails, but are led on rides around the property.

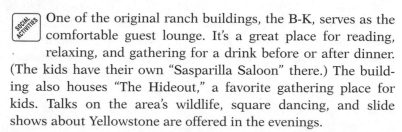 One of the original ranch buildings, the B-K, serves as the comfortable guest lounge. It's a great place for reading, relaxing, and gathering for a drink before or after dinner. (The kids have their own "Sasparilla Saloon" there.) The building also houses "The Hideout," a favorite gathering place for kids. Talks on the area's wildlife, square dancing, and slide shows about Yellowstone are offered in the evenings.

FOR CHILDREN: Between June 12 and Labor Day, the ranch offers a daily children's program for children between 4 and 12, and a few supervised activities for 2- and 3-year-olds. The focus is really on older children, and families with younger children are gently forewarned by the management that they may feel tied down if they choose this ranch for a vacation. A special rate is offered for nannies; children under 2 stay for free.

Four- and five-year-olds cannot ride on trails, but are led on pony rides. Six- and seven-year-olds take special horse classes early in the week, and work up to trail rides. Older children may ride with their families or go on special kids-only rides.

The program also features cookouts, rodeos, arts and crafts, nature walks, and outdoor games. In general, the activities coincide with the adult trail rides.

One night a week, the children have a special nature walk and party at the North Fork Cabin. The cookout and camp-out on Wednesday nights are something your children will remember for years to come. An 8-year-old boy we met here talked excitedly for the rest of the week about the seven shooting stars he'd seen from his berth in the sheepherder's wagon!

The ranch has a well-designed playground.

NICETIES: There's a coin laundry for guests' use.

Each cabin has an eclectic collection of paperback books, and board games can be borrowed to help while away evening hours. The office has a small library of historical novels, natural history works about Montana, Yellowstone guide books, and diaries of trappers.

OF INTEREST NEARBY: Yellowstone National Park is only an hour away. It's hard to imagine being this close to the nation's oldest national park and not taking time to visit.

Bozeman, an old cowboy town, is about an hour's drive. If it rains during your week at Lone Mountain, you'll probably be offered an outing to Bozeman, with a visit to the Museum of the Rockies, which has interesting exhibits on dinosaurs and western history.

The Big Sky ski area is just above the ranch (Lone Mountain is the peak that provides the most challenging skiing there). During the summer months, you can ride a gondola up the mountain. In the winter, there's downhill skiing.

FOR MORE INFORMATION: Write Lone Mountain Ranch, Box 160069, Big Sky, MT 59716, or call (406) 995-4644.

MOUNTAIN SKY GUEST RANCH
Emigrant, Montana

The Mountain Sky Guest Ranch is the oldest guest ranch in Montana, but in some ways it may also be the most modern. Founded in the 1880s as a working cattle ranch, it began welcoming guests (under a different name) in the 1920s, and some of its most sought-after log cabins date to that era. But you can't find much more modern facilities anywhere than the ranch's heated outdoor swimming pool, sauna, and hot tub, or its mirror-walled dance and exercise studio, or its more recently built guest units, complete with all the comforts of home.

The 5,000-acre ranch in the Gallatin National Forest, a 75-minute drive from Bozeman, Montana, has been owned by the Brutger family since 1980. The ranch experience here reflects what owners Mary and Alan Brutger have always sought for their own family vacations: good food, comfortable accommodations, spectacular surroundings, and a variety of activities for all age groups, but no pressure to participate.

Situated on the eastern slope of the Gallatin Mountains, the ranch is a roaming ground for moose, deer, elk, and an occasional bear. Every trail is more scenic than the one you took yesterday, whether on horseback or on foot. You'll feel like you're a million miles from anywhere, alone among the towering lodgepole pines and the Milky Way. There are no highway noises, buzzing power lines, or airplanes passing overhead to disturb your solitude—only the bubbling of Big Creek and the call of a passing coyote. And if it's companionship you seek, there are always the other guests. Guest ranches seem to attract nice people.

ACCOMMODATIONS: $$$$ Mountain Sky has accommodations for about 75 guests in two dozen cabins or duplex-type units. You can choose from a half dozen or so wonderfully rustic old log cabins, with either a fireplace or wood-burning stove, or from among 20 newer units.

Our preference is for the older cabins, which have large

screened-in porches, one, two, or three bedrooms, and a living room—and plenty of atmosphere. But the modern cabins are also lovely. Those appropriate for families have a sitting room with a hide-a-bed and a separate bedroom; the largest have two bedrooms, a sitting room, and two baths. All cabins have refrigerators and coffee pots that come with a selection of coffees and herbal teas.

The rate structure is based on both the size of the cabin and the number of occupants. Children receive a nominal discount from adult rates. The ranch is open from the end of May through mid-October.

In the summer, cabins are rented on a weekly basis, beginning on Sundays. Shorter stays can be arranged in the spring and fall.

DINING: The bell rings 10 minutes before mealtime to summon guests to the rustic dining hall in the main ranch building, where most meals are served. The chef is exceptionally good.

For early risers, a continental breakfast is served at 7 A.M. The regular breakfast is served between 8 and 9 A.M. and alternates between a bountiful buffet and sit-down, order-from-a-menu meals. Lunch is served at 12:30 P.M., outdoors. Everyone looks forward to the cookie of the day.

Dinner is served at 6:45 P.M. Sunday night, the day of arrival, is a get-acquainted night, with a family dinner served buffet style (lots of good, hearty food, but nothing fancy). Children eat with their parents at this meal, and over coffee and dessert Shirley Arsenault, the ranch manager, explains the ranch's rules (safety first) and routines.

Thereafter, special children's dinners are served most nights at 5:30 P.M. in a separate children's dining room, while parents have their cocktails nearby. After dinner, the children are taken up to the activities center for a few hours of games, songs, and storytelling while parents enjoy their meals alone.

Tuesday night is gourmet night, featuring haute cuisine accompanied by a group of Austrian accordion players. Wednesday night is country music night, with an outdoor barbecue for families by the pool followed by a hayride and campfire sing-along. Friday night is another family night, with the menu featuring seafood flown in from the Pacific Northwest. Saturday night is another adults-only adventure in gourmet cooking.

The chef will gladly prepare special meals for guests with special diet requirements.

ACTIVITIES

 Two courts.

 Heated pool, sauna, and hot tub. A poolside bar serves up favorite drinks from 11 A.M. to 5 P.M. daily.

 The fishing is fabulous in the nearby Yellowstone River or the Armstrong or Nelson creeks, two nearby blue-ribbon trout streams. Big Creek flows through the ranch property and has been known to reward anglers for just an hour of effort. The ranch also has a trout pond stocked with whoppers.

Excursions by van are offered once or twice weekly to Yellowstone National Park, less than an hour away (there's an extra charge). Rafting on the Yellowstone River is offered once each week. Children as young as 5 are welcome on the trips, which offer a nice diversion from the ranch routine and a spectacular way to see the scenery in the Yellowstone Valley (extra charge).

The ranch has a string of 100 horses. Twice-daily rides are offered at 9 A.M. and 2 P.M. Mondays through Saturdays; on Sundays, the horses have the day off. An all-day ride is offered Thursday to those guests who feel comfortable enough in the saddle, and on Tuesday and Friday there are breakfast rides, beginning at 7 A.M.

The ranch's trails feature spectacular views of the surrounding Absaroka and Madison mountain ranges. Be sure to take a ride up into the ranch's overnight pasture, where you'll have a panoramic view of Big Sky country, with Emigrant Peak (elevation 10,960 feet) in the background. For a fee, an in-house massage therapist will tend to your sore muscles.

Evening activities are frequently scheduled following dinner, ranging from softball games open to all ages, to Western dancing to a live band, to an impromptu pool tournament. A popular gathering place for adults before and after dinner is the Mountain View Lounge, next to the dining room, where homemade hors d'oeuvres and a full selection of cocktails (and 25 or so different beers) are served up.

FOR CHILDREN: Mountain Sky has something to offer children of all ages, from attentive baby-sitting for the very youngest to an active, outdoors-oriented program for those 3 and over. The program is usually run by a young woman with a degree in early childhood education and extensive preschool experience.

A wooden playground structure outside the activities room has a gigantic, shaded sandbox, swings, a wide slide, and climbing equipment, and serves as the focal point for the children's activities. The children's program meets from 9:15 to 11:30 A.M., 1:45 to 4:30 P.M., and for dinner and after-dinner activities three or four evenings a week.

The log-walled activities center is a favored hangout for teens, who like the pool and Ping-Pong tables. There's often someone banging out a song on the piano, or looking for a partner for chess or checkers. Younger children also use this building for arts and crafts and games.

Children 7 and over are permitted to go on trail rides. A special children's wrangler first assesses their skills and provides whatever instruction is needed. For younger children, an old gentle horse is frequently saddled up for rides around the playground area.

NICETIES: A basket of fresh fruit is placed in your cabin daily, which helps tide children over between meals.

The children's activity center has a variety of baby equipment available—a backpack carrier for hikes, a stroller, car safety seats, and a playpen—that you can borrow.

There's a laundry, complete with iron and ironing board, in the pool area. Water coolers filled with the tastiest—and coldest—water imaginable are placed strategically around the property so that guests don't get dehydrated in the dry mountain air.

OF INTEREST NEARBY: Yellowstone National Park is only an hour or so away, and you shouldn't miss an opportunity to visit it. It's too vast to be appreciated in the one-day outing offered by the ranch, so plan to add on a few days to your vacation and experience it at your leisure.

FOR MORE INFORMATION: Write Mountain Sky Guest Ranch, P.O. Box 1128, Bozeman, MT 59715, or call (406) 587-1244 or (800) 548-3392.

BISHOP'S LODGE
Santa Fe, New Mexico

Two centuries ago, this land was a farm worked by Spanish colonials, who borrowed irrigation techniques from nearby Pueblo Indians and turned the dry soil into fields of wheat, corn, beans, and fruit trees.

Then came the property's most famous resident, Bishop Jean-Baptiste Lamy, who used this corner of the Little Tesuque Valley, which he named the Villa Pinctoresca, as a retreat from the dust and disorder of Santa Fe.

Then came some private owners—among them a local dairy farmer and the Pulitzer newspaper publishing family of St. Louis.

But since 1919, this wonderful 1,000-acre spread in the "Land of Enchantment" has been the province of private paying guests, coddled and cared for by the Thorpe family. It has earned four stars from the Mobil Travel Guide for the last 15 years.

Bishop's Lodge is in a category all its own. Its adobe-style architecture lends a distinctly regional flavor, and its beautifully landscaped 1,000-acre site in the pink and orange foothills of the Sangre de Cristo Mountains ensures peace and quiet and magnificent views. Yet it is only a 10-minute drive from Santa Fe, possibly the most interesting and beautiful small city in the United States.

ACCOMMODATIONS: $$ to $$$$ Bishop's Lodge has 88 rooms or suites that can accommodate about 170 guests. The rooms range from modest, hotel-type rooms to luxurious suites. Some of the standard doubles have separate sleeping alcoves that can easily accommodate a child or two. All deluxe rooms have fireplaces and balconies or patios. Suites can accommodate a family of six.

The lodge's newest rooms (finished in 1994) are in Chamisa Lodge, a 14-room addition overlooking Little Tesuque Creek. Each room features a kiva-style fireplace, sitting area, wet bar, oversized bathroom and patio.

During the summer, a Modified American Plan package is available that includes breakfast and lunch or dinner daily and the children's program.

Beginning in 1994, the lodge has been staying open year-round.

DINING: A week of dining at Bishop's Lodge is guaranteed to send you home with a tummy bulge. The kitchen prepares "New American" cuisine with a southwestern flair. It's served in an attracting dining room decorated with beamed ceilings, chandeliers, old Navajo rugs and murals by the early Santa Fe artist W.E. Rollins.

The day begins with an elaborate breakfast buffet served from 7:30 to 10 A.M. (room service is also available). The trailside breakfasts are popular in the summer.

Lunch is ordered off the menu; box lunches can be requested if you're going on a family outing. The lodge's Sunday brunch draws diners from throughout New Mexico.

Dinner is cooked to order and features some regional favorites and continental dishes. Among the offerings on the menu: crab cakes with black bean puree, charbroiled zucchini salad, ranch-raised elk noisettes with jalapeno corn cakes, and a double-dip chocoloate-coffee creme brulee.

Children's portions are available, as are hamburgers, chicken strips, spaghetti, and sandwiches.

Cocktails are served in the El Charro Bar, decorated with Mexican and American cowboy gear, and, weather permitting, on the Firelight Terrace. During the summer, a trio provides background music on the terrace, which has a lovely view.

ACTIVITIES

Four tournament-grade Omni-Court tennis courts. Resident pro, round-robins, tournaments, and private, semi-private, and group lessons. Special instruction for "shorty swatters," ages 6 to 11, is offered three times a week. Court fees.

Privileges at the nearby Santa Fe Country Club, the Los Alamos Country Club, and the Cochiti Lake course.

Heated outdoor swimming pool and cabana, with an indoor sauna and whirlpool nearby.

New Mexico offers some of the finest white-water rafting and kayaking opportunities in the nation, including the famous Taos Box on the Rio Grande River. Day outings are easily arranged.

 A picturesque fishing hole chock-full of hungry trout is popular with children, who can borrow equipment from the counselors. Nearby stream and lake fishing for adults.

 The Santa Fe National Forest and the Pecos Wilderness Area abut Santa Fe. There are scenic and rugged mountain trails, with good fishing. Families will enjoy a drive through the Santa Fe National Forest, whose peaks rise to 12,000 feet. In the summer, you can ride the chairlift to the summit. The temperature drops about 30 degrees as you work your way to the top along a winding, scenic drive. Bishop's Lodge offers occasional guided nature walks.

 The lodge has a string of about 65 horses for guests' use between April and Thanksgiving (they winter at Rancho de los Caballeros). You won't want to miss the opportunity for a guided ride up into the foothills of the Sangre de Cristo Mountains for the panoramic view. There are two daily two-hour rides; children over 7 are welcome. Breakfast rides and picnic rides are offered each week during July and August. Pony rides are offered between April and October.

 Skeet and trap shooting are available at an automatic range on the lodge's grounds for a charge; minimum age 12.

Exercise room. Massage by appointment.

Downhill skiing at the Santa Fe Ski Basin.

FOR CHILDREN: During the summer, Bishop's Lodge offers a fun-filled, well-supervised children's program free of charge to Modified American Plan guests (European Plan guests pay a fee). Children between 4 and 12 are supervised by a staff of four college-age counselors in planned activities and games seven days a week.

A typical day begins at 8:30 A.M. with a group breakfast in the special children's dining room, just behind the main dining room, followed by play on the playground, which has an Indian teepee and standard playground equipment, as well as a nearby kids' fort (a sign proclaims "No Grown-ups Allowed"). After that, it's pony rides in a ring for younger children or a trail ride for those over 7. By then it's time for lunch, which the children eat together.

Then they're off on a hike, followed by arts and crafts and a swim at the pool. After their afternoon snack, they're returned to their parents at 4 P.M. But the group convenes again at 6:15 P.M. for dinner, followed by games, arts and crafts, or a movie that lasts until 8:45 P.M., which allows parents ample time for a dinner alone.

Your child is welcome to take part in all or some of the activities each day. There are typically 15 to 30 kids in the program.

The lodge tries to help teenage guests get to know each other by reserving a special table for them in the main dining room and organizing pool parties and pizza parties.

Babysitting is available.

NICETIES: Kindling and firewood are laid out every morning in guests' fireplaces.

A topographical map showing the main trails through the lodge's property and a bird-watchers' field checklist are available at the front desk.

Early-risers' coffee is available each morning in the lobby.

The lodge has a small library off the lobby, where guests can grab a quiet moment or check out some bedtime reading. Lots of recent-issue magazines are available.

OF INTEREST NEARBY: In 1987, Santa Fe was judged the most livable small city in the United States because of all its cultural amenities. It is truly a culture lovers' paradise—as well as a nature lovers' dream—with more to see and do than is possible in a week.

The heart of the city is the Plaza, which bustles with activity day and night. During the day, three or four dozen Native American merchants set up shop under the portico at the adjacent Palace of the Governors, built in 1609; beautiful silver and turquoise jewelry and pottery are offered for sale. Each of the streets bordering the Plaza is lined with interesting little shops and galleries that sell everything from souvenirs to fine art.

Santa Fe is also rich is museums. Children will especially enjoy the International Folk Art Museum, featuring folk art from over 50 countries and a scale model of an old-fashioned rail-car circus. For tourists with an interest in Indian art, the nearby Wheelwright Museum has a rotating collection of Indian objects in a stunning building. The Museum of Fine Art, on Palace Avenue, has a reputation as one of the country's leading centers for the arts.

There are several dozen Indian pueblos near Santa Fe. The Taos Pueblo is famous for its pueblo-style architecture and is worth a visit; it's a full day trip, but you can combine it with lunch in Taos, a visit to the nearby Millicent Rogers Museum, which has a fantastic Indian art collection, and a stop at the Rio Grande Gorge Bridge, which will give you a stomach-churning view into this famous gorge.

Bandelier National Monument is less than an hour from Bishop's Lodge; it protects remnants of ancient cliff dwellings that children will love exploring. You can combine a visit there with a stop in Los Alamos, the atomic research center, which has a fascinating museum. A little farther are the Puye Cliff Dwellings.

FOR MORE INFORMATION: Write the Bishop's Lodge, P.O. Box 2367, Santa Fe, NM 87504, or call (800) 732-2240. FAX: (505) 989-8739.

FLYING L GUEST RANCH
Bandera, Texas

Bandera, a tiny western town about an hour northwest of San Antonio, boasts that it's the "Cowboy Capital of the World." You'll see hitching posts outside the general store on Main Street, though there are more pickup trucks than ponies parked there these days. A souvenir shop reserves one whole wall for the autographs of rodeo winners in a town that's called home by seven world champion rodeo riders.

The Flying L, about a mile south of town, is the area's most luxurious ranch. Unlike most of the area's other dude ranches, Flying L was never a working ranch. A San Antonio business-man founded the ranch in the 1940s as a place to entertain friends, many of whom were pilots. He constructed some simple bungalows and built a private landing strip. Then his guests flew in for weekends of real Texas fun—barbecues, horseback riding, and camp fires.

The property was sold in the 1970s and redeveloped as a 542-acre ranch resort.

ACCOMMODATIONS: $$$ Don't expect bunkhouses here. Guests stay in bungalows, condominiums, and villas, some equipped with whirlpool baths.

The ranch's 38 units fan out from the main clubhouse to form a small compound where it would be hard for children to get lost. There are three types of rooms, all with a western flair. The Golfview suites, bordering the ninth fairway, are ideal for guests who want to be within putting distance of the golf course. Each two-room condominium suite has a refrigerator, cooking unit, wet bar, color television, and private balcony.

The Ranchview suites, the resort's most deluxe and spacious accommodations, can comfortably sleep a family of four. The suite's enormous kitchen is a perfect gathering place, with built-in banquettes and every convenience of home, including a washer and dryer. The living room has a stone fireplace and a sofa that opens to a queen-size bed. The bedroom has a king-size bed and a Texas-size bathroom. The Ranchview suites are only a horseshoe pitch from the swimming pool and dining hall. Each one also has a covered patio, equipped with lawn furniture and a big barbecue pit.

The original guest houses, nestled under huge live oaks, are bungalow-style units. They have color televisions, refrigerators, and even some fireplaces. The larger units sleep up to six people, with two double beds in the bedroom and a sofa with a double bed in the living room.

The ranch's rate covers the room, two meals a day, golf and horseback riding, and maid service. Children between 3 and 11 are charged a small flat daily rate, and there are reduced rates for children 12 to 17.

DINING: Meals are served family style in the cozy dining room in the main house.

The breakfast menu changes daily, but on a typical day you'll find stacks of buttermilk pancakes, platters of fluffy scrambled eggs, toasty English muffins, spicy sausages, sweet rolls, and all the milk, orange juice, and coffee you can drink. If you miss breakfast in the main dining room, head for the Pro Shop, where you can order from a menu.

Lunch may be purchased at the Pro Shop or in town.

Guests are summoned to dinner by a cowhand ringing a metal triangle. Every night of the week there's a different theme—Mexican Fiesta, Back to the 50s, Hawaiian Luau, German/Polish night, and everyone's favorite: Get Western. On Sundays, the spread is the kind of food you'd expect to find on a farm—oven-baked ham, turkey, roast beef, and fried fish with stuffing, homemade rolls, and baby carrots.

When weather permits, the buffets are served outside with all the food piled on long tables covered with red-checked table-cloths.

ACTIVITIES

 Two lighted hard-surface courts; racquets and balls available.

 Eighteen-hole course (6,787 yards, par 72); driving range, pro shop, rental equipment.

 Outdoor swimming pool. Tubing in nearby creek.

 Cane fishing poles available for use at the San Julian Creek, about three-quarters of a mile away.

 The ranch has miles of established hiking trails.

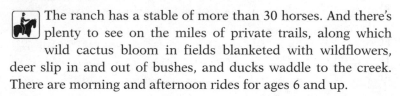 The ranch has a stable of more than 30 horses. And there's plenty to see on the miles of private trails, along which wild cactus bloom in fields blanketed with wildflowers, deer slip in and out of bushes, and ducks waddle to the creek. There are morning and afternoon rides for ages 6 and up.

Volleyball, Ping-Pong, shuffleboard, bingo, movies, card games. In the evening you can swap trail stories in the Branding Iron Saloon, a small bar in the main lobby. There's nightly entertainment, including musical shows, twilight hayrides, marshmallow roasts, softball games, square dancing, hoe-downs, country-western dancing, and performances by a snake handler and expert trick roper.

FOR CHILDREN: The ranch's free formal children's program runs during the summer and over the Thanksgiving, Christmas and spring school breaks. Activities are held daily from 9:30 A.M. to 12:30 P.M. and 2 to 4:30 P.M. for children ages 3 to 12.

Daily activities vary, depending on the weather, the children's ages, and their preferences. They can choose from pony rides, fishing, hiking, movies, swimming in the pool or spring-fed creek, having sack races, going on fossil hunts, or learning rope tricks or western crafts. A low adult-child ratio is maintained.

If you visit when the children's program is not operating, the ranch will provide a list of sitters so you can get away for several hours of golf or horseback riding.

NICETIES: Each guest unit has a clock-radio in the bedroom, and larger ones have a second in the kitchen. But you won't find any telephones in the units; they've been deliberately omitted to make your vacation as relaxing as possible. If you must make a call, there are pay phones at the main house, pro shop, and service room of the Golfview condominiums, where you'll also find coin-operated washers and dryers.

There are two Shetland ponies available for the pint-size cowboys to ride around the ring.

OF INTEREST NEARBY: A goat farm just across the entrance from the ranch on Highway 173 is a great destination for a 10-minute after-dinner walk. Also popular with families are the Frontier Museum in Bandera; dinosaur tracks at a creek bed in Tarpley; Medina Lake, a nearby boating, fishing, and recreational area, and Sea World, 45 minutes away in San Antonio.

FOR MORE INFORMATION: Write Flying L Guest Ranch, P.O. Box 1959, Bandera, TX 78003, or call (800) 292-5134 or (210) 460-3001.

PARADISE GUEST RANCH
Buffalo, Wyoming

Webster's Dictionary defines paradise as "any place of great beauty and perfection," and it would be hard to think of a more apt description for this ranch in north-central Wyoming.

This former cattle ranch is surrounded by close to 2 million acres of Bighorn National Forest—some of the most remote and scenic territory to be found in this arid country. To the west are the snowy peaks of the Bighorn Mountains. Bull moose, deer, and other wildlife graze against a backdrop of ponderosa pine and aspen.

The ranch has taken in paying guests since 1905 and is one of the oldest ranches in the West. Author Owen Wister, who stayed at the ranch in the 1920s, is said to have drawn on his experiences here for his Western epic "The Virginian." Since 1981, the ranch has been totally renovated and expanded to accommodate about 70 guests at a time. Its congenial owners are Jim and Leah Anderson.

The ranch buildings are attractively clustered at the foot of a hill. A two-story bar-lodge with open loft is the center of evening activities. A few steps away is the dining hall, which has been built around the ranch's original registration center. Parked outside is an antique chuck wagon that is called into use each week to deliver the victuals to an upper meadow for a cookout dinner. Down the road is the corral, where guests saddle up each day.

The ranch's cattle brand, FUN, which hangs from the gate as you cross over French Creek, tells you clearly what to expect during your week here.

ACCOMMODATIONS: $$$$ Eighteen log cabins with inviting front porches and stone chimneys are perched on a hillside over-looking the ranch buildings and, in the distance, the grazing meadows. The log cabins have rustic appeal, but have been fully up-dated with modern bathrooms and kitchenettes. Four of the cabins have one bedroom, 11 have two bedrooms, and three have three bedrooms. As at many other ranches, no keys are issued.

The ranch's season runs from Memorial Day through the second week of September. Guests come for week-long visits, beginning each Sunday. Children's rates are available, including a greatly reduced rate for children under 6 who do not take part in trail rides.

Besides lodging, the rates include all food, riding, the children's program, and entertainment. The only extras are alcoholic beverages, fishing licenses, an optional 3-day pack trip, and gratuities.

DINING: Exceptionally tasty meals are served at tables long enough to seat several families. All breads and desserts are made fresh each day. The pastry chef's repertoire includes baklava, carrot cake, ice cream in a meringue shell, lemon pie, and strawberry flan.

Breakfast is a hearty affair, designed to tide you over if you're taking a morning horseback ride. Lunch features a choice of two entrées, or sandwiches, if you're on an all-day outing.

Dinners are special. Sometimes, they're planned around an activity like a late-afternoon ride to a high meadow called Bald Eagle Park, culminating in a chuck-wagon supper of barbecued ribs, potatoes, corn on the cob, and sourdough bread. There's a gourmet dinner each Thursday night for adults only. Saturday night's dinner features thick, juicy steaks barbecued on an open grill.

ACTIVITIES

 Heated outdoor pool, whirlpool.

 French Creek is stocked with 12-inch rainbow trout. Fishing gear can be borrowed.

 The ranch has 90 horses from which to choose; you can stick with the one you're assigned for the whole week or, if you prefer, switch daily. You'll want to do lots of riding here to cover as much of the varied terrain as you can. One trail follows along French Creek, another winds through thick groves of aspen and pine trees, and yet another goes uphill between steep mountains. You can ride as a family or split up according to your level of experience.

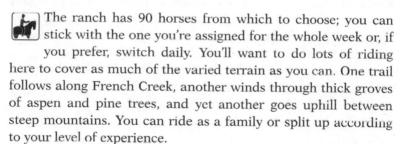 Volleyball, horseshoes, pool, Ping-Pong. In the evenings: bonfires, sing-alongs, marshmallow roasts, slide shows, guest talent shows, rodeos and square dancing.

The ranch has designed a three-day guided pack trip into a base camp at Frying Pan Lake. Tacked onto the end of the week-long ranch stay, the pack trip carries an additional charge. Horse, sleeping bags, cots, food, and cook are supplied. The trip takes you to a 9,700-foot elevation, where you can catch cutthroat, brook, or rainbow trout in one of several lakes or rushing streams.

FOR CHILDREN: The ranch offers a free children's program directed by four counselors; in generaly, they're college students on their summer breaks. The program varies each week depending upon the ages of the children in residence. The Andersons' own children, Kate and Travis, take part in many of the activities.

Each morning after breakfast, the counselors call the children together for circle time to talk over the day's activities. Those who aren't riding that morning will do nature-oriented crafts: watercolor mountains, grass rubbings, or pine-cone and dried-flower pictures. Then they'll spend some time in active play, like relay races, badminton, or floating boats in the creek.

After lunch, an activity like Capture the Flag or a scavenger hunt is planned before the older kids trot out for their afternoon ride. Some time is spent on a second art activity or on a special event like learning roping from a wrangler or throwing a fishing line in the creek. Ping-Pong and horseshoe tournaments are often scheduled. Each child's art treasures are kept in a folder during the week and are bound together on Saturday.

One of the highlights of the week for children is an overnight camp-out in a walled tent in the woods across French Creek on Thursday night, planned to coincide with the adults' gourmet night. The kids hike up to the woods with the activities director and some of the ranch hands for a weenie roast and s'mores, followed by relay races and camp-fire songs. (There's a separate campout for teens.)

But the favorite weekly event is the rodeo, in which all but the smallest children demonstrate their skills in handling horses.

NICETIES: In your cabin you'll find coffee and herbal tea. You also can ask the kitchen staff to stock your small refrigerator with snacks and soft drinks.

Each day, the fireplace is serviced and the wood bin outside the door is replenished with firewood and diesel-soaked sawdust.

Some of the cabins are equipped with washers and dryers. For those that aren't, guests may use the laundry machines in the recreation hall after 3:30 P.M., at no charge.

When you check in, you'll get a list of the other guests' names, hometowns, and their children's ages, along with a "horse sense" handbook that offers tips on how to handle horses.

OF INTEREST NEARBY: There are few attractions nearby, but many people combine a ranch visit with a trip to Yellowstone National Park, four hours west of Buffalo, or to the granite presidential images at the Mt. Rushmore National Monument in the Black Hills National Forest in western South Dakota, about four hours to the east.

Cody, Wyoming, the home of Buffalo Bill Cody, is about three hours to the west and displays memorabilia from the American West in four museums under one roof. And 125 miles away in southern Montana, you can visit the Custer battlefield monument in Little Bighorn, where Custer made his last stand against the Indians.

FOR MORE INFORMATION: Write Jim and Leah Anderson at Paradise Guest Ranch, P.O. Box 790, Buffalo, WY 82834, or call (307) 684-7876.

SKI AREAS

MONT-TREMBLANT
GRAY ROCKS
Mont-Tremblant, Quebec, Canada

Americans can experience the ambience of European skiing by driving just 75 miles north out of Montreal into the world of French Canadian hospitality. After a one and a half-hour ride into the Laurentian Mountains, skiers can find themselves at any one of about 30 picture-book, snow-covered hostelries—with ski tows, runs, and trails rising behind them.

Getting there is part of the experience. Driving up the Laurentian Autoroute brings a delightful vista with every turn— a small village clustered in a valley, a steeple pointing high above the white rooftops, a chalet perched on a mountainside with ski trails converging behind it.

This is where recreational skiing began in North America, when the world's first rope tow was installed in the village of Shawbridge in 1932. In 1951, a young man named Réal Charette furthered the industry by instituting the "ski week" at a resort named Gray Rocks. Even today, most of the skiers who come to the Laurentians sign up for ski weeks, at all-inclusive prices.

New owners and a $43 million facelift in 1993 have turned Mont-Tremblant into a world-class destination.

Whether staying at an intimate chalet, an inn, or a larger resort, guests find themselves basking in their hosts' courtesy and warmth, comfortable accommodations, French-influenced cuisine, and the *joie de vivre* of the Quebec lifestyle.

ACCOMMODATIONS: $$ to $$$ The Mont-Tremblant area has numerous chalets, inns, and hotels, several with their own ski schools on the mountain. Most hotel provide package plans that include meals and skiing.

Gray Rocks, the *grande-mere* of them all, is a large, rambling lodge and cottage complex with 150 spacious rooms and 56 housekeeping units, each with a picture-window view of either Lake Ouimet or Sugar Peak.

At the base of the Mont-Tremblant ski area, the new condo hotel, the St. Bernard, offers one- to three-bedroom units overlooking a pedestrian plaza.

DINING: Meals at Gray Rocks are served in a dining room with the tables dressed in linen and fresh cut flowers. Each family or group is assigned a table for the duration of its stay.

A new base village at Mont-Tremblant features such electic restaurants as the Grain de Cafe, The Shack, and Aux Truffles. At Vieux-Tremblant, you can dine at The Savoie where the specialties are fondue and raclette.

For lunch, skiers can remain at the mountain and eat in one of several cafeterias or at the new mountaintop restaurant, Le Grand Manitou, with spectacular views.

THE SKIING: Above the sweeping valleys and the gently rounded mountaintops of the Laurentians rises Mont-Tremblant, at 3,000 feet the highest skiable peak in eastern Canada. Abundant natural snowfall—170 inches a year—provides for skiing from mid-November until mid-April. In addition, 75 computer-controlled snowguns spray forth each night to cushion the trails evenly. The manufactured snow provides a minimum base of 46 inches.

Gray Rocks has its own ski area on Sugar Peak, and most Gray Rocks guests ski there. The area is also open to non-guests.

 Mont-Tremblant: 20 percent novice, 45 percent intermediate, 25 percent advanced, 10 percent expert.

Gray Rocks: Five novice, eight intermediate, seven advanced trails.

 Mont-Tremblant: Six high-speed quads, gondola, three triples.

Gray Rocks: One quad chair, three double chairlifts.

 Mont-Tremblant: 2,130 feet.
Gray Rocks: 620 feet.

Mont-Tremblant: Three and one-half miles.
Gray Rocks: One mile.

At the Mont-Tremblant Ski School, the 80 instructors are members of the Canadian Ski Instructors Alliance. For the ski week, guests are organized into classes of similar skill levels; groups stay together for the duration. Gray Rocks' Snow Eagle Ski School has 65 full-time instructors; all but advanced classes are taught on Sugar Peak.

The area has a network of 69 miles of regularly groomed cross-country ski trails. The trails wind up and around hills, through vales, and across frozen lakes. Numerous lodges sit along the trails; skiing to one for a leisurely lunch makes for a delightful day.

ACTIVITIES FOR NON-SKIERS: Gray Rocks offers a complete evening social program featuring ski movies, wine and cheese parties, and a karaoke casino night. An attractive and spacious indoor sports center has a heated swimming pool, hot tubs, saunas, massage, aerobics classes, Nautilus and Global equipment, and a beauty shop.

FOR CHILDREN: Gray Rocks offers ski classes for all children over 3, and from 4 to 11 P.M. daily there's an après-ski program featuring cider and cheese parties, swimming, sleigh rides, games, and dances. There's a recreation room and a snack bar. The Snow Eaglet Day Care Service provides care for 1- to 6-year-olds in the Lucile Wheeler Chalet.

Garderie pour les Enfants, on the edge of the Mont-Tremblant ski slope, offers care for 3- to 5-year-olds. There children can learn to ski, participate in indoor and outdoor group activities, and eat lunch. Each class has about five children. The classes ski on terrain appropriate to the children's ages and skills. The cost includes lift tickets.

Children 7 and older who are in classes get priority access to all lifts at Mont-Tremblant. The older group of children and adults must buy lift tickets in addition to ski school tickets.

Child-care options for younger children are a day-care center in Tremblant Village or private baby-sitting; hotels will help make arrangements.

IN THE SUMMER: All the lodges offer extensive activities in the summer—boating, swimming, water skiing, and wind surfing on the numerous lakes; tennis; golf; horseback riding; hiking; and other outdoor recreation. Special children's activities are also offered.

FOR MORE INFORMATION: For information about Gray Rocks call (800) 567-6767; for Mont-Tremblant call (800) 461-8711 or (819) 681-2000.

For general information about tourism in the Laurentians, call (514) 436-8532.

KILLINGTON SKI AREA
Killington, Vermont

Killington is a vast ski area of six mountains laced with 155 trails and 829 acres of skiable terrain. Killington has skiing for every member of the family, from the mogul maniac to the slightly bewildered novice. Killington also offers a lot of activity off the slopes, with scores of restaurants and shops, dozens of night spots, and ample entertainment for every family member.

Although Old Man Winter has provided an average 250 inches of snow a year over the last decade, Killington leaves nothing to chance. The ski season is extended at both ends—from October to June—with the use of snowmaking equipment on trails from all 19 lifts and on intermountain connecting trails. Come April, when other eastern ski areas are closing down, Killington skiers greet the spring skiing season with T-shirts and suntan lotion. Those long, sweeping vistas from the top of the mountain include views of the Killington golf course greening up at the base. In fact, the golfing season is well under way when the last skiers leave the slopes.

ACCOMMODATIONS: $$ to $$$ The Killington area offers a staggering variety of accommodations, with a choice of over 100 lodges, country inns, motels, and condominium groupings. Some offer no meals as part of the basic rates; others have Modified American plans or breakfast plans. Some are at the foot of the slopes, others are 10 or more miles away. The Killington Lodging Bureau helps you find your way through this maze of options by providing a single source of information on accommodations. A wide variety of packages is available that offers lessons, lifts, equipment, and lodging in almost every combination.

Killington Village has seven condominium complexes, a swimming pool, a health club, restaurants, and shops. There's no extra charge for children staying in a unit with parents.

DINING: Everything from fast food to fine New England country inn fare is a few minutes' walk or drive from your room. Killington offers five cafeterias and one full-service restaurant at the slopes and one mountaintop restaurant.

THE SKIING: Killington has one of the longest ski seasons in the east, thanks to good snowfalls and snow-making equipment that cranks all winter long. The six mountains feature an interconnected system of trails and lifts and offer the greatest diversity of ski terrain in the eastern United States and the highest lift-serviced skiing in New England.

 Sixty-six novice, 36 intermediate, 53 advanced. (Outer Limits, the steepest mogul slope in New England, has vertical drops and pitches up to 62 degrees.)

 One gondola, seven quad chairs, four triples, five doubles, two Pomas.

 3,175 feet.

 Ten miles.

Group lessons, private lessons, lesson packages, and family workshops are available at both Snowshed and Killington Base Lodge. Intermediate and advanced skiers can sign up for the Master's Ski Week. In this five-day program you and four other skiers receive intensive instruction as you ski together for three hours a day on all kinds of terrain. Killington's four acres of Mountain Training Stations are included in accelerated learning programs and Master's Ski Week programs. Here instructors give individualized on-the-spot instruction on a wide variety of skiing terrains.

Touring centers in the Killington area, and the nearby towns of Chittenden, Stockbridge, and Woodstock.

ACTIVITIES FOR THE NON-SKIER: Killington has all the traditional winter activities of a quality ski resort, including ice-skating, snowshoeing, and sleigh rides. You'll find racquetball facilities at the Killington Health Club and at Summit Lodge. Indoor tennis is available at Vermont Sport & Fitness in Rutland, 20 miles away. The bowling alleys and the multi-screen cinemas in the Rutland area are possibilities for evening entertainment.

FOR CHILDREN: The Killington Children's Center offers child care for children from 6 weeks to 6 years. Excellent facilities include a reading corner, block area, science and music areas, jungle gym, large toy area, a housekeeping area, and a games, puzzles, and arts and crafts area. The program is divided between structured and individual activities. Outdoor activities are scheduled, weather permitting. A lunch and two snacks are included in the full-day charge.

The "First Tracks" program for 3- through 5-year-olds gets children skiing in short order with two one-hour lessons in each full-day session. These lessons can be combined with the child-care program so that your child gets day care and skiing from 8 A.M. to 4 P.M.

The "Superstars" all-day skiing program caters to children 6 through 12, with unlimited use of the lifts, ski instruction, ski videos, and indoor activities. Lunch is included.

Your teenage child, 12 through 15 years, can participate in the "Killington Teen Ski" program, offered during certain peak winter vacation weeks. The program includes two hours of lessons per day, ski races, movies, and social activities.

NICETIES: Complimentary "Meet the Mountain" tours provide a two-hour introduction to Killington's mountains by Killington guides. Tours leave daily from Snowshed and Killington Base lodges. Killington provides Your Ski Week, an excellent pocket-size guidebook to the area, with maps and information on lifts, trails, lodging, restaurants, and services. The guide includes skiing courtesy and safety tips.

OF INTEREST NEARBY: Vermont is a patchwork of small shops and crafts makers and vendors. It is roadside shopping at its best. In addition to the shopping, consider visits to the New England Maple Museum near Rutland, which will give your family the complete lowdown on maple sugar and other maple products. The Vermont Marble Exhibit, also near Rutland, tells the story of the rock for which Vermont is known.

IN THE SUMMER: When the snow finally leaves the slopes, summer activities are already under way. Rates on Killington condominium units plunge, making it a very affordable summer family vacation destination. Ten golf courses within 10 miles of Killington Village offer a new golfing challenge on every day of a golfing vacation. Killington's own 6,300-yard, par 72 course is one of New England's most scenic. From mid-May through mid-September the highly acclaimed Killington School for Tennis offers two-day and five-day tennis programs, which include five hours of daily instruction, tennis videos, ball machines, and all meals and lodging. Killington is on the straw-hat trail, with Broadway-quality theater each July and August in the Killington Playhouse at Snowshed Lodge. And the fine arts get their due in the annual Killington Musical Festival, the Summer Showcase.

Horse riding is another summertime Green Mountain favorite. The Killington Mountain Equestrian Festival, held each July, brings in hundreds of top hunters and jumpers to compete.

FOR MORE INFORMATION: Write Killington Lodging Bureau, 203 Killington Rd., Killington, VT 05751-9708, or phone (802) 773-1330.

MOUNT SNOW RESORT
Mount Snow, Vermont

That 8-year-old skiing down the mountain with a teddy bear strapped to his back isn't eccentric. Nor is the 7-year-old clutching her Barbie doll (all decked out in ski wear) or the 10-year-old with a threadbare stuffed dog tucked into his belt. They're all skiing Mount Snow during Teddy Bear Week, one of the most attractive family-aimed promotions of any ski resort. They're skiing free and then going on to have fun at the special activities that await them at the end of the ski day

Mount Snow, long a favorite destination for day-trippers from Boston and smaller New England cities, has gone after the family business in a big way in recent years, offering four weeks during the winter—the Teddy Bear Weeks—when children under 12 who bring along their stuffed animals ski free for five days, and also get to take part in lots of special activities. But Mount Snow is a good place for families anytime during the ski season. The atmosphere is unpretentious, and there's a wide variety of terrain. And there are plenty of restaurants nearby to sample at night.

Mount Snow is one of the most accessible of the New England ski resorts. And its part of southern Vermont has all the ambience you expect—charming country villages dominated by Victorian-era architecture, antiques shops galore, and inviting country inns.

ACCOMMODATIONS: $$ to $$$$ Mount Snow Vacation Services is a one-call service (800-245-SNOW) that handles reservations at all the on-site facilities and about 60 nearby country inns, motels, condominiums, and guest lodges as well. The reservation clerks can assess your needs and resources and recommend the place that's most appropriate.

Snow Lake Lodge, owned and operated by the Mount Snow Ltd., is a 103-room lodge on Snow Lake at the base of Mount Snow, a short shuttle ride from the slopes. It features lakeside dining, a cocktail lounge with nightly entertainment, indoor hot tub, outdoor Jacuzzi, a game room, and a fitness center. Rates include two meals.

Snowtree Condominiums has 115 units, ranging from efficiencies to town houses that can accommodate 10. Guests here have the use of a sports center with whirlpool, sauna, and exercise room.

Seasons on Mount Snow offers ski-in-ski-out accommodations, in the deluxe range. There are 165 units, ranging from two to four bedrooms, with a sports center with an indoor pool, platform tennis, exercise and game rooms, and whirlpool and sauna.

DINING: During the day, quick meals are available at the main base lodge, which has a cafeteria, a Mexican food outlet, a pastry counter, and the Starloft Cafe, a full-service restaurant on the fourth floor. On nice days, outdoor barbecues provide a convenient, tasty alternative. There are cafeterias and lounges at the Sundance and Carinthia base lodges, and the Summit Lodge, which has a gorgeous view of four states.

Snow Lake Lodge and several of the other private lodges near the area all have dining rooms. And restaurants on the road to nearby West Dover and in Wilmington welcome families. A fun place for both adults and kids is Poncho's Wreck on South Main Street in Wilmington, which features idiosyncratic Mexican foods in a casual, rustic atmosphere. TC's Tavern is a good pizza and spaghetti place just a short drive from Mount Snow; kids can keep themselves occupied with the Junior Trivial Pursuit cards that fill a coffee mug on each table.

THE SKIING: Mount Snow is a big 3,600-foot mountain, with trails ranging from narrow, tree-lined runs (beginners, beware) to 100-yard-wide "highways." Mount Snow has four interconnected mountain areas, each with a different character. It boasts the greatest variety of terrain from one summit in the East and the greatest summit lift capacity in New England.

 Thirty-seven novice, 65 intermediate, 25 advanced.

 Nine triple chairs, 10 doubles, one T-bar, two rope tow, one high-speed quad, one quad.

 1,700 feet.

 Two and one-half miles.

 Mount Snow has a large ski school staff and offers a special Introduction to Skiing package to encourage novices to take a lesson before they hit the slopes. For intermediate and advanced skiers, Mount Snow offers EXCL, 45-minute workshops for small groups.

Four cross-country skiing centers in the area. A directory is available at most lodges. The top of the southern Green Mountain range is the site of a 3.1-mile cross-country skiing trail called the Ridge Trail, which connects the summits of Mount Snow and Haystack Mountain and offers gorgeous vistas from six peaks.

ACTIVITIES FOR THE NON-SKIER: There are numerous shops and night spots in nearby Wilmington, as well as a nice skating rink at Carinthia. Sleigh rides are offered several times a week at the Matterhorn (802-464-8011) and Adam's Farm (802-464-3762). Guided snowmobile tours through the Vermont countryside can be arranged through Wheeler Farm Snowmobile Tours; call (802) 464-5225.

FOR CHILDREN: For children between 6 weeks and 8 years, the state-licensed Pumpkin Patch Day Care offers a variety of indoor activities and attentive caregivers. The center operates daily from 8:30 A.M. to 4:30 P.M. and from 5:30 to 9:30 P.M. Wednesdays; parents must provide lunch, drinks, and snacks for children under 3. The center is in the Vacation Center, next to the Main Base Lodge. Reservations are required. Multi-day discounts are offered.

The staff is caring and competent; a ratio of one adult to 3 or 4 children is maintained at all times for children under 1. Children between 18 months and 3 years are segregated from the babies and cared for in slightly larger groups.

Children ages 3 and 4 are offered a daylong program that balances ski instruction and indoor and outdoor activities. Lessons for this age group, called SKIwee, are held on a separate slope a short walk from the Pumkin Patch; a rope tow helps them get up the slope. Between the two daily ski lessons, children enjoy arts and crafts, songs, games, cooking, and free play with toys. Two snacks and lunch are served.

Six- to 12-year-olds can enroll in a six-hour program that includes five hours of ski instruction and lunch. Beginning lessons are conducted on the children's slope, but those children with intermediate or above skills use the whole mountain as their classroom.

NICETIES: There's a protected box of tissues at the entrance to most lifts, a real godsend to snifflers.

Mount Snow issues a daily newsletter that lists special activities and offers tips to save time at lunch.

FOR MORE INFORMATION: Call Mount Snow Vacation Service, at (802) 464-8501; (800) 245-7669 from outside New England, New York, and northern New Jersey. Write Mount Snow Resort, Mount Snow, VT 05356.

SMUGGLERS' NOTCH RESORT
Smugglers' Notch, Vermont

It's no wonder that Smugglers' Notch Resort has garnered family travel awards from Family Circle, Better Homes and Gardens, and Snow Country magazines. This is truly "kid country." Whether summer or winter, this self-contained resort feels like a family camp.

Nestled at the base of three interconnected mountains in the heart of Vermont's Green Mountains, Smugglers has skiing options for everyone in a family. While there is plenty of terrain for beginners, including their own special lift, the trails on the two upper mountains were cut for the intermediates to enjoy and the experts to conquer.

Smugglers' is a 45-minute shuttle ride from Burlington International Airport, or a convenient drive from New York, Boston or Montreal, mostly along interstate highways. From Washington, New York, and communities along the Amtrak line, you can even take the train, and be met at the Amtrak Station in Essex Junction, Vt.

ACCOMMODATIONS: $ to $$$$ Smugglers' Notch Resort Village features cozy condominium-style housing, from compact studios up to five bedrooms. All are within 250 yards of the Village Lift, clustered like a little community around the facility's activities centers.

The resort is big on all-inclusive packages. A Modified American Plan is available for use at any of a dozen or so on-site restaurants.

All lodging, package vacations, activities and special programs can be reserved by calling (800) 451-8752.

DINING: Within the Resort Village, you will find several options for convenient meals. The Club Cafe specializes in a light fare menu and quick service. The Village Restaurant menu offers children's prices pegged to their ages. The Pizzaria provides quick takeout service, and seems to be a place teens like to congregate.

In the summer, the Scoop Shop is a popular place. There's a country store and deli on site for families who prefer to cook in their condos.

On the slopes, there are two cafeterias and a pub.

In the evening, there's often entertainment at the Smugglers' Sports Bar and Lounge.

Within a five-mile drive of the Resort Village, you'll find Italian, Mexican, French, American and continental cuisine in country inns, renovated barns, a grist mill and a log lodge. A dining guide with sample menus is included in your arrival packet.

THE SKIING: Smugglers' Notch offers Northern Vermont's highest vertical drop, and a variety of trails that wind, twist and weave, providing surprises and great views around every turn. The trails are groomed every evening to assure good skiing the next day.

 57 trails: Twelve novice, 26 intermediate, 19 advanced.

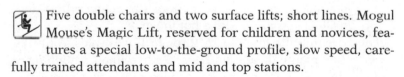 Five double chairs and two surface lifts; short lines. Mogul Mouse's Magic Lift, reserved for children and novices, features a special low-to-the-ground profile, slow speed, carefully trained attendants and mid and top stations.

 Vertical Drop: 2,610 feet.

 Longest Run: 3.5 miles.

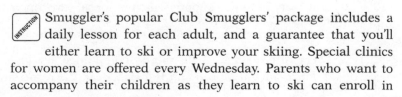 Smuggler's popular Club Smugglers' package includes a daily lesson for each adult, and a guarantee that you'll either learn to ski or improve your skiing. Special clinics for women are offered every Wednesday. Parents who want to accompany their children as they learn to ski can enroll in

"Mom & Me" or "Dad & Me" classes. The Ski Learning Center uses video analysis and Sybervision to help skiers reach their potential.

 An on-site touring center includes 23 kilometers of groomed and tracked trails; lessons, rental equipment, guided night tours. Snowshowing and sleigh rides.

ACTIVITIES FOR NON-SKIERS: There's plenty for the non-skier to do, right within the Resort Village. In the daytime, you can go ice-skating, snowshowing, swimming, sleding, trail riding, or shopping, or play tennis, have a massage, or attend an arts and crafts class.

Evening entertainment includes Family Game Night, Pictionary parties, Showtime Theater, pool parties, fireworks and torchlight parades, a comedy club, dances, family sing-alongs, and old-fashioned sledding parties.

FOR CHILDREN: Smugglers' Notch promises your money back if your kids don't have fun. It's doubtful the resort has ever had to make good on the guarantee.

Children between six weeks and six years are cared for at Alice's Wonderland, a fully certified 10-room child-care center with a special curriculum for each age group. Three- to six-year-olds who want to ski can take part in the center's Discovery Camp, an all-day program with a hot lunch.

The Adventure Program for 7- through 12-year-olds features a variety of on-mountain adventures and a hot lunch. Children are grouped by ability for a full day of instruction and interactive outdoor games.

Teenagers can take part in the Explorer Program, which keeps them busy from noon through the evening. The afternoon is devoted to skiing instruction, with a taste of snowshoeing, tele-mark skiing, snowboarding and cross-country skiing for those who want it. Organized social events and games are offered from 5 to 7 P.M., and Teen Central, a supervised club house, stays open until 11 P.M.

NICETIES: Every afternoon at 3:30, there's complimentary hot cocoa by a bonfire. Mogul Mouse and Bill Bob Bear, the resort's mascot characters, interact with the kids and congratulate them on a successful day on the slopes.

Showtime Theater, produced by the Ski School every Thursday night in ski season, uses videos, an emcee, audience participation, and live music to teach lessons on ski safety.

IN THE SUMMER: The ski area becomes a mountain hideaway in the summer. Just up the road from the resort is an entry point to the Long Trail, a hiking path that travels the entire length of Vermont.

The same care in programing that skiers appreciate in the winter is evident in the all-day camps for kids, the TenPro Tennis School, and the specialty camps offered during the summer. In addition, scheduled summer activities include guided mountain hikes, mountain biking expeditions, ropes course adventures, horseback riding, and Tai Chi clinics. Golf is available at nearby Stowe Country Club and several other courses.

The resort's Water Playground is a popular place in the summer. It features three water slides, 2 full-size pools, and 2 wading pools.

Evening events such as the Vermont Country Fair, Moonlight Watersliding and Bingo Bonanza are fun for families.

Rates are about 30 percent lower in June than in July and August. During selected weeks, look for special packages that include free child care, arrival gifts, sport shop certificates, and brunch.

OF INTEREST NEARBY: There are numerous one-of-a-kind shops in the area that sell quality Vermont products. Among the most distinctive are Quilts by Elaine, the Vermont Rug Makers, and the Johnson Woolen Mills. Antique shops abound, and there are covered bridges along many country roads.

From mid-May to mid-October, a visit to the Shelburne Museum in Burlington will give your family easy-to-absorb lessons in Americana.

A ferry ride across broad Lake Champlain is a treat in the summer.

FOR MORE INFORMATION: Call (800) 451-8752, or write to Smugglers' Notch Resort, Smugglers' Notch, VT 05464.

STRATTON
Stratton Mountain, Vermont

It's no accident that this ski area has the look of a Tyrolean village. Many of the principals involved in its development since the 1960s were Europeans attracted to the picturesque charm of Vermont's Green Mountains and the skiing terrain of Stratton Mountain, the highest mountain in southern Vermont. Even today, a few members of the top management are Europeans, as well as many of the instructors. They lend the area an international air.

Stratton is a top-quality ski resort and planned community. Nothing looks out of place; there's no chance of a honky-tonk joint opening down the street from the base lodge. The architecture looks like it all came out of the same shop—and, in large part, it did, $60 million worth since 1984. It attracts many families because of its fine ski school and its easy accessibility to the slopes. There may be no closer-to-the-slopes accommodations anywhere.

And after the day's skiing is done, you have the wonderful small towns and country inns of southern Vermont just a short drive away. Although you can easily spend your time cloistered in the Stratton Village, it also provides a good base from which to explore.

ACCOMMODATIONS: $$ to $$$$ The Stratton Corp. operates a one-call lodging service that handles reservations for the Stratton Mountain Villas and two dozen other lodgings, from lodges to country inns.

The Stratton Mountain Inn offers 125 beautifully decorated rooms just a short shuttle ride from the slopes. Better suited to families is the newer Stratton Village Lodge, right behind the base lodge, which has 91 rooms, some with lofts and each with a kitchenette (children are free in their parents' room).

The Stratton Mountain Villas have one- to five-bedroom condominium units that you can ski in and out of.

Also very close to the mountain are two European-style lodges, the Birkenhaus and the Liftline Lodge, which have a cozy ambience. They are suitable for families with older children.

Special package rates are available at all Stratton Corp. lodgings.

DINING: Stratton has a busy, but friendly, slopeside cafeteria, and another cafeteria at the Sun Bowl Base Lodge; there are outdoor barbecues in spring. The base lodge also has a sit-down restaurant, the Bear's Den, which provides good cooked-to-order food at lunchtime. The Mid-Mountain Restaurant at the base of the North American lift offers complete cafeteria service, as well as a special fast-food kiosk.

Many skiers at Stratton make dinner a real event, trying a different restaurant each evening. For families with children, the best bets on the premises are Sage Hill, Birkenhaus and Liftline Lodge or Mulligans and La Pizzeria in The Village Square.

In the nearby town of Bondville, four miles from the slopes, the River Café is a nice place for dinner, and it welcomes children. Three of the area's finest restaurants, Bear Creek, Sweet Woodruffs, and Jamaica House, are in nearby Jamaica.

THE SKIING: Stratton is in the middle of Vermont's snow belt and receives an average of 170 inches of snow a year, guaranteeing reliable skiing from late October until well into April. Stratton also makes its own snow; 60 percent of the terrain can be covered with machine-made snow.

 Thirty-two novice, 35 intermediate, 25 expert.

 Four quad chairs, one triple, six doubles, one gondola, two surface lifts.

 2,003 feet.

 Three miles.

 Stratton's Ski School has 175 professional instructors, who use the American Teaching Method. Group lessons last one hours each and are held daily at 9:45 A.M. and 1:15 P.M. Individual lessons available.

 Eleven miles of tracked and groomed trails at the new Sun Bowl Cross-Country Ski-Touring Center. Guided moonlight tours along the trail are offered Wednesday nights. Skating trails and 50 kilometers of back country skiing trails available.

ACTIVITIES FOR NON-SKIERS: Stratton offers a full range of other activities each day, including snowshoeing, snowboarding, shopping in The Village Square, après-ski entertainment, and movies in the Bijou Theater.

The Stratton Sports Center is a fully equipped exercise center and spa that offers aerobics and water exercise classes, golf lessons, indoor tennis, and racquetball. Massages and tanning beds are available.

Numerous social activities are offered each week at the base lodge. The Stratton Mountain Boys provide lively après-ski entertainment—yodeling and Tyrolean folk dancing—a few days a week in the Bear's Den. On other days, there's rock and jazz music. The Stratton Village Square has 30 shops and restaurants.

FOR CHILDREN: Stratton is serious about putting kids on skis at an early age; it began one of the first bona fide ski schools for children in the United States, using the SKIwee system. From 8 A.M. to 5 P.M., children between 4 and 6 can attend the "Little Cub" all-day program, which includes between four and five hours of skiing, lunch, and some indoor play. Children under 7 do not need lift tickets.

Children between 6 and 12 go into the "Big Cub" program, running from 8:30 A.M. to 3:45 P.M., which provides all-day supervision and lunch. At 10 A.M. and again at 1:15 P.M., they join the Junior Ski School for lessons. Reservations for both programs are strongly suggested at the time you make your lodging reservations.

For children younger than 4, Stratton provides care in the state-licensed child-care center in the Base Lodge. About 80 children can be accommodated; reservations are suggested. The child-care center operates from 8:30 A.M. to 4:30 P.M. and takes children as young as 6 weeks. With advance notice, extra hours also can be scheduled before the regular program and from 4:30 to 11 P.M. The charge is by the hour (minimum of two hours).

The center provides a variety of activities for infants and toddlers, including arts and crafts, games, storytelling, and songs. There's a separate sleeping room for infants. Lunch and two snacks are served.

NICETIES: The Villager Lift, which provides access to a nice, gentle beginners' slope, is free at all times. That's nice for parents who want to do some skiing with their children—or for a beginner who wants to put in a lot of practice on turns.

A shuttle van and buses operate between all of the on-property lodging, the ski-touring center, the sports center, and the slopes.

Stratton has a multi-level parking garage that is a great alternative to the mud flats at many other New England ski resorts.

OF INTEREST NEARBY: Stratton is about a 20-minute drive from Manchester, Vermont, a charming New England community with dozens of Victorian mansions, lovely country inns and restaurants, and The Equinox, a famous old hotel. It's also a major center for factory outlets; ski wear, sportswear, designer clothes, and kids' clothes can be had for a song. A cross-country touring center is operated on the grounds of the estate of Abraham Lincoln's son in Manchester Village, just beyond the Equinox. The home is operated as a museum in the summer.

IN THE SUMMER: Stratton is a full-service golf and tennis resort in the summer months, with one of the nation's finest golf schools and plenty of other activities for families, too, including horseback riding, expert tennis instruction, carriage rides, windsurfing, and gondola rides. LPGA and women's tennis tournaments are held each summer.

FOR MORE INFORMATION: Call (800) 843-6867 from outside Vermont or (802) 297-2200 or write the Stratton Corporation, R.R. 1, Box 145, Stratton Mountain, VT 05155.

SOUTHWEST AND MOUNTAIN STATES

ASPEN AREA SKI RESORTS
ASPEN MOUNTAIN

TIEHACK MOUNTAIN

SNOWMASS

ASPEN HIGHLANDS

Aspen, Colorado

The silver mines of Aspen had just fallen silent when adventurers began clearing trees so they could streak down the snow on Aspen Mountain. The Aspen area's four slopes now offer a skiing experience that many consider one of the best in the world—and an après-skiing experience that is definitely unparalleled in the United States.

Aspen is an area of high fashion and cowboy boots. It is, as its promotional literature says, at once "rustic and cosmopolitan, tranquil and trendy, historic and futuristic." People go there to ski, and also to be seen.

But that doesn't mean that Aspen isn't for families. Since it was a real town before it became a ski resort, it has lots of inherent charm. Its streets are lined with colorful Victorian houses, and its sizable year-round population means that it has such real-town amenities as playgrounds and good supermarkets and a library.

The Aspen area offers four separate ski areas, each with a different atmosphere and clientele. Aspen Mountain, sometimes called Ajax, overlooks the city of Aspen. Aspen Highlands is located on Maroon Creek Road, southwest of Aspen. Tiehack (formerly called Buttermilk) is located just down Highway 82 from the Highlands. And Snowmass, one of North America's largest mountains, is just a 20-minute drive down Highway 82.

ACCOMMODATIONS: $$ to $$$$ Aspen Central Reservations (800-26-ASPEN) offers a convenient, one-stop reservations service. Prospective visitors can book lodging alone or ski packages that include lodging, lift tickets, airfare, ground transportation, and ski lessons. The agency can book you into a variety of lodgings, from hotels and condominiums to private homes and bed and breakfasts.

The heartbeat of Aspen can be felt at the magnificently restored Hotel Jerome; call (303) 920-1000. Originally opened in 1889, the Belle of the Roaring Fork Valley regained her crown in the mid-1980s after a $30 million renovation and addition.

For something off the beaten track, consider staying at the moderately priced T Lazy 7 Ranch on Maroon Creek Road, just up the road from Aspen Highlands. The ranch offers cabins ranging from rustic to very rustic; many have fireplaces, and all have kitchens. There's a hot tub and sauna and a bar for après-ski gatherings. Transportation is available to the slopes. Phone (303) 925-4614.

Snowmass has 750 comfortable guest rooms in modern lodges ranging from luxurious to the casually simple, including the newly renovated Silvertree Hotel (303-923-3520) and Hotel Wildwood (303-923-3550). And there are more than 1,450 spacious condominiums, many with ski-in-ski-out convenience.

DINING: You can easily dine somewhere different every night. Restaurants like the Hallan Caviar and Abetone Ristorante offer cuisine of international reputation. Most restaurants require reservations.

Families on a budget will like the Hickory House Restaurant and the Aspen Grove Café. Asia Restaurant is a Chinese restaurant specializing in gourmet Mandarin and Hunan cuisine. The Red Onion is a popular local spot serving fine homemade American and Mexican food.

And no trip to Aspen is complete without a meal at Little Annie's, which serves home-cooked foods, such as ribs and chicken.

In Snowmass, there's the Mountain Dragon, the village's only Chinese restaurant; Mama Maria's Pizza & Subs, and La Piñata, famous for double Margaritas and great Mexican food. For elegant mountaintop dining try the High Alpine Restaurant, located at the top of the Alpine Springs lift in the Snowmass ski area.

THE SKIING: All four local ski areas—Aspen, Snowmass, Tiehack and Aspen Highlands—are operated by the Aspen Skiing Co. The skiing season typically extends from Thanksgiving weekend through the Easter week-end, and sometimes beyond. Multiday tickets are available that permit skiing at all four areas.

 Aspen Mountain: 35 percent more difficult, 35 percent most difficult, 30 percent expert.

Snowmass: 10 percent easiest, 62 percent more difficult, 21 percent most difficult, 7 percent expert.

Tiehack: 35 percent easiest, 39 percent more difficult, 26 percent most difficult.

Aspen Highlands: 20 percent novice, 50 percent intermediate, 30 percent advanced.

 Aspen Mountain: One gondola, one high-speed quad chair, two regular quads, four doubles.

Snowmass: Three detachable quad chairs; two triple chairs, nine doubles.

Tiehack: Six double chairs.

Aspen Highlands: Five double chairs, two highspeed quads, two surface lifts.

 Aspen Mountain: 3,267 feet.
Snowmass: 3,615 feet.

Tiehack: 2,030 feet.

Aspen Highlands: 3,800 feet.

 Aspen Mountain: three miles.
Snowmass: four miles.

Tiehack: three miles.

Aspen Highlands: three and one-half miles.

 Ski schools at all areas.

 The largest free cross-country system in the country, with more than 40 miles of groomed trails radiating from the heart of Aspen through forested hillsides to Snowmass Village.

ACTIVITIES FOR NON-SKIERS: Just a few blocks from downtown Aspen is the municipally operated Aspen Ice Garden. Public skating sessions are scheduled throughout the week.

A year-round program of theater, dance, music, and film classics is offered in the historic Wheeler Opera House. Aspen also boasts two public museums, the Aspen Historical Society Museum and the Aspen Art Museum. The Aspen-Snowmass area has more than 50 art galleries and an assortment of eclectic shops.

A guided snowmobile ride is an ideal way to explore the mountains above the Roaring Fork Valley. The T Lazy 7 Ranch on Maroon Creek Road has nearly 50 miles of groomed trails ready for exploring by competent snowmobilers. The trail to secluded Maroon Lake is about seven miles long through towering stands of willowy white aspen trees. The ranch also offers a snowmobile caravan up Independence Pass to the gold-mining ghost town of Independence.

Sleigh rides and guided evening dinner ski tours are available at Pine Creek Cookhouse (303-925-1044) at nearby Ashcroft.

If you'd like to experience the Jack London life-style, you can contact Krabloonik Kennels (303-923-4342) in Snowmass and arrange for a sled and team of dogs. Teams of 13 dogs and a crack guide take guests on two-hour tours of the winter wilderness.

Hot-air balloons ascend each morning for voyages over the Roaring Fork Valley. Several balloon companies offer regular flights.

FOR CHILDREN: Call (800) 525-6200 for detailed information about children's ski schools at all four mountains. Reservations are advisable.

Aspen Mountain: No ski school or on-site day care for children. A special shuttle, "Max the Moose Express," transports children morning and late afternoon between the Aspen Mountain Gondola Building and the children's ski school at Tiehack.

Snowmass: "Snowmass Snow Cubs" is a state-licensed children's ski-and-play school for children ages 1 through 3 in the Timbermill Building on the Snowmass Mall. Three-year-olds are introduced to skiing on a contoured slope. Full and half days available; reservations required.

"Big Burn Bears" is a ski program for children ages 4 through kindergarten. It offers ski instruction in small groups of similar abilities, and provides hot lunches and snacks. Full and half days available.

A special picnic on Wednesdays and a "Fun Race" on Thursdays are highlights of the week.

Special classes for teens only are offered daily at Snowmass. Activities include races, picnics, ice-skating and pizza parties.

Apres-ski care is available from 4 to 11 P.M. for 3- through 12-year-olds for an hourly fee at Nighthawks Evening Child Care.

Tiehack: "Powder Pandas" is a learn-to-ski program from 8:30 A.M. to 4 P.M. daily for children between 3 and 6. It meets at the Panda House off Tiehack Road. The fee includes a hot lunch, snacks and indoor play activities.

Children from first grade through age 12 can attend ski school together, in classes divided by ability; the fee includes a supervised lunch.

Except over the Christmas and Easter holidays, children's ski rentals (12 and under) are free with an adult rental at Buttermilk Sports, at the base of Tiehack.

Teens-only classes are offered over the Christmas and Eastern holidays. And Tiehack's "Learn to Snowboard" program will appeal to the hot dogs in your family. Both Snowmass and Tiehack have special snowboard-only parks and half-pipes.

Fort Frog is an on-the-slopes children's adventure and video center at Tiehack.

Aspen Highlands: "Snow Puppies" is the ski school for 3- to 6-year-olds. Supervised by specially trained and very patient instructors, children are taught skiing safety, etiquette, and basic skills. The program operates from 9:30 A.M. to 3:30 P.M. daily; the fee includes lift tickets, lessons, and lunch. Aspen Highlands also offers the "Kids Camp" for kids 7 to 12. It meets daily from 10:15 A.M. until 3:30 P.M. The charge includes lifts, lessons, and a variety of fun activities.

Baby-sitting for younger children can be arranged only on an individual basis (ask the Snow Puppies staff for referrals).

Children 12 and under ski free with a paying adult.

NICETIES: Many winter visitors find car rental is unnecessary because of the free shuttle buses connecting the town with the slopes.

IN THE SUMMER: Aspen is a terrific summer destination for families, with boundless opportunities for hiking, fishing, whitewater rafting, ballooning, and just plain sightseeing. The nearby Maroon Bells Wilderness Area is a wonderful place for hiking, fishing, and camping. In the summer Aspen becomes Colorado's cultural arts center, with a dizzying schedule of performances by the Aspen Music Festival, the DanceAspen Summer Festival, and the Aspen Theatre Company.

FOR MORE INFORMATION: Call Aspen Central Reservations at (800) 26-ASPEN or (303) 925-9000. Call Snowmass Central Reservations at (800) 332-3245.

For detailed information about ski programs at all four slopes, call the Aspen Skiing Co. at (800) 525-6200.

CRESTED BUTTE MOUNTAIN RESORT
Crested Butte, Colorado

Crested Butte isn't a ski area you just stumble upon. It's at the end of a paved road, nowhere near an interstate highway, 230 miles from Denver, and decidedly not on the way to anywhere else. You have to set out for Crested Butte in order to end up there. Yet tens of thousands of skiers make it their chosen destination every year.

The reason? There are many: the charm of an authentic Old West town whose downtown area is a National Historic District; locals who love living here year-round; a spectacular setting amidst six mountain peaks that exceed 14,000 feet, and absolutely free skiing for children who are accompanied by a paying adult.

And from just after Thanksgiving to mid-December, everybody skis free at Crested Butte (no kidding).

ACCOMMODATIONS: $ to $$$$ The area offers lodging for 6,000 visitors in condominiums, lodges, bed and breakfasts, and a luxury hotel, the Grande Butte Hotel. Crested Butte Vacations offers a one-call booking service (800-544-8448).

For a family of intermediate to expert skiers, secluded Irwin Lodge, North America's highest-year-round, full-service resort, provides the most unique skiing experience in the area. Snocats gives skiers access to untouched powder and natural terrain with a thrilling 2,000-foot vertical drop; after skiing, you can retreat to one of the 25 cozy guest rooms atop a convivial lodge with a gourmet restaurant. Call (800) 2-IRWIN-2.

DINING: When you get there, pick up a copy of Menu Magazine for a quick look at the offerings of almost all of the area's restaurants.

The Bakery Cafe has wonderful breads, pastries, soups, sandwiches and natural food offerings. The Slogar Bar & Restaurant is famous for its skillet-fried chicken and family-style service. In the evenings, families will feel welcome at the Powerhouse Bar & Grill, which serves Mexican food in the town's old water-driven powerhouse, and the IdleSpur, a restaurant and micro-brewery that serves sandwiches and steaks in surroundings with a western motif.

THE SKIING: Over the last three decades, Crested Butte has had the highest average snowfall of any ski town in Colorado: 229 inches a year, compared with 153 at Aspen and 145 at Dillon. The expert-only North Face contains some of the most daring ski terrain in the country.

 Eighty-five trails, 22 percent beginner, 60 percent intermediate, 18 percent advanced, 48 percent expert (plus 550 acres of double black diamond ungroomed terrain).

 Three triple chairs, four doubles, four surface lifts, two high-speed quads.

 3,062 feet.

 2.3 miles.

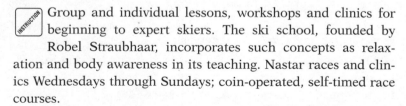 Group and individual lessons, workshops and clinics for beginning to expert skiers. The ski school, founded by Robel Straubhaar, incorporates such concepts as relaxation and body awareness in its teaching. Nastar races and clinics Wednesdays through Sundays; coin-operated, self-timed race courses.

On a 30-km groomed track system at the downtown Nordic Ski Center at the Crested Butte Club; rentals, instruction.
Guided backcountry tours through Elk Mountains and Paradise Divide, including overnight excursions utilizing wilderness huts. Periodic Nordic races through the winter.

ACTIVITIES FOR NON-SKIERS: Until you've ridden a horse over a snow-packed trail, you've no idea what a special experience that can be. Call (303) 349-5425 to arrange.

Hot-air balloon rides are available year-round from Bighorn Balloon, the highest altitude balloon company in North America; call (303) 349-6335.

Adventurers will enjoy snowmobiling through the Elk Mountains, including lunch and dinner tours (303-349-5031) or special Snocat powder tours from Irwin Lodge (303-349-5308).

FOR CHILDREN: Crested Butte's big lure for families is free skiing almost every day of the season for each child, 12 and under, accompanied by a ticket-purchasing adult (a few blackout days apply).

The Crested Butte Mountain Resort Children's Ski Center, in the Whetstone Building right on the mountain, offers half- or full-day nursery care for infants through 2-year-olds in a cheerful setting; reservations are mandatory (303-349-2259).

Children ages 3 to 7 can be enrolled in either day-care (no skiing) or the "ABC's on Skis" program. Graduates of the ABC program and children who are experienced lift riders can take half- or full-day group lessons. One-on-one lessons for 2 to 7-year-olds are also offered. (For a small extra fee, parents can tag along with the private lessons and learn how to coach their child on basic skills.)

For children between 8 and 12, the "Butte Buster" program offers half- and full-day instruction.

NICETIES: There's a free shuttle bus between Mt. Crested Butte and the downtown area.

For intermediate skiers, there's a free two-hour guided tour of the mountain three times a day; advanced skiers can sign on for a free tour of the Extreme Limits of the North Face and Phoenix Bowl twice daily.

IN THE SUMMER: Crested Butte is the official "Wildflower Capital of Colorado," and in the summer the ski slopes, roadsides, and mountain meadows are ablaze with millions of blooms, including the heavenly Colorado columbine. The famed Rocky Mountain Biological Laboratory (303-349-7231) in nearby Gothic offers special adult nature walks, family field tours, and children's nature workshops through the summer.

There's golf at the Skyland Country Club on a 7,200-yard course designed by Robert Trent Jones Jr.

FOR MORE INFORMATION: Call Crested Butte Mountain Resort at (800-544-8448) or (303) 349-2281.

STEAMBOAT SKI AREA
Steamboat Springs, Colorado

Steamboat has been playing host to skiers since 1962, when local developers built a ski lift and modest warming house on Storm Mountain in northern Colorado. The area's commitment to family skiers was evident almost from the start; the nursery building was added just two years after the opening. But it wasn't until 1969 that the development of Steamboat Village Resort began in earnest. A series of regular improvements nearly every year since then has resulted in one of the nation's premier ski resorts. The ski area boasts that it has Colorado's biggest lift system, "trails so long you have to stop to catch your breath, and mountain panoramas so vast they will leave you breathless."

Steamboat has the feel of a family resort; fancy furs and Ferragamos are few and far between, and in the parking lots, minivans and Suburbans predominate over sports cars and imported sedans.

ACCOMMODATIONS: $ to $$$$ The selection is eclectic. The area offers everything from the inexpensive downtown Rabbit Ear's Motel to expensive mountainside luxury condominiums like Torian and Bearclaw. Less expensive condominium accommodations are available at Ptarmigan House, Storm Meadows, and Thunderhead Lodge. The Steamboat Reservations Service (800-922-2722) can match you with a place that suits your needs.

DINING: A range of food, with an emphasis on western specialties, is available in more than 60 restaurants on and around the mountain and in town.

On one of the nights when the stars came out with a special brilliance, we took the ski area's 8-passenger high-speed gondola to a place called Hazie's. The menu offers everything from steak to sushi. The view of the setting sun and, later, the twinkling lights of Steamboat Springs and the sprawling Yampa River basin were spectacular. It's a special place for a parents' night out. Reservations are necessary.

Also at the ski area, the Thunderhead facility at the upper terminal of the Silver Bullet has a cafeteria and a barbecue sun deck. The Rendezvous Saddle facility, in the Priest Creek area, offers fine dining, with unusual Norwegian specialties at Ragnar's. There's also a barbecue deck and a cafteria on the second and third floor.

For those who choose to prepare some or all of their meals in a condominium kitchen, there are two supermarkets near the mountain (and on the bus loop).

THE SKIING: Steamboat's season normally runs from late November to mid-April, with the regular season beginning around mid-December. The ski area covers a mountain range that includes Sunshine Peak, Storm Peak, Thunderhead Peak, and Christie Peak, and encompasses 2,500 acres, of which 1,400 are groomed. The elevation is 10,568 feet at the top; 9,080 midway, and 6,900 at the base. Snowfall can hit 350 inches a season. Steamboat's snow is among the best in the West.

 107 cut trails, plus glades: 15 percent novice, 54 percent intermediate, 31 percent advanced.

 One gondola, two high speed detachable quads, one quad chair, six triples, eight doubles, two surface lifts.

 3,668 feet.

 Three miles.

Fully staffed ski school, all levels of instruction. NASTAR Racing Clinics for youngsters and grown-ups Tuesday through Sunday (two hours of coaching and a videotape analysis). There's a timed race course open from 9:30 A.M. to 3:30 P.M. daily. Billy Kidd is the head counselor at two- and three-day race camps throughout the season.

The Steamboat Ski Touring Center maintains 33 miles of trails, with guided tours and moonlight journeys by appoint-ment. Some area inns offer their own cross-country programs.

ACTIVITIES FOR NON-SKIERS: The ski area's promoters put together a series of special events every year, including torchlight parades and the popular Winter Carnival, which features ski racing and jumping, hot-air balloon racing, parades, and fireworks.

Regular offerings at Steamboat include hot-air balloon rides, bobsledding, sleigh rides, ice-skating, bowling, and movies.

Don't miss a soak in one of the area's hot springs, either downtown or at Strawberry Fields.

FOR CHILDREN: Except over the December holidays, kids under 12 stay and ski free at Steamboat if their parents book a minimum of five nights at a Steamboat Springs Chamber/Resort Association member lodge and if they purchase lift tickets for themselves for five or more days. Children also get free ski rentals when their parents rent skis for five or more days.

The Kids' Vacation Center gives 2- to 6-year-olds all-day or half-day classes that include instruction, games, and lunch. Children must be out of diapers in order to participate.

"Rough Rider Ski School" is open to children from 6 to 15.

The Kiddie Corral Child Care facility at the lower Silver Bullet terminal operates from 8 A.M. to 5 P.M. daily, with half-day care available, morning or afternoon. The facility welcomes children as young as 6 months, but food for children under 2 years must be supplied by the parents.

Evening care is offered for children from 6 months through 12 years on Tuesdays through Saturdays during the ski season.

NICETIES: Steamboat operates a "host and hostess" program in which employees are stationed on the mountain and in the information center to give directions, inform visitors about activities, help reunite parents with lost children, and generally keep the peace.

IN THE SUMMER: Summertime here offers vigorous hikes into the surrounding Routt National Forest, horseback rides through Aspen groves, llama trekking, rafting on the Colorado and

Yampa rivers, the Friday night rodeo, golf at two public courses, including Robert Trent Jones Jr.'s 18-hole course at the Sheraton Steamboat, fishing for mountain trout, boating on Steamboat Lake and Stagecoach Reservoir, bicycling on the new trail system along the Yampa River or on mountain-bike trails, gondola or balloon rides, and thrill-filled voyages down the municipal waterslide.

Steamboat is also known for its summer festivals: Cowboy Roundup Days in July; Strings in the Mountains Chamber Music Festival in July and August, Steamboat's Summer Children's Jubilee, Rainbow Weekend, a ballooning competition, and the annual Vintage Auto Race & Concours d'Elegance.

FOR MORE INFORMATION: Call (800) 922- 2722 or (303) 879-6111 or write 2305 Mt. Werner Circle, Steamboat Springs, CO 80487.

SUMMIT COUNTY SKI RESORTS

BRECKENRIDGE

COPPER MOUNTAIN

KEYSTONE

Summit County, Colorado

Summit County, Colorado, has one of the greatest concentrations of world-class ski resorts, skiable terrain, diverse accommodations and après-ski activities of any county in the nation.

Just 90 miles west of Denver's new international airport via Interstate 70, Summit County offers skiing conditions that will please skiers of any ability. And through "Ski the Summit," the ski areas' joint marketing program, skiers can purchase coupons that entitle them to ski at all of the areas for less than the price of a lift ticket at a single area. On a week-long ski vacation, you may find you never have to ski the same trail twice! Each area has its own appeal and an army of diehard loyalists who proclaim it their favorite.

Breckenridge, the largest and most popular of the county's ski areas, has the charm of an old Victorian mining town, complete with a 350-building historic district.

ACCOMMODATIONS: $ to $$$$ You can stay at any one of more than 100 condominium complexes with one- to four-bedroom units, quaint bed and breakfasts, cozy country lodges, or the Keystone Lodge, which has earned a four-diamond rating from AAA.

Each of the ski areas offers its own central reservations service. At Breckenridge, accommodations are found both in town and at the Village at several slopeside hotel complexes; Breckenridge boasts more ski-in-ski-out lodgings that any ski resort in North America. Call the Breckenridge Resort Chamber at (800) 221-1091 (800-822- 5381 within Colorado).

All of Copper Mountain's accommodations are within walking distance of the ski slopes. Guests who stay anywhere at Copper Mountain have privileges at the Racquet and Athletic Club, which offers year-round tennis, hot tubs, saunas, steambaths, exercise classes, and therapeutic massage. For Copper Mountain reservations, call (800) 458-8386.

Keystone Lodge, a member of Preferred Hotels Worldwide, offers luxury hotel rooms right next to the Keystone slopes; in addition, Keystone Resort has almost 1,000 rental condominiums and private homes. For lodge reservations, call (800) 541-0346; for Keystone condominium reservations, call (800) 222-0188.

A cozy alternative is the rustic Ski Tip Lodge, which offers 22 quaint rooms decorated with antiques in a restored stagecoach stop next door to the cross-country center (303-468-4202).

DINING: Breckenridge alone has more than 100 restaurants, including 14 on its three ski mountains and their bases. Many others are in the lovingly restored Victorian-era bulidings in the downtown historic district.

Copper Mountain has about 20 eating establishments, ranging from O'Shea's Copper Bar at the base of the American Eagle Lift to the elegant Pesce Fresco restaurant in the Mountain Plaza.

Keystone has about 20 restaurants, ranging from very casual to highly elegant. The Edgewater Cafe in Keystone lodge and Razzberry's at the Keystone Inn are popular for breakfast. Lunch is usually a quick bite at one of the base lodges. At night, the Last Lift Bar at the mountain and Montezuma's in the village are popular watering holes. Garden Room Restaurant in the Lodge, the mountaintop Outpost, and Ski Tip Lodge are nice places for dinner.

THE SKIING: Breckenridge offers three distinct ski mountains, each with its own personality. Copper Mountain is widely regarded as a "skier's mountain," with an award-winning trail system that features naturally separated terrain for beginning, intermediate and expert skiers. And Keystone offers four distinct ski experiences: the groomed boulevards of Keystone Mountain, the moguled challenges of North Peak, the exhilaration of Arapahoe Basin (the continent's highest lift-served ski area), and the untamed ski experience of The Outback, with above timberline, gladed and trail skiing. With many of its trails lighted, Keystone can guarantee 13 hours of skiing every day.

 Breckenridge: 126 trails; 18 percent beginner, 27 percent intermediate, 55 percent advanced.

Copper Mountain: 98 trails; 22 percent beginner, 27 percent intermediate, 51 percent advanced.

Keystone: 89 trails; 13 percent beginner, 34 percent intermediate, 53 percent advanced. (At Arapahoe Basin: 61 trails; 10 percent beginner, 50 percent intermediate, 40 percent advanced.)

 Breckenridge: four quad superchairs, one triple, eight doubles, three surface.

Copper Mountain: two quad superchairs, six triples, eight doubles, four surface.

Keystone and Arapahoe: two gondolas, four quad superchairs, four triples, 10 doubles, four surface.

 Breckenridge: 3,400 feet.
Copper Mountain: 2,760 feet.
Keystone: 2,680 feet;
Arapahoe Basin: 2,250 feet.

 Breckenridge: Three and one-half miles.
Copper Mountain: Almost three miles.
Keystone: Three miles;
Arapahoe: One and one-half miles.

 Ski schools at all areas. Breckenridge offers special "women only" lessons with female instructors upon request, and Copper Mountain offers several Women's Skiing Seminars throughout the season. Breckenridge also has one of the most complete programs for disabled skiers anywhere.

In the county, a total of 73 miles of groomed cross country and ski-skating trails, plus more than 320,000 acres of skiable backcountry terrain. Breckenridge has 13 miles of double-set cross country trails next to the ski area; the Breckenridge Nordic Center offers torchlight skiing and a nordic program for disabled skiers. Copper Mountain's Trak Cross Country Center has 15 miles of groomed trails. Keystone has 16 miles of groomed trails, plus guided tours into national forest lands.

Helicopter skiing in the backcountry can be arranged for groups.

ACTIVITIES FOR NON-SKIERS: There's ice-skating on the largest outdoor rink in the country (at Keystone) and the West Lake at Copper Mountain. Romantic horse-drawn sleigh rides depart in the evening for swings through the village at Copper Mountain and historic Breckenridge. You can take Keystone's gondola to the summit for a candlelit fondue dinner. The Keystone Science School (303-468- 5824) offers talks by naturalists on Friday nights from January through mid- April. For the adventuresome, there's snowmobiling in the backcountry and even dogsled rides. Theatrical performances and tours of Breckenridge's Historical District are offered through the winter.

FOR CHILDREN: At Breckenridge, the "Fanta-Ski Kingdom" program offers a full day of skiing instruction, supervised skiing, and just plain fun for children 6 to 12.

Three-year-olds can take an introductory skiing course, with lessons no more than 90 minutes in length; 4- and 5-year-olds can be enrolled in the Junior Ski School for 90-minute lessons. The resort's specially designed terrain gardens make learning fun. (Parents must provide the skis and boots.)

Two daycare centers, at the Peak 8 and Peak 9 base areas, provide child care for non-skiing children as young as two months. Half-, full-day, and hourly rates available. Up-to-date immunization records must be provided for children under 12 months. Reservations are essential; call (303) 453-2368.

At Copper Mountain, the "Belly Button Bakery" at the base of the mountain provides care for children from 2 months on up. The center has special areas for arts and crafts, reading, storytime, creative play, and outdoor snow play. Children 3 and older can try to ski. A highlight of each day is baking cookies, cakes, pizza, and other goodies, which are presented to parents at the end of the day. The Junior and Senior Ranch skiing programs meet on the ground floor of the center.

Copper Mountain's "Junior Ranch," for ages 4 to 6, enjoys its own ski lift close to indoor facilities that have games, cubbies for storage, and overnight ski storage. The "Senior Ranch," for ages 7 through 12, gives children easy access to the entire mountain with a small group of children of similar age and ability. Children stay with the same instructor all day, eat lunch with their class, and ski as much as time allows.

The Keystone children's programs operate out of two Children's Centers, one at Keystone Mountain and the other at Arapahoe Basin, from 8 A.M. to 5 P.M. At Keystone Mountain, care is provided for children ages two months on up; at Arapahoe Basin, the minimum age is 18 months. Call (303) 468-4182 for reservations.

The "Mini-Minor's Camp," for 3- and 4-year-olds, and the "Minor's Camp," for 5- to 12-year-olds, include lift tickets, lessons, lunch, and equipment rental in the fee. Call (303) 468-4170 for reservatons.

NICETIES: Getting around the Summit County ski areas is made easy by the Summit Stage, the free shuttle service that runs from early morning until late evening.

Breckenridge offers free skier evaluations every day from 12:30 P.M. to 1:15 P.M. at the mountaintop restaurants.

IN THE SUMMER: The Breckenridge Golf Club features the only public course in the world designed by Jack Nicklaus. Bicycling is popular along miles of country roads or the paved two-lane bicycle path that links Breckenridge with Copper Mountain, and the mountain's water slide attracts thousands of tourists.

Tiger Run Tours (303-453-2231) offers backcountry jeep tours, gold-panning, and whitewater rafting. The Breckenridge Music Institute's summer festival runs from late June through July, with numerous chamber orchestra concerts, workshops, and lectures. (The 90-piece National Repertory Orchestra performs through the summer.) Other special summer events include fishing contests, arts and crafts fairs, a water toy festival, mountain-bike races, and a jazz festival.

Copper Mountain lures summer vacationers with paddleboat and chairlift rides, miles of paved bike paths, whitewater rafting, fly-fishing in Ten Mile Creek, a mid-mountain nature center, a special kids' fishing pond, boundless hiking opportunities, and guided horseback rides. The Copper Creek Golf Club, designed by Pete Dye, has the highest altitude championship course in the United States. The Belly Button Bakery operates through the summer.

Keystone has one of the most comprehensive summer activity programs of any ski resort. Many summer visitors don't even think of it as a ski resort; to them, it's a mecca for golf, sailing, tennis, hiking, and just relaxing. It's famous for its Keystone Tennis Center and for its championship 7,090-yard golf course designed by Robert Trent Jones Jr. For children, Keystone offers all-day or half-day summer programs, beginning at 2 months of age. Activities include hiking, swimming, boating, arts and crafts, and pony rides.

FOR MORE INFORMATION: Write Ski the Summit, P.O. Box 98, Dillon, CO 80435, or phone (303) 468-6607.

TELLURIDE SKI RESORT
Telluride, Colorado

The secluded town of Telluride is as attractive a ski resort as you'll find anywhere in Colorado. Nestled in a valley deep in the San Juan Mountains, this old mining town, with its brightly painted Victorian houses and cosmopolitan atmosphere, exudes charm.

With the awesome beauty of the surrounding mountains as a backdrop, the skiing here is a special experience too. The slopes on the San Juan mountains rise up on the very edge of town, and the views from the ski trails are spectacular enough to prompt a skier to pack a camera on a sunny day. Ski round a bend on a trail on the mountain and you will find Telluride almost straight down, several thousand feet below you, literally at your ski tips.

Named for a kind of ore in which gold is found (tellurium), the town itself is tiny, about six streets wide by 12 streets long, with a year-round population of about 1,200. You will find no Dairy Queen here; Telluride's strict zoning codes ensure the town's quaintness. The downtown area is a National Historic District.

But Telluride and the ski resort are expanding to meet the growing number of skiers that come here. And there's no shortage of après-ski activity, with interesting restaurants, shops, and pubs to try out after the day's skiing is done.

Telluride opened in 1972 with five lifts and 20 ski trails. In 1979, the resort was purchased from the original developer by Benchmark Companies, which also developed property at Avon, Colorado. Much has since been spent on new lifts and trails, and the development of Mountain Village Resort, where the $68 million Peaks at Telluride Hotel & Spa (formerly the Doral) is located.

ACCOMMODATIONS: $$ to $$$$ Telluride's accommodations are concentrated in the town, where 80 percent are within walking distance of the base facilities, and at Mountain Village Resort, where 95 percent are ski-in-ski-out. You can choose from condominiums, bed and breakfasts in old Victorian homes, and rooms in the Peaks at Telluride Resort and Spa. The staff answering the central reservation number (800-525-3455) can direct you to accommodations that best suit your needs and budget. You can also use this number to arrange lift tickets and air or ground transportation.

DINING: Telluride has about 25 restaurants, many of them with interesting interiors and menus, ranging from ethnic cuisine to continental cuisine and seafood.

At the base of lifts 3 and 4 in Mountain Village Resort, the Cactus Cafe offers Mexican food and the Paradise Cafe offers pizza, soup and sandwiches. At mid-mountain, the Gorrono Ranch and Saloon offers a full cafeteria, self-service deli, barbecue, and full-service bar. Once the site of an old ranch, the Gorrono Ranch has magnificent mountain views. Giuseppe's Restaurant is at the top of Telluride's expert slopes, and offers pizza, Italian sandwiches, soup, beer and wine.

THE SKIING: With an average snowfall each year of 300 inches, Telluride usually has snow when other ski resorts may not. The mountain has a summit of 12,247 feet and a base of 8,735 feet.

Sixty-four trails: 21 percent novice, 47 percent intermediate, 32 expert.

 One quad chair, two triples, six doubles, one surface lift.

 3,522 feet.

 Almost three miles.

 Ski school with 75 instructors. Beginners learn the basics at the Meadows and Sunshine Peak. Sunshine Peak has gentle glades and broad, well-groomed trails for the beginner and the "never-ever" skier.

 Fifty miles of groomed trails and backcountry skiing maintained by the Telluride Nordic Center. Equipment rentals, private and group lessons and guided backcountry tours.

Experience helicopter skiing over spectacular scenery in the Uncompahgre and San Juan national forests. A high Alpine tour designed for skiers of all abilities includes a gourmet lunch and ground transportation (303-728-4904).

ACTIVITIES FOR THE NON-SKIER: Deep Creek Sleigh Rides will take you on a dinner ride on a 16-passenger sleigh; call (303) 728-4142. Another option is snowmobiling around the high country meadows of Alta Lakes and Beaver Park; call Telluride Outside at (303) 728-3895. Telluride Outfitters offers trail rides in the foothills of the Black Canyon even in the deep of winter; call (303) 728- 3895. San Juan Balloon Adventures offers dawn and brunch rides; call (303) 728-3895.

Telluride's Town Park Ice Rink offers free ice-skating parties every Wednesday night in the winter, with hot refreshments, music and a roaring fire in the warming shelter; call (303) 728-3851. You can take a self-guided walking tour of the Telluride National Historic District using a map available at the Visitor's Center. Or visit the San Miguel County Historical Museum at 317 N. Fir St.

Indulge yourself at the Peaks' full-service spa, which offers an indoor lap pool (with a slide down to an indoor/outdoor pool), a circuit weight-training facility, squash and racquetball courts, steam baths, sauna, indoor and outdoor whirlpools, and massage and skin therapies.

FOR CHILDREN: Telluride offers a variety of children's programs, starting with the Village Nursery for children 2 months to 3 years old. Day care is provided from 8:30 A.M. to 4:30 P.M. in Le Chamonix Complex near the Mountain Village base facility; lunch is included. The adult-to-child ratio is one-to-two for children under 2.

The resort's "Snowstar" program introduces 3- to 5-year-olds to skiing with a combination of snow play, ski lessons, and indoor play. Children learn the parts of the ski and the basic movements indoors in front of a mirror; the emphasis is on fun. The adult-to-child ratio is one-to-three. For information and reservations, call (303) 728-4424.

The "Telstar Ski School" offers lessons to children age 6 to 12. Lunch is included in the daily fee.

NICETIES: A free shuttle bus to the ski resort operates every 12 minutes during the ski season from the city of Telluride. Another free shuttle bus takes skiers from Telluride to the Mountain Village Resort.

There are protected tissue boxes at each of the chair lifts.

IN THE SUMMER: Summer is special here. The mountain meadows are ablaze with wildflowers, and the town hops with festivals, special events, and seminars. Among them: the Telluride Balloon Rally, Bicycle Classic, and Bluegrass Festival in June; the Telluride Wine Festival, Firemen's Barbecue, Alpine Wildflower Photography Workshop, and Rotary 4 X 4 Rally in July; the Telluride Jazz Festival and Chamber Music Festival in August, and the Film Festival, Hang Gliding Festival, and Bicycle Tour of the San Juans in September.

The Telluride Institute (303-728-4981) offers special interest camps, seminars, and retreats through the summer.

A new lure to golfers: the 18-hole, high-country golf course with a 7,009-yard championship tee, which opened in July 1991 at the Telluride Mountain Resort Village. Summer also offers horseback riding, tennis, fishing, hiking, horseback riding, mountain biking and kayaking.

FOR MORE INFORMATION: Call the Telluride Ski Resort at (303) 728-3856 or write Box 11155, Telluride, CO 81435. For ski school, child care, and rental equipment reservations, call the Telluride Ski Resort at (303) 728-4424.

VAIL/BEAVER CREEK
Eagle County, Colorado

It can't be just good luck that continually earns Vail the highest ratings by readers of national ski publications. Skiers vote with their feet as well, and more choose to ski at Vail every year than at any other Colorado ski resort (and all but one other in the nation).

One reason for its phenomenal allure is that Vail has the country's largest ski mountain, with 4,014 acres of runs. It also has perhaps the best children's ski programs anywhere, and some of the most impressive nursery and day-care facilities we've seen. Add to that its easy accessibility, a natural, gladed bobsled run, a snowboarding park, plenty of breathtaking upper-mountain intermediate ski areas, a dazzling array of après-ski activites, and a world-famous reputation, and it's easy to understand why many families return to Vail year after year.

For the last decade, part of the draw has also been Vail's nearby sister ski area, Beaver Creek, a beautifully designed resort that is particularly attractive to families because of its self-contained, intimate feeling.

ACCOMMODATIONS: $ to $$$$ Vail offers accommodations in every price range, from motels affiliated with most of the national chains to on-mountain condos to in-town guest houses and bed and breakfasts. The Westin Resort-Vail (303-476-5031) has its own ski lift direct to the top of the mountain. For all reservations in Vail, call (800) 525-2257.

There are 4,700 beds within the Beaver Creek Resort, all luxurious and all quite close to the slopes. Among the hotels are the Hyatt Regency Beaver Creek, with its year-round outdoor pool and its own children's program; the Beaver Creek Lodge, an all-suite hotel, and the Park Plaza, which offers elegant two to three-bedroom apartments, many with a family-sized Jacuzzi in the master bath. For all reservations in Beaver Creek, call (800) 622-3131.

DINING: Vail and Beaver Creek together have more than 100 restaurants, with cuisines ranging from haute French to Malaysian to Mexican to Western.

At Vail, the Two Elk Restaurant, new in 1991, offers Southwestern, Western, and American food in a beautifully decorated cafeteria-style facility, elevation 11,200 feet, overlooking the majestic China Bowl.

Spruce Saddle, at Beaver Creek, is a mid-mountain restaurant that serves skiers coq au vin, red or green chili, and fresh deli sandwiches. Its upstairs adjunct, Rafters, serves pastas, salmon, salads, and hearty stews in a clublike atmosphere.

A very special dining experience is offered at Beano's Cabin on Beaver Creek Mountain. For a fixed price, visitors can enjoy a sleigh ride from the mountain base to the log restaruant, followed by an elegant dinner in front of a blazing fire. (In the summer, the restaurant is reachable by van, horseback, or horse-drawn wagon.)

THE SKIING: Only the front side of Vail's mountain is visible to skiers at the base. There are runs there suitable for skiers of all levels of expertise. But it's the back side, with its expansive bowls, that has made Vail legendary.

Beaver Creek's newest terrain, Grouse Mountain, opened to skiers in 1991 on a ridge on the western section of the mountain. It features undulating terrain and long, sweeping expanses, with enough steep, gladed parks to thrill any expert.

 Vail: Front side, 32 percent beginner, 36 percent intermediate, 32 percent advanced; back side, 36 percent intermediate, 64 percent advanced.

Beaver Creek: 18 percent beginner, 39 percent intermediate, 43 percent advanced.

 Vail: Eight high-speed quads, two fixed-grip quads, one gondola, two triples, six doubles, two surface lifts.

Beaver Creek: Two high-speed quads, five triples, four doubles.

 Vail: 3,250 feet.
Beaver Creek: 3,340 feet.

 Vail: Four and one-half miles.
Beaver Creek: Almost three miles.

Vail's 700 ski instructors and Beaver Creek's 400 offer classes that aim to make any skier better, from the novice to the black-diamond connoisseur. Among the tools: video analysis with on-slope viewing centers, SyberVision role-model tapes, and express lift-lanes for ski-school participants. Expert skiers can sign on for a session with a "super guide"; in this program, small groups receive light coaching as they explore seldom-skied areas of the mountains.

The Vail and Beaver Creek Cross-Country Ski School (303-476-5601) offers instruction for every level of Nordic skier, including telemarkers. Also offered are all-day nature tours in the White River National Forest, gourmet tours, and overnight hut tours along the Tenth Mountain Trail.

Vail's Nordic Center has 11 miles of groomed trails. At Beaver Creek, McCoy Park, reachable by its own lift, offers 18 miles of machine-set double track that meander through aspen groves and alpine glades.

ACTIVITIES FOR THE NON-SKIER: You needn't ever put on skis to have a good time at either of these resorts. Among the options for the adventuresome are snowmobile tours at secluded Piney River Ranch, backcountry tours by a 12-passenger heated Snocat, horsedrawn sleigh rides and guided snowshoe walks. All arrangements can be made through the Adventure Co. (303-949-9090).

The free Hot Winter Night ski shows, generally on Wednesday nights at Vail, combine synchronized skiing, technical displays, comedy demonstrations, and aerials with a light show, music, and fireworks. On Thursday nights at Beaver Creek, the torchlight ski-down is a must-see. The best viewing spot is on the Hyatt Regency patio.

For shoppers, Vail and Beaver Creek offer dozens of interesting shops.

FOR CHILDREN: Both Vail and Beaver Creek take children's ski instruction very seriously, but one of their goals is to ensure that children also have the time of their lives. At both ski areas, instruction takes place on a Children's Adventure Mountain, which integrates a taste of Colorado's colorful history with teaching as children ski through attractions like a "gold mine," an "Indian village," or a "frontier town." Sport Goofy, the resorts' ambassador of skiing and good sportsmanship, stops by every day to check on the kids' progress.

All-day classes are offered for 3- to 12-year olds at the children's skiing centers at Lionshead and Golden Peak in Vail and at the base of the mountain at Beaver Creek. There are special children's rental shops in the Golden Peak and Beaver Creek Children's Skiing Centers.

For non-skiing children between 2 months and 6 years, the on-mountain Small World Play Schools provide licensed day-care with low adult to child ratios (evening care for an hourly fee is available at Beaver Creek). Advance reservations are required for the nursery: call Golden Peak at (303) 479-5044 and Beaver Creek at (303) 845-5345.

Teenagers will be attracted to the special snowboarding and racing programs.

Special family activities include Family Night Out on winter Tuesdays, featuring dinner and a performance by the Beaver Creek Children's Theatre; Kids' Night Out Goes Western, on winter Thursdays at Golden Peak Children's Skiing Center; K2/Sport Goofy Challenge on Fridays at Vail's Gitchegumee Gulch and Beaver Creek's Buckaroo Bowl, and Après-Ski with Sport Goofy. Call the Family Activity Line at (303) 479-2048 for details.

NICETIES: Parents with infants in the nursery can borrow a personal beeper so that they can be reached in an instant.

At Vail, there's a free intra-resort bus system. Beaver Creek has a free "dial-a-ride" service. Regular bus service also links the two ski areas.

Cindy Nelson, an Olympic medalist, offers free pointers every Wednesday at Beaver Creek and every Thursday at Vail. Other free extras include daily ski trips for intermediate to expert skiers and a "Meet the Mountain" tour several days a week.

IN THE SUMMER: Vail and Beaver Creek are wonderful family vacation destinations in the summer. Marked hiking trails and separate mountain-biking trails crisscross both mountains, and hundreds of miles of trails meander through the nearby White River National Forest and the Eagle's Nest Wilderness as well. Vail's Lionshead Gondola and Beaver Creek's Centennial Express chairlift operate throughout the summer.

There are five 18-hole golf courses in the valley. At Piney River Ranch, 13 miles north of Vail, families can rent rowboats or canoes and take guided horseback rides (there's even a supervised play area for children too young to ride). One night each week, there's a special Western night for families featuring a performance by the excellent Beaver Creek Children's Theater.

Beaver Creek's children's programs operate through the summer. Visiting children can be enrolled in several short overnight camps, run by the resort, that are exceptionally well-run: Winona's Art Camp, Chief Passamaquoddy's Fishing Camp, and Camp Matawin, where campers dress, live, and sleep like Indians (the teepees are spectacular!)

"Bravo! Colorado," the state's summer music festival, offers a program of music and dance from early June through early August at the amphitheater in Vail. The Vail Nature Center (303-479-2291) offers guided walks, campfire talks, and nature discovery programs for families in the summer. Also possible: swimming, jeep adventures, hot-air balloon rides, whitewater rafting, guided fishing expeditions, tours of ghost towns, and overnight pack trips.

FOR MORE INFORMATION: Write Vail Associates, Inc., P.O. Box 7, Vail, CO 81658 or call (303) 476-VAIL or (303) 949-5750.

WINTER PARK RESORT
Winter Park, Colorado

Winter Park is known as "Colorado's favorite ski resort," and with good reason. It's the place Colorado skiers choose to ski more than any other, partly because of its proximity to Denver (90 minutes from downtown), but also because of its good mixture of slopes and its friendly family atmosphere. People come to Winter Park to ski, not to gawk at celebrities, bar-hop, or shop for designer clothes. Skiing is first and foremost, and whether you're a 3-year-old putting on skis for the first time or a middle-aged pro, the skiing is fabulous.

In the 1993–94 season, Winter Park spent $2 million to create Discovery Park, a contained learn-to-ski area with nearly 30 terrain stations, race facilities, and adventure trails. This beginner terrain offers novices, children, ski school classes and disabled skiers their own playground for practicing basic skiing skills.

Parsenn Bowl offers the adventure of above tree-line skiing. Parsenn offers skiers 203 acres of open bowl and gladed tree skiing that fans out from the 12,060-foot summit and merges with the terrain on Mary Jane's Backside.

Other recent improvements include the opening of 200 acres of intermediate and expert terrain on Mary Jane's Backside, with service on the new Sunnyside triple chairlift, and the opening of the resort's third mountain, Vasquez Ridge.

ACCOMMODATIONS: $ to $$$ Winter Park offers a range of accommodations including basic motel rooms, bed and breakfasts, mountainside lodges, condominiums, and deluxe ski-in-ski out hotel rooms. Winter Park Central Reservations (800-729-5813) can book accommodations to suit your needs and budget. One call also arranges lift-ticket purchases, ski school, retals, day care and reservations for the children's programs.

One of the best condominium values is Snowblaze. Located one block from shopping, dining and nightlife, this property also features an on-site athletic club with weight room, racquetball courts and indoor swimming pool.

Hi Country Haus offers studios to three-bedroom condominiums, most with fireplaces, just a short drive or bus ride from the slopes. The complex includes an indoor swimming pool.

The Vintage represents one of the finest full-service properties. It's within walking distance of the slopes, and also offers free shuttle service. Most rooms include fireplaces and kitchenettes. Amenities include a swimming pool, sauna and jacuzzi.

Several charming mountain inns provide rooms with breakfast and dinner daily at reasonable rates. Woodspur Lodge is known for its cozy living room, home-baked cookies and children's rates.

DINING: The Winter Park-Fraser area has more than 45 restaurants, including a variety of ethnic options, such as Cajun, German, Chinese, Swiss, and Mexican.

All visitors to Winter Park should indulge in at least one meal at the award-winning Lodge at Sunspot, located at the 10,700-foot summit of Winter Park mountain. For lunch, try the full-service Sunspot Dining Room, specializing in roasted chicken and wild game. One side of Sunspot houses the Provisioner food marketplace, featuring freshly baked breads and cookies, baked potato bar, grilled sandwiches, soup and salad bar, and gourmet delicatessen.

In the base lodges, the Derailer Bar and Club Car Restaurant serve good food and drinks with great views of the slopes. A cafeteria is available for those in a hurry. The mid-mountain Snoasis serves sandwiches, snacks, and light meals, cafeteria-style. (Skiers can phone in a pizza order from the "Pizza Hot Line" at the top of the mountain, and their order will be ready when they arrive!)

THE SKIING: Winter Park Resort comprises three separate but interconnected mountains and an alpine bowl: Winter Park Mountain, Mary Jane (including Parsenn Bowl), and Vasquez Ridge. The latter two are favored by intermediate and expert skiers.

Winter Park gets more frequent snowfalls than other parts of the Rockies and averages 360 inches annually. Snowmaking equipment extends the ski season from mid-November to mid-April.

 Twenty-two percent beginner, 58 percent intermediate, 20 percent expert. Mary Jane has some of the best moguls in the nation.

 Six high-speed detachable quads, five triples, nine doubles.

 3,060 feet.

 5.1 miles.

 Winter Park offers a variety of ski school otions. For first timers, a special learn-to-ski package makes learning affordable and fun. For upper-level skiers, the ski school offers a variety of workshops, including bumps, parallel break-through, and technique tuneups. Winter Park also offers women-only classes. For all ability levels, private lessons for up to four people are offered.

The National Sports Center for the Disabled, recognized as the world leader in recreational skiing for people with disabilities, is located at Winter Park. Each year, the center teaches skiing to hundreds of disabled children and adults from around the world.

Dozens of miles of cross-country skiing trails nearby. Equipment can be rented at Beaver Village and Idlewild Touring Center in Winter Park, Devil's Thumb, and at the YMCA's Snow Mountain Ranch.

ACTIVITIES FOR NON-SKIERS: Daily tours by Snocat bring guests to the summit to enjoy spectacular views of the Continental Divide. Snowmobiles can be rented for touring through mountain meadows. Dogsled rides offer an exciting daytime adventure. The Fraser Tubing Hill is a local landmark. Kids and adults alike love riding giant inner tubes down a snow-covered hill.

Several different outfitters provide moonlit sleigh rides through the snowy woods; some end with a gourmet dinner around a warm bonfire. Jim's Sleigh Rides go through the forest and meadows by the Fraser River.

FOR CHILDREN: Winter Park has one of the highest-ranked children's ski programs in the country, headquarters in the 32,000-square foot Children's Center, with its own lesson meeting rooms, kitchen, day-care service, rental shop and specially trained ski school staff.

Child care is provided from 8 A.M. to 4 P.M. daily in the ski season for children between 2 months and 5 years, with ski instruction available for children 3 and over. The infants and toddlers are kept apart from the older children and spend their days playing; the adult-to-child ratio is about one-to-five. A separate nap room has private cubicles with cribs. At the end of the day, parents get a written report about the child's naps, diaper changes, and meals.

In the Ute program, 3- and 4-year-olds alternate indoor play with skiing. A typical first day is spent becoming familiar with equipment and playing games indoors and outside. As skills improve, the Utes practice sidestepping, gliding, and stopping on the center's short ski slope. A "Magic Carpet" makes it easy to get to the top of the hill.

Five-year-olds are called Cheyennes. They spend more time skiing in Discovery Park, and have their own large playroom for indoor activities.

First, second and third graders are called Navajos. They convene in their own room in the Children's Center and spend most of each day skiing with children of similar ability.

Fourth graders and children up to age 13 go into the Arapaho program, where they are assigned to classes according to ability. Arapahos spend the entire day on the mountain and have lunch at one of Winter Park's on-mountain restaurants.

NICETIES: The Lift, a free bus with several different routes, transports skiers to and from their accommodations and to restaurants and shops.

Winter Park offers "preference pricing," which means that visitors can choose the lift ticket that best fits their needs and pocketbooks. Children under 5 and adults over 70 ski for free.

IN THE SUMMER: Golfers can play at the Pole Creek Golf Course. Mountain-bikers will enjoy 45 miles of mountain trails, accessible by lift; the Fraser Valley has over 600 miles of bike trails. The lift also takes visitors to the top of the mountain for lunch at the Lodge at Sunspot. Children will beg to try Colorado's longest alpine slide, with 30 linked turns.

The Winter Park area offers innumerable opportunities for water sports such as boating, fishing, rafting, and wind-surfing. A two-day music festival and a wine and food festival are held each summer, and the High Country Stampede Rodeo is held every Saturday night in July and August.

FOR MORE INFORMATION: Call Winter Park Central Reservations at (800) 729-5813.

PARK CITY AREA SKI RESORTS
DEER VALLEY SKI AREA

PARK CITY SKI AREA

PARKWEST SKI AREA

Park City, Utah

A common criticism of ski resorts is that they are colorless, high-tech recreation machines, providing interchangeable slopes to ski on by day and indistinguishable accommodations by night. Park City, Utah, is a different story. Its three ski areas are located in a landscape enriched by landmarks from its century-old mining days, and the lively town itself is no monochromatic "concept," but rather a colorful jumble of independent businesses. It offers a combination found only in the West—spectacular natural scenery, old mining buildings and Victorian homes, and great, plentiful snow.

Another major selling point is that it's only an hour's drive from Salt Lake City's airport.

Deer Valley is the newest and poshest of the area's ski resorts. It offers the best intermediate skiing and on-site child care, as well as incomparable restaurant fare. Not surprisingly, everything costs a little more.

Then there is ParkWest, at the other end of the spectrum; uncrowded, catering more to local skiers, but with tough, long runs down the mountain, and a very relaxed, unpretentious atmosphere. It's a favorite with teens, because it's Utah's snowboarding headquarters.

Finally, there is the granddaddy of the three, Park City Ski Area, Utah's largest ski resort. From the steep chutes to the satin smooth groomed slopes, Park City has a lot to offer to each skill level. The fact that it's the home of the U.S. Ski Team says a lot.

ACCOMMODATIONS: $ to $$$$ A broad range of accommodations is available. For Victorian-style, but recently constructed, homes just west of the ski areas, contact Park City Management Services at (801) 545-7669; For inexpensive motel rooms just a short walk from the Park City lifts, try Acorn Chalet Lodging at (800) 443-3131 or Budget Lodging at (800) 522-SNOW. And there are quaint bed-and-breakfasts like the Washington School Inn (800-824-1672) or the more affordable Imperial Hotel on Main Street (800-669-UTAH). The Inn at Prospector Square (800-453-3812) offers moderate to deluxe rooms, with an excellent athletic club that offers free baby-sitting while you work out.

A pleasant alternative would be to stay at the Homestead Resort, 20 minutes south of Park City, with a hot spring-fed pool and relaxing country inn atmosphere; call (800) 327-7220. If you don't have to ask the price, book into Stein Eriksen Lodge, with two restaurants and a health spa (800-453-1302). It's a gorgeous lodge with a rustic look, providing such niceties as tea in the lobby every afternoon.

DINING: It would take several vacations to thoroughly explore the more than 45 dining rooms of Park City. Cisero's on Main Street offers inexpensive pasta dinners and a selection of veal and chicken dishes at moderate prices. Adolph's, at the Park City Golf Course, serves international cuisine at high prices.

The restaurants in the various lodges at Deer Valley are top of the line, with prices that reflect their reputation. The Silver Lake Restaurant offers a sumptuous buffet; also good is the more casual Stew Pot at the Deer Valley Plaza and the two fine European-style restaurants at Stein Eriksen Lodge.

The oddly named Irish Camel, on Main Street, is renowned for its Mexican dishes. There are numerous steak and seafood restaurants, among them the Brand X Cattle Company on Park Avenue and the Columbine at the Park City Resort Center.

THE SKIING: Many skiers regard the snow in this part of the country—light, dry powder—as the greatest on earth. Excellent skiing conditions are guaranteed from mid-November to May. The average annual snowfall is more than 350 inches.

 Park City: Eighty-six runs, 17 percent novice, 50 percent intermediate, 33 advanced, 650 acres of open bowls.

ParkWest: Fifty-eight trails, 22 percent beginner, 22 percent low intermediate, 48 percent advanced and expert.

Deer Valley: 66 runs and three bowls, with 15 percent novice, 50 percent intermediate, and 35 percent advanced.

 Park City: one gondola, three quads, five triple chairs, five doubles.

ParkWest: seven double chairs.

Deer Valley: two high-speed detachable quads, nine triple chairs, two doubles.

 Park City: 3,100 feet.
ParkWest: 2,800 feet.
Deer Valley: 2,200 feet.

 Park City: Three and one-half miles.
ParkWest: Two and one-half miles.
Deer Valley: Two miles.

 All three ski areas offer ski lessons for adults and children.

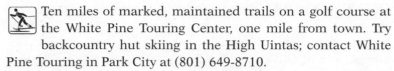 Ten miles of marked, maintained trails on a golf course at the White Pine Touring Center, one mile from town. Try backcountry hut skiing in the High Uintas; contact White Pine Touring in Park City at (801) 649-8710.

Helicopter skiing is available in the mountains around the ski resorts.

ACTIVITIES FOR NON-SKIERS: There's a lot more to do in the winter at Park City than ski. You can ice-skate at the Park City Ski Area Plaza, or snowmobile to Guardsman's Pass. Several outfits offer sleigh rides, usually in the evening, with dinner and entertainment following the ride.

The Norwegian School of Nature Life (801-649-9321) offers ski touring and lessons, as well as dogsled adventures.

The ultimate thrill may be to lift off one bright morning in a gondola attached to a hot-air balloon and view the mountains and valley from that perspective. Contact Balloon Affaire at (801) 649-1217 or Park City Balloon Adventures at (801) 649-3866. Children older than 5 are generally allowed on the flights.

Nightlife is plentiful. Live theater at the Egyptian, on Main Street, is an unusual diversion for a ski area. The Brickyard Playhouse offers more serious plays.

There are several nightclubs in town; to enjoy them, Utah's liquor laws require you buy a club membership. Favorites on Main Street are the Alamo, popular with local residents, and the Club, next door, which attracts more high-lifers.

FOR CHILDREN: Probably the most convenient system for skiing families is at Deer Valley, where a licensed day-care center is located in a roomy facility at the resort center (they take children in diapers and can accommodate 48 non-skiers). Reservations are a must for infants, particularly during the holiday seasons. Call (800) 424-DEER.

For children between 3 and 5, Deer Valley offers a combination of ski instruction and supervised play; children between 6 and 12 have their own program, with a heavier emphasis on skiing. Both programs include lunch.

Park City Ski Area and ParkWest have "Kinderschule" programs (3- to 6-year- olds at Park City, 18-month-olds to 9-year-olds at ParkWest), and youth lessons for older kids. Neither provides infant care. The Park City facility is in a basement, but parents who have used it praise it for its equipment and activities. It can handle 140 kids and is extremely crowded during holidays. It is much less expensive than Deer Valley's facility.

ParkWest's "Kids Central" offers a full day of lessons for children for the lowest cost in the area. Children 3 and under ski free.

There are some off-slope alternatives for infants and young children if you're not going to ski at Deer Valley. One of the best is Miss Billie's Kid's Kampus, located near ParkWest on Highway 224. Kid's Kampus has a big outdoor play area, an upstairs nursery, and well-equipped playrooms downstairs. It's state-licensed and open seven days a week, from 9 to 5. Call (801) 649-KIDS for more information and reservations.

Another option is K.I.D.S. Hotel (Kid's Individualized Daycare and Skiing Hotel) at the Ramada Hotel in Park City, (801) 649-2900. It offers full day care at a daily rate, and nighttime care for an hourly fee from 7 P.M. to midnight.

Baby-sitting service in your motel or condominium can be obtained through several agenies.

NICETIES: Free bus service is offered throughout the town, and a free chair lift carries you from downtown to the Park City Ski Area.

Cars can be rented in town for just a day if you want to go on an excursion elsewhere.

Utah ski resorts have joined forces to offer multi-area ticket books containing ski checks usable for all-day lift passes at the three Park City resorts, as well as Brighton, Alta, Snowbird, and Solitude in the Cottonwood Canyons, an hour's drive away.

OF INTEREST NEARBY: Both children and adults will enjoy a ride on the Heber Creeper, an old steam engine that takes travelers up into the mountains 18 miles south of Park City. You can dine on the train in the evening, or take a day trip. For schedules and information call (801) 534-1779.

IN THE SUMMER: The historic feeling of Park City makes it a pleasant place to base oneself for summer vacations that feature hiking in the Uintas, mountain-biking on lift-serviced trails, golfing at the Jeremy Ranch Golf Course of the Park Meadows Country Club, horseback riding, and virtually any other outdoor activity imaginable. Summer accommodations are quite inexpensive. And many provide amenities like swimming pools, racquetball courts, and health clubs.

ParkWest stages a series of outdoor jazz, pop, and country music concerts throughout the summer at the ski area, and Deer Valley holds a jazz festival, a bluegrass festival, and symphony concerts. The city of Park City offers a Shakespeare festival.

Fishing at nearby Echo Reservoir is popular, and many cycling competitions are held. The valley ballooning industry is in full flower in September, when the annual Hot Air Balloon Festival is held.

FOR MORE INFORMATION: Write the Park City Ski Area at Box 39, Park City, UT 84060, or call (801) 649-8111. Write ParkWest at 4000 ParkWest Drive, Park City, UT 84060, or call (800) 754-1636. Write Deer Valley at Box 3149, Park City, UT 84060, or call (800) 424-3337.

For general tourist information, call the Park City Area Chamber of Commerce/Convention and Visitors Bureau at (800) 453-1360.

LAKE TAHOE AREA SKI RESORTS

SQUAW VALLEY U.S.A.

ALPINE MEADOWS

NORTHSTAR-AT-TAHOE

HEAVENLY

KIRKWOOD

SIERRA-AT-TAHOE

Lake Tahoe, California

The Tahoe area is home to the biggest concentration of ski resorts in the country—15 within a 100-mile radius. Most ring the north or south shores of Lake Tahoe and some, particularly Heavenly, offer top-of-the-world views of this turquoise-blue, 22-mile-long lake. The offerings range from small "Mom and Pop" resorts with a couple of lifts to the mammoth Heavenly and Squaw Valley U.S.A. ski areas, the latter the home of the 1960 Winter Olympics. Because of the array of choices, many skiers choose to sample several different areas if they're going to be here for more than a few days.

Probably best known among the Tahoe ski resorts are "The Big Six"—Squaw Valley, Alpine Meadows, and Northstar on the North Shore and Heavenly, Kirkwood and Sierra-at-Tahoe on or near the South Shore. Though South Lake Tahoe tends to be a fast-paced vacation spot because of the casinos on the Nevada portion of the shoreline, North Lake Tahoe offers a quiet and relaxed atmosphere.

A still-burning Olympic flame at the entrance to Squaw Valley reminds visitors of the resort's venerable past. The variety and number of slopes make Squaw a skier's paradise. The beginner's area is set apart, so novices can enjoy wide open runs without worrying about faster, more aggressive skiers whooshing by.

Just a few minutes down the road is Alpine Meadows, the favorite of locals and the home of the area's ski school for the disabled. Less than a half hour away is Northstar-at-Tahoe, which prides itself on being an all-in-one ski area, with lodging, restaurants, and entertainment all wrapped into its tidy boundaries. All three are close to the folksy, lakeside town of Tahoe City, which is chock-full of specialty shops, delis, restaurants, condos and bed-and-breakfast lodges.

At the other end of the lake sits Heavenly, which claims to have more acres of skiable terrain—21,000—than any other resort in the country. Nearby Sierra-at-Tahoe is known for its fine teaching terrain and ski school. And Kirkwood boasts the highest base elevation in northern California and a complete cross-country ski center.

ACCOMMODATIONS: $ to $$$$ On the North Shore, the busy little resort town of Tahoe City has lodging ranging from relatively inexpensive motel rooms to posh condominiums.

Granlibakken is a charming resort that was the site of the 1932 Olympic ski jump trials. A former lodge for alumni of the University of California, Granlibakken (916-583-4242) has been transformed into a pleasant resort and conference center. For very young or novice skiers, Granlibakken also offers an added plus: it has its own free mini-ski slope, which is served by a rope tow. Adjoining it is one of the area's few sanctioned "snow play hills." An overnight stay in a two-bedroom townhouse at Granlibakken includes a buffet breakfast.

Also on the North Shore, Northstar-at-Tahoe (800-533-6787) is a completely self-contained ski resort, with 220 rental units ranging from hotel-style rooms to fully equipped four-bedroom homes. The Ski Trails condos here are within 100 yards of the Northstar slopes, providing ski-in-ski-out convenience.

Squaw Valley's accommodations are pricey, but within walking distance—or a short shuttle ride—of the slopes. Among them are the Squaw Valley Lodge (800-922-9970), which has apartment-type units with kitchens; Olympic Village Inn (800-VIL-LAGE), which served as housing for the 1960 Olympic athletes, and the 405-room, deluxe Resort at Squaw Creek, with ski-in-ski-out access (916-583-6300).

Skiers at Heavenly can select from such accommodations as the inexpensive Flamingo Lodge (800-544-5288) and the expensive Tahoe Chalet Inn (800-821-2656). Kirkwood has six different condominium complexes within walking distance of the lifts; call (209) 258-7000. Sierra-at-Tahoe runs a shuttle service that stops at 30 different properties, with a total of 20,000 rooms or housekeeping units. Call (800) AT-TAHOE for recommendations on accommodations.

DINING: On the North Shore, Tahoe City offers hungry skiers everything from Texas-style barbecue to more elegant steak and seafood dining.

Hearty and tasty German meals are served up in a cozy family atmosphere at Pfeifer House. Jake's on the Lake specializes in seafood and steaks, and, as its name suggests, has lakeside views. A favorite among local residents is moderately priced Rosie's Café, decorated with a collection of old sleds. Tahoe House serves Swiss and California cuisine at dinner only. And in the old railroading town of Truckee, O.B.'s Pub and Restaurant is recommended.

On the South Shore, the Beacon has a great view of the lake, the 89th Street Bar and Grill features live jazz and blues with its steaks and chops.

Northstar-at-Tahoe has about a half-dozen restaurants, delis, and bars either on the mountain or in the little village below.

THE SKIING: Skiing ranges from the thrills of Squaw and Heavenly to the tamer, more family-oriented slopes of Northstar and Kirkwood. Alpine Meadows considers itself a compromise— big enough to offer variety, but not so large as to be overwhelming. Because of its sheer size and variety of slopes, Squaw Valley is the best known of the Tahoe ski resorts. Yet because of the crowds, it is not the place for families looking for a quiet day of skiing. Northstar-at-Tahoe, built on 1,700 acres on the hips of 8,600-foot Mt. Pluto, limits the number of daily ski passes it sells to minimize waiting time in lift lines.

Multi-day passes, as well as interchangeable passes good at the six largest ski areas, are available.

 Alpine Meadows: 100 runs, six open bowls; 25 percent novice, 40 percent intermediate, 35 percent advanced. (No snowboarding.)

Heavenly and Northstar-at-Tahoe: 25 percent novice, 50 percent intermediate, 25 percent advanced.

Kirkwood: 15 percent novice, 50 percent intermediate, 35 percent advanced.

Sierra-at-Tahoe: 25 percent novice, 50 percent intermediate, 25 percent advanced.

Squaw Valley: 25 percent novice, 45 percent intermediate, 30 percent advanced.

 Alpine Meadows: one high-speed quad, two triple chairs, eight doubles, two Pomas.

Heavenly: one aerial tram, detachable quad, seven triple chairs, nine doubles, six surface lifts.

Kirkwood: six triple chairs, six doubles, one surface lift.

Sierra-at-Tahoe: three high-speed detachable quads, one triple chairlist, five double chairlifts.

Northstar: one gondola, two high-speed quads, three triple chairs, three doubles, two surface lifts.

Squaw Valley: one aerial tram, one gondola, two detachable quad chairs, five triples, 16 doubles, two surface lifts.

 Alpine Meadows: 1,797 feet.
Heavenly: 3,600 feet.
Kirkwood: 2,000 feet.
Northstar: 2,200 feet.
Sierra-at-Tahoe: 2,212 feet.
Squaw Valley: 2,850 feet.

 Alpine Meadows: Two and one-half miles.
Heavenly: Seven miles.
Kirkwood: Two and one-half miles.
Northstar: Almost three miles.
Sierra-at-Tahoe: Two and one-half miles.
Squaw Valley: Three miles.

 Ski schools at all areas.

 The North Lake Tahoe area has eight cross-country ski areas offering almost 400 miles of groomed trails, including those at the country's largest Nordic area, Royal Gorge. A nordic ski center is located in a clearing just behind the mid-mountain lodge at Northstar; there are 25 miles of groomed and tracked courses that wind through woods on logging roads. Kirkwood's Nordic Center has 45 miles of groomed trails.

ACTIVITIES FOR NON-SKIERS: Non-skiers can take in stunning views by riding the trams and gondolas at most resorts. Strolling through quilt and handicraft shops in Tahoe City is a pleasant way to spend a few hours. Along the way, kids can drop some bread or crackers to the rainbow trout swimming under the Fanny Bridge at Highways 28 and 89.

And, of course, there are the casinos on the South Shore and in nearby Reno, which routinely present big-name entertainers and shows. Harrah's on the South Shore has a supervised, check-in and check-out arcade for youngsters aged 6 to 14 and a movie room.

Sleigh rides can be arranged through the Hilltop Lodge in Truckee at Kirkwood, Richardon's Resort, Northstar-at-Tahoe, and next to Caesar's Tahoe.

Mountain Lake Adventures in Kings Beach has guided snowmobile tours of the backcountry along the North Shore. Phone (702) 831-4202 for more information.

Mountain High Balloons has hot-air balloon trips that lift off, weather permitting, during the winter. Phone (916) 583-6292.

For a different kind of commute to the slopes, skiers staying on the South Shore can hop aboard a Mississippi-style sternwheeler and ride across the lake to the North Shore resorts. A shuttle then takes skiers to either Squaw Valley, Alpine Meadows, or Ski Homewood. On the way home, there's dancing to a live band, plus appetizers and cocktails. For more information, call the Tahoe Queen Ski Shuttle at (916) 541-3364.

FOR CHILDREN: All "Big Six" resorts offer full-day ski schools for children from age 3 or 4. Only Northstar, Sierra-at-Tahoe and Squar offer care for younger children.

Alpine Meadows operates a "snow school" for kids aged 3 to 6, open from 8:30 A.M. to 4:30 P.M. For youngsters aged 6 to 12, a day of lessons and lift tickets at the children's ski school is available.

Heavenly's ski school is for children 4 to 12 years of age.

An entire slope festooned with balloons and dubbed "Mighty Mountain" has been set aside for children at Kirkwood. There's an all-day ski school for youngsters 4 to 12, and day care is available for children 3 and over.

Northstar has an especially attractive nursery program, called "Minors' Camp," which includes low-key ski lessons, for potty-trained children aged 2 to 6. It's in the Village Mall and open from 8 A.M. to 4:30 P.M. daily. The adult-to-child ratio is one-to-six. An all-day ski program, "Star Kids," also is available for children aged 5 to 12.

Sierra-at-Tahoe operates a licensed day-care facility, the Wild Mountain Children's Center, for children from 24 months to 5 years. Ski instruction is offered for children 4 to 12. Children under 5 ski free.

Squaw cares for children as young as 6 months at its "10 Little Indians Snow School." The fee includes lunch and snacks. Ski lessons are available starting at age 3.

NICETIES: Free shuttle service is widely available to and from the bigger condo complexes and ski resorts.

A parking spot can be reserved ahead of time at Sugar Bowl.

OF INTEREST NEARBY: The tragic tale of the Donner Party, a group of pioneers who got trapped in these mountains during the winter of 1846–47, is detailed at the Donner Memorial State Park in Truckee. Open daily from 10 A.M. to noon and 1 to 4 P.M., the museum includes displays on the pioneer movement, railroading, local Indians, and geology. Call (916) 587-3841.

The history of skiing from 1860 to the present is covered at the free Western American Ski Sports Museum off Interstate 80 near Boreal Ridge. Phone (916) 426-3313.

IN THE SUMMER: The Lake Tahoe area provides innumerable recreational opportunities in the summer, from boating to fishing, golf, tennis, hiking, horseback riding, sightseeing, jet skiing, wind-surfing, bicycling, rafting, miniature golfing, hot-air ballooning and seaplane rides. There are also such special events as the Lake Tahoe Summer Music Festival, Music at Sand Harbor, Shakespeare at Sand Harbor, Truckee Tahoe Airshow, Truckee Championship Rodeo, Concours d'Elegance Wooden Boat Show, and the Izuzu Celebrity Golf Championship at Edgewood Tahoe Golf Course.

There are seven golf courses in the area, including the 18-hole, 6,897-yard, par 72 course at Northstar-at-Tahoe designed by Robert Muir Graves.

Northstar-at-Tahoe is an especially attractive summer destination for families. Ten acrylic tennis courts and an Olympic-size pool are available, and the Northstar stables offer guided rides along mountain trails. Children between the ages of 4 and

10 can take part in a summer day camp that features swimming lessons, storytelling, nature walks, tennis, arts and crafts, and horseback riding from 10 A.M. to 5 P.M.

A striking waterfall and stream help make The Resort at Squaw Creek an attractive summer vacation spot, along with an 18-hole golf course, bike paths, eight tennis courts, an aquatic center with three pools and a slide, and miles of riding and hiking trails through the surrounding mountains.

FOR MORE INFORMATION: The direct numbers for each of the six largest ski areas are as follows: Squaw Valley, (916) 583-6955; Alpine Meadows, (916) 583-4232; Northstar-at-Tahoe, (916) 562-1010; Heavenly, (916) 541-1330; Kirkwood, (209) 258-7000, and Sierra-at-Tahoe, (916-659-7453).

Call the Tahoe North Visitors and Convention Bureau (800-824-6348) for lodging reservations on the North Shore.

On the South Shore, the Lake Tahoe Visitors' Authority (800-288-2463) provides general tourist information.

HISTORY
PLACES

MYSTIC SEAPORT
Mystic, Connecticut

Today's children may associate boats with pleasure—boarding an ocean liner for a long vacation cruise or paddling in a canoe on a camping trip. But long, long ago, boats were a way of life for entire communities, whose residents built them at a local shipyard and then went to sea to catch fish and whales and even fight wars.

Nowhere is the adventure, romance, and hard work of the high-seas life experienced more vividly than at Mystic Seaport, a picturesque 17-acre museum on the Mystic River 50 miles northwest of New Haven.

One day is sufficient to stroll through the indoor and outdoor museum areas, see a movie on whaling and a show in the planetarium, and even visit the nearby Mystic Marinelife Aquarium, operated by a separate non-profit organization. But to really steep yourself in the rhythm of a 19th-century maritime village, plan on staying for a few days and participating in one of the programs offered by the museum's Education Department. You can even learn to sail.

Mystic Seaport owns more than 400 sailing vessels, making it the largest maritime museum of its kind in the country. Ships are maintained through a working preservation shipyard. About 150 ships are usually on display; visitors can board four.

The seaport also contains approximately 60 authentic buildings that house shipbuilding activities and vestiges of 19th-century life. Some of the buildings are original; others were moved there.

Exquisite examples of scrimshaw, portraits of famous sea captains, and elaborately carved ships' figureheads are among the exhibits. Also worth visiting are the buildings that display machinery and photographs showing how the 19th-century division of labor made seagoing life possible. For example, in the oyster house, moved to Mystic from New Haven, oysters were sorted by size and shipped to markets as far away as California. In the ropewalk building, rope was made to rig boats. In the cooperage, barrels were assembled to hold provisions for long journeys.

Among the biggest attractions for children are the "role players," who dress in period outfits and demonstrate life from another era.

Mystic was first settled by fishermen and farmers in the 1600s. Shipbuilding was important from early days and fueled the growth of the area. The War of 1812 further spurred its growth. Other 19th-century events necessitated building other types of boats. For example, the California Gold Rush of 1849 called for clipper ships, which could sail quickly around Cape Horn. Many of the clippers built at Mystic set speed records. The Civil War required steamships for moving men and arms. Demand for wooden boats decreased after 1870, and many shipyards were shuttered. World Wars I and II revived demand briefly.

Mystic Seaport was founded as the Marine Historical Association, a non-profit maritime museum and educational institution, by three Mystic residents in 1929. In addition to charming visitors, it houses the G. W. Blunt White library, with more than 350,000 manuscripts and 56,000 ships' plans and charts for study.

Mystic Seaport hours are 9 A.M. to 5 P.M. daily, May through October, and from 9 A.M. to 4 P.M. daily, November to April. The museum is closed Christmas Day. The aquarium is open daily from 9 A.M., except Thanksgiving, Christmas, and New Year's Day.

ACCOMMODATIONS: $ to $$ The town of Mystic offers at least 10 different places to stay, including several large chain-affiliated motels.

Locally owned hostelries include the Taber Motor Inn, within walking distance of the museum (call 203-536-2621); the Seaport Motor Inn, overlooking the Mystic River (call (203) 536-2621); the nicely landscaped Inn at Mystic, on Long Island Sound (call (203) 536-9604); and the Red Brook Inn, an authentically furnished bed-and-breakfast with nine rooms (call 203-572-0349). The Mystic Hilton is across from the Marinelife Aquarium (call 203-572-0731).

Families that like to camp can pitch their tents at Seaport Campgrounds on Route 184; Rocky Neck State Park on Route

156; Camp Niantic by the Atlantic on Route 156, or Ponderosa Park and Campgrounds on Chesterfield Road, Route 161.

DINING: The Galley on the grounds of Mystic Seaport, near the South Gate, offers cafeteria-style New England fare.

The Seamen's Inne, a full-service restaurant near the North Gate, offers lunch and dinner. It has an oyster saloon for snacks and drinks and a terrace for warm-weather meals.

Ten miles west of Mystic is the Lighthouse Inn in New London, which has an elegant restaurant for lunch and dinner.

ACTIVITIES: Take your time to explore Mystic Seaport's buildings. In the Aloa Meeting House, you can see a black-and-white movie about whaling, with footage from the 1920s. In the planetarium, you can learn how the stars, moon, and sun helped sea captains and their crews navigate safely.

Special activities abound, especially from May through October. On Memorial Day, Mystic Seaport stages a lobster fest near Lighthouse Point. In June, the Sea Music Festival brings together musicians from both sides of the Atlantic to play popular sea and folk music. On July 4, the museum holds a parade with a 19th Century wreath ceremony and country dance. At Christmastime, evergreens top the masts of tallships, and Lantern Light Tours are held in the evenings.

The museum offers numerous classes throughout the year in woodcarving, blacksmithing, fireplace cooking, boatbuilding, and sailing. Subjects vary from year to year.

FOR CHILDREN: The Children's Museum provides a hands-on environment for children and their parents to explore together. The theme of the exhibit is "It's a Sailor's Life for Me." Children seven and under can swab the deck, move cargo, cook in the galley, dress in sailors' garb and pretend to sleep in sailors' bunks.

Four of the museum's old ships can be explored: the 1841 111-foot-long wooden whale ship *Charles W. Morgan*, whose whaling days ended in 1921; the 1882 square-rigged training ship *Joseph Conrad*, which was moored permanently at Mystic in 1947; the 1921 fishing schooner *L. A. Dunton*, which had been used to catch haddock and halibut; and the 1908 57-foot *S.S. Sabino*, the last coal-fired steamboat still in operation. The Sabino makes 30-minute daytime and 90-minute nighttime cruises from Mystic Seaport every day from mid-May through mid-October, which children will love.

Other boats to look for: the 1891 oyster sloop *Nellie*, the 1866 Noank smack *Emma C. Berry*, and the *Estell A.* sloop, which had been used as a lobster boat. It's fascinating to children to pick out the differences among the boats.

Through the year, Mystic Seaport offers special activities for children; write the Education Department and ask for the schedule. Among the usual offerings are Family Days, over Thanksgiving weekend; a children's winter program in mid-February, the highlight of which is an overnight program aboard the tall ship *Joseph Conrad*; games and special children's tours daily through the summer; two-week summer day camp sessions; a children's field day in late fall, and Victorian Christmas activities.

For children 10 to 15, the *Joseph Conrad* program offers a crash course in the fundamentals of sailing, rowing, small boat safety, weather prediction, marlinspike seamanship, and aspects of maritime history, while living on board the tall ship, *Joseph Conrad*, for six days.

In the summer, children 15 to 19 can cruise the New England waters for six to 10 days on the *Brilliant*, a classic schooner yacht.

OF INTEREST NEARBY: Plan to take the one-mile side trip to the Mystic Marinelife Aquarium, where you can see 6,000 specimens of marine life in 45 exhibits, including sharks and performing dolphins and sea lions.

New London has an impressive historic district with many buildings dating from the late 18th century. Old Lyme, Stonington, and Norwich also are pleasant towns to visit.

FOR MORE INFORMATION: Write Mystic Seaport, 75 Greenman ville Avenue, P.O. Box 6000, Mystic, CT 06355-0990, or call (203) 572-0711.

OLD STURBRIDGE VILLAGE
Sturbridge, Massachusetts

Life in the 1830s had its share of daily surprises, so don't be surprised if you encounter a farmer rolling a broken wagon wheel to the blacksmith's shop while you're strolling the paths of Old Sturbridge Village. If you accompany the farmer on his errand you might discover that 19th century blacksmiths did not shoe horses; they primarily used their iron-making skills to forge tools and farm implements.

Most of the "villagers" you encounter at this living history museum will gladly respond to questions as they go about their chores: making cheese or candles, fixing the split rail fence, and grinding corn at the mill.

Old Sturbridge Village is set on 200 acres in Sturbridge, Massachusetts. The museum comprises more than 40 structures, most of them restored buildings brought from other areas. Each building is staffed by costumed men and women who are well versed in the details of daily life in a New England town during the early part of the last century.

Visitors will need at least a full day to get around to all parts of Old Sturbridge Village. Starting at the Village Common, where sheep are often seen grazing, you can visit the bank, the law office, the parsonage, and various other residences or meeting houses. Your children might enjoy taking their places on a wooden bench in the small district school, where the schoolmaster or mistress explains the daily lessons. Wander down the dirt roads or take a detour onto one of the quiet, wooded trails, and eventually you'll find yourself near the Pliny Freeman Farm, a complete, working historical farm. By the time you work your way through the Mill Neighborhood and see the large bellows working in the blacksmith shop or the grist mill grinding a variety of grains, your family will be ready for a horse-drawn ride along the edge of the millpond.

Old Sturbridge Village is open year-round, with the seasons determining the special events and demonstrations. Throughout each season, various demonstrations, activities and performances are held at different spots in the Village, so be sure to check the daily schedule printed on your map guide.

ACCOMMODATIONS: $ to $$$ The Sturbridge area offers a variety of accommodations that are convenient to both the highways and Old Sturbridge Village. The Old Sturbridge Village Lodges and Oliver Wight House, (phone 508-347-3327) are adjacent to the Village entrance. The restored house, which is listed in the National Register of Historic Places, has 10 moderately priced rooms furnished in the style of the Federal period. The Lodges offer inexpensive first-floor rooms with private entrances, and two luxury suites. Restaurants are nearby.

Across from the entrance to Old Sturbridge Village is the Sturbridge Host Hotel and Conference Center (formerly a Sheraton), which offers accommodations in the same price range; phone (508) 347-7393. The resort, located on the edge of a lake, has a private sand beach for swimming, boat rentals, and plenty of hungry ducks. Rooms overlook the lake or a lovely indoor pool. A miniature golf course, outdoor tennis courts, and a health club with racquetball courts and Nautilus equipment are also on the resort grounds.

DINING: Visitors to Old Sturbridge Village may dine at the Bullard Tavern, which has a Buffet and Tap Room serving lunch and a cafeteria serving continental breakfast and lunch. The Buffet serves a variety of traditional hot foods, such as chicken pot pie and Indian pudding. There are also two snack bars on the Village grounds; the Miner Grant Store and Bake House sells freshly made cookies. Picnic tables are available.

Outside the Village grounds there are many dining choices, ranging from the typical assortment of fast-food stops to full-service restaurants.

ACTIVITIES: The seasons dominate life at Old Sturbridge Village, much as they dominated life in the 1830s. Demonstrations and exhibits, as well as special events and workshops, vary as the chores necessary for each season change. Some programs require reservations and extra fees.

Your family could enjoy a special New England fall by attending the Village's Harvest Weekends, when the farmers bring in the crops and the Village women start storing food for the coming winter. Thanksgiving week is a wonderful time to visit and learn how families prepared for the holiday more than 160 years ago. Thanksgiving Day itself is celebrated with services at the Center Meetinghouse; a traditional holiday dinner is available at the Bullard Tavern (reservations must be made well in advance).

Seeing the Village under a fresh blanket of snow is a special winter experience, particularly when combined with holiday shopping in the lovely gift shop and bookstore. February brings a weekend birthday celebration for George Washington, complete with speeches and toasts. Maple sugaring in late winter is a sure sign that spring is just around the corner. Spring brings new arrivals in the barnyard, as well as "Shearing, Spinning and Weaving," which offers an opportunity to watch sheep shearing and wool processing. "Muskets, Music and Merriment," "Spring Gardens in Bloom" and "Summer Garden Week-end"are popular spring and summer events.

Independence Day is grandly celebrated with speeches, a parade, games, and picnic. Or you might arrange to visit the Village during the "Charitable Society Fair," when the Village ladies hold their annual meeting and fair to raise money and make plans to help the poor.

An Activities Guide describes all the special workshops, week-end and evening programs and concerts held through the year. An especially appealing program is Crafts at Close Range, which offers hands-on experiences in a variety of 19th-century crafts and activities, such as spinning, hearth cooking, and black-smithing. These workshops, for adults and children 14 years or older, are offered from November to May.

FOR CHILDREN: Everything that goes on at Old Sturbridge Village is designed with children in mind, but there are several programs operated periodically during the year that focus even more on children's interests.

Summershops are five-day workshops, providing time travel back to the 19th century for children ages 8 to 14. The children, wearing costumes, learn firsthand about life during the period. Eight- to 10-year-olds make their own 19th-century tools, toys and decorative arts in hands-on workshops. Older chidren learn about weaving, hearth cooking, basketmaking and toolmaking. All the children spend time in the Village. The sessions, directed by the Museum Education Department, run Monday through Friday from 9 A.M. to 2 P.M.

During the week between Christmas and New Year and again in February, Old Sturbridge Village offers several programs designed for the entire family. And several "Family Fun Weekends" are scheduled each summer.

FOR MORE INFORMATION: Write Visitor Services, Old Sturbridge Village, 1 Old Sturbridge Village Road, Sturbridge, MA 01566, or call (508) 347-3362, extension 325. The TDD number is (508) 347-5383.

PLIMOTH PLANTATION
Plymouth, Massachusetts

To most people, Plymouth Rock means Pilgrims, and Pilgrims mean Thanksgiving, with a huge feast featuring turkey and cranberries on the side. A trip to Plymouth, Massachusetts, an hour south of Boston, can provide families with a much deeper understanding of the annual holiday and early American history.

Plymouth bills itself as "America's Hometown," and nearly everything ties into the Pilgrim theme in one way or another. Most of the Pilgrim Americana here is in good taste. Your visit seems like a trip back through time, more than 360 years ago, when people seeking a better way of life braved a treacherous trip across the ocean.

The centerpiece for this Old World atmosphere is Plimoth Plantation, a living museum set on a 105-acre site along the Eel River. In the 1627 Pilgrim Village, Pilgrim "townspeople" who have been steeped in the customs and the way of life of their 17th-century counterparts are available for questions and demonstrations of how things were done then. The adjacent Wampanoag Homesite presents the history and culture of the Indian natives whose friendship and support were so important to the new settlers.

Also available to satisfy your curiosity about the lives of the Pilgrims is Mayflower II, a reproduction of the type of ship that brought the voyagers to Massachusetts in 1620. Nearby is the famous Plymouth Rock, now only a fraction of its original size. A seasonal guide tells the story of the Pilgrims' crossing and answers questions.

Other attractions include authentically restored buildings and museums to deepen your knowledge of Pilgrim lore, and the cemetery high atop a hill where names such as Carver and Bradford adorn many of the tombstones, reminding you of the town's importance in early American history.

Plimoth Plantation is open daily from 9 A.M. to 5 P.M., April through November. Children under 5 are admitted free.

ACCOMMODATIONS: You can either commute from Boston or choose from several bed-and-breakfast accommodations, motels, and campgrounds in the area.

If you prefer a motel, the choices include the Sheraton Plymouth at Village Landing, phone (508) 747-4900, which is right on the waterfront, and a pair of inns known as the John Carver and the Governor Bradford. The Sheraton offers a heated indoor pool, saunas, whirlpool, and exercise room, as well as an attractive, glassed-in restaurant with a view of Water Street.

The Governor Bradford Inn, phone (508) 746-6200, overlooks the harbor and has a small outdoor swimming pool. The John Carver Inn, phone (508) 746-7100, on the town square, was redecorated in the mid-1980s and also has a pool and restaurant.

DINING: Plimoth Plantation offers a snack bar for a midday break. Reservations are required for the 17th-century dinner and many other special theme dinners. Picnic tables are available in summer. There are numerous family restaurants in Plymouth.

ACTIVITIES: After a visit to the orientation center at the plantation, including a multi-media presentation, you will go to the Pilgrim Village. There, interpreters portray individual pilgrims such as William Bradford and John Alden.

As visitors swirl about them, the residents of the Pilgrim Village go about their normal daily lives. If no one approaches them, they carry out their daily chores—cooking, cleaning, and tending to the variety of duties that were second nature to their forebears. If someone asks them a question, they will answer in period dialect, with knowledge that stops in the 1620s. One young visitor, for example, asked why there weren't any kids in the area. A village resident, pretending to be momentarily befuddled, quickly pointed out that there were many baby goats all around.

The sights, sounds, and smells of the village are accurately re-created, down to the heavy clothes that the residents wear even in the heat of the summer. Asked why he would not doff some of his clothing to cool off, one of the residents, who was wearing handmade leather boots, replied, "We've come to an uncivil place, but we did not come to uncivilize it, just because of its warm climate."

When one young visitor came up with a case of the hiccups, two village residents began an earnest consultation of the best way to cure the affliction they called "the hikkets." Their prescription: sassafras bark or root.

After wandering around the Pilgrim Village, visitors can go to Hobbamock's Indian Homesite, the re-created Indian encampment. Inside a dome-shaped home (wetu) made of bent saplings and woven reed mats of bark, they can sit on a bed covered with beaver pelts and listen to tales of the history and culture of the Wampanoag people.

The homesite does not carry over the Pilgrim Village premise of role-playing; instead, it features actual members of the Wampanoag tribe plus trained guides explaining Native American ways.

FOR CHILDREN: School-age children will delight in imagining that they are back in "the olden days." A favorite game is trying to trick the guides into answering a question with knowledge gained since the 17th century.

The Education Department schedules special activities for children daily during the summer and holiday tourist seasons and on weekends at other times.

OF INTEREST NEARBY: The *Mayflower II*, is located on the Plymouth waterfront, about three miles north of Plimoth Plantation. It's staffed by costumed workers who speak the language as it was spoken in the Pilgrims' time. They describe the long voyage across the ocean and talk about why they left their known world for a new land where they could worship as they wished.

The full-scale reproduction was built in England and sailed across the Atlantic in 1957. Visitors first see a dockside exhibit that introduces the passengers who sailed for 66 days on the ship's namesake. Aboard the ship, there are both the hired hands who are looking forward to returning to England and Pilgrims, facing the challenge of building a new colony.

The original *Mayflower* did not first touch land at Plymouth. Rather, it reached the tip of Cape Cod at Provincetown, which was deemed an unsuitable spot for settlement. Today, Plymouth Rock, now surrounded by a Parthenon-like structure on Water Street, is only about a third of the size of the original rock; over the years people have chipped away at it, removing thousands of pounds. A guide gives a brief talk on the history of the site.

A walk along Water Street should also include a visit to Ocean Spray's Cranberry World, where not only admission but small samples of juice and other cranberry delicacies are available free of charge. You can look at exhibits on the life and times of a cranberry bog, showing how the berries are grown, harvested, and processed.

FOR MORE INFORMATION: Write Plimoth Plantation at P.O. Box 1620, Plymouth, MA 02362, or call (508) 746-1622.

For general tourist information, write the Plymouth County Development Council, P.O. Box 1620, Pembroke, MA 02359, or call (508) 826-3136.

SOUTHEAST

PARENT & CHILD SPACE CAMPS
Huntsville, Alabama
Titusville, Florida

One of our children announced not too long ago that he wanted to go to the moon on vacation.

Until vacationing in outer space become a reality, parents and children have to settle for going to the Parent & Child Space Camp.

But what an alternative it is!

Using a simulator, you can experience the weightlessness of outer space.

With the Multi-Axis, you'll understand how astronauts felt while the Mercury space capsule tumbled through space.

With the Microgravity Simulator, you'll feel like the astronauts did as they walked on the moon, which has one-sixth the Earth's gravitational pull.

Space Camp is the place to get a sense of the physical and intellectual challenges of conquering the next frontier—and have fun besides.

The U.S. Space and Rocket Center, part of NASA, offers Parent & Child Space Camp programs in two locations—Huntsville, Alabama, near the Marshall Space Center, and Titusville, Florida, near the Kennedy Space Center. Both camps use the nearby space museums as classrooms, along with facilities dedicated specifically to the camps themselves.

Parent and child campers are separated into teams of 12, each with its own camp leader. From arrival Friday morning to departure on Sunday morning, there's no down time (except for sleep).

Like so many things in the U.S. space program, Space Camp was the dream of rocket scientist Wernher von Braun. He envisioned a space camp as as an opportunity to inspire, motivate, and educate children. Since 1984, Space Camp has been offering specialized camps for elementary, middle, and high school students, adults, educators and families.

The Parent & Child program is open to children 7 through 11 years age, accompanied by a parent or legal guardian. (Legal guardians include grandparents, aunts, uncles, or a sibling 19 and up.) Parent & Child sessions are scheduled most weekends from early May through mid-September and once or twice a month at other times.

ACCOMMODATIONS: $$$$ At the Huntsville camp, accommodations are in the "Habitat I" or in the Aviation Challenge facility, which are used by school-age campers during the week. The Habitat I rooms were designed to look like the living quarters of an inter-galactic space vehicle; each parent-child pair has their own room. The Aviation Challenge facility is a dormitory. In both facilities, restrooms are down the hall.

At the Titusville site, housing is in single-sex dormitories. Parents and children of different sexes are housed in different dormitories.

Tuition was $250 per person in 1994. It includes meals, housing, educational programs and materials, and a t-shirt and hat for each participant.

DINING: Dining is cafeteria-style, with a choice of several entrees at each meal and a host of side dishes. The food is wholesome, filling and unlimited. A meatless dish is an option at every meal.

ACTIVITIES: The camp's 48-hour schedule is crammed with activities. Parents engage in exactly the same activities as their children. Safety is a top priority, with shoulder and lap belts and helmets required in the simulators.

Campers experiment with different methods of movement, including the slow motion jog and the Kangaroo hop. The Manned Maneuvering Unit Trainer allows campers to drift effortlessly across the floor on a cushion of compressed air, while using controls to turn themselves upside-down and get the feel for working in space. In simulated voyages to distant planets, campers sit in space capsules that move realistically while they view a video presentation of a space flight.

Each parent-child team builds a rocket and launches it. Rockets have a small payload compartment and a parachute to slow their descent. Campers can experiment with the basic design to see how placement of the fins or composition of the payload affects the performance.

Each group practices and performs a simulation of a Space Shuttle mission, complete with launch, scientific missions and landing. The shuttle and mission control mock-ups are very realistic; all communication between team members is through microphones and headsets.

A session on living in the weightlessness of space answers campers' questions on everything from the kinds of food the astronauts eat (samples are passed around) to how the astronauts go to the bathroom.

Campers have several opportunities to learn some astronomy, both in a miniature planetarium and from observing the sky at night.

Evening programs center include films in the Omnimax theaters at the adjacent space museums. The films include wonderful footage of the Earth, photographed from space, and of astronauts aboard orbiting space craft.

Campers visit the Marshall Space Center in Alabama or the Kennedy Space Center in Florida.

OF INTEREST NEARBY: If you're going to the Alabama camp, allow some extra time to visit the U.S. Space & Rocket Center, including the Spacedome Theater, on your own. The center is the nation's premier showcase for space technology. It features America's only full-scale Space Shuttle Exhibit, the actual Apollo 16 command module, the high fidelity model of Skylab, and dozens of rockets.

In Florida, you'll want to plan extra time at the U.S. Astronaut Hall of Fame, including its Shuttle to Tomorrow exhibit, which features a multi-sensory video inside the cargo bay of a full-size space shuttle orbiter replica.

Both museums display space suits, capsules from the Mercury, Gemini and Apollo space programs, a lunar rover, moon rocks, and full size mock-ups of the lunar modules that carried U.S. astronauts to and from the moon.

Titusville is within easy driving distance of the Orlando area's theme parks.

FOR MORE INFORMATION: Phone (800) 63SPACE.

OZARK FOLK CENTER STATE PARK
Mountain View, Arkansas

The Ozark Folk Center celebrates a bygone way of life and a vanishing culture.

The pioneers who settled in the Arkansas mountains were known for their strong religious views, ingenuity and work ethic. Isolated in the misty blue mountains known as the Ozarks, they developed a culture and music all their own. Beginning in 1920, outside influences started permeating the old Ozark way of life. The Ozark Folk Center State Park was founded in 1973 to keep Ozark traditions alive.

Because of it dedication to the region's history and folklore, the Ozark Folk Center State Park is among the nation's most unusual state parks. It sits on the edge of Mountain View, Ark., a small town nestled within the highest part of the Ozarks in northern Arkansas. No matter where you look, the view is spectacular.

The folk center and lodge fill more than 80 stone and cedar buildings situated within easy walking distance of each other on 80 wooded acres. The state has expansion plans for the 600 neighboring acres.

The heart of the Ozark Folk Center is the Crafts Area, a cluster of 24 small craft demonstration buildings nestled among the hills within a fort-like enclosure. Within each of those round, contemporary structures, artisans practice what they dub "lost skills". They make brooms, spin thread, and create dolls from cornhusks.

Demonstrating such crafts is only part of the center's purpose. It is also dedicated to keeping such arts alive. Apprenticeship programs are offered through the center's April-October season for tourists, as well as serious craftsmen. An archive—the Ozark Cultural Resource Center—is open by appointment for research in Ozark regional music, crafts, history and lore.

The craft area features a few bona fide log cabins, including a one-room school, which give tourists a glimpse into the primitive Ozark way of life in the 1800s. At the General Store, you can buy many of the items produced by the craftsmen. Their brooms are said to last forever.

The complex includes the 1,000-seat Ozark Folk Center Theater, where near-nightly concerts showcase everything from blue-grass to gospel music to clogging. Local Musicians perform several times a day in a smaller auditorium in the nearby Conference Center.

The Ozark Folk Center has conference facilities, but its emphasis is on attracting families. About 100,000 tourists visit each year. The center is open year-round, but April through October are the premier months for visiting.

ACCOMMODATIONS: Dry Creek Lodge, the park's hotel, has 60 rooms in 30 round, window-lined cabins bordering the woods. Each room has two double beds, a television, phone and bath. There is no charge for children under 13. No pets are allowed in the rooms.

Among the guest amenities are an outdoor swimming pool and recreation room can near the lodge office.

Numerous other motels, hotels, bed and breakfasts and campsites are available in the area. The camping areas include some federally run sites within the lovely Ozark National Forest.

DINING: Iron Skillet Restaurant, the lodge's 150-seat dinery, is the best and most economical place to eat within miles of the folk center. The restaurant is walled with windows and decorated with Ozark craft items. Diners sometimes have to wait in line, but it's worth it. Bowls of the center's tasty apple or peach butters are served with every meal. Dinner features such regional specialties as hickory-cured ham, chicken and dumplings and corn bread. Children's portions are available.

The craft area has two snack bars. The Smokehouse offers a make-your-own sandwich buffet, hot fried pies and drinks, while the Confectionery offers hot cider, fudge and ice cream sundaes.

Mountain View has a handful of fast-food places.

ACTIVITIES: In the craft area, you can watch a craftsman make a gun from scratch and observe women making lye soap and apple butter in huge pots over an outdoor fire (you might just be offered a taste of a buttermilk biscuit baked in a wood stove!) You can touch a rattlesnake skin, try your hand at dipping candles, weave a white oak basket, or create your own cornhusk doll.

At the Heritage Herb Garden, you can learn about the native and exotic plants that have naturalized throughout the countryside, and the uses to which Native Americans and early settlers put them. The Garden for the Physically Challenged features raised beds planted with herbs that you can touch, pinch and smell. The Native Plant Wildlife Garden was planted with the tastes of birds, bees and butterflies in mind.

The Ozark Folk Center hosts several special events during the year. For example, the Ozark Invitational Fiddle Competition is always held in April, before the center's official opening, and there are several other fiddle competitions throughout the season. There's also a dulcimer jamboree, numerous herb workshops and "feasts", and many crafts and music festivals.

If you're serious about learning a craft or new musical skill, consider enrolling in the 2- to 5-day workshops in basket-making, playing the dulcimer or autoharp, furniture-making, spinning, and folk-dancing.

Music shows featuring national and local artists are held nightly except Sunday in the outdoor theater. One Sunday a month, there's a gospel concert.

FOR CHILDREN: The center's regular craft demonstrations are engaging enough to interest most school-age children. Every Saturday in April, May, September, and October, special hands-on activities, such as making yarn, square-dancing, and using feather pens are offered for "Young Pioneers," ages 7 to 14. They are offered three times daily, Tuesday through Saturday, in the summer.

An extra effort to engage children is made during the two Youth Weeks, in June and August. During those weeks, the craft centers offers 3 1/2-hour excursions for children only, called "Learning from Yesterday," which give them a chance to try their own hands at the various crafts and old children's games. They also have special "hands-on" opportunities, such as handling animal pelts. Each day is capped with party games, singing and dancing.

In the Craft Area, children will love the mule swing ride, where a mule pulls a primitive, old-time swing carousel.

OF INTEREST NEARBY: Mountain View calls itself the "Folk Music Capital of the World." Numerous dinner theaters, hoedowns, and music shows offer live entertainment every night during the summer and on week-ends in the spring and fall. The town also has many crafts and antique shops.

About 15 miles away, in the Ozark National Forest, are the Blanchard Springs Caverns. Two underground trails offer a fascinating look at cave features.

The Buffalo National River, which runs through northern Arkansas, offers opportunities for fishing, canoeing and rafting. The nearby White River is known nationally for its spectacular trout fishing.

FOR MORE INFORMATION: Write the Ozark Folk Center at Box 500, Mountain View, Arkansas, 72560, or call (501) 269-3851. For lodging inquiries, call (800) 264-3655 or (501) 269-3871. For general tourist information, write Mountain View Chamber of Commerce, P.O. Box 253, Mountain View, Arkansas 72560 or call (501) 269-8068.

COLONIAL WILLIAMSBURG
Williamsburg, Virginia

Families come to Williamsburg to learn about an important time in history. In this small, restored town in tidewater Virginia, once a colonial capital, they see for themselves what life was like in the 18th Century. They gain a different perspective on democracy in the Hall of the House of Burgesses where the patriots—Patrick Henry, George Washington, and Thomas Jefferson—came together to discuss and debate the inalienable rights to life, liberty, and the pursuit of happiness. Williamsburg inspires children to look at history in a new way.

In 1926, the Reverend Dr. W. A. R. Goodwin, rector of the Bruton Parish Church in Williamsburg, persuaded John D. Rockefeller to help in the restoration of Colonial Williamsburg. Altogether, 88 18th-century buildings were restored. Nineteenth and 20th-century buildings were torn down, and, in their place, more than 50 reconstructions of their 18th-century predecessors were built, including the Governor's Palace, the Capitol, and the Public Hospital.

When children think about "the olden days," they often focus on what people *didn't* have—electricity, modern plumbing, telephones, computers. At Williamsburg, they're made aware of what the people *did* have, as well as how they worked and played. Artisans and costumed interpreters bring the 18th century to life. On a walk down Duke of Gloucester Street, you'll see the printer and bookbinder at work. You'll learn who subscribed to the Virginia Gazette and how many books the average person owned. The wigmaker will show you how a wig is made and explain why wigs were a status symbol. The apothecary will give you a lesson in the medicinal use of leeches.

The costumed interpreter at the Geddy House will tell you about 18th Century family life. You'll see the toys the children played with and maybe watch an 11-year-old do needlework. Outside, your children will play the same games children played 200 years ago. You can participate in an auction, dine in a colonial tavern, attend a service at the Bruton Parish Church, see the public "gaol" where prisoners were given "salt beef damaged, and Indian meal," or tour the Capitol, where the House of Burgesses met.

A visit to Williamsburg will show you how people from many walks of life lived—the craftsman, the innkeeper, the slave, and the governor.

ACCOMMODATIONS: $ to $$$$ Colonial Williamsburg operates a variety of accommodations, all of which can be booked through a central reservations service (call 800-HISTORY). Numerous package plans are available; under some, children stay free.

The Mobil 5-star Williamsburg Inn is the most elegant hotel, furnished in the Regency style. The Williamsburg Lodge, right next to the Historic Area, offers comfortable rooms, an indoor pool, and underground parking. Williamsburg Woodlands, located next to the Visitor Center, has a casual atmosphere and many recreational options—three swimming pools, a putting green and miniature golf course, shuffleboard, table tennis, and a playground. The Governor's Inn is located three blocks from the Historic Area and has inexpensive to moderately priced rooms.

If you're looking for the total "colonial experience" and your children are mature enough so that you don't have to worry about their noise, you may enjoy staying in one of the colonial houses or taverns in the Historic Area. These range from a 16-room tavern to a small cottage and sleep 2 to 12.

Guests at all the Colonial Williamsburg properties qualify for lower ticket prices to the Historic Area, free guided walking tours, use of the Tazewell Club Fitness Center, unlimited use of the Historic Area transportation system, and preferred seating times in the Historic Area's restaurants.

Most national hotel and motel chains have affiliates here.

DINING: Dine in the colonial manner at one of the four taverns that offer traditional southern cooking, served by costumed servers. Choose from the King's Arms Tavern, which has an excellent chicken pot pie; Shield's Tavern, perhaps the most authentic; Christiana Campbell's Tavern (George Washington's favorite), and Chowning's Tavern, known for its Welsh rarebit and Brunswick stew. At Chowning's, the "gambols" (colonial games and entertainment) begin at 9 P.M .

All are open for lunch and dinner; children's menus are available.

One block from the Visitor Center, you'll find the Cascades, famous for its hearty Hunt Breakfast Buffet (with scalloped oysters, grits, and hotcakes). Friday and Saturday evenings, the Bay Room at the Williamsburg Lodge features a Chesapeake Bay Feast.

Right across from the Visitor Center, at Williamsburg Woodlands, you'll find quick service, good food, and reasonable prices at the Woodlands Grill.

ACTIVITIES: Colonial Williamsburg is made for walking. Even if you never sign up for a special activity, your family will soak up history. But the more hands-on activities you take part in, the more meaningful the experience will be.

The "Visitor's Companion" provides a calendar of special events and a map of the Historic Area. Here's just a sampling of what you might find in any given week:

- Take a carriage or stage wagon ride through the Historic Area.
- Listen to the Fife and Drum Corps or attend a militia review.
- Visit selected crafts shops on an evening Lanthorn Tour.
- Take a special tour led by a costumed interpreter. "According to the Ladies" portrays women of 18th-century Williamsburg. "The Other Half" explores slave life.
- Enjoy "Bruton by Candlelight," a recital at Bruton Parish Church.
- Attend an 18th-century play in the Williamsburg Lodge.
- Take in evening entertainment at the Capitol, which may include a "Musical Diversion," or "An Assembly" (an evening of dance and music), or "A Capitol Evening" (with political debate, court drama, and period music).

A separate admission is charged for some of these events.

FOR CHILDREN: Hands-on activities through the Historic Area will help children learn about the 18th Century. At the Military Encampment, they can march and drill (and even pretend to fire a cannon). At the Geddy House, they can play games their colonial counterparts played. At the wigmaker's, they can be measured for a powdered wig. At every stop, costumed actor-historians talk to them about what it was like to be a child in colonial Virginia.

On holidays and over the summer, special programs are offered for families at Benjamin Powell House, where actors impersonating 18th-century family members (including children) act out the relationships between family members and household slaves. Visitors get to help with the chores.

For guests of the Williamsburg Inn and Williamsburg Lodge, supervised children's activities are offered daily through the summer (free for guests on the Family Getaway Plan). The Little Patriot's Club (for children aged 5-7) and the Capitol Kid's Club (for 8- to 12-year-olds) offer a "Talk to the Animals" tour, outdoor games such as croquet, hoop rolling and badminton, story time and swimming. Some nights, there's a "Kid's Night Out" program in which children dine and play together while their parents enjoy a quiet dinner.

Williamsburg Woodlands and the Governor's Inn offer the Young Colonial's Club for 5- to 12-year-olds for a nominal fee (free for guests on the Patriot's Package Plan). Kids go on a special tour of the Historic Area, during which they may go lawn bowling, attend a musket-firing demonstration, observe a Fife and Drum Corps march, and get lost in the Governor's Palace Maze. Some evenings, the club offers supervised swimming, miniature golf, Ping Pong, arts and crafts, and games.

OF INTEREST NEARBY: Take the seven-mile Country Road, passing by woodlands, marshes, and ravines, to Carter's Grove, a beautiful 800-acre estate with a 200-year-old mansion. There you'll find reconstructed slave quarters. As you look out at the James River from the mansion, you'll see the 17th-century remains of Wolstenholme Towne. The six sites, which date from between 1619 and 1710, were excavated between 1976 and 1981. An archaeological museum displays artifacts. Admission to Carter's Grove is included in the Patriot's Pass.

Jamestown, Williamsburg, Yorktown—historians say that it is

here that the British Crown acquired a vast empire, debated it, and lost it. Try to include a visit to both Jamestown and Yorktown while you're in the area.

At Jamestown, see the statues of John Smith and Pocahontas and the Old Church Tower (the only standing ruin of the 17th-century town), visit replicas of the James Fort and Powhatan's Lodge, and board replicas of *Susan Constant*, *Godspeed*, and *Discovery*, the vessels that brought the first English settlers to Virginia. Call (804) 229-1607 for hours and fees.

At Yorktown, visit the battlefield; you'll find the auto tours well-marked. Also plan to stop at the National Park Service Visitor Center (804-898-3400) and the Yorktown Victory Center (804-887-1776) for interesting films and exhibits.

Busch Gardens, a 360-acre theme park, features nine authentically detailed 17th Century European hamlets and some thrilling rides. Call (804) 253-3350 for information.

FOR MORE INFORMATION: Write the Colonial Williamsburg Foundation, P.O. Box 1776, Williamsburg, VA 23187-1776, or call (804) 229-1000.

CONNER PRAIRIE
Fishers, Indiana

The year is 1836, only 20 years after the state of Indiana was carved out of the old Northwest Territory. President Andrew Jackson's term is coming to an end, and in the small frontier village of Prairietown, Indiana, the residents are talking about the upcoming election, which pits Martin Van Buren against William Henry Harrison.

Mrs. Zimmerman, the proprietress of the Golden Eagle Inn, is preparing the noonday meal for the Inn's guests, who pay 12 cents a night to sleep in the common sleeping chamber.

Outside the inn, a traveling gunsmith and his son have set up shop under a canvas awning beside their wagon. They are in the village for a week or two repairing the rifles and muskets of the men of Prairietown and nearby villages. On this day, they expect business to be good because Mr. Whitaker, the storekeeper, is staging a shooting match in Prairietown.

You and your family head toward the shooting match over the dirt streets of Prairietown, a historically accurate re-creation of a 19th-century frontier village. You stop on the way and knock on doors, enter houses or workshops, chat with Prairietown "residents" and listen in on their conversation and gossip.

A visit to Conner Prairie is a visit into the daily lives of Indiana's first-generation settlers. Prairietown villagers, by their dress, mannerisms, food, speech, and interactions with the social, religious, political, and economic issues of 1836, convey history in the first person. This is living history at its best.

The Conner Prairie settlement grew out of the keen interest in Indiana history and archaeology of pharmaceutical magnate Eli Lilly. In the 1930s, Lilly purchased and restored the 1823 home of William Conner, a prominent resident and key player in the early development of Hamilton County, Indiana. The land and buildings were eventually given to Earlham College to develop as a museum. In the 1960s and 1970s, more authentic 19th-century buildings were moved to Conner Prairie and grouped into the fictional, but historically accurate, Prairietown.

Prairietown at Conner Prairie is open from early April to late November. But programs take place elsewhere at Conner Prairie throughout the year.

ACCOMMODATIONS: $ to $$ Conner Prairie has no regular overnight accommodations. But on selected weekends in the winter, spring, and fall, your family can rent a pioneer log cabin for Friday night, Saturday night, or both. The Lilly Cabin is a genuine one-room log cabin furnished with all the amenities available to Indiana pioneers—a double bed with a straw-stuffed mattress, a simple table and benches, a fireplace with 19th-century cooking equipment, candle lanterns, and an ample supply of firewood. You bring your own food, blankets or sleeping bags, and other necessities. Toilets (but no showers) are a short walk from the cabin.

Special rates are available through Conner Prairie at six local hotels. The Quality Inn in Castleton, six miles away, offers king- and queen-size suites, each with a wet bar and refrigerator; a full breakfast is included in the rate. The Frederick-Talbott Inn, across the street from Conner Prairie, is a bed-and-breakfast country inn with 12 individually-styled guest rooms.

Other hotels that offer special rates are the Hampton Inn Northeast (six miles away); the Guest Quarters Suite Hotel (eight miles away), the Signature Inn Castleton (seven miles), and the Holiday Inn North (a 20-minute drive).

DINING: During the winter months, Conner Prairie offers special dinners for groups of up to 12 people in the dining room of the William Conner home. The menu for Hearthside Suppers includes roast game hens, pickled beets, warm slaw, hearth bread, orange fool and Shrewsbury cakes. Costumed interpreters prepare your dinner on the kitchen hearth using traditional recipes and cooking implements. The dinner is served by candle-light on a table in the Conner dining room. Nineteenth-century parlor games and a tour of the Conner home conclude the evening. Reservations are required.

Summer Suppers at the Inn, on select Friday evenings in June, July and August, allow visitors to experience what a relaxing summer night might have been like in 1836. As a weary traveler passing through Prairietown, you are welcomed to the

Golden Eagle Inn for an evening of refreshing summer fare and pleasant conversation. You assist innkeeper Martha Zimmerman as she prepares an authentic 19th Century supper—cold ham and chicken breast, mustard potatoes, and bread pudding with cherry sauce.

Throughout the year, Governor Noble's Eating Place in the Conner Prairie Museum Center serves daily lunches and Sunday Brunch. Picnic facilities are located on the grounds.

ACTIVITIES: Conner Prairie offers four windows into the early 19th century. The first is Prairietown, the living history village. The second is the newly re-restored Federal-style home of William and Elizabeth Conner. The third is the Pioneer Adventure Area, and the fourth is the Weaver Gallery.

Fifty Conner Prairie staff members recreate the roles of Prairietown residents each day from early April through late November. In addition to the Golden Eagle Inn, the village contains a pottery, blacksmith's and carpenter's shops, a village store, a school, and a number of homes, including the doctor's house. Special events like weddings, temperance society meetings, and local elections are scheduled.

The Conner home is listed in the National Register of Historic Places. In the home and its outbuildings, interpreters recount the life and times of the Conner family and explain the origins and function of the estate's furnishings and equipment. Cooking demonstrations take place in the kitchen. At intervals throughout the year, interpreters demonstrate spinning, weaving, and dyeing in the loom house. The barn contains farming equipment from the early 19th century. Candlelight tours of the 1836 Village of Prairietown are conducted at Christmas time.

The Pioneer Adventure Area is the hands-on aspect of the Conner Prairie experience. Here you and your children can spin, weave, cook, make soap, split logs, or play frontier games. Perhaps a spelling bee is in progress, or an itinerant violinmaker is in residence. Special theme weekends focus on one particular aspect of frontier life.

Other special events are scheduled from time to time. Your visit might coincide with a hayride, a pig roast and picnic, or a barn dance. In the Halloween season, the Sleepy Hollow legend is reenacted.

FOR CHILDREN: Children on the staff of Conner Prairie play roles in the re-enactment of history in Prairietown. Learning how children lived more than 150 years ago provides your own children with a fascinating lesson in cultural history.

The Pioneer Adventure Area is the focus of activities for children. The schedule of events changes weekly and includes naturalist programs as well as history-related activities.

Conner Prairie will appeal mainly to children over 5. Since much of the mission of Conner Prairie involves working with schools, the staff is skilled in relating to children and their interests.

OF INTEREST NEARBY: The Children's Museum of Indianapolis is the largest children's museum in the world. Galleries focus on the physical and natural sciences, history, foreign cultures, and the arts. Don't miss it. It's one of the best children's museums anywhere.

The Indianapolis Museum of Art is in a park with a botanical garden designed by Frederick Law Olmsted, the designer of Central Park in New York. In the park you'll find restaurants, shops, a wildlife refuge, lakes, and a greenhouse.

Union Station is Indianapolis's train station, which has been restored and converted into a "festival marketplace" with shops, restaurants, nightspots, entertainment and an Amtrak station. The Holiday Inn, located in the original train shed, features 26 suites in fully restored Pullman cars from the 1920s.

White River State Park houses the Indianapolis Zoo, with its cageless design and excellent exhibits on marine life.

FOR MORE INFORMATION: Write Conner Prairie, 13400 Allisonville Road, Fishers, IN 46038-4499, or phone (317) 776-6000.

HISTORIC NEW HARMONY
New Harmony, Indiana

On the banks of the Wabash River, near Indiana's border with Illinois and Kentucky, lies a small town of 1,000 that is unlike any other in the United States. New Harmony is a living history village in the most literal sense, for modern-day folks go about their daily tasks in the midst of a setting that is steeped in history.

New Harmony was the site of two of the most ambitious utopian experiments in the nation. It was founded in 1814 by a Lutheran separatist group called the Harmonie Society. Its charismatic leader, Father George Rapp, devised a plan for the construction of a model town in what was then the wilderness of the Indiana Territory, and within a year the community housed 800 people in 150 structures. It thrived for 10 years, exporting more than 20 products throughout the South and Midwest. Its per capita income and cultural amenities rivaled those of many long-established cities in the East.

The entire town was bought in 1825 by a Welsh-born industrialist, Robert Owen, of New Lanark, Scotland, after the Harmonists decided to move back to Pennsylvania. Owen had his own vision of a model community where education and social equality would serve as the watchwords. William Maclure, the nation's most eminent geologist, joined Owen's venture a year later, and brought with him a group of pre-eminent thinkers. Owen stayed for only two years, and his vision was never fully realized. But his sons stayed behind, and from 1830 to 1860 New Harmony was one of the most important training and research centers for the study of geology in America. Its residents also made pioneering contributions to education, women's rights, science, architecture, and the arts.

The visonary focus of the town weakened over the next century, but in 1959 a trust established by one of Owen's descendants began a restoration process that led to the re-emergence of New Harmony as a center of progressive thought and innovative design.

Today, many of the original buildings have been restored and furnished with period pieces, and Historic New Harmony, which is affiliated with the University of Southern Indiana, operates a series of year-round cultural programs and historic tours.

A visit here is both a step back in time and a look towards the future, for the spirits of the Harmonists and the Owenites hover over the town, inspiring visitors in the belief that a better life is possible.

ACCOMMODATIONS: $ The New Harmony Inn, on the edge of the historic district, was built in 1974 according to a design that captures the Harmonist spirit. There are 90 lovely rooms, ranging from doubles to unusual bi-level suites with sleeping lofts. Three rooms have kitchenettes, and 18 have working fireplaces. Furnishings feature original designs crafted by an artist in Posey County. The hotel, which is featured in many country inn guides, has a glass-enclosed heated swimming pool for year-round use, a sauna, a Jacuzzi, and several tennis courts. Call (812) 682-4491 for rates and information.

Campsites and cabins, both primitive and modernized, are available in Harmonie State Park, four miles south of New Harmony. The park has an Olympic-sized swimming pool with a 110-foot water slide, picnic areas and nature trails; call (812) 682-4821.

DINING: The Inn has two restaurants, the famous Red Geranium, which draws diners regularly from three states, and the more casual Bayou Grill. The Red Geranium serves regional and continental cuisine for lunch and dinner (except Mondays, when it is closed). Its memorable baked goods are available to take home.

ACTIVITIES: Tours start at the Atheneum, a striking building designed by architect Richard Meier, which houses an excellent gift shop, an 1824 model of New Harmony, an observation deck, exhibition space, and a theater in which a 20-minute orientation film is shown.

There are almost 20 historic buildings or points of interest open to visitors. Among them are the David Lenz House, where children will marvel over the outdoor baking oven; the West Street Log Cabins; the Salomon Wolf House, which houses an automated model presentation of 1824-era New Harmony, the John Beal House, which has exhibits on natural science and education from the Owen era, and the Victorian-era doctor's office, which has one of the most complete collections of medical and apothecary objects in the Midwest.

The historic district is open daily from April through October, and weekends only in March, November, and December.

The town's famous Roofless Church, opened in 1960, is an interdenominational church designed by the noted architect Phillip Johnson, with bronze entrance gates and sculpture by Jacques Lipchitz. Nearby is Tillich Park, where German theologian Paul Johannes Tillich is buried.

The New Harmony Theatre, affiliated with the University of

Southern Indiana, offers theatrical productions in the summer. Call (812) 465-1635 for a schedule.

FOR CHILDREN: New Harmony will appeal to any child with an interest in "the olden days." Children will especially love visiting the Labyrinth, a restored garden maze, which to the Harmonists symbolized the twists and turns along life's pathway.

Throughout the year, special events are held with particular appeal to children. Among them are the traditional Easter egg hunt in the Harmonist Cemetery, Heritage Week in April, during which 19th-century crafts are demonstrated, and the Kunstfest in September.

FOR MORE INFORMATION: Write Historic New Harmony, P.O. Box 579, New Harmony, IN 47631 or call (812) 682-4482.

SHAKER VILLAGE AT PLEASANT HILL
Harrodsburg, Kentucky

Utopian movements are a distinctive part of American history. Groups that held divergent religious beliefs and practiced non-conformist life-styles flourished on the American frontier in the 1800s. These movements typically dispersed and died within a few generations. But their achievements in agriculture, science, architecture, design, and commerce still linger today.

One such group was the Shakers, followers of a messianic woman who immigrated to the United States from England about the time of American independence. A dissident Quaker group whose name evolved from the writhing, whirling body movements of the faithful during worship, the Shakers expanded from a single colony near Albany, New York, to 18 colonies scattered from New England to the Ohio valley.

The Pleasant Hill community in what is now Mercer County, Kentucky, 25 miles southwest of Lexington, was one of the westernmost colonies. Founded in 1805, it grew to about 500 members at its zenith in 1840, and then gradually faded away. The history and achievements of the Shakers are celebrated here in a faithful restoration of 30 of their nearly 300 buildings, in the display of more than 2,000 items they crafted, and in demonstrations of early-19th-century Shaker crafts like broom making, spinning, and weaving.

ACCOMMODATIONS: $ The Village has 80 guest rooms in 15 original Shaker buildings. Pleasant Hill is the only historic village in the United States in which all guest services are in original buildings. Concessions to modern times include central heating and air-conditioning, ice machines, telephones, TV sets, and bathrooms with each guest room. Otherwise, your room at Shaker Village is furnished and decorated much like the rooms the Shakers inhabited 150 years ago.

Furniture is in the simple Shaker style, with high beds, hard wooden chairs and rocking chairs, a simple writing table and a high bureau. Some rooms have a trundle bed for a child. Broad plank floors are covered with rag throw rugs. The only wall decorations are candles (now with electric bulbs) and a single mirror. There are no closets. The Shakers ringed the walls of their rooms with pegs and hung many things from them, including chairs. In all of Shaker Village there are more than 30,000 pegs.

In addition to large single rooms with baths, there are some two-bedroom combinations, and some two-bedroom suites with sitting rooms. Most guest rooms are located in the East Family House and the West Family House. These buildings have common lounges for guests with reading lamps and ice and soda machines.

One-price packages that include lodging, meals, and programs are offered throughout the year. There is no charge for children who stay in the same room as their parents.

DINING: The Village dining room occupies the first floor of the Trustee's Office, a building completed in 1839 as the administrative center for Shaker business with the outside world. Guests are seated in low-back Shaker-style chairs at plain wood tables. Hurricane lamps are the only table decoration. In this simple setting, wonderful southern food is served at breakfast, lunch, and dinner.

An afternoon tea is offered between November and February. Special dinners are presented in the Thanksgiving and Christmas periods. A children's menu is available.

There are three seatings for lunch and two for dinner year-round; make reservations at the time of your arrival. Mercer County, Kentucky, is a dry county, so no alcoholic beverages are served in the dining room.

ACTIVITIES: Exploring the restored community is the major activity here. Shaker Village is best seen at a leisurely pace.

Start your tour in the Centre Family House. Guides in 19th-century dress will orient you to Shaker beliefs and way of life; the house itself serves as the museum of Shaker Village. With original articles made and used by the Shakers, various rooms depict how the Shakers cooked, ate, slept, cared for the sick and infirm, and raised orphaned and abandoned children. There are exhibits on the industries the Shakers created in vegetable seeds and the manufacture of household items.

From Centre Family House you might go directly across the road to the cantilevered Meeting House, which was the site of worship services. Or you could turn in either direction down the Old Turnpike road, once Pleasant Hill's main street, to watch demonstrations of furniture making, medicine making, spinning and weaving, barrel making, quilting, or broom making. In each exhibit, well-informed guides demonstrate how the Shakers worked using tools from the last century. They also point out the many inventions of the Shakers, including a washing machine, clothespins, and circular saws.

Buildings and exhibits are open from 9 A.M. to 6 P.M. daily from April through October. Children under 6 are admitted free.

FOR CHILDREN: Any child with an interest in history will be fascinated by Pleasant Hill. Shaker Village may not be appropriate for children under 5, depending on their individual interests and attention spans, although many will enjoy sleeping on a trundle bed, playing with door latches and bolts, or exploring spiral staircases. Children also enjoy the horse-drawn wagon rides in summer and sleigh rides in winter.

OF INTEREST NEARBY: From late April through October, the paddle-wheel riverboat Dixie Belle leaves Shaker Landing below Shaker Village for 1-hour excursions on the Kentucky River. The captain comments on the importance of the river to the Shaker economy and the natural history of the Kentucky River valley. Special extended excursions are held from time to time, including nature cruises and a cruise through Lock and Dam No. 7 on the Kentucky River. Box lunches can be arranged at the Inn. Guided nature walks in early spring and winter are a special feature.

Harrodsburg is the nearest community to Pleasant Hill. The town dates from the frontier days of the 18th century and bills itself as Kentucky's oldest town. A replica of the 1775 fort stands in Old Fort Harrod State Park. Beaumont Inn dates from 1845 and is renowned for its traditional Kentucky fare. From late June through August, outdoor dramas on the lives of Daniel Boone and Abraham Lincoln are presented in the James Harrod Amphitheater.

FOR MORE INFORMATION: Write Shaker Village at Pleasant Hill, 3500 Lexington Road, Harrodsburg, KY 40330, or phone (606) 734-5411.

HENRY FORD MUSEUM & GREENFIELD VILLAGE
Dearborn, Michigan

What do American heroes Thomas Alva Edison, Harvey S. Firestone, Noah Webster, Henry Ford and the Wright Brothers all have in common? Their homes or their workplaces have been brought together at Henry Ford Museum & Greenfield Village, a unique 93-acre outdoor museum commemorating the agents of change in our society.

The Greenfield Village buildings, just 20 minutes from the Detroit Metro Airport, are scattered around a beautifully land-scaped 81-acre site. As a visitor to this shrine to American innovativeness, you can tour 80 historic buildings, many with original furnishings, and hear costumed interpreters relate the life stories of the persons whose innovations shape our modern world.

Thomas Edison's Menlo Park, N.J., Laboratory, sometimes called the "Invention Factory," was moved here in its entirely. More than 400 inventions arose out of this laboratory, and it looks much like it did at the time Edison invented the light bulb and the phonograph.

The boyhood home of Orville and Wilbur Wright is at Greenfield, along with their workshop and original models of the machine that would first put man aloft.

Encircling the village green are buildings that speak volumes about America's political, social and religious life—the Logan County Courthouse where Abraham Lincoln practiced law and the Scotch Settlement School where Henry Ford started classes in 1871. Greenfield also has a variety of mills, shops, and small factories that teach about the development of American industry and crafts in the 19th century. Blacksmithing is demonstrated at Cotswold Forge, and in other parts of the village you can observe weaving, pottery making, printing, tinsmithing and glass blowing.

The adjacent Henry Ford Museum showcases a century and a half of change. The exhibits here function as a three-dimensional encyclopedia of the American experience. The most renowned section is "The Automobile in American Life." It includes more than 100 historically significant autos representing every stage in the development of the motor car industry. And there are many auto-related artifacts, such as a 1946 diner, a 1940s Texaco service station, and an early '60s Holiday Inn guest room.

ACCOMMODATIONS: $ to $$$ No accommodations are available right at the Museum and Village, but a wide selection of motels and hotels can be found nearby. The Hyatt Regency-Dearborn (313-593-1234), the Best Western Greenfield Inn (313-271-1600), and Marriott Hotel (313-271-2700) are all family-friendly.

DINING: The Eagle Tavern in Greenwich Village is an 1850s stagecoach stop serving up authentic meals and hospitality of the period. Suwanee Park has an 1870s vintage soda fountain and ice cream parlor where you will want to stop for a treat.

In the Ford Museum, the neon-lit American Cafe serves up a wide variety of modern-day favorites. Fast food snacks are offered at kiosks throughout the complex.

ACTIVITIES: The Greenwich Village Town Hall, on the village green, is the headquarters for hands-on activities and old-fashioned games. At the Scotch Settlement School, students are initiated into the discipline of a 19th century school room.

The Ford Museum Activities Center invites families to participate in a simulated assembly line, operate a printing press, ride a high-wheeled bicycle or try on clothes from a different era. You can also lead your family on a self-guided treasure hunt.

Check the brochures for special exhibits and events scheduled throughout the year. Plays and musicals are performed in the Henry Ford Museum Theater.

The complex is open 9 A.M. to 5 P.M. daily, except Thanksgiving and Christmas. The interiors of the Greenfield Village buildings are closed from January 2 through mid-March. Children under 5 are free; a two-day combination ticket is the best bargain for adults and older children.

FOR CHILDREN: The Museum and Village have attractions to delight children of all ages. Younger children will find the hands-on activities most appealing. Older children will like catapulting back in time to a pre-Civil War slave house from Hermitage Plantation, Georgia, or to the Wright Brothers' workshop. These experiences touch children and give them a real sense of history.

Visitors of all ages will delight in riding the 1913 carousel in Suwanee Park. And a ride on the paddlewheel steamer or the steam-powered train that circles the village is sure to be a hit.

OF INTEREST NEARBY: Belle Isle Park, in the middle of the Detroit River, offers swimming, canoeing, tennis, golf, boating and bicycling on a beautiful 1,000-acre site. The park includes a great playground for children and an aquarium, nature center, zoo and the Dossin Great Lakes Museum.

The Children's Museum in Detroit has variety of exhibits and activities for younger children; call (313) 494-1210.

The Motown Historical Museum (313-867-0991) celebrates the Motown Sound.

FOR MORE INFORMATION: Write the Henry Ford Museum and Greenfield Village, 20900 Oakwood Blvd., Dearborn, Michigan 48121, or call (800) 343-1929 or (313) 271-1620. For TDD service, call (313) 271-2455.

For general tourist information, call the Metropolitan Detroit Convention & Visitors Bureau at (800) DETROIT.

MACKINAC STATE HISTORIC PARKS
Mackinac Island and Mackinaw City, Michigan

When visitors disembark from the ferry on Mackinac Island, Michigan, they have three choices for getting around: foot, bicycle, or horse-drawn carriage.

That's right. Horse-drawn carriage. There are only three vehicles with internal combustion engines on the whole island: a fire engine, a police car, and a maintenance truck. Instead of cars, Mackinac Island has the largest fleet of radio-dispatched horse-drawn taxis in the world. There are so many horses on the island—600 at last count—that the city's small staff includes several employees whose sole job is cleaning up after them.

It is this quaint insistence on maintaining some of the vestiges of 19th-century life that brings thousands of visitors to the island every day through the spring, summer, and fall.

Your visit to Mackinac Island should start in Mackinaw City, Michigan. This was where French settlers in 1715 established Fort St. Philippe de Michilimackinac (pronounced MISH-ili-mack-i-naw) as a trading post and fort guarding the Straits of Mackinac, which link Lake Michigan with Lake Huron.

Now called Colonial Michilimackinac, the fort today is one of three living history museums in the area that are operated by Mackinac State Historic Parks. (A combination ticket admits you to all three.) The fort's buildings have been painstakingly reconstructed and authentically refurnished so that 20th-century visitors can get a sense of early life in what was once the greatest fur trading center in North America.

A few miles down U.S. 23 is Historic Mill Creek, another state historic park. Here, in 1790, settlers built a water-powered sawmill that provided much of the finished lumber for Fort Mackinac.

Fort Mackinac, on Mackinac Island, was the successor to Fort Michilimackinac, and was built in 1780, largely of limestone. Today, period displays and costumed interpreters impart a sense of military life in the 1880s, about 10 years before it was decommissioned.

Mackinac Island is reached by ferry from Mackinaw City or St. Ignace; there are scores of departures every day.

ACCOMMODATIONS: $ to $$$$ There are 1,400 tourist beds on the island distributed among 11 hotels and eight bed-and-breakfasts.

The most famous is The Grand Hotel (800-334-7263), which has become synonymous with the island and represents one of its most lasting images. The expansive white frame structure occupies a postcard-perfect perch overlooking Lake Huron, and the hotel's public rooms and guests room are decorated with period furniture and Victorian era-inspired wallpapers and rugs.

Although the atmosphere here is sedate and reserved, The Grand Hotel is a great place for families to stay. There's a fabulous serpentine-shaped pool where Esther Williams once swam, and two 9-hole golf courses. The hotel's youth counselor supervises a special children's barbecue lunch and nature walk almost every day, as well as a separate children's dinner at night.

The Mission Point Resort, on the opposite end of the downtown area from the Grand, is as unlike the Grand as possible, but no less inviting. Its lobby, with a cathedral ceiling crafted from gigantic rough-hewn logs, gives it the look of a northwoods lodge. The atmosphere here is casual, and the emphasis is on relaxation and fun.

There are special children's activities here, too, three hours of games and arts and crafts for 5- to 12-year-olds on Tuesdays, Thursdays, and Saturdays and a free half-hour story-time for children every morning. Mission Point has a heated outdoor pool, tennis courts, a fitness center, and the island's only movie theater. Call (800) 833-7711.

Many inexpensive motels and bungalow colonies can be found in Mackinaw City.

DINING: The Grand Hotel is famous for its cuisine, especially its luncheon buffet. The hotel also operates the Tea Room at Fort Mackinac; the terrace there has some of the best views on the island.

Zach's Delicatessen, on Huron Street, packs excellent picnic lunches for bicyclists, and even provides a backpack!

ACTIVITIES: Every day through the summer, employees of Colonial Michilimackinac dress as villagers, soldiers, traders, and priests and perform tasks out of the 1770s—horseshoeing, cooking over a fireplace, tending farm animals, paddling a birchbark canoe, and even taking part in a wedding (performed in French, the settlers' language).

At Historic Mill Creek, visitors can watch informative sawmill and sawpit demonstrations and a slide show, and hike several trails through the surrounding 625-acre wooded park. A staff naturalist leads nature discovery tours five days a week.

Fort Mackinac features guided tours, rifle and cannon firing demonstrations, costumed soldiers on parade, re-enactments of a military court martial, special children's programs and military music concerts.

Taking one of the carriage rides operated by Mackinac Island Carriage Tours is a great way for families to get a sense of Mackinac Island. Two Belgian draft horses pull a 16-seat, roofed carriage along the island's streets while the driver provides a running commentary about historic sites and what island life is like for the 600 permanent residents.

Bicycling the eight-mile length of State Highway 185, which hugs the Lake Huron shoreline, is another must-do. Bring your own bicycles, or rent them from any of the outfitters along Huron Street. They have everything from tandems with a rear seat specially adjusted for a child's short legs to adult bikes with trailer attachments for toddlers.

FOR CHILDREN: At Colonial Michilimackinac, separate tours are offered for children that emphasize what it was like to be a child in the 18th-century.

At Fort Mackinac, there are special tours for families and a children's discovery room where children can pretend to be soldiers or laundresses (pretty much the only options for islanders in the 1880s) and press buttons to hear such sounds of history as a horse clopping down the street, a steamboat arriving from the mainland, or a laundress scrubbing on a washboard.

The interpreters at all three sites are attuned to children's interests and draw them into their activities, whether it is sawing a log, playing a drum, dancing a jig, or firing a cannon.

FOR MORE INFORMATION: For information about the state parks, call (906) 847-3328 or write Box 370, Mackinac Island, MI 49757. For general tourist information about Mackinac Island, call (906) 847-3783. For general tourist information about Mackinaw City, call (800) 666-0160.

WEST

CROW CANYON ARCHAEOLOGICAL CENTER
Cortez, Colorado

For more than 14 centuries the Anasazi Indians inhabited the Four Corners region of the United States. They built pueblos of magnificent masonry on a scale unequaled anywhere in the United States. Their settlements spread from the Grand Canyon in the west to the Great Plains in the east, and from central Arizona and New Mexico north into southern Utah and Colorado.

Suddenly, in the 13th century, the Anasazi abandoned the Four Corners area. Why? No one knows for certain. The mystery of the Anasazi has fascinated archaeologists for decades.

Crow Canyon Archaeological Center, a not-for-profit organization, is dedicated to investigating the Anasazi civilization. Its scientists are attempting to answer questions concerning how the Anasazi lived, how they were organized socially, and why they abandoned their magnificent dwellings.

In addition to its exacting research and scholarship, the center has pioneered a program of public archaeology and education in which families can learn about the Anasazi and participate in archaeological field work. This is not a stuffy, boring college course in disguise, but a fun and challenging vacation adventure in which you help unearth the past and solve the mystery of the Anasazi.

ACCOMMODATIONS: $$$ Accommodations are provided in the Crow Canyon Lodge and in comfortable log hogans, patterned on the eight-sided Navajo ceremonial house. The hogans are located on a piñon and juniper-covered hillside above the lodge, with doors that face the rising sun, as Navajo tradition prescribes.

The lodge has dormitory-style rooms that sleep 2 to 11 people in bunk beds. Hogans contain four beds each. Both lodge and hogans have shared bath facilities. The toilets and showers for the hogans are in a separate building in the hogan complex. Guests bring their own linens or sleeping bag.

During Family Week, Crow Canyon attempts to house each family together, but it is sometimes necessary to separate families and provide accommodations in the sex-segregated dormitory rooms.

Housing is only available for participants of week-long programs. Participants in shorter programs can stay in motels in nearby Cortez or camp in Mesa Verde National Park.

DINING: The Crow Canyon dining room serves three delicious homestyle meals a day. The food is quite a few cuts above typical camp cuisine. Breakfasts always include fresh fruit, and when egg dishes are served, there's a low-cholesterol egg substitute. Box lunches are provided when your schedule takes you away from the center on field trips. Dinners often feature Southwest-inspired dishes. Tea, coffee, and lemonade are available throughout the day.

ACTIVITIES: Crow Canyon will appeal mostly to people who have a strong interest in native Americans or archaeology. The Crow Canyon experience gives them an appreciation of prehistoric culture, an understanding of the continuity of the human experience through time, and a sense of their place within that experience.

Crow Canyon offers a wide variety of educational programs, including excavation archaeology, environmental archaeology, workshops, seminars, cultural explorations, Family Week, and one-day programs.

The week-long excavation and environmental archaeology programs are centered on field work and laboratory analysis of artifacts found in the field. The area surrounding Crow Canyon has one of the highest concentrations of Anasazi sites anywhere in the Four Corners region. The center always has several excavations in progress.

Families who can't schedule a full week at Crow Canyon can experience the excitement of archaeology and the richness of Anasazi culture through a day program. The one-day programs include an examination of Anasazi artifacts, experience in Anasazi lifestyles, and a visit to a working archaeological site. One-day visits are available from late May through mid October. The program fee includes lunch. Reservations are essential.

FOR CHILDREN: Crow Canyon is as dedicated to its educational mission as it is to research. Its staff is especially skilled in relating to children. Children learn through hands-on activities which include handling artifacts and relating them to the lives of an ancient people.

Family Week, held each August, is geared to parents or grandparents with children in seventh grade or above. Children excavate in the field alongside their parents and the Crow Canyon research staff. The week-long program includes an introduction to Southwest prehistory, an ecology hike, experience in handling and classifying aritifacts in the laboratory, a visit to Mesa Verde National Park, and such Anasazi activities as grinding corn on a stone metate, throwing a spear with an atlatl, and starting a fire with a fire bow.

Each evening finds amateur archaeologists sitting in the rockers on the lodge porch watching the sun set against the La Plata mountains in the distance and swapping stories of experiences in the field that day.

OF INTEREST NEARBY: Crow Canyon is located in the heart of the Four Corners area, near numerous national parks and monuments, including Mesa Verde, Hovenweep, Chaco Canyon, Canyonlands, Arches, Natural Bridges, Black Canyon, and Canyon de Chelly. It is a day's drive from the Grand Canyon and five hours from Sante Fe.

Nearby are Navaho and Ute Indian reservations, which offer various cultural events throughout the summer. In Cortez and Durango, many vacation activities are offered, including hiking, mountain biking, horseback riding, rafting, fishing, swimming in pools fed by hot springs, and llama trekking. The famed Durango-Silverton narrow gauge railway is popular with families.

Both Durango and Cortez are located on the San Juan Skyway—a highway loop through some of the most scenic mountain country in Colorado.

FOR MORE INFORMATION: Write Crow Canyon Archaeological Center, 23390 County Road K, Cortez, CO 81321 or phone (800) 422-8975, extension 142.

MEXICO

THE MAYA ROUTE
The Yucatan Peninsula, Mexico

Superbly sculptured temples, tropical rainforests, glorious beaches and quaint villages are the scenic features along *La Routa Maya* (The Maya Route) which passes through the Mexican states of Yucatan and Quintana Roo on the Caribbean coast on its 2,600-mile route across Mesoamerica.

The Maya civilization reached its height between 300 and 900 A.D., when Europe was in the Dark Ages. During this creative period, the Maya people built temples and ceremonial centers, excelled in astronomy and mathematics, developed a system of hieroglyphic writing, and built roads whose straightness confounds modern engineers.

By the tenth century, most centers of Maya civilization were abandoned. No one knows whether it was because of war, drought, disease, or a combination of all these factors. As with North America's lost Anasazi culture, that mystery is part of the civilization's appeal.

The Maya Route links the archeological sites and colonial cities of the Yucatan and Quintana Roo—as well as Belize, Guatemala and parts of Honduras and El Salvador—as a way of promoting the historical and cultural heritage of the five nations. Traveling along part of the route by rental car in Mexico, either out of Cancun or Merida, is an excellent way to introduce your family to the heritage of the Maya. Allow five days to a week to do the trip justice.

Uxmal (oosh-MAHL), south of Merida, is one of the most important and beautiful Maya sites in Mexico. Its buildings are adorned with elaborate stone figures and geometric designs. The Pyramid of the Magicians is the highest structure (it's 118 steps to the top). A sound and light show is presented twice nightly (once in English).

Chichen Itza (che-CHEN EAT-sa) was a great Maya city and is one of the archeological wonders of the world. Its richly carved pyramids, temples, and shrines cover almost four square miles. At different times, it was both a Maya and Toltec center. Climbing the steep nine-level pyramid, *El Castillo* (The Castle), will be a challenge for any family. The Ballcourt (the largest in the pre-Hispanic world), the Temple of Warriors and the Astronomical Observatory are all structures worth exploring. Sound and Light presentations are given nightly.

Tulum (tuh-LUM), "City of the Dawn," perches on cliffs by the Caribbean and is best visited early in the morning or late in the day to avoid the crowds arriving daily from Cancun. It is smaller than the other ruins, but the setting is spectacular. Gray-black buildings contrast with the white sand beaches and the turquoise waters of the sea. Bring along your bathing suits for a dip in the placid waters of the Caribbean.

Coba (co-BA) is close to Tulum and is less frequently visited because only five per cent of this 50-square mile city, with an estimated 6,500 structures, has been excavated. You can climb to the top of the Nohock Mul pyramid. At 130 feet in height, it was one of the tallest structures constructed by the Maya.

ACCOMMODATIONS: Uxmal: Hacienda Uxmal is a pleasant colonial-style hacienda whose rooms feature tile floors, colorful ceramics and iron grillwork. The large courtyard shelters a lovely garden, a pool and a restaurant. For reservations, call Mayaland Tours at (800) 235-4079; FAX: 011-99-25-23-97. Another option here is the Club Med Archaeological Villa, which has an attractive central courtyard with a pool; call (800) CLUB-MED.

Chichen Itza: The Hotel Hacienda Chichen was originally built to house the archaeologists when they excavated Chichen Itza. Its bungalows with ceiling fans and private baths are set in a lovely tropical garden with the swimming pool nearby. The food in the patio restaurant is delicious. The hotel and restaurant are open only from November through Easter Week. Phone (800) 624-8451. Also in Chichen Itza and very close to the ruins is the very comfortable Mayaland Hotel, which is open year-round. Phone (800) 235-4079. Club Med has another Archaeological Villa here; call (800) CLUB-MED.

Tulum: The best place to stay is at Akumal, 15 miles north of Tulum on the Caribbean sea shore. Akumal is well-known for its snorkeling and scuba diving, and the beach is beautiful. The Hotel-Club Akumal Caribe offers economical bungalows (Villas

Mayas) set in a garden, a small hotel facing the pool and ocean, and four beachfront villas (Villas Flamingos), which share a swimming pool. All units have full baths, air conditioning, fans and refrigerators. The villas have full kitchens and up to three bedrooms. A small grocery store is located at the entrance to the complex. An optional meal plan (breakfast and dinner) is available; children's rates are reasonable. For information and reservations, write Hotel-Club Akumal Caribe, P.O. Box 13326 El Paso, Texas 79913, or call (800) 351-1622.

Coba: Coba is only a day trip from Akumal, but for those who prefer to spend the night here, Club Med's Archaeological Villa is close by the ruins. It is air-conditioned and has an attractive swimming pool and tennis courts. Phone (800) CLUB-MED.

DINING: All the hotels listed above have restaurants. The Hotel-Club Akumal has a choice of four restaurants, a pizza parlor, snack bar and ice cream shop.

ACTIVITIES: Exploration of the Maya ruins can be done on your own or with a guide. Registered guides are available, for a fee, at each of the archeological sites. Whether or not you hire a guide, a good guide book is a must.

Mid-day weather in this part of Mexico can be hot at any time of year. It might be best to do your exploring first thing in the morning or late in the afternoon, and plan a swim and siesta in the middle of the day.

FOR CHILDREN: Before you leave home, go to the library and find books on the culture and language of Mexico. This trip provides a wonderful opportunity to learn some Spanish and explore remnants of one of the world's great ancient civilizations.

The Mexican archeological parks allow visitors to climb on many of the restored ruins, something most children will love. The pyramids are particularly challenging and engaging. Watch for the lizards that scamper among the ruins.

At Hotel-Club Akumal Caribe, a children's program is offered Monday through Saturday, featuring snorkeling, pool and beach play, arts, movies, bike trips and games. Morning, afternoon and evening activities are scheduled. There's a playground on the beach.

OF INTEREST NEARBY: Families staying at Akumal can easily spend a day at the amusement park Xcaret, which is north on the highway to Cancun. There is much to see and do here—idyllic beaches, snorkeling, boat rides, horse shows, a wonderful bird zoo, scale models of all the major Maya ruins, several restaurants, and a unique underground river ride in which you don a life jacket and float through a series of caves for about a quarter mile.

On your way to or from Tulum, be sure to stop at Xel-Ha Natural Park (pronounced shel-HA), a marine park 10 miles north of Tulum. Here you can picnic, kayak or snorkel in a spring-fed freshwater lagoon populated by tropical fish and coral (rental equipment and locker rooms on site).

If you have a few extra days, spend them on Cozumel, an island 12 miles off the east coast of the Yucatan Peninsula. It's one of the best sites in the Caribbean for snorkeling and scuba diving. Palancar Submarine National Park protects a 20-mile stretch of the island's most pristene coral reefs.

FOR MORE INFORMATION: Write the Mexican Government Tourist Office at 405 Park Ave., Suite 1402, New York, NY 10022, or call (212) 755-7261 (FAX: 212-753-2874).

CRUISES

AMERICAN HAWAII CRUISES
S.S. Constitution
S.S. Independence

The waters surrounding the Hawaiian islands are perfect for cruising. The climate is deliciously tropical, and every island is attractive and unique. The smell of frangipani wafts through the air, and the water's color is surreal. As an added bonus, humpback whales can be spotted from the ship's deck at certain times of the year!

American Hawaii Cruises is only major year-round cruise operator in the Hawaiian Islands. Its sister ships, the *S.S. Constitution* and the *S.S. Independence*, have been cruising Hawaii since the early 1980s and are the only major cruise ships sailing anywhere under the American flag with all-American crews.

One of the nicest things about these cruises is their emphasis on Hawaiian culture. *Kumus* (Hawaiian teachers) accompany each sailing and help integrate Hawaiian lore, music, crafts and cultural traditions into the cruise experience. In addition, an on-board hands-on exhibit created by the Bishop Museum helps passengers learn about Hawaii.

The ships themselves are a treat for anyone interested in the history of water travel. Both were launched in the early 1950s for the trans-Atlantic passenger trade. Each longer than two football fields, these former North Atlantic speed demons carried politicians, movie stars, and tourists between New York and Southampton until sidelined by the rise of jet travel. They have more character than newer ships. Both were refurbished in 1994 at a total cost of $60 million.

The ships travel the same route, but in opposite directions. They depart Honolulu on Saturday evenings (*Independence*) and Tuesday evenings (*Constitution*) and visit ports on Maui, Hawaii, and Kauai. The major Hawaiian islands are relatively close together, so there is only one full day at sea in a seven-day itinerary. The ships travel between islands at night, dock first thing in the morning, and depart for the next port between 6 and 9 P.M.

ACCOMMODATIONS: $$$$ Each ship's capacity is 798 passengers. Staterooms range from deluxe outside suites to budget inside cabins, each with a private tub or shower and toilet. Sleeping configurations include double, king, and twin beds, and upper berths. All are decorated in light pastels.

Many of the outside staterooms have large picture windows. Some two-room suites have king-sized beds and marble bathrooms. Cribs should be requested in advance.

Among the packages American Hawaii offers are the 7-day cruise, 3-day cruise and 4-day hotel, and 4-day cruise and 3-day hotel combinations. The cruise line also offers optional vacation extensions in luxury hotels at special rates.

On many sailings, children 16 and under travel for free when staying with two full-fare adults in certain cabin categories. At other times, children pay $195. Reduced airfares are available from most U.S. cities.

DINING: Cruises are famous for food, and the *Constitution* and *Independence* are no exceptions. The feasting begins with an early buffet breakfast on deck and continues through regular breakfast, lunch, late afternoon tea, dinner, and a late-night buffet.

At each meal there's a choice of traditional American and continental favorites, plus at least one Polynesian-influenced offering, such as Kona coffee lamb noisette, mahi-mahi Polynesian style, and chocolate macadamia nut cream pie. The Hawaiian pupu plate, offered on Polynesian night, includes smoked marlin, Hawaiian prawns, and scallops. Fresh papaya and pineapple are always available. The options at every meal include a selection of health-conscious items that are clearly marked. Kona coffee is served at every meal. Each dinner revolves around a different theme.

ACTIVITIES

 Each ship has two fresh water pools. While in port, you can swim at a some of the most beautiful beaches in the world.

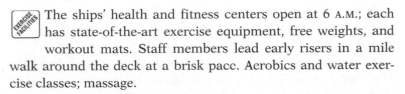 The ships' health and fitness centers open at 6 A.M.; each has state-of-the-art exercise equipment, free weights, and workout mats. Staff members lead early risers in a mile walk around the deck at a brisk pace. Aerobics and water exercise classes; massage.

 The daily newsletter, "Tradewinds," lists a panoply of traditional cruise activities (except for gambling): cards, reading, games, crafts, films, quizzes, trivia contests, musical reviews, comedians, talent shows, and dancing.

A nice extra is the emphasis on Hawaiian culture and heritage. Passengers can learn the hula, take ukulele lessons, make their own leis, weave with coconut palms, and take Hawaiian language lessons. The nightly entertainment is frequently Polynesian as well. On selected cruises, a naturalist travels along and lectures on the native flora and fauna, including whales.

Six whale-watching theme cruises are offered each February and March. Eight special "Big Band" theme cruises are offered each year.

FOR CHILDREN: Both the *Constitution* and *Independence* have year-round children's and teens' programs. Each also has a video arcade and Youth Recreation Center.

The program for 5- to 12-year-olds begins at 8 A.M. with breakfast and includes beach parties and games at the swimming pool, scavenger hunts, Ping-Pong, putt-putt golf, bingo, hula lessons, movies, crafts, dancing, shuffleboard, and parties.

Thirteen- to 16-year-olds have pool parties, dances, mystery games, talk shows, and a junior olympics. Activities in both programs end at 10 P.M. Parents pick up children for lunch and dinner.

NICETIES: The purser's office will be happy to arrange a wake-up call so that you can view the lava flow that has been active on the Big Island of Hawaii since 1983.

Children receive pictures of their group prior to docking in Honolulu.

The kitchen staff will pack a picnic lunch for your on-shore explorations.

PORTS OF CALL: Each ship offers 45 organized shore excursions, for an extra charge. Among the ships' shore excursions of most interest to families are Zodiac raft adventures off the coast of Kauai, snorkeling and sailing near Kona, and bicycling down Haleakala. Children's rates are available.

But the Hawaiian islands are also easy to explore on your own. Rental cars can be arranged at the ship's shore excursion office or on your own at each port of call.

The outdoor-loving family will find many fascinating hiking trails on every island. On the island of Hawaii, the most interesting walks are in Volcanoes National Park. On Maui, the best walks are on the flanks of Haleakala in Haleakala National Park. On Kauai, the legendary Kalalua Trail traverses the Na Pali Coast; you'll also find good hiking trails in Waimea Canyon in Kokee State Park.

Temple sites, the only vestiges of ancient native Hawaiian architecture to survive, dot the islands. One of the most interesting is at Puuhonua O Honaunau National Historical Park on the Kona coast of the Island of Hawaii.

On Oahu, don't miss the Bishop Museum in Honolulu, which houses one of the world's best collections of artifacts from the Pacific Islands, and Brigham Young University's Polynesian Cultural Center. At Sea Life Park you can learn about the undersea world. The Arizona Memorial in Pearl Harbor is a sobering reminder of the price of war.

FOR MORE INFORMATION: Call (800) 765-7000 for a brochure. Contact your travel agent for reservations.

CARNIVAL CRUISE LINES
Holiday
Tropicale
Jubilee
Festivale
Fantasy
Ecstasy
Celebration
Sensation
Fascination
Imagination
Inspiration

Carnival Cruise Lines has mastered the art of mass-market cruising. Each year, the line's nine ships carry more than one million happy sailors—including 86,000 kids—off to sea. Carnival ships carry nearly twice as many passengers as the nearest competitor; fully one-fourth of all the North Americans who cruise in any given year go Carnival. Carnival must be doing something right.

What Carnival does for its passengers is pack a 24-hour day with nearly 24 hours of activities, earning its ships the nickname

"Fun Ships." Its ships are sleek and well-maintained, its staff professional and friendly. Families are present on nearly every sailing. Over Christmas, the staff doesn't even blink at the prospect of having 500 children aboard.

Part of the reason for Carnival's overwhelming success is that it maintains an even standard of quality of all its ships, from the older two—the *Carnivale* and *Festivale*—to its three superliners—the *Holiday*, the *Jubilee*, and the *Tropicale* —to its state-of-the-art mega-liners, the *Fantasy*, the *Ecstasy*, the *Sensation*, and the *Fascination*. Two other giant ships, the 2,600-passenger *Imagination* and *Inspiration*, will be launched by 1996, as well as an as-yet-unnamed 3,300-passenger ship, the largest passenger ship ever to be built, which will bring the total fleet to 12.

Carnival ships cruise the Bahamas, the Caribbean and the Mexican Riviera, on cruises lasting 3 to 7 days.

We sailed on the *M.S. Holiday* through the eastern Caribbean.

ACCOMMODATIONS: $$$ to $$$$ Most of the staterooms have twin beds that convert to king-size beds, and some have one or two upper bunks that are perfect for children. Carnival claims its staterooms are 50 percent bigger than those offered by other cruise lines (an average of 185 square feet, to other ships' 117 square feet). A big plus is the large picture window in most of the outside staterooms. On most ships, outside suites are available.

Children sharing a stateroom with their parents pay reduced rates. For adults, special "Fly Aweigh" rates include round-trip airfare to port cities and transfers to the ship.

DINING: There are only a few hours a day in which there's no scheduled eating, and even then, room service is available. In general, the food is tasty and ample, with a recently introduced emphasis on innovatively prepared seafood and poultry, and fresh fruits as an alternative to calorie-laden desserts. At each meal, you'll find specially marked "Nautica Spa" selections, which are lower in calories, sodium and fat than the other menu offerings. In the main dining room, vegetarian alternatives are available at all meals. Some special diets can be accommodated with advance notice.

Early risers will find coffee and sweet rolls in one of the ship's casual restaurants. For a full breakfast, passengers can choose from a menu in the main dining room or go through a cafeteria line elsewhere, where an abbreviated menu is served and bathing suits are acceptable attire. Coffee, tea and bouillon are served from 10 to 11 A.M. daily, followed a half-hour later by a buffet lunch and sandwiches by the main pool. A sit-down lunch is also served in the dining rooms, but is usually sparsely attended.

Each afternoon, there's afternoon "tea"—sandwiches, cakes, and hot drinks, for the adults, and ice-cream sundaes and cookies for the kids. After that, there's just enough time to dress for happy hour and the main sitting dinner. Among the entrees you'll find are lobster ravioli with watercress coulis, bouillabaisse, Norwegian salmon coulibiac, and blackened swordfish. If you're still hungry after all this, you can try to stay awake for the late-night (around midnight) buffet, followed an hour later by the mini-buffet.

Children can choose from the regular menu, but the waiters will offer sure-fire child-pleasers—hamburgers, hot dogs, and pizza—as well. High chairs and boosters are available.

ACTIVITIES

 Three small saltwater pools on each ship. Some have water slides (children must be 7 to use them).

 The *Fantasy, Ecstasy, Sensation* and *Fascination* have identical 12,000-square-foot Nautica Spas, featuring state-of-the-art exercise equipment and separate men's and women's saunas. Each of the other ships has a jogging track, workout facilities, saunas, steam rooms and whirlpools, as well as daily aerobics classes and "walk-a-mile" activities while at sea. Carnival touts its Nautica Spa program, which features such exotic body and facial treatments as ionothermie and cathiodermie, as the most elaborate at sea.

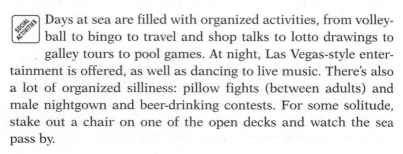 Days at sea are filled with organized activities, from volleyball to bingo to travel and shop talks to lotto drawings to galley tours to pool games. At night, Las Vegas-style entertainment is offered, as well as dancing to live music. There's also a lot of organized silliness: pillow fights (between adults) and male nightgown and beer-drinking contests. For some solitude, stake out a chair on one of the open decks and watch the sea pass by.

FOR CHILDREN: Camp Carnival offers supervised children's activities on all sailings year-round, whether there are 10 or 500 kids on board. In general, the program runs from 9:30 A.M. to 9:30 P.M., with group babysitting available after-hours for a fee. Separate activities are offered for 2- to 4-year-olds; 5- to 8-year-olds, 9- to 13-year- olds, and 14- to 17-year-olds (except on the *Tropicale* and *Festivale*, which don't have programs for toddlers).

Each of the ships has a special playroom, well-stocked with games and toys, where many children's activities are held. The line's program is staffed by almost four dozen children's coordinators, who rotate among the ships as bookings of families require. During the summer and school holidays, extra counselors are brought on board.

On a typical day at sea, the younger children will engage in face- and finger-painting, water play in the splash pool, puppet-making and shows, and ice-cream parties. The "Juniors" make shell boxes and mobiles, attend movies, participate in talent shows and have pizza parties. The "Intermediates" get together for bingo, charades, scavenger hunts, swimming, and newspaper production (their product is called the Fun Club Newspaper, and it goes to all passengers on the last day of each cruise). The "Teens" get together mainly in the evenings for dances, lip sync contests, and Ping-Pong tournaments.

Babies under 4 months are not permitted on the ships.

NICETIES: The dining room waiters and busboys will delight your children by creating comical animal puppets out of napkins. They are also great about serving children quickly.

Complimentary hors d'oeuvres are served during the cocktail hour on most of the nights at sea.

PORTS OF CALL: The *Fantasy* and the *Ecstasy* specialize in 3- and 4-day cruises, out of Port Canaveral or Miami, to the Bahamas and the Gulf coast of Mexico. In the Bahamas, the ships stop in Nassau or Freeport and Nassau. The cruises to Mexico stop in Key West, Cozumel and Playa del Carmen.

The *Tropicale* offers 7-day cruises to the southern or western Caribbean, and 10- or 11-day cruises to the Panama Canal. On its southern Caribbean itinerary, the *Tropicale* goes from San Juan to St. Thomas, Guadeloupe, Grenada, Venezuela, and Aruba. On its western Caribbean itinerary, the *Tropicale* goes from New

Orleans or Tampa to Grand Cayman, Cozumel and Playa del Carmen, Mexico. On its 10-day cruises to the Panama Canal, it sails from San Juan to St. Thomas, Guadeloupe, Dominica, Grenada and Curacao. The 11-day cruises sail from San Juan to St. Thomas, Virgin Gorda, Tortola, St. Lucia, Aruba, the Panama Canal and Ocho Rios.

The *Festivale* and the *Fascination* offer 7-day cruises from San Juan to St. Thomas, St. Maarten, Dominica, Barbardos, and Martinique. The *Jubilee* offers 7-day cruises from Los Angeles to Cabo San Lucas, Mazatlan, and Puerto Vallarta.

The *Holiday* and the *Sensation* sail from Miami through the western Caribbean to Ocho Rios, Grand Cayman and Cozumel and Playa del Carmen. The *Sensation* also offers an eastern Caribbean itinerary (along with the *Celebration*) from Miami to San Juan, St. Maarten and St. Thomas.

The itineraries for the three newest ships have not yet been announced.

FOR MORE INFORMATION: Call (800) 438-6744 for a brochure. Contact your travel agent for reservations.

NORWEGIAN CRUISE LINE
Starward
Southward
Westward
Dreamward
Windward
Seaward
Norway

Norwegian Cruise Line is one of the masters in the American cruise business. Its 3- to 7-day cruises crisscross the Caribbean from the Bahamas to South America, and from Mexico to the West Indies, calling at 25 different ports. Other 7-day cruises take passengers from the East Coast to Bermuda and back, and from Vancouver to Alaska, with two different itineraries.

The line's seven ships range from a group of smaller ships in the 725-to-830 passenger range—the *Starward*, *Southward* and *Westward*—to mid-size ships, the *Dreamward*, *Windward* and

Seaward, which accommodate 1,200 to 1,500 passengers—to the 2,032-passenger *Norway*, the world's largest cruise ship and the flagship of the fleet.

We cruised out of San Juan, Puerto Rico, on the *Starward* for one week to the lower Caribbean islands of Barbados, Martinique, Antigua, St. Maarten, and St. Thomas. The line's other cruise ships start from different ports and visit different islands. But the on-board amenities and programs of all the ships are similar.

ACCOMMODATIONS: $$$ to $$$$ Norwegian Cruise Line has "one class" ships, with the staterooms varying very little in decor and amenities. All staterooms are above the water line. Rates reflect differences in location. Deluxe suites are much larger than standard rooms.

Rates include round-trip airfare from more than 100 American cities to the port of embarkation. Passengers who do not require air transport can deduct $250 from the rates. Children occupying the third or fourth bed in a cabin are charged a reduced rate. Children under 2 travel free.

Standard cabins feature a double bed or twin beds and one or two bunkbeds that are stowed during the day. The bunks are suitable for children, but a large teenager or adult would feel cramped. All cabins have private baths, with showers, and 110-volt electrical service to handle hair dryers, electric razors, and small travel irons.

Cabin service is excellent. Your steward will straighten up during the day, provide turn-down service at night, and make sure you have a constant supply of fresh towels for bathroom and pool.

DINING: Norwegian Caribbean ships, like most cruise ships, offer more food each day than any rational human would ever consider consuming: early-morning wake-up snacks, six-course breakfasts, luncheon buffets, afternoon teas with pastries and finger sandwiches, marvelous dinners, and a sumptuous midnight buffet.

Food quality is excellent, and the variety astounding. Among the courses offered at every meal are "light options" for calorie watchers. Buffet breakfasts and lunches are served in poolside cafés. Room service is available on all ships.

ACTIVITIES

 Two pools on each ship except the *Southward*, which has one. Snorkeling instruction. On Caribbean sailings, the "Dive-In" program offers snorkeling at every stop. Fees include snorkeling equipment. Children 5 and up are welcome.

 Early-morning fitness program, workout facilities, basketball, Ping-Pong. Active or retired NFL players mingle with passengers on every 7-day cruise.

 Backgammon tournaments, beauty demonstrations, perfume and cosmetics seminars, sightseeing lectures, tours of the ship's bridge, arts and crafts classes, card and Ping-Pong tournaments, movies, trapshooting. After dinner, the ship's nightclub offers a music, comedy, or magic show; sometimes, the ship's entertainment staff puts on a comedy review. Casino, disco, movies.

FOR CHILDREN: The *Norway*, *Dreamward*, *Windward* and *Southward* offer supervised "Kids Crew" programs year-round for both teenagers and younger children; the other NCL ships, the *Seaward* and the *Starward*, offer them during summer months and over major holidays. The minimum age for participation is 6, although supervised morning activities are offered to 3- to 5-year-olds during summer and holiday sailings on the *Norway, Dreamward, Windward* and *Southward*. As many as 100 children are aboard each ship during holiday periods.

The children are divided by age into four groups. While at sea, children's activities start at about 10 A.M. Activities include a tour of the captain's bridge, swimming pool games, bingo, scavenger hunts, drawing contests, movies, word games, ice-cream sessions, stories, and masquerade parties. On most cruises, children practice songs, dances, and magic tricks and perform a "Circus at Sea" for parents one night.

On some days, children eat lunch with parents; on others they eat with the children's program coordinators. Parents collect children at about 4 P.M. to prepare for dinner. The children's program usually meets for an hour or two in the evening as well.

Teens have their own on-board program, with games, sports, and social events.

Baby-sitting can be arranged.

The *Dreamward* and the *Windward* each has a children's playroom, called Kids Korner, as well as a separate teen activity center, complete with a jukebox and large-screen TV. The *Norway's* playroom is called Trolland; *Seaward's* is Porthole. All the play-rooms feature SEGA Genesis video game systems, as well as play equipment, arts and crafts materials, and board games. The *Starward* has no special facilities for children.

NICETIES: Let your dining room waiter know about birthdays and anniversaries in your family. A chorus of waiters will present a cake and sing for the honoree.

Under the air/sea package, NCL staff members meet your flight, whisk away your baggage, and place it at your cabin door a few hours later. On the way back home, NCL takes your bag to customs and makes sure it gets on your homeward flight.

PORTS OF CALL: In the late fall, winter, and early spring, the *Dreamward* sails from Ft. Lauderdale to the Western Caribbean. From May through October, it sails round-trip from New York City to Bermuda.

In the winter, the *Windward* sails on seven-day cruises from San Juan to the southern Caribbean; from May through September, it offers Alaska cruises from Vancouver. In between the two itineraries, the ship offers cruises through the Panama Canal.

The *Westward* offers seasonal itineraries to Bermuda and the Mexican Riviera.

The *Seaward* offers 3- and 4-day cruises from Miami to the Bahamas and Mexico's Gulf coast. The *Norway* offers 7-day voyages year-round from Miami to St. Maarten, St. John, St. Thomas and NCL's private island in the Bahamas.

NCL offers a half dozen or more shore excursions in every port of call; separate fees are charged.

FOR MORE INFORMATION: Call (800) 327-7030 for a brochure. Contact your travel agent for reservations.

PREMIER CRUISE LINES
Star/Ship Oceanic
Star/Ship Atlantic
Star/Ship Majestic

From the moment you step off the gangplank onto one of Premier Cruise Lines' gleaming "Big Red Boats," there's no doubt what these cruise ships are all about. The first thing you're handed are schedules of all the activities the ship's youth counselors have planned for the next three or four days. There's something to do for children until midnight the night before they get off!

The *Oceanic* makes three- and four-day cruises each week from Port Canaveral, on Florida's east coast, to Nassau, Salt Cay (a private out-island) and Port Lucaya, all in the Bahamas. The three-day cruises leave on Fridays, and the four-day cruises, which include a full day at sea, depart on Mondays.

The *Atlantic* cruises the same route, with four-day cruise departures on Sundays and three-day cruise departures on Thursdays.

Their smaller sister ship, the *Majestic*, offers four-night cruises, departing Mondays, between Tampa and the Gulf coast of Mexico, and three-night cruises, departing Fridays, between Tampa and Key West.

Premier Cruise Lines began offering family-focused cruises in 1984, well before the other cruise lines woke up to the potential in the family market. It's still a leader in the field.

All three ships were refurbished in 1991 and 1992. They range in size from the smallest, the *Majestic*, with a capacity of 1,006 passeners, to the *Atlantic*, which can handle 1,550 passengers, to the *Oceanic*, which can accommodate 1,800 passengers. On a cruise during the summer or some school holidays, a third to a half of the passengers are likely to be children, which makes these cruises decidedly family affairs.

ACCOMMODATIONS: **$$** to **$$$$** The ships' passenger cabins range from tiny inside cabins with one double bed to suites with private patios that can easily accommodate extended families. The majority of cabins can accommodate up to five passengers. They all have private bathrooms and ample closet and drawer space. Many of the four-passenger cabins use upper bunks for the third and fourth passengers. Cribs can be arranged.

Children pay a reduced rate if they occupy the same cabin as their parents. Premier offers packages that include the cruise, airfare, hotel accommodations at Walt Disney World, admission fees, a rental car and tours of Spaceport USA.

DINING: As on most cruise ships, meals are a memorable experience. You can begin your day at 6 A.M. with early-risers' coffee and pastries and end it with the midnight buffet, with in-between stops for a hearty sit-down breakfast, late-morning coffee, a luncheon buffet or sit-down lunch, afternoon tea and cakes, cocktails, and an elegant dinner. On the nights the *Oceanic* and the *Atlantic* are docked in Nassau, there's even an additional repast—French onion soup and made-to-order eggs Benedict from 1 to 3 A.M.

The food on the ships is exceptionally good and beautifully presented. There are two seatings for dinner in the ships' Galaxy Dining Rooms, at 6 and 8:15 P.M. Special children's menus ensure happy children.

Each night of your cruise, dinner is organized around a different theme. The first night out is usually "A Stop in the Italian Riviera." On the second night, it's "An Evening in Paris." A night in Nassau is, not quite appropriately, "The Caribbean Isles." The last night at sea is "A Salute to America the Beautiful."

ACTIVITIES

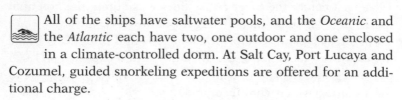 All of the ships have saltwater pools, and the *Oceanic* and the *Atlantic* each have two, one outdoor and one enclosed in a climate-controlled dorm. At Salt Cay, Port Lucaya and Cozumel, guided snorkeling expeditions are offered for an additional charge.

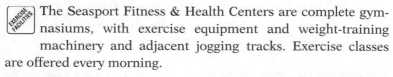 The Seasport Fitness & Health Centers are complete gymnasiums, with exercise equipment and weight-training machinery and adjacent jogging tracks. Exercise classes are offered every morning.

Bingo games, scavenger hunts, mock horse-racing competitions, trivia quizzes, talent shows, shuffleboard, costume parties, dance classes, ice-cream sundae socials, special teas for parents, vegetable carving demonstrations, lectures about the Bahamas, and movies. Casino with slot machines, several blackjack tables, and a roulette wheel. At night, the lounges hop with a variety of entertainment. In the show "Legends in Concert," convincing look-alikes pretend to be some of America's most favorite entertainers.

FOR CHILDREN: Each ship has several separate indoor play areas for children, as well as private open decks with great play-ground equipment, cute riding toys, and splash pools. The *Oceanic's* play areas are the largest.

Each ship carries up to 30 youth counselors, most of them cheerful young men and women who have had previous experience in child care. For supervised activities, children are divided into groups by age: "First Mates" for children 2 to 4; "Kids Call" for ages 5 to 7; "Starcruisers" for ages 8 to 10; "Navigators" for ages 11 to 13, and "Teen Cruisers" for ages 14 to 17.

Scheduled kids' activities begin at 10 A.M. and end at 10 P.M., with breaks for meals with parents. Children can spend as little or as much time in the programs as they wish.

The 2- to 4-year-olds spend time listening to stories, singing songs, making arts and crafts, having their faces painted and going on treasure hunts in the First Mates Club House. They also go on tours of the bridge, build sand castles, and help make costumes for each boat's current play.

Each evening, as the young children begin to wind down, the counselors dim the lights, lay out mats, and give each child a blanket and a pillow to curl up with in front of a video. After 10 P.M., group baby-sitting is available in Pluto's Playhouse until 1:30 A.M. for an hourly fee. In-room baby-sitting is not available.

Children 8 through 13 meet in the Space Station, where they have video game competitions, go on scavenger hunts, play water basketball, make crafts and play games.

On each ship, a separate lounge for children over 13 features a dance floor, jukebox, and video games. Pool volleyball, bridge tours, karaoke contests, basketball shootouts, Ping-Pong tournaments, and dances are scheduled during each cruise.

When the *Oceanic* and *Atlantic* are at Salt Cay, supervised beach activities are offered for children.

The ships' new "Voyages of Discovery" programs enable parents and children to engage in hands-on, multimedia activities designed to enrich their understanding of natural phenomenon and maritime history.

NICETIES: A bagful of chocolate "ship" cookies awaits children in their cabin.

Looney Tunes characters such as the Tasmanian Devil, Road Runner, Tweety and Bugs Bunny roam the ship signing autographs and creating photo opportunities. For an extra fee, you can have one of the characters tuck in your children one night!

PORTS OF CALL: The *Oceanic* and the *Atlantic* are in Nassau until 2 A.M., so with a little planning you can get a good taste of the city and even lose some money at the casinos on Paradise Island. Should you wish to leave the children behind, Pluto's Playhouse remains open for supervised free play.

Children will enjoy walking up the 65 steps of the Queen's Staircase, which leads to another popular historical site, the ship-shaped Fort Fincastle. Ardastra Gardens, a short taxi ride from downtown, is Nassau's private zoo; it features the only flamingos in the world that have been trained to march. Coral World is a marine park and underwater observatory on Silver Cay. Children will enjoy watching the shark, stingray, and turtle tanks and observing action in the reef tank 20 feet under the sea.

During the daylong stopover in Port Lucaya, on Grand Bahama Island, you can participate in a "dolphin encounter," go deep-sea fishing, golf, parasail, snorkel or scuba dive, ride in the Seaworld Explorer (a semi-submarine) or simply loll on a beach.

In Mexico, the *Majestic* stops in Playa del Carmen and Cozumel. You can snorkel in the Chankanaab Nature Park or the Xel-Ha National Park, loll on a beautiful beach, attend the Ballet Folklorico, ride horses through a jungle, go on a glass-bottom boat ride, or take a side trip to the ancient Maya ruins at Tulum or Chichen Itza.

Key West, where the *Majestic* spends 12 hours on its three-day cruises, is famous for its street life. Be sure to drop into the charming Key West Aquarium, and take a trolley ride around town. Kids will enjoy the Ripley's Believe It or Not Museum.

FOR MORE INFORMATION: For a brochure, call (800) 473-3262. For reservations, see your travel agent.

ROYAL CARIBBEAN CRUISE LINE
Majesty of the Seas
Monarch of the Seas
Sovereign of the Seas
Nordic Empress
Viking Serenade
Song of America
Song of Norway
Nordic Prince
Sun Viking

When Royal Caribbean Cruise Line's ships depart from Miami, Florida, for their seven-day cruises to the Caribbean, a band plays and streamers fly. The departure is every bit as exciting as it was when steamships were the only means of transport across the Atlantic and "making the crossing" was only within the reach of the upper class. Before you know it, you've left Miami behind and are out in the middle of the deep blue sea. During your seven days on the ships, you'll sail through tropical waters, feast on elegant meals, and sample a few foreign countries.

We cruised on the *Song of America*, which made its maiden voyage in 1982. The third-largest of the Royal Caribbean ships, *Song of America* can accommodate 1,390 passengers, a small town's worth. There were sun decks on several levels, an outdoor café, two swimming pools, and the Viking Crown Lounge—the Royal Caribbean hallmark. This glass-enclosed lounge rises 10 stories above the sea, cantilevered from the ship's funnel stack.

The staff of 500 included Norwegian officers and employees of dozens of nationalities, which gave the ship an international flavor. The passenger list usually contains names from all over the world as well; your children are as likely to make friends from Canada and France as from New Jersey or Missouri. And it's not uncommon to have more than 200 passengers under the age of 18, especially during the summer and holiday periods.

ACCOMMODATIONS: $$$ to $$$$ Royal Caribbean staterooms are comfortable, well-designed, and attractive. You'll find ample closet and drawer space, a tabletop that can be used as a desk or dressing table, and single beds, some of which convert to queens. In many of the standard staterooms, Pullman upper beds are available to accommodate families of three or four. Larger families will have to reserve two cabins.

Each stateroom has a private bathroom with shower, a telephone, a three-channel radio, and 110-volt outlets for small appliances. Cribs can be reserved, but it's advisable to bring your own porta-crib.

Children sharing a stateroom with their parents qualify for third- and fourth-person rates, which are substantially lower than double rates. Rates include round-trip air transportation to Miami from most major cities, all meals, services, and entertainment. The fares do not include gratuities, shore excursions, and port taxes.

DINING: On the *Song of America*, breakfast options include a modest continental breakfast delivered to your cabin, a served breakfast in the dining room, or a buffet breakfast outside at the Verandah Café.

The Verandah Café is also a popular spot for lunch. You'll find a hot entrée, barbecued hamburgers and sandwiches, as well as salads and desserts. If you'd like a more formal luncheon, you can always retreat to the dining room for a five-course meal. Afternoon tea is also served in the Verandah Café. The pièce de résistance for kids is serve-yourself ice-cream sundaes.

Dinner is always an event, complete with music, costumed waiters, and flaming desserts. One night, the theme is French; another night, it's the exotic cuisine of the Caribbean. As a band plays, waiters parade with dessert cakes balanced on their heads. The passengers cheer and twirl red napkins above their heads.

Passengers request one of two sittings (6:30 or 8:30 P.M.) and receive table assignments. A children's menu features such child pleasers as hot dogs, tuna fish sandwiches, macaroni and cheese and popcorn shrimp. High chairs are available.

Dress for several evenings is casual (men won't even need a jacket) but on at least two nights, dress-up clothes are required.

ACTIVITIES

 Small saltwater pools on each ship. In many of the Caribbean ports, beach outings are offered, or you can find a beach on your own.

 Children and their parents can join in the ShipShape program, where they earn ShipShape "dollars" that can be redeemed for a ShipShape T-shirt and sun visor. Activities include a walkathon, aerobics classes, golf driving and putting, Ping-Pong and basketball tournaments, and aquacize.

 A mind-boggling array of daily activities, including cash bingo, Trivial Pursuit, gambling (slot machines, blackjack, or American roulette), movies. Dancing, cabaret shows, a masquerade ball, a country and western night, and a passenger talent show are among the evening possibilities.

FOR CHILDREN: Children's programs are offered on all of the Royal Caribbean ships, though the dates and hours vary. Generally, they're offered year-round on *Majesty of the Seas*, *Monarch of the Seas*, *Sovereign of the Seas*, *Viking Serenade* and *Nordic Empress*. On the other ships, they're generally offered during the summer months and over the Christmas, New Year's, and Easter holidays.

On each ship, children are divided into three age groups: "Kids", 5- through 8-year-olds; "Tweens", 9- through 12-year-olds," and "Teens," 13- through 17-year-olds. Participation is voluntary, and kids can drop in and out as they please. On days the ships are at sea, activities are generally scheduled between 9 A.M. and noon, 1:30 P.M. and 4:30 P.M., and 8 and 10 P.M.

On a typical day, children may meet their counselors for breakfast and then take part in a walkathon, golf-putting tournament, shuffleboard competition, or pool games. In the afternoon, a scavenger hunt, kite flying, or Ping-Pong tournament might be offered. After dinner, kids play bingo, see a movie, or join the masquerade parade.

Older kids enjoy disco dances, mock casino games, and pizza parties. Teens are usually regulars at the midnight buffets!

Facilities for children vary from ship to ship. *Sovereign of the Seas*, *Monarch of the Seas*, *Majesty of the Seas*, *Nordic Empress* and *Viking Serenade* have special children's playrooms, and the *Majesty of the Seas*, *Monarch of the Seas* and the *Viking Serenade* have teen centers. The other ships use the regular public rooms for children's activities.

In-room baby-sitting can be arranged (three-hour minimum).

NICETIES: The bellmen provide cabin service 24 hours a day. Coffee, drinks, sandwiches, and continental breakfast are available.

On the last day of the cruise, the youth counselors distribute autograph books and pens to all the children.

PORTS OF CALL: Five of Royal Caribbean's nine ships specialize in the Caribbean cruise market.

Sovereign of the Seas sails every Saturday from Miami on 7-night cruises to St. Thomas, San Juan and Coco Cay. *Monarch of the Seas* offers four different 5- to 8-night itineraries, generally in the Southern Caribbean. *Majesty of the Seas* also offers four 5- to 8-night itineraries, generally in the northern Caribbean.

Song of America offers seven different itineraries in the Caribbean in the winter; in the summer, it cruises between New York and Bermuda. The *Nordic Empress* offers 3- and 4-night cruises between Miami and Nassau.

Viking Serenade plies the waters of the Pacific on 3- and 4-night cruises from Los Angeles to Catalina Island, California, and Ensenada, Mexico. The *Nordic Prince* offers longer cruises in the Pacific, with eight different itineraries, including the Mexican Riviera, the Pacific Northwest, and Alaska.

Song of Norway offers 12 different itineraries as far afield as Scandinavia, Russia, the Mediterranean and the Panama Canal.

Sun Viking, the line's smallest ship, offers cruises from San Juan to the Southern Caribbean in the winter, a Panama Canal voyage in April, and 10-night cruises from Vancouver through the Inside Passage to Alaska in the spring and summer.

FOR MORE INFORMATION: See your travel agent.

ADVENTURE TRIPS

CHEWONKI WILDERNESS TRIPS
Wiscasset, Maine

The Chewonki Foundation has shaped the leadership skills of four generations of American youth. The Chewonki summer camp for boys, begun in 1915, still thrives as the oldest ecologically oriented camp in the country. Its alumni include Roger Tory Peterson and Kingman Brewster; Rachel Carson sent her nephew there.

Happily, in recent years the Chewonki program has expanded in many other directions with workshops, wilderness trips and expeditions, school semester and outreach programs, and environmental education programs for families.

The Chewonki experience has as its starting point an encounter with nature, whether on a canoeing, sailing or hiking trip, or in a natural history workshop. Through the skill of the Chewonki staff, these encounters challenge participants individually and as a group through observation, problem solving, communication, and decision making. The result is a sense of community, a growth in personal insight and self-confidence, and a greater appreciation of the natural environment.

Chewonki takes the great out-of-doors as its classroom. Headquarters are 400 acres of beautiful, heavily wooded peninsula not far from Wiscasset, Maine. Various trips explore the spectacular coast, mountains, forests, and streams of Maine.

Chewonki programs operate in every month of the year, but the programs designed for families are held in the summer. Chewonki trips vary in length, type, degree of challenge, and emphasis. Groups of 8 to 12 are encouraged to organize themselves and approach Chewonki to design a trip that will serve that particular group.

THE OUTFITTER: The Chewonki Foundation is a tight-knit community made up of people with shared values and beliefs. Of the full-time staff of 50, 17 are environmental educators. Most have formal training in ecology or environmental education, and all are skilled in the ways of the out-of-doors.

THE ITINERARY: Samples of family trips scheduled in recent years include the following:

- Seven days on the Allagash River in the Allagash Wilderness Waterway, with both lake and river paddling, from Churchill Dam to the town of Allagash.
- Five days on the Moose River.
- A 7-day sailing and rowing trip among the Maine islands in traditional boats built at Chewonki.
- A 5-day hiking trip in beautiful Baxter State Park, including a climb of Mt. Katahdin
- A 5-day sea kayak trip from Chewonki Neck downeast to Muscongus Bay or beyond.

During each trip, Chewonki leaders teach trip members about the local ecology, through both formal lectures and hands-on observation. Every Chewonki trip produces a journal that represents the combined efforts of the group. Group members take responsibility for recording a day's activities or a special event. Poems, recipes, drawings, and short essays are included. Children too young to write contribute drawings. Finally, names and addresses are added, and the resulting record of the trip or workshop is photocopied and distributed to all group members.

A journal entry from a week-long sailing/rowing trip from Jonesport to Northeast Harbor tells of the camaraderie the group feels with a group of curious dolphins that circled the boat so closely that their breathing could be heard.

Each night the group gathers around a fire to sing and exchange reflections on the day.

FOR CHILDREN: The canoeing, hiking, and sailing trips are suitable for age 8 and above; the minimum age for sea kayaking is 13. The guiding rule for all Chewonki activities is capability. Chewonki requires only that participants be physically capable of engaging in the activities that are necessarily part of a trip.

On each trip with children, the leaders make a special effort to involve them at their developmental level.

RATES AND PERSONAL GEAR: Costs vary based on the itinerary and each group's special needs. Rates include meals and all general camping equipment, such as tents, cooking equipment, saws, axes, and the special equipment required for any trip, such as canoes, paddles, life jackets, and the like. Families bring their own sleeping bags, packs, and clothing. Detailed equipment lists are sent out in advance. Early reservations are advisable.

An important part of a Chewonki experience is the food. Good nutrition is part of the Chewonki creed. Rather than load up backpacks and boxes with highly processed foods, Chewonki trips carry the real thing—vegetables, whole-grain cereals, flour, and fresh meat. The results are gratifying: pancakes for breakfast, delicious sandwiches for lunch, stir-fry dishes for dinner, and a cake from the reflector oven or biscuits from the Dutch oven.

Chewonki counselors do not take on the role of outdoor servants who do all the grunt work. Rather, work that supports the welfare of the group is a shared responsibility.

FOR MORE INFORMATION: Write Greg Shute, Wilderness Trip Director, Chewonki Foundation, RR 2, Box 1200, Wiscasset, ME 04578, or call (207) 882-7323.

MAINE WINDJAMMER CRUISE
Penobscot Bay, Maine

Since the early 1970s, the jagged coast of Maine has been one of America's favorite summer playgrounds. Water, sun, delightfully cool weather, great scenery, and marvelous seafood all contribute to the Maine experience. But popularity has its price. In the summer invasion of the Maine coast, tourists fight monumental traffic jams on U.S. 1 to crowd into hotels and restaurants.

A cruise on a windjammer is the answer for families who want to get away from it all on the Maine coast. A vacation on one of these great sailing ships combines solitude, history, adventure, relaxation, good food, and wonderful scenery in half-week or full-week sails among the islands off the coast of Maine.

America's rich maritime history comes alive on an authentic coastal schooner. Many of the ships in the Maine Windjammer Assocation fleet date from the turn of the century—the golden age of sail when "coasters" dominated the eastern seaboard, engaged in the work of fishing and hauling cargo and passengers.

Most Maine windjammers are schooners—an American sailing craft specially rigged to accommodate the variable winds off American coasts. Schooners have great maneuverability, allowing the craft to change course quickly and to sail equally well on either tack without lowering or resetting sails.

The oldest ships in the Maine windjammer fleet were built more than 100 years ago. The newest were inspired by the traditional boats and were built as recently as the 1980s. Every boat in the fleet is U.S. Coast Guard-inspected and carries a ship-to-shore radio. The boats range in length from 64 to 132 feet.

THE OUTFITTER: The Maine Windjammer Association got its start in the 1930s, when steamships and railroads were putting schooners out of business. Today the Maine Windjammer Association is made up of individual and family owners of 10 ships.

The renovated boats in the Maine windjammer fleet have been completely refitted below decks with galleys, comfortable guest cabins, and heads (toilets). Each boat accommodates 22 to 44 passengers in cabins that sleep one to four persons. Schooner accommodations are comfortable, but not luxurious. Electric lights and portholes are standard features in most cabins.

Meals are served family-style. The "buffet deck" is the choice in good, warm weather. The long varnished tables in the galley are the scene for breakfast, special dinners, and for all meals in cool or rainy weather.

The food is first-rate. On most of the windjammers, the cooking, including fresh-baked breads and pastries, is done on wood-burning stoves. The crew rises long before first light to bake a breakfast treat for you to enjoy when you climb to the deck in the morning—pancakes, blueberry muffins, eggs, and bacon.

At lunch, there's likely to be chili or chowder, corn bread, and cookies. Dinners feature fresh fish, turkey, breads, pies, and cakes. A lobster feast or roast turkey dinner are the culinary highlights of the week.

THE ITINERARY: Before sailing, the captain holds an informal meeting to familiarize all passengers with the ship and with safety procedures; a welcome-aboard get-together follows. Sailing time is usually set for late morning. Your ship is slowly towed out of the harbor at Camden or Rockland past rows of smaller boats. As your vessel clears the channel markers, the sails are raised, and you move backward in time. The shapes of modern society—buildings, cars, and such—recede and disappear into the beauty of the Maine coast.

This is not like a cruise on an ocean liner; there are no schedules with a half dozen activities to choose from every hour, nor a staff of social directors. On a windjammer, there are no pressures, schedules, or deadlines, no phones, no television sets. Instead, you can lie on the deck and watch clouds drift above the wind-tautened sails. Stand at the rail as your vessel silently treads the narrow passage between uninhabited islands. Watch and listen to the sea as it constantly changes with the weather and time of day. Soak up the sun. Read the books you've been storing up. Play chess or Scrabble or cards. Get to know the other passengers.

A chance pass by another windjammer results in a flurry of picture taking and perhaps a spontaneous "race." Fishermen can troll from the stern of the boat. Nature lovers will be on the lookout for eagles, diving cormorants, and the occasional minke whale. The captain will let you take the helm and show you how he or she navigates among the islands sprinkled along the Maine coast.

The crew needs help each morning in raising the nearly half-ton anchor and in hauling up the sails. The cook always has vegetables and salad ingredients to prepare and cookie batter to mix.

In the late afternoon, the captain consults the charts and selects a safe anchorage in an island cove or small village harbor. The dinghy will be lowered into the water so that photographers and sightseers can row out to explore the surrounding shores and take photographs of the windjammer against the setting sun. The general store at the nearby village may be the destination of others.

After dinner, passengers either gather to tell stories and sing or sit on the deck talking quietly or gazing upward at an unrivaled display of stars.

FOR CHILDREN: Because of the relaxed pace of shipboard life and the desire on the part of most guests to experience the quiet and solitude of sailing, windjammer trips are most appropriate for families with older children. If you want to take a windjammer trip with children less than 16 years of age, check with the captain first. The *Nathaniel Bowditch* (800-288-4098) accommodates children over 10 years old. The *Roseway* (800-255-4449) accommodates children 10 and up on a four-day voyage every August; in the winter, it offers cruises in the Virgin Islands (minimum age 16).

RATES AND PERSONAL GEAR: $$$ Rates are comparable on all boats in the fleet. The peak months for sailing are July and August. Rates are somewhat lower in June and September, when wind and weather are often ideal for sailing. Rates include all meals and parking for your car.

Dress on the ships is casual. Some guests like to bring along small musical instruments so they can contribute to the entertainment at night. Passengers wishing to drink carbonated beverages, beer, wine, or liquor must bring their own; large ice chests are provided. You'll certainly want to bring a camera and a pair of binoculars.

OF INTEREST NEARBY: En route to the Penobscot Bay area (a two-or three-hour drive from Portland), consider visiting some of the attractions of coastal Maine.

Wiscasset has one of the finest groups of colonial era buildings in the country. The Maine Maritime Museum and Sewall House Mansion in Bath recall the age of sail. Boothbay is the site of the Railway Village and the Marine Resources Aquarium, with its touch tanks and tidepools. Pemaquid, near Bristol, was one of the earliest settlements in North America and is still one of the most picturesque; its small museum is worth a visit. Rockport has Shore Village Museum, a transportation museum, and historic Owls Head Light. Camden Hills State Park near Camden boasts Mount Megunticook, the highest point along the Atlantic seaboard.

FOR MORE INFORMATION: Write the Maine Windjammer Association, P.O. Box 1144, Blue Hill, ME 04614, or phone (800) 807-WIND.

SOUTHEAST

CUMBERLAND ISLAND CAMPING ADVENTURE
Cumberland Island, Georgia

"Geologic Gussie," "Nudibranch Nancy," "Jungle Jim!" No, these are not endangered species, but the nicknames that participants in a Wilderness Southeast camping adventure took on as they introduced themselves on disembarking from a ferry at Cumberland Island National Seashore off the coast of Georgia.

This unusual round of introductions fits with the philosophy of Wilderness Southeast, a non-profit educational organization whose programs emphasize learning about the natural world in a fun, exciting, and non-stressful way. Wilderness Southeast runs trips for families and individuals that encourage participants to look at nature, the environment, and themselves in new ways.

Cumberland Island National Seashore, with its rich social and natural history, is a perfect destination for families. Cumberland is the southernmost and largest of Georgia's barrier islands. It is 18 miles long and three miles across at its widest point; an occasional sand dune rises 50 feet above sea level.

The island includes beaches and dunes, live oak forests, freshwater ponds and salt marshes. Although it has felt the impact of society's presence, most of the island is wild and uninhabited. Congress guaranteed the island's preservation when it established the Cumberland Island National Seashore in 1972; 85 percent of the island is protected.

THE OUTFITTER: Wilderness Southeast was founded in 1973 by ecologists Dick and Joyce Murlless as a not-for-profit "school of the outdoors," with the belief that learning about nature should be com-fortable and fun. The organization's board of directors is sprinkled with naturalist writers and educators.

Wilderness Southeast offers quality outdoor experiences throughout the Southeast for those who seek something beyond a luxury tour. Among the options for families with children as young as 8 are cabin-based canoe trips through the Okefenokee Swamp and camping and hiking trips in the Great Smoky Mountains. In addition, children 12 and up are welcome on 4-day canoe trips in the Florida Springs area and 5-day sea turtle watches. Children 14 and up are welcome on canoe-camping trips through the Okefenokee and hiking and rafting trips on the Big Bend River. And children 16 and up are welcome on kayak and canoe trips through the Everglades; snorkeling trips in Belize; backpack trips through the Blue Ridge Mountains, and sea kayak trips off the Georgia coast.

On each trip, campers are made comfortable, but not pampered; they are invited to live with nature, not conquer or merely endure it.

Trip leaders are experienced naturalists who put heart and soul into maximizing a camper's contact with nature while relieving him or her of the chores of wilderness travel. Groups are kept small to allow group members to form closer bonds and to minimize the ecological impact of camping.

THE ITINERARY: On the Cumberland Island trip, the group gathers at Park Visitors Center in St. Marys, Georgia. You then board the ferry for a 45-minute trip through the St. Marys River coastal marshes and Cumberland Sound to the island. Gear is loaded on to hand carts, and the group walks a half mile to beautiful Sea Camp campground, set in a live oak forest just behind barrier dunes and Sea Camp Beach on the ocean side of the island.

Sea Camp is a well-equipped campground with rest rooms and shower blocks built of attractive native oak. The rest rooms have electric outlets for hair dryers or electric shavers.

At the campfire on the first evening, the group and leaders set a tentative agenda for the next three and a half days, allowing ample free time.

A typical day begins in a leisurely way. Early risers have the beach, the morning mist, and the sunrise to themselves. Together, the leaders and participants prepare breakfasts of fresh fruit, bagels and cream cheese, pancakes or omelets, and hot chocolate, tea or coffee.

Each day brings explorations of different parts of the island. On some days, the group takes a lunch on a full-day trip; on other days the group returns to camp for lunch. Explorations are leisurely walks to the beach, salt marsh, forest, dunes, and historical sites on the island. The group sets the pace. Group members disperse to explore and collect shells, with members returning to the leader from time to time with interesting finds.

Leaders are schooled in the local ecology, and are fully capable of presenting an academic lecture on the subject. But the learning process is experiential, not pedantic. Leaders allow group members to engage nature, and assist them in the process. They explain the ecology of the island using the plants, animals, and land forms encountered on a walk.

The beach is a magnificent stretch of white sand, always changing. The beach here rivals the best in the world. Each high tide washes up millions of shells. Shore birds—sea gulls, terns, black skimmers, pelicans, and sanderlings—can always be seen; more than 300 species have been sighted here. Female loggerhead turtles lay eggs here during the summer months.

Live oak and pine forests occupy the central part of the island. Trails crisscross the forests, making access easy. Freshwater ponds attract raccoons, deer, and feral horses (descendants of horses released by the Carnegie family). Armadillos waddle everywhere. Wild pigs are more elusive.

Salt marshes line the sound side of the island. These wetlands are among the most productive habitats in the world and are the home of ducks, fiddler crabs, wading birds, shrimp, and numerous fish.

Man's impact on the island may be the subject of another walk. Shell middens are reminders of the coastal Indian society. The 19th-century agricultural economy is represented by ruins of plantation buildings. And the ruins of the Carnegie Dungeness mansion evoke insights into the leisure activities of early industrialists.

Two Visitors' Centers are located at the south end of the island, with a half-mile trail between them along the St. Marys River and Cumberland Sound. Each has a museum. The museum at Sea Camp Dock illuminates the natural history of the island. Human history is the subject of the museum at Dungeness Dock.

After group activities, there is ample time for families or individuals to explore, or swim, or just relax. Dinner is always an extremely appetizing and appealing culinary experience. A soup may begin the meal, followed by a chicken and vegetable casserole. Fresh corn bread baked at the camp fire in a Dutch oven and a tossed salad are accompaniments, with a pudding or strawberry shortcake for dessert. Fresh fruit is offered at every dinner.

After dinner, the evening's entertainment begins around a campfire and frequently ends with a game on the beach. The campfire is a time for discussing that day's activities and planning the following day. Campfire games all have an ecological theme and are appropriate to all ages. "Emerald hunts" with flashlights reveal insect eyes and beach creatures that glow in the dark. In a guessing game, each group member uses "magic clay" to sculpt an animal found on Cumberland Island.

FOR CHILDREN: Each Wilderness Southeast trip varies in sleeping arrangements, activities, and strenuousness. The Cumberland Island trip is appropriate for children 8 and older. It is best that your child have some camping experience.

In addition to its regularly scheduled group trips, Wilderness Southeast will custom design trips for one or more families to any of its regular nature destinations or to other mutually agreeable destinations.

RATES AND PERSONAL GEAR: $ to $$ There's a 15-percent discount for children under 18 who are accompanied by one parent, and a 25-percent discount for children accompanied by two parents.

Wilderness Southeast provides two person tents, all food, and eating gear. You may bring your own tent, if you prefer. Sleeping bags, air mattresses, and a day pack may be rented. A list of recommended personal clothing and equipment is mailed to all group members. When trips involve canoes or snorkeling, Wilderness Southeast provides the equipment. The outfitter even brings a small "library" of field guides appropriate to the area and ecology. Bring sun block, insect repellent, sunglasses, and comfortable walking shoes.

OF INTEREST NEARBY: Okefenokee National Wildlife Refuge is an hour's drive from St. Marys, Georgia, and is an ideal area for camping and canoeing adventures.

FOR MORE INFORMATION: Write Wilderness Southeast at 711 Sandtown Road, Savannah, GA 31410, or call (912) 897-5108.

WHITE-WATER RAFT TRIP ON THE NEW RIVER
Fayette County, West Virginia

An outfitter on the New River in West Virginia has found a way to remove the barriers to white-water rafting for many families. Class VI River Runners of Lansing, West Virginia, provides a number of trip options that allow children to accompany parents on the calmer sections of the New River—and then take part in stimulating off-river activities while their parents run the more demanding sections.

The New River is a great white-water stream and a geological curiosity. It is one of the few rivers outside the Arctic region that flows northward; its headwaters are in North Carolina, and it flows into the Ohio River. It also has one of the deepest river gorges east of the Mississippi, well over 1,000 feet deep at points. The New's descent is gradual over much of its course, but a 16-mile stretch descends more rapidly, with a gradient of 12 feet per mile.

The history of settlement along the New River adds to the fascination of a raft trip. The completion of the C & O rail line in 1873, linking the Ohio valley with the Eastern Seaboard, opened the valley to coal mining. More than 20 coal towns sprang up on the riverbanks over the next 50 years—towns like Prince, Dunfee, Rushrun, Beury, and Nuttall. But the coal industry is depressed now, and as you raft down the New River you pass the ghost towns of that once- thriving coal economy.

The history and the scenic beauty of the New River led the federal government to designate a 53-mile stretch a National River in 1978. It is managed by the National Park Service.

THE OUTFITTER: Class VI is one of more than 15 outfitters on the New River. What sets Class VI apart is the quality of its services and the services it offers families.

Class VI offers a large variety of raft trips on the New and the nearby Gauley. You can choose a casual one-day float down calm, scenic portions of the New River or a hair-raising ride down the most difficult sections of the New or the Gauley.

The most popular trip is the one-day raft trip down the most challenging section of the New River, which includes some good solid Class IV rapids and maybe a Class V, depending on how the water is running.

Class VI's headquarters and stylish reception building over-look the New River Gorge near the small town of Ames Heights, West Virginia. Its equipment is first-rate. Rafts accommodate six to nine people. All rafts are guided by expert members of the Class VI staff, who have knowledge of the local history and train-ing in first aid and CPR. No prior rafting experience is required of passengers; you need not even be a swimmer. Good-quality life jackets are provided, as well as instruction.

THE ITINERARY: The section of the New River from Prince to Thurmond is a good one-day family trip. When you assemble at the Class VI headquarters, sweet rolls, coffee, and hot chocolate are available. Use the change rooms to don swimsuits or shorts, and then board the Class VI bus for the 45-minute ride to Prince.

There, your guide fits you with a life jacket and explains pro-cedures. No alcoholic beverages are allowed on this or any other Class VI river trip. A waterproof rubber bag is available for cam-eras.

Your trip will have one or more rafts. Inflatable kayaks, better known as "rubber duckies," are also used on this relatively calm portion of the river. They accommodate one adult or an adult and a child. The duckies are great fun. Even a novice can man-age them.

Near midday, the group stops for lunch. An upside-down raft serves as a table. You'll be offered make-your-own sandwiches with appropriate relishes, and perhaps marinated mushrooms, potato salad, a salmon pasta salad, dessert, and cold drinks (there's also peanut butter and jelly for balky kids).

There are several Class II rapids in the afternoon. These are fun rapids that are easily run. The trip ends around 4 or 5 P.M. at a take-out point just above Thurmond. Soda is served before the bus departs for Class VI headquarters.

Class VI serves dinner on the upper deck of its reception building on Friday through Monday evenings during the sum-mer. Charcoal grilled roast beef, turkey, ribs, or chicken are on the menu, along with a salad bar, fresh vegetables, potatoes, baked beans, and a homemade dessert, plus an eclectic selection of beer and wine. During busy periods, reserve in advance.

An alternate raft trip is from Thurmond to Fayetteville, the most challenging part of the New River. Your raft glides by the old railroad town of Thurmond, and a series of small rapids sharpen paddling skills in the first seven miles of this trip. Later in the day, you'll crash through the three Keeneys, the river's best known rapids, with a total vertical drop of 45 feet from the top of Upper Keeney to the bottom of Lower Keeney.

FOR CHILDREN: The age minimum for children on raft trips in the popular Thurmond-Fayette Station section of the New River is 14 years until July 1 and 12 years afterward.

Other portions of the New are more appropriate for family trips. The 12 miles of river above Thurmond, starting at Prince, have calmer water, with Class I and II rapids, which is perfect for a family raft trip. The minimum age for children in the Prince-Thurmond section is 6 years.

Class VI will take children 6 and older on a raft trip on the calmer portions of the New River while their parents get their kicks in the heavy rapids. Both the adults' and children's trips depart and return to headquarters at about the same time.

An alternative is to do a two- or three-day trip by combining two or three one-day family trips on the upper New River. There are three different sections of the river on which Class VI will take children 6 and older.

Class VI will attempt to arrange a schedule that will meet your needs and will even arrange baby-sitting for your younger children. Trips depart almost every Friday, Saturday and Sunday from mid-March through October.

RATES AND PERSONAL GEAR: $ In peak periods, and particularly on weekends, it is best to make reservations. Children under 17 are half-price for the upper New River trips.

The water is cold in March, April, and May and again in late September and October. You may need a wet suit then, which can be rented for a nominal fee. It's a good idea to have sunglasses or a hat, sunscreen, and a windbreaker in all seasons on the river.

Class VI will send you a recommended personal gear list for overnight trips. You provide sleeping bags and a tent (or rent the latter). Class VI provides waterproof bags for packing your gear and all food for overnight trips.

OF INTEREST NEARBY: Highway 19 spans the New River Gorge over one of the longest arch construction bridges in the world. Class VI's headquarters is a short distance away. Stop at the

Visitors' Center on the north rim of the gorge and walk to the observation platform for a good view of the bridge.

FOR MORE INFORMATION: Write Class VI River Runners, Ames Heights Road, P.O. Box 78, Lansing WV 25862-0078, or call (304) 574-0704 or (800) CLASS VI (252-7784).

CANOEING ON THE BUFFALO NATIONAL RIVER
The Ozarks, Arkansas

In 1972, as the last of America's free-flowing streams seemed destined for damming, Congress acted to protect some of those that were still untamed. The Buffalo River, one of the nation's finest streams, was the first to be designated a national river. Development was banned along its entire length of 132 miles, and most of the vestiges of previous development were removed. So a float from the river's source in the Boston Mountains to its junction with the White River is truly a wilderness experience.

Unlike the rivers in the West, which are known for their thrills and spills, the Buffalo is very much a river for families, with long languorous stretches lined with hardwood forests and towering limestone bluffs. The scenery is lovely, with rushing streams, caves, natural arches, and feeder springs at almost every turn. Clear, deep pools, perfect for swimming, alternate with narrow sections that provide just enough challenge to make it interesting.

The river is perfect for day trips, with evenly spaced put-in and take-out points, but it also offers one of the few opportunities in the central United States for a canoe-camping trip of 10 days or more.

While the primary activity is canoeing, self-guided raft trips are increasing in popularity. And a hiking trail along the river's entire length is being built, with about 26 miles completed between Ponca and Pruitt. Marked trails leading from many gravel bars and riverside campgrounds also offer opportunities for shorter hikes.

THE OUTFITTER: The Buffalo Outdoor Center is the largest authorized concessioner on the river, with 90 canoes based in

Ponca and 150 more downriver in Silver Hill. Mike and Evelyn Mills, the owners, met at the University of Arkansas at Fayetteville and spent their courtship exploring the Buffalo. In 1978, they started up their own river outfitting business with a goal of providing the best service on the river.

Since then, the Millses have custom-designed float trips for thousands of canoeists each year from early spring through late fall. They have two young daughters of their own, so they are attuned to family needs. Mike Mills is the author of a picture book, "The Buffalo, America's First National River," which he dedicated "to the families who gave up their land so that all might enjoy it, and to the individuals that strove to protect this free-flowing stream forever."

THE ITINERARY: The Millses will suggest a stretch of river that suits both your canoeing ability and the depth of your desire to escape from civilization. Anything from a five-hour, 10-mile float to a 10-day, 132-mile voyage is possible. You can leave your car at the offices in Ponca or Silver Hill and have it shuttled, for a fee, to your destination.

The upper Buffalo above Ponca boasts some of the greatest white water in the region in spring, when it's suitable only for experts. Come late May, the level drops to levels more appropriate for amateurs, and by early summer it's too low to be floatable. The 11-mile stretch from the Steel Creek put-in near Ponca to Kyles Landing is an easy first-day float for families. It's particularly scenic, with landmarks such as 500-foot Big Bluff, the tallest bluff in the Ozarks; Hemmed-In Hollow, with the tallest waterfall between the Appalachians and the Rockies; and Bear Cave Hollow, which was carved out of the mountains by a scenic cascading stream.

Another nice stretch for families goes from Pruitt to Hasty. It's particularly good for rafting in the summer months, with many deep holes for swimming, lots of nice gravel bars for picnicking, and plenty of bluffs.

In July and August, the only reliably floatable stretches are on the middle and lower Buffalo, from Woolum Ford to White River. There are many good stretches for fishing and wildlife sighting. From Rush to the White River is the most isolated section of the river; it requires at least one or two overnights. Most of the area below Rush has been designated a wilderness area.

For a first-time canoeing experience, we recommend renting

one of the Buffalo Outdoor Center's cabins at Ponca or Silver Hill and taking several day-long trips on the river. Families with canoeing experience may want to try canoe-camping, stopping overnight on isolated gravel bars or in the National Park Service campgrounds.

FOR CHILDREN: There are no special programs for children along the river, but they will enjoy the summer ranger programs at Buffalo Point, Lost Valley, and Still Creek. They include campfire programs, guided walks and hikes, guided canoe trips, and Ozark crafts and folk music demonstrations. For a schedule, call the National Park Service.

Children age 6 and over will find the whole canoeing experience wonderful if the pace allows plenty of time for swimming and exploring the riverside by foot. There are fossils to be found on most gravel bars, fish to be caught, and deer, turtles, and great blue heron to be spotted.

RATES AND PERSONAL GEAR: $ The Buffalo Outdoor Center's cabins (14 at Ponca, 10 at Silver Hill) are comfortably furnished and fully equipped for housekeeping. They sleep six in three double beds, two of them upstairs in a sleeping loft. Each of the log cabins has a massive stone fireplace, cathedral ceiling with ceiling fans, front porch (some with double swings), and barbecue grills. The cabins are situated in the wooded hills next to the river.

The National Park Service operates 14 campgrounds along the river, each about 10 miles apart. Thirteen are considered rustic (outhouses only) and are free. The campground at Buffalo Point, where fees are charged, has water and electrical hookups, restrooms, showers and trailer dump stations, group sites, and day-use pavilions.

Buffalo Outdoor Center provides paddles, lifejackets, and good-quality plastic canoes, which glide easily over the river's low sections. All you need to bring for day floats are a cooler, water bottles, sunscreen, hats, and a good hearty lunch. Put anything you need to keep dry in a dry bag (available for purchase at the center), and tie everything to the canoe. Wear bathing suits, because you'll surely want to swim.

For multi-day floats, you can either keep your camping and overnight gear in your car and have it shuttled to your destination, or carry it in your canoe.

OF INTEREST NEARBY: While off the beaten path, Ponca is a good base for a family vacation. You can alternate canoeing days with sightseeing forays into the countryside. Mike Mills was director of tourism for Arkansas in the mid 80s, so he knows the state's tourist attractions intimately. Among those worth visiting:

Eureka Springs, about an hour away, drew visitors from all over America to its mineral-water baths in the 19th century, and today it is a charming enclave of former hippies, New Age devotees, folk art craftsmen, and artists. Its hilly streets are lined with beautifully renovated Victorian homes that house bed-and-breakfasts, shops, and restaurants. Mineral baths, eucalyptus steam treatments, facials, and massages are still offered at the Palace Bath House (call 501-253-8400 for reservations). Children will enjoy a ride on the Eureka Springs and North Arkansas steam-powered train.

Somewhat further afield, the Ozark Folk Center State Park in Mountain View celebrates the culture and way of life of the Ozark mountain region before 1920, and its music before 1940. Call (501) 269-3851 for a brochure.

Blanchard Springs Caverns, about 15 miles from the folk center in the Ozark National Forest, has two underground trails.

FOR MORE INFORMATION: Write Buffalo Outdoor Center, P.O. Box 1, Ponca, AR 72670 or call (800) 221-5514. For park information, write Superintendent, Buffalo National River, P.O. Box 1173, Harrison, AR 72602-1173 or call (501) 741-5443.

APOSTLE ISLANDS SAILING ADVENTURE
Madeline Island, Wisconsin

The Apostle Islands are scattered off the tip of the Bayfield peninsula, the westernmost of the three large peninsulas that jut northward into the clear waters of Lake Superior, the largest of the Great Lakes. The 22 Apostles range in size from the three-acre dot of Gull Island to the 14,000 acres of Madeline Island. Twenty-one of the Apostles and a 12-mile-long strip of the mainland shoreline make up the Apostle Islands National Lakeshore.

What a wonderful place for family sailing! The Apostles are a vacationer's paradise of sunshine, clear water, and deep green islands edged with red sandstone cliffs, perfect for any family that loves sailing or has ever dreamed of taking a family sailing vacation. Many protected coves provide safe anchorages, and several marinas in the area also rent slips or anchorages for overnight stays.

The Apostle Islands are a dream spot for nature lovers, too. They have a mixed forest ecology with hardwoods and conifers that provide good habitat for bear, deer, beaver, smaller mammals, and a diverse population of birds, whose numbers and species swell with spring and fall migrations. Terns, ringbill gulls, loons, great blue heron, and the ruby-throated hummingbird are commonly seen here. From May to October, waves of wildflowers bloom in successively bolder hues. Orchids, bog laurel, and sand cherry are seen here, too.

The Apostles are also rich in history. Vestiges of human excursions through these islands remain in abandoned quarries and fishing camps, old lighthouses, and in the Ojibway cemetery on Madeline Island. Many of the Ojibway Indians, also known as the Chippewa, were driven from their home along the eastern Great Lakes by more aggressive tribes. They eventually made their way to the southern shores of Lake Superior and the Apostle Islands. The Madeline Island Historical Museum in La Pointe and the National Lakeshore Visitors' Center in Bayfield house historical relics of these eras and are worth visiting.

THE OUTFITTER: The Apostle Islands Yacht Charter Association (AIYCA) is a co-operative formed by individual boat owners at the Madeline Island Marina. AIYCA was the first charter fleet on Lake Superior to organize in this fashion. The association's offices are in the marina headquarters building on Madeline Island, accessible by car ferry from Bayfield, Wisconsin. Charter guests have full marina privileges, including use of bathrooms and showers.

Each boat in the fleet is owned by an individual co-op member, and each boat and skipper must pass stringent qualifications to be included in the charter fleet.

AIYCA offers a wide selection of boats, from day sailers to large yachts that sleep six or more people and can be sailed the length and breadth of Lake Superior. Interior appointments range from the spartan to the luxurious. Boats suitable for overnight cruising all have bunks with mattresses, a head, and a galley (sink, stove, and ice chest). An assortment of pots, pans, plates, cups, and flatware is provided.

If you opt for an AIYCA skipper, he or she will involve your family in sailing the charter boat and teach you some sailing and water safety fundamentals. But a family that wants to learn to sail, as opposed to being chauffeured, would do well to investigate the Blue Waters Sailing School. The school is headquartered at Madeline Island Marina and is directed by Captain Ann M. Larson, an AIYCA member. Larson and her staff of Coast Guard qualified instructors have 20 years of accumulated teaching experience.

To give its students extended sailing experience on big yachts, the Blue Waters Sailing School periodically offers a 9-day scheduled cruise on a 42-foot ketch from its base at the Madeline Island Marina around Isle Royale in Lake Superior. The sailing party is usually made up of unrelated individuals or several family groups, which makes it an excellent way to share the cost of a yacht-training experience. The Isle Royale training cruise spends four days at Isle Royale itself, circling the National Park, anchoring at night in protected coves, and allowing plenty of time during the day for sightseeing and hiking.

For bare-boat charters, the association requires a certificate from a recognized sailing school or appropriate references.

THE ITINERARY: Firm itineraries are not always possible in sailing. The winds and weather help determine where and when you go. The best approach is to sit down with an AIYCA representative and a chart of the Apostle Islands and sketch a tentative route for your sailing adventure. Consider the amount of time you want to devote to sailing and land exploration, the places you might want to visit, the anchorages available in the islands, and the weather forecast, including wind speed and direction.

Before you start, mark the location of the 11 public docks scattered throughout the islands. These are prime locations for picnic lunches and the starting points for exploring many of the islands. Campgrounds with picnic tables and toilets usually adjoin them.

Come prepared with information on other facilities and programs provided by the National Park Service. Rangers are stationed on some of the larger islands. Stockton Island has a National Lakeshore Visitors' Center with evening programs for campers in the summer months. The larger islands have trail systems linking historic sites like old lighthouses, quarries, or abandoned fishing camps with sand dunes, bogs, and lovely red sand beaches. Trails frequently follow the course of old railroad beds and logging roads.

FOR CHILDREN: If there is one common mistake in family sailing, it is spending too much time sailing and not enough time having fun in the places you can reach by water. The Apostles are a good place for spur-of-the-moment stops. Camping, fishing, hiking, beachcombing, scuba diving, and animal watching experiences await the sailing family in numerous spots. Allow for plenty of shore time and remain flexible enough to change schedules as the needs of family members dictate.

Even young children will enjoy life on a boat if you remember to bring games and activities to amuse them.

RATES AND PERSONAL GEAR: $$$ to $$$$ Charter rates vary with the size of boat. Hiring a skipper or crew member raises the cost considerably. Weekly rates are available.

You will probably want to stop at one or more of the towns and marinas in the Apostle Islands to replenish your food supply as your cruise progresses. You'll find a supermarket in Bayfield and a small grocery store near the marina on Madeline Island. If you prefer, the Association will stock your boat, for a charge.

AIYCA charters are fully equipped with all the gear necessary to sail the boat. A dinghy is provided with most boats, which allows you to get ashore.

Your personal items should include deck shoes, foul-weather gear, warm sweaters or jackets, hats, windbreakers, sunglasses, sunscreen, and sleeping bags or sheets and blankets for every member of your party.

FOR MORE INFORMATION: Write Apostle Islands Yacht Charter Association at P.O. Box 188, La Pointe, WI 54850, or call (715) 747-2983 May through October or (800) 821-3480 year-round.

Tourist information is available from the Apostle Islands National Lakeshore, Route 1, Box 4, Bayfield, WI 54814.

BOAT-CAMPING IN VOYAGEURS NATIONAL PARK
International Falls, Minnesota

Voyageurs National Park is a 218,000-acre expanse of beautiful lakes set in towering forests on the Canada-Minnesota border. It is among the least well-known of our national parks.

These lakes and the narrow passages between them were once the highway of the *voyageurs*, the French-Canadian adventurers who paddled heavy canoes 12 to 16 hours a day to bring trade goods from Montreal into the vast northern wilderness. Life then centered on the waterways, and even today many of the ridges and hilltops in this region are without names. Fifty-six miles of the *voyageurs'* route lie within the park's boundaries.

The park is made up of four major lakes—Rainy, Kabetogama, Namakan, and Sand Point—and more than two dozen smaller lakes. More than a third of its acreage is covered by water. Only three small areas of the park are directly accessible by road, so boats are the only practical way to explore and enjoy its beauty.

THE OUTFITTERS: The Voyageurs area has many outfitters who can provide your family with the essential equipment for an outdoor adventure in the National Park. The Crane Lake Commercial Club is an organization of outfitters who serve the Crane Lake access area; call (800) 362-7405 or write the club in Crane Lake, MN 55725. The National Park Service can provide you with a list of authorized outfitters in all four access areas.

Outfitters will provide you with charts of the lake system, help you select an itinerary, and provide you with a well-maintained motorboat and all the equipment and provisions you might need. They will also teach those not familiar with power-boating how to read channel and hazard markers. They will alert you to Indian pictographs, rookeries, and particularly beautiful islands and coves along the way. Some outfitters can arrange for a guide to accompany your party and to help with fishing, setting up and striking camp, and cooking.

Renting a houseboat is an alternative for families who want to experience the wilderness without roughing it.

THE ITINERARY: You can retrace the route of the voyageurs or just casually cruise the shallow bays and narrow passages between islands, ever on the lookout for deer, beaver, otter, moose, and bear. You're sure to see numerous species of birds, including bald eagles, loons, great blue herons, mergansers, and ducks of many stripes.

Your wanderings may take you to Kettle Falls at the juncture of Namakan and Rainy lakes, where a shuttle is available to take your boat and belongings around the falls. All water-born commerce through the vast North had to pass this spot. Indians, *voyageurs*, loggers, gold miners, and fishermen all converged here. The historic Kettle Falls Hotel has been restored by the national park Service. Located in the wilderness and accessible only by boat, its rooms and furnishings—especially the barroom with the nickelodeon and the uniquely slanted floor—all speak of the heritage of the great northwoods. Call (800) 322-0886 to arrange a stay.

There are 120 designated boat-in camp sites in the national park and countless other sites suitable for camping. Camping is on a first-come, first-served basis (no charge). Each designated site is equipped with a picnic table, fire grate, pit toilet, and tent pad. Most of the campsites on the mainland and on larger islands are also equipped with "bear boxes" for storing food at night.

If camping is not your thing, consider one of the many resorts near the national park that cater to families. Several resorts have children's programs. Nelson's Resort on Crane Lake (phone 218-993-2295) has first-rate cabins, a gourmet dining room, a naturalist program for children, and one of the largest sand beaches in the Voyageurs area. Sandy Point Lodge and Resort, an informal family- friendly place on Kabetogama Lake, has a half-day nature-oriented children's program. It offers a choice of housekeeping cabins or full American plan dining with special children's rates. Call (800) 777-8595.

FOR CHILDREN: Boat-camping is naturally appealing to children.

Many campsites in the park have spectacular vistas, and some have sandy beaches nearby. Avoid campsites with no room for children to play, and choose spots that have safe approaches to the water.

The national park visitor centers at Rainy Lake, Kabetogama, and Ash River offer naturalist-guided activities such as canoe trips, puppet shows, and walks around a beaver pond. The "Kids Explore Voyageurs" program for children 7 to 12 years of age includes a ride in a 26-foot long "Duck" boat, a chat with a "*voyageur*," and an exploration of a beaver pond.

RATES AND PERSONAL GEAR: $ to $$ Rates vary by outfitter and with the amount and kind of equipment and provisions you require. Contact several outfitters and compare services and rates. If you rent a large boat, you will be able to take many camping luxuries—a comfortable tent, camp stove, lantern, ice chests, lawn chairs, fishing gear, extra fuel, and enough food to tide you over until the fishing gets going.

Be sure to bring appropriate clothing. The summer weather here can range from very hot to very cool; it's usually between 60 and 85 degrees Fahrenheit. Bring good rain gear and all the potions you'll need to ward off insects, which can be fierce.

OF INTEREST NEARBY: The Boundary Waters Wilderness Canoe Area is just east of the park. This western entrance is the preferred entrance for those who want the wilderness to themselves. Outfitters in Crane Lake can set you up for the Boundary Waters; they can shuttle your canoe right up to the area by power boat, if you like.

FOR MORE INFORMATION: Write Superintendent, Voyageurs National Park, 3131 Highway 53, International Falls, MN 56649-8904, or phone (218) 283-9821 for general information on the park and lists of outfitters and resorts.

For general travel information, call the International Falls Chamber of Commerce at (800) 325-5766 or the Kabetogama Lake Association at (800) 524-9085.

HOUSEBOATING ON LAKE POWELL

GLEN CANYON NATIONAL RECREATION AREA

Arizona and Utah

There are few more serene experiences than sitting on the deck of a houseboat and drifting by the most spectacular scenery in the Glen Canyon National Recreation Area, with its multi-colored canyons and riveting mid-lake peaks.

Although Lake Powell has been a water playground for millions of Americans since it was opened to boats in the mid 1960s, it is so vast in size—161,390 acres and 186 miles long, with 1,900 miles of zigzagging shoreline—that houseboating vacationers not infrequently find themselves alone with the scenery, with only an eagle soaring overhead for company.

Renting a houseboat is the best way for families to experience the glories of the area, as well as an adventure unto itself. Children of all ages will delight in making themselves at home in these compact floating houses. Even just a few days spent here will present you with innumerable opportunities to fish, swim in the crystal-clear water, hike into otherwise inaccessible canyons, spot wildlife, and visit ancient Indian ruins.

THE OUTFITTER: ARA Leisure Services operates all facilities at Lake Powell, including 308 houseboats out of four marinas: Wahweap Lodge & Marina, on the south shore six miles north of Page, Arizona; Bullfrog Resort & Marina, in Utah, midway on the lake; Hall's Crossing Resort & Marina, across the bay from Bullfrog at mid- lake, and Hite Marina, on the upper lake.

All of the rental boats are in impeccable shape. Three sizes are offered: 36 feet, which sleeps six in three beds; 44 feet, which sleeps 10 in six beds; and 50 feet, which sleeps 12 in eight beds. Each size contains a fully equipped galley, a bathroom with shower, a 12-volt light system (no outlets), a gas grill, and an outdoor deck. The two larger sizes have a separate sleeping area.

Many renters also rent a small tag-along boat—a skiff or a powerboat—and tie it onto the houseboat while they traverse the lake. Families can then waterski or motor into the smaller canyons.

THE ITINERARY: The outfitter purposefully avoids handing out suggested itineraries to houseboat renters to avoid overcrowding particular areas of the lake. But the staff will make informal suggestions based on renters' interests.

No special skills are needed to operate a houseboat. Renters are given about an hour of instruction when they take possession of the boat. Instruction manuals are aboard each boat in case you run into problems. The detailed "Boating and Exploring Map," available at all marina stores, is a good thing to pick up before you embark.

Keep to a leisurely pace, and let a commitment to serendipity be your guide. Plan on beaching frequently throughout the day to permit fishing, swimming, or hiking onshore. With 96 major canyons ringing the lake, there's plenty of spectacular scenery to explore.

Be sure to cruise by Rainbow Bridge, one of the seven natural wonders of the world. It is a designated national monument because it contains the largest known natural stone bridge. You'll also want to see Hole-in-the-Rock, where the Mormons crossed the Colorado River in 1879 and 1880.

Two of the most wellknown Indian ruins are off the Escalante River and in Forgotten Canyon. They are old Anasazi Indian dwellings that have been sheltered by cliff overhangs and stabilized by the Park Service.

Among the suggested hikes for families is an hour or two walk into Dungeon Canyon, just above Padre Bay. Along it you'll find a slickrock mound with remnants of Moki steps carved by Anasazi Indians 600 years ago, as well as the ruins of a Navajo hogan and its nearby rock sheep corral.

Other hiker-accessible canyons include West Canyon, with spectacular examples of erosion, Davis Gulch, with its impressive Bement Natural Arch, and the beautiful San Juan Arm's Alcove Canyon.

FOR CHILDREN: Houseboating is suitable for children of all ages, provided precautions are taken. State regulations require that anyone 12 or under wear a lifejacket at all times when on deck. (If parents set an example, there should be little resistance from children. By calling it a "magic jacket," one family we know got their 3-year-old to regard wearing the lifejacket as a treat!)

Children will enjoy frequent stops for fishing, swimming, and exploring the shoreline; looking for birds and other wildlife is also an adventure for them. Don't expect young children to be as enchanted with the scenery as you are; bring along plenty of their favorite toys to occupy them in the cabin.

You may want to plan to spend a night or two moored at a marina such as Wahweap, which has restaurants, a laundry, video games, gift shops, and other tourist facilities.

Most families rent houseboats in the summer; although the days are hot, the evenings are pleasant, and the water temperature can reach 80 degrees. But spring and early fall are the best times to visit to avoid crowds. Temperatures are moderate, and fishing is at its best.

RATES AND PERSONAL GEAR: $$ to $$$$ Rates depend on the size of boat you choose, the length of the rental (it's less expensive to rent by the week) and the time of year (summer rates are highest). Houseboating can be surprisingly inexpensive if two or more families share the cost.

It's a good idea to bring children's lifejackets from home to ensure that they fit properly and comfortably. The outfitter's promotional literature contains a detailed list of other items to bring. The actual necessities are surprisingly few, since the houseboats are completely outfitted, except for bedding, which can be rented. Food can be brought from home or purchased at the marina stores.

OF INTEREST NEARBY: You can make a houseboating adventure on Lake Powell the centerpiece of a tour of some of the seven national parks and seven national monuments in what's called the Grand Circle area. They include Grand Canyon, Bryce Canyon, Capitol Reef, Zion, Canyonlands, Mesa Verde, and Arches national parks and Natural Bridges, Hovenweep, Canyon de Chelly, Navajo, Rainbow Bridge, Pipe Spring, and Cedar Breaks national monuments.

Special points of interest include the Anasazi Indian village near Boulder, Utah, which contains an excavation of Indian ruins that date back to 1050 A.D. Newspaper Rock State Park, at Blanding, Utah, preserves a rock with 1,000-year-old petroglyphs. The Monument Valley Navajo Tribal Park, near Valley, Utah, preserves hundreds of acres of naturally carved red sandstone buttes and weather-carved arches. Canyon de Chelly National Monument, near Chinle, Arizona, memorializes the slaughter of Navajos by Kit Carson in the 1860s and preserves the spectacular 1,000-foot sandstone walls of the canyon. The Navajo National Monument, near Tonalea, Arizona, preserves three major ruins dating to 1274 A.D.

FOR MORE INFORMATION: Call Lake Powell Resorts and Marinas, at (800) 528-6154, from Phoenix, call (602) 278-8888. Other tourist information is available from the Grand Circle Association, P.O. Box 987, Page, AZ 86040. Call (602) 645-3232.

RAFTING ON THE GREEN RIVER
BILL DVORAK'S KAYAK & RAFTING EXPEDITIONS
Utah

The Green River is one of the most famous rivers in the Southwest. Its major canyons, Desolation and Gray, are known for their pristine desert ecologies. And its more than 60 rapids, which progress from unnamed riffles to the challenging Three Fords, Steer Ridge, Coal Creek and Rattlesnake rapids, provide enough thrills to satisfy even the most experienced river rat. Yet the river is safe enough to permit children as young as 5 to learn what a river trip is all about.

The 86-mile Green River trip is a special favorite with families because of its wild desert canyon scenery and its rich history. Children will revel in campfire stories about Butch Cassidy, the mysterious "D. Julie," Flatnose Curry and Major John Wesley Powell, who passed through this canyon wilderness. Another lure: Dvorak's family-friendly pricing policy. On five trips each summer, kids under 14 go free!

Bill Dvorak's Kayak and Rafting Expeditions is one of the most responsible outfitters in the Southwest; it was the first to be licensed by the Colorado Division of Parks and Outdoor Recreation. Dvorak's offers trips through 29 canyons on 10 rivers; they vary in difficulty and traverse some of the most beautiful and historic regions of the Southwest. Some trips are limited to children over 10.

THE OUTFITTER: Dvorak's started in 1969 as Partners' River Program, a non-profit agency dedicated to bringing boating to special populations, such as youths, families, and the disabled. Partners' became Dvorak's in 1984 and has maintained its dedication to serving special populations; about 30 percent of Dvorak rafters are members of youth groups. Bill and Jaci Dvorak, the owners, are also committed to making the river accessible to the disabled with special services, adapted boats, and substantial discounts.

The basis of Dvorak's philosophy is participation. Dvorak prefers to take vacationers in paddle boats, which they paddle themselves, rather than oar boats, which are paddled by guides. (Vacationers can request an oar boat if they're skittish about having so much control. Children under 10 float only in oar boats.)

Dvorak employs licensed professional guides who are trained in first aid, CPR, and lifesaving skills. All the guides are knowledgable about the flora, fauna, geology, and history of the canyons.

The rafting season on the Green, as on most western rivers, runs from May through September.

THE ITINERARY: The Green River trip is a five- or six-day trip with over 60 rapids, ranging from Class II to Class III. Early in the spring, the white water is faster; later, the river is lower and calmer, perfect for a relaxed float. On July and August floats, swimming in the river provides a perfect antidote to the heat.

Participants on a Green River trip are advised to arrive in Grand Junction, Colo. the day before the trip embarks. From there, rafters are flown to the put-in point.

The first day on the river, you learn paddle strokes and commands, and soon your crew is working together as a team, moving the boat backward and forward, left and right, as if you had been doing it all your life.

Your boats will probably pull into camp early enough to allow you to take a swim or a walk before dinner. Watch for cougar tracks, old deer bones, and other signs of wildlife. You might want to just sit on the beach after unloading and look at the bluffs and the river. Or the crew will happily take you up on any offers of help in setting up camp and cooking dinner.

The camping is wilderness camping, following the "take only pictures, leave only footprints" philosophy. Tarps are provided for cover, though vacationers can rent or bring their own tents if they wish.

The food does not suffer from the primitive surroundings. Dvorak follows a long-established tradition of good eating among boaters. Breakfasts feature fresh juices, all-style eggs, pancakes or French toast, fruit and cereal. Lunches are usually served buffet-style, with salads, sandwiches, fruits and cookies among the offerings. Dinner entrees include barbecue steak, Mexican chile, baked fish, chicken enchiladas and Dutch oven-baked desserts and breads. Vegetarians are happily accommodated. Wine is served with dinner; adults are welcome to bring along beer and alcohol (only in unbreakable containers, and a limit of one case of beer per person).

Most of the Dvorak trips include at least one side trip a day to a point of interest along the river. On the Green River trip, expect to hike in to explore Indian petroglyphs, abandoned homesteads and shadow-filled grottoes.

The final day of the trip is spent on several miles of white water. The trip ends mid-afternoon. From the takeout, it's an hour and 40 minute drive back to Grand Junction.

FOR CHILDREN: The Dvoraks have young children themselves; the youngest took his first raft trip at the age of 7 weeks. The Dvoraks believe a river trip is especially suited for a family vacation, since boating allows families to come together on neutral ground with no distractions.

The minimum age on the Green River trip is 5. Children under 10 must ride in an oar boat; older children may ride in a paddle boat. Children are generally happier if there are other children in the group. Check with Dvorak's to see if you can book your trip when another family is signed up.

Half of the fun of a river trip is listening to the staff tell tales (some of them tall) about the rapids they have run and those you can look forward to. There are nightly activities for children, such as scavenger hunts, "Capture the Flag," and word games.

Inflatable kayaks can be rented for use on nearly every trip. These are especially fun for children.

RATES AND PERSONAL GEAR: $$ to $$$$ Dvorak's trips range in length from a half day to 12 days. Children's prices are approximately 10 percent less than adult prices, but substantial family discounts are offered on specified trips. Besides the "Kids Go Free" policy on some of the Green River trips, Dvorak's offers reduced rates for family groups on some of the Colorado, Rio Chama and North Platte trips.

The rates include use of tarps, ground sheets, dry bags, water-resistant camera boxes, and cooking utensils, as well as food and wine. Dvorak's will rent other equipment as needed.

OF INTEREST NEARBY: Grand Junction borders the Colorado National Monument, with hiking and driving trails, picnic areas, and campgrounds. Evening camp-fire programs are offered by the National Park Service.

While in Grand Junction, stop at Dinosaur Valley at Fourth and Main streets, which displays dinosaur skeletons as well as one of the world's largest exhibits of animated lifelike dinosaurs. Walk through the nearby "Rabbit Valley Trail Through Time Paleontological Area" to see the excavation sites.

Especially appealing to young children in Grand Junction is the Moon Farm, with farm animals, pony rides, and an "international playhouse."

FOR MORE INFORMATION: Write Dvorak's Kayak and Rafting Expeditions at 17921 GFV-Highway 285, Nathrop, CO 81236, or call (800) 824-3795 or (719) 539-6851; FAX: (719) 539-3571.

WEST

WHITE-WATER RAFTING ON THE AMERICAN RIVER
Coloma, California

The American River is the most floated river in California, attracting more than 140,000 rafters and kayakers each year. One reason is its guaranteed flow. Every morning, the keepers of the Chili Bar Dam release water from the dam to create hydro electric power; in the process, they create 21 miles of rapids and chutes downstream. Another reason is the spectacular terrain— the rolling foothills of the Sierra Nevadas and the river's long rocky gorges. This is Gold Rush country, which means it's rich in human history, too.

Thirty-three outfitters are licensed to take adventurers down the river's popular South Fork. No others serve families quite so well as Mariah Wilderness Expeditions, which specializes in providing high-quality, non-competitive wilderness experiences.

The South Fork is particularly well-suited to families because it has enough thrills to keep an intermediate-level rafter happy, but is manageable enough to permit children to sample the sport. Mariah offers a two-day trip that offers families the opportunity experience the entire 21 miles of raftable river and to camp, with somebody else doing most of the work.

THE OUTFITTER: Mariah Wilderness Expeditions is one of the few outfitting companies owned solely by women. Co-owners Donna Hunter and Nancy Byrnes are known for their family-only and women-only trips, though they also offer many trips open to anybody.

Mariah operates half-day, full-day and two-day trips on the South Fork from April 15 through September. Among Mariah's other offerings are one- or two-day trips on the more challenging Middle Fork, one-day trips on the North Fork (dependent on a healthy snow pack), one- or two-day trips on the Merced amd one-day trips on the Stanislaus.

THE ITINERARY: Participants on the two-day South Fork trip arrive about 7 p.m. the night before their scheduled departure and pick a campsite at Mariah's riverside base camp near Coloma. No meals are served on the first night. Plan to eat on the way, or bring a picnic with you to enjoy at one of the picnic tables at the base camp.

The next morning, the aroma of cooking bacon alerts campers that breakfast is being prepared. It's generally a hearty buffet featuring banana or blueberry pancakes, bacon and sausage, homemade granola, juice and coffee. After breakfast, the lead guide gives a 30-minute talk on river safety. Depending on when water is released from the dam, the trip begins either mid-morning or after lunch. In either case, salad and sandwich fixings are served buffet-style.

Mariah runs the South Fork in self-bailing paddleboats; passengers are expected to wield a paddle and help get through the rapids. Depending on their size, one to three families share a raft, with a trained river guide in the stern. Mariah prides itself on employing guides who are smart, skilled and fun-loving, as well as certified in first aid and CPR.

For logistical reasons, Mariah generally rafts the Lower Canyon on the first day and the Upper Canyon on the second day. On the first day, the rafts leave from Mariah's base camp for the 11-mile run downstream to Folsom Lake. The first six river miles traverse the Bacchi Ranch, a fifth generation cattle-ranching operation that started during the Gold Rush. Here, the river is gentle and confidence-building. The thrill-seekers in your family will want to swim the Swimmers' Rapid about a mile downstream from the base camp. By the time you reach The Gorge, everyone in your boat will be ready for a thrill. The Gorge delivers—dropping 33 feet per mile. When you get through Satan's Cesspool, the biggest rapid in the Gorge, you'll feel a great sense of accomplishment.

Among the sights you'll see on your first day out are several gold-recovery operations, which look like gigantic vacuum cleaners. They suck silt and small rocks from the river bottom, along with gold flecks and nuggets.

The first day's trip concludes as the river is entering Folsom Lake. From there, you'll be bused back to your campsite, where hors d'oeuvres, soft drinks, beer and wine await you. The energetic among you will strike up volleyball or ping pong games;

those with sore muscles will seek out the wood-fired hot tub (water supply permitting).

Dinner is always a memorable affair, with thick, charcoal-grilled beef and salmon steaks and chicken breasts, stir-fried vegetables, baked potatoes and salad. After dinner, a professional photography company shows slides of each raft's passage through Satan's Cesspool (prints are available for purchase). As the sky darkens, the campfire is lighted, and a professional storyteller begins spinning bedtime tales.

The next morning, another ample breakfast—mushroom and cheese omelettes, bacon and sausage, and fresh fruit—gets you ready for your second day on the river. The put-in point today is just below the Chili Bar Dam. In the three miles below Chili Bar, the river's average gradient is 40 feet per mile, which makes for nearly constant thrills. Almost immediately, your raft enters the Meatgrinder Rapid, a Class III or IV rapid, depending on the water flow. A professional photographer will again be on hand.

The rest of the second-day float is fairly sedate. The historical high point comes at mile 5.7, where you'll see Sutter's Mill, site of the accidental gold discovery that changed California's history. The day concludes with a buffet lunch at the base camp.

FOR CHILDREN: Mariah operates eight two-day trips on the South Fork each summer strictly for families. One trip is set aside for fathers and children, another for mothers and children, another for single parents and children, and five for families of any kind. On these special trips, a professional storyteller spins tales before meals, on breaks between rapids, and around the campfire at night. Our children delighted in learning yarn tricks and Indian lore from the storyteller on our trip.

Children must be 8 years old to raft the South Fork, and 14 to raft the Middle Fork. On the two-day family trips, younger children are welcome to join in the meals, campsite activities and storytelling sessions for a nominal charge. You can bring a babysitter along to stay behind during the raft trip.

RATES AND PERSONAL GEAR: $$$$ The rate includes two nights camping, five meals, and the raft trip. A tip of $10 to $20 per person is recommended for your guide. You can bring your own camping gear or rent tents, sleeping bags and one-inch pads from Mariah. Be sure to reserve equipment in advance.

On the river, wear a swimsuit or quick-drying shorts, a t-shirt, shoes that can get wet, a hat, sunglasses, and plenty of sun screen. A wet suit is recommended from April through mid June; you can rent one from Mariah.

OF INTEREST NEARBY: The history of the Gold Rush comes alive at Marshall Gold Discovery State Park, a few miles down State Route 49 from Mariah's base camp. Sutter's Sawmill has been reconstructed, and there's a visitors' center and numerous displays of gold-discovery technology (ranging from the classic pan to several Rube Goldberg-type contraptions). Call (916) 622-3470 for hours.

FOR MORE INFORMATION: Call (800) 4-MARIAH or (510) 233-2303 or write P.O. Box 248, Point Richmond, CA 94807.

ECUADOR

EXPLORING GALAPAGOS NATIONAL PARK
Galapagos Islands, Ecuador

After visiting the *Islas Encantadas* (the enchanted isles) in October 1845, Charles Darwin wrote, "The natural history of these islands is eminently curious, and well deserves attention."

One hundred and fifty years later, what an understatement that seems! Simply put, there is no other place on Earth like the Galapagos Islands, the re-named *Islas Encantadas*. The Galapagos lie 650 miles off the coast of Ecuador. The archipelago consists of 13 major islands and six smaller islets. More than 90 percent of the land area is unspoiled national park. Because of their isolation, they harbor animal and plant species found nowhere else on the planet. Today, families can still see what Darwin saw, for the islands have changed very little.

Traveling here is an unforgettable experience in nature. Most of the animal inhabitants are not afraid of humans and will allow you to approach within a few feet. You can walk right up to land and marine iguanas, sit a short distance from hawks and owls, stand beside nesting marine birds, and swim with penguins, sea lions, and fur seals. You may even see baby sea turtles leave their nests on the beach and scramble for the sea.

The Galapagos are also memorable for their stark beauty. The islands were formed by volcanic activity, so they are mountainous and darkly beautiful.

Because a trip within the park is made entirely by boat, the magic of ocean travel enhances an already unique vacation.

A family vacation in the Galapagos is, without exaggeration, a once-in-a-lifetime experience. It will redefine your standards for family vacations.

OUTFITTERS: Choosing the right outfitter is critical. One option is to join a scheduled tour group. The other is to interest another family in going and charter your own boat directly.

If you go with a group, be sure it is no more than 15 or 20 people. Smaller groups on smaller boats have access to some parts of the park that larger groups and larger boats cannot visit. Smaller groups also tend to develop more camaraderie.

A group outfitter will charter the boat, obtain a registered park guide, and make all other arrangements. Inca Floats is an experienced and very reputable group tour operator in the Galapagos.

If you charter a boat yourself, you should do first do extensive research. Information on boat operators is available from the Galapagos National Park Service.

For a personal charter, we highly recommend Andando Tours, run by Galapagos native Fiddi Angermeyer. Fiddi began sailing these waters and exploring the islands as a child. He has an unusual depth of knowledge, and his boats and crews are first class. Angermeyer runs two boats, the deluxe *Andando*, a 105-foot-long brigantine motor-sailer that accommodates 12 people in six cabins, each with shower and toilet and forced air ventilation, and the *Samba*, a steel-hulled yacht built in Holland with six two-person, air-conditioned cabins with private hot water showers. Not the least of the reasons for our recommendation of Andando Tours was the memorable food the crew prepared from locally caught fish and fresh fruits and vegetables.

If you want to travel over a holiday period, you should plan a year or more in advance.

THE ITINERARY: The majority of Galapagos tours are seven to 14 days long. Each boat's itinerary must be approved in advance by Galapagos National Park. If you join a group you will have no influence over the itinerary. If you charter your own boat, you can request that certain places be included in your itinerary.

Each island has its own unique collection of plants and animals, so the more islands you visit, the more variety you will see. Some species are found on only one or a few islands and only in certain seasons. For example, to see the waved albatross you must go to Hood Island starting in late March. The red-footed booby lives only on Tower Island. You will also want to see the famous giant land tortoise that gives these islands its name. The giant tortoises are sometimes hard to locate, particularly in dry weather. To ensure that you see the Galapagos, make the Darwin Research Station and its tortoise exhibit part of your trip. The research station is at the town of Puerto Ayora on the island of Santa Cruz.

Boats generally travel between islands at night. During the day, your party will make several shore excursions with your naturalist-guide. Guides are trained and certified by the National Park Service.

First thing in the morning, at mid day, and in the evening you are likely to be on deck watching for whales, reading, sunning or simply enjoying the vistas. The sunsets are spectacular.

Swimming and snorkeling are highlights of every day.

FOR CHILDREN: It's hard to think of an activity more inherently compelling to children than watching a bottle-nose dolphin or a baleen whale swim alongside their yacht, swimming with sea lions and penguins, or hiking across lava fields that resemble a lunar landscape.

But landing on a beach in the breaking surf is something of a physical challenge, and good medical care may be more than a day's travel away. For these reasons, wait until your youngest children is at least 10 before making your Galapagos trip.

RATES AND PERSONAL GEAR: $$$$ The cost of tours varies by their length. The rates quoted by tour operators do not include airfares, park entrance fees, and tips for boat crews and guide-naturalists. The bottom line: this is a very expensive vacation.

Bring casual, outdoor clothing. The Galapagos Islands are on the equator, and the sun is intense, so bring a broad brim hat and more sunblock than you can imagine you'll need. Those who are sensitive to the sun will need light cotton long sleeve shirts and long pants. Although the weather is warm year-round, bring a jacket for early morning and late evening excursions on deck. Tennis shoes or sandals are essential for beach landings.

Binoculars are a must for observing wildlife. Bring books, magazines and travel games for quiet times. Many boats have stereo systems. Bring a few of your favorite tapes.

You will need to stay in Quito, Ecuador for at least one night to make plane connections early the next morning to the Galapagos. You will need a jacket or sweater for Quito, whose elevation is close to 9,000 feet.

FOR MORE INFORMATION: Write Inca Floats at 1311 63rd Street, Emeryville, CA 94608, or call (510) 420-1550, or FAX (510) 420-0947. Write Andando Tours at P.O. Box 17-21-0088, Quito, Ecuador, or phone (59) 32 24 18 13 or (59) 32 46 51 13; FAX 59 3332 44 31 88.

NATURE
PLACES

ECHO LAKE CAMP
Mount Desert Island, Maine

Mount Desert Island, the largest rock-based island on the Atlantic coast, is best known for its centerpiece, Acadia National Park. The island's temperate summer climate and 100 square miles of rugged coastline, mountains, forests and lakes have attracted vacationing families for 200 years, long before Acadia National Park was founded.

Mount Desert Island is also the home of the Appalachian Mountain Club's Echo Lake Camp. The club was founded in 1876 to promote the protection, enjoyment and wise use of the mountains, rivers and trails of the Northeast. In the 1920s, the club sought a permanent site in Maine for use by its burgeoning membership. It found it on Echo Lake, a two-mile-long lake on the edge of the national park, near Southwest Harbor. Ever since, Echo Lake Camp has been serving as a retreat for families, many of whom return summer after summer to enjoy a wholesome, inexpensive summer getaway.

In keeping with the values of the Appalachian Mountain Club, now 55,000 members strong, Echo Lake Camp emphasizes conservation. Showers have water-saving showerheads, and toilets are of the high-efficiency water-saving type. Most trash is recycled. Compostable refuse is recycled for use by local farmers.

The Appalachian Mountain Club operates three other full-service facilities for families in the Northeast: Cardigan Lodge and Reservation, in Bristol, N.H. (open late June through mid October); Cold River Camp, at Center Conway, N.H. (open late June through late September), and Three Mile Island, at Lake Winnipesaukee, N.H. (open late June through late August). Each offers rustic accommodations, hearty, family-style meals, guided hikes, and other nature-oriented activities.

At all of the AMC sites, you can be assured of sharing a vacation with people who love and respect the natural world.

ACCOMMODATIONS: $ At Echo Lake, campers sleep in large tents in wooded areas near the lake shore. All tents are on raised wooden floors; cots, mattresses, pillows and bedding are supplied, but you must bring your own towels. Most tents house only two people, but there are a few three-person tents, and two tents that can accommodate up to six. Large families can request adjoining tents.

The camp's permanent buildings include an administrative office, kitchen and dining hall, and a library and recreation room. The common spaces have fireplaces that take the chill out of foggy mornings and cool evening gatherings.

Echo Lake is open from the first week of July through Labor Day, with stays of one week required. The camp always has more applications than spaces. Camp applications must be postmarked before April 1 of the year you hope to vacation there. Places are assigned by lottery for each of the nine camp sessions. If you apply after April 1, your chances of being accommodated diminish greatly.

All rates include meals, activities, tent space and state lodging taxes. Children 15 and younger and Appalachian Mountain Club members pay reduced rates. No credit cards are accepted.

DINING: Delicious, fresh, home-cooked meals are served family style in the rustic dining room. Two oceanside meals are part of every week's dining program—a lobster picnic on the shore at Sea Wall and a clam bake at Pretty Marsh. Special diets cannot be accommodated.

ACTIVITIES

 Echo Lake is warm enough for swimming, in contrast to the Atlantic Ocean here. The camp has two offshore floats.
A sand beach with lifeguards is located in a state park a short distance away.

 Rowboats, canoes, a kayak and sunfish-type sailboat are available at no charge. You are free to bring your own canoe or sailboat. No powerboats are allowed on the lake. Each week, the camp offers tour boat trips in the waters surrounding Mount Desert Island.

 Mount Desert Island offers 120 miles of hiking trails, allowing everything from a leisurely stroll to a strenuous climbs. They run from sea level to the peak of 1,532-foot Mt. Cadillac, the highest point on the island. More than 500 species of wildflowers, including many Arctic varieties, can be found within the park. The camp offers a daily guided hike, usually three to five miles in length. Hikers are transported to the starting point by bus.

When John D. Rockefeller, Jr. donated about a third of the land for Acadia National Park, he specified that 51 miles of carriage roads be built. These are now set aside for walking and the most spectacular cycling anywhere in Maine. There are also 27 miles of motorways in the park that can be used for cycling. Bring your own bikes or rent them in Bar Harbor by the day or week.

Three or four members of the Appalachian Mountain Club are assigned as leaders each week. Many are naturalists who willingly share their knowledge with campers. Through daily activities, they help participants explore the unique geology, rich diversity of marine life, and the plants and birds of the area. Evening programs center on nature themes. Many campers also take part in the nature programs of Acadia National Park, including naturalist-led walks, children's programs, hikes, sketching workshops, and boat cruises. A listing of these is available in the "Acadia Beaver Log", the park's visitors' guide.

Campers can help on trail maintenance in nearby Acadia National Park.

Horseshoes, volleyball, group games, square dancing, slide shows, and evening talks. Music is an integral part of camp life; campers are encouraged to bring their musical instruments and favorite songs.

FOR CHILDREN: Echo Lake Camp is a place for families to have fun together. All programs are designed with participation by children in mind. No child care services are available.

The camp is not suitable for children under four.

OF INTEREST NEARBY: Golf, tennis, deep-sea fishing, and sailing can be arranged in Bar Harbor. From the Opp Golden Anchor Inn Pier in Bar Harbor, you can take the *Acadian Whale Watcher* to Mount Desert Rock. You're likely to see harbor seals and whales during the four-hour cruise. Shorter cruises are also offered.

The U.S. Coast Guard maintains five lighthouses in the area: Egg Rock, Bass Harbor Head, Bear Island, Baker Island and Great Duck Island. You can visit the Bass Harbor Head Light by car. The others are visible only from afar.

Near Southwest Harbor, a few miles from Echo Lake, the Mount Desert Oceanarium displays harbor seals in a 50,000-gallon tank, and has a touch tank, exhibits on local marine life, and a boardwalk across a marsh. On the same site, the Maine Lobster Museum teaches you about the life of a lobsterman.

Within Acadia National Park, visit the Abbe Museum of Stone Age Antiquities, near the spring, and the Nature Center, with its adjacent Wild Gardens.

FOR MORE INFORMATION: Write the Appalachian Mountain Club, 5 Joy Street, Boston, MA 02108, or phone (617) 523-0636. For information on the national park, write Acadia National Park, Bar Harbor, ME 04609 or call (207) 288-3338.

GASTON'S WHITE RIVER RESORT
Lakeview, Arkansas

The Ozarks, extending across much of Arkansas, is a distinct geographical region with ancient rocks, rugged terrain, and steep valleys cut by fast-flowing, spring-fed fishing streams. The Ozarks area has long been a paradise for anglers. Old timers in Arkansas claim they remember the days when "the fish were so plentiful that they pushed one 'nother out of the water and clear up on th' bank."

The White River, which rises out of the Boston Mountains in northwest Arkansas, is one of the best of the many Ozark fishing streams. Its waters are calmed momentarily behind Bull Shoals Dam and then released in a clear, cold flow that provides a perfect environment for trout. In the five to 10 miles below the dam, browns reach unbelievable sizes—25 or 30 pounds is a not uncommon catch. The world record brown (38 pounds, eight ounces) was caught here on a humble kernel of corn and blob of marshmallow. And trophy rainbow trout weigh in at 20 pounds or more.

The great size of trout in the White is due in no small part the White and North Fork River Outfitters Trophy Trout Release Program. More than 1,000 trophy trout were caught and voluntarily returned to the White last year. Catch-and-release anglers of trophy trout are rewarded with a pin and a certificate.

In the eyes of many anglers, Gaston's is synonymous with the best fishing the White has to offer. Gaston's has catered to anglers and their families since 1958, and its second-generation owner, Jim Gaston, has made it one of the best-known fishing resorts in the Ozarks.

Gaston's has none of the "old-boy fishing camp" image that steers many families away from fishing vacations. It meets the non-fishing needs of its guests, too.

ACCOMMODATIONS: $ Gaston's offers accommodations ranging from motel-like units to housekeeping cabins to lodges suitable for large family gatherings or multi-family vacations. The largest cottages and the lodges have four bedrooms; the River Villa accommodates 20 people in 10 bedrooms.

Nearly all the units are located on the banks of the river, and most have decks that face the water. Each cottage comes with a 20-foot johnboat. The largest accommodations come with four.

The housekeeping units each have a small kitchen and an outdoor charcoal grill on which you can grill your trout. Each unit has cable TV and air-conditioning (important during an Arkansas summer!) Several units have large stone fireplaces.

Fishing packages are available. Children under 7 are free; children 7 and over pay $12 a day. Pets are welcome. As a lure to visitors in the winter, Gaston's offers two nights for the price of one.

DINING: The long, narrow dining room seems to float over the White River. There's a a great view from every part of the room. The room is decorated with antiques and old photographs; vintage bicycles are suspended from the ceiling.

The menu features a wide range of cocktails and family favorites (naturally, it includes trout). The dining room will prepare a box lunch for your day on the river. If you chose to hire a fishing guide, he will prepare a wonderful shore lunch of your freshly caught trout, fried potatoes, salad, and chocolate chip cookies.

ACTIVITIES

 In an outdoor pool.

 On a nearby 18-hole course.

 One outdoor court.

 Rental johnboats available.

Fishing is, of course, the major activity at Gaston's (license required). Try a single-day float with a guide (fees begin at $85 per person). Float fishing is the leisurely kind of trip families can enjoy. Floats leave the dock at about 7:30 A.M. All you need do is bring your rod and reel and your guide will organize the rest. Everything is provided, including the shore lunch. Most anglers use spinning gear when fishing the White, but you may want to experiment with fly fishing.

Trout fishing is possible year-round; winter fishing produces many lunkers.

Gaston's also offers guided bass-fishing trips on Bull Shoals Lake.

 Be sure to bring binoculars for the birdwatching, both on the river and off it. Great blue heron and kingfishers abound. A 1.7-mile nature trail is a great place for walks.

FOR CHILDREN: Your older children can go off and fish with their own guide, if you like, and meet you later for lunch along the river.

There's a game room stocked with video games and nice outdoor playground. Baby-sitting can be arranged.

NICETIES: Gaston's has a 3,200-foot grass airstrip for guests who prefer to fly in.

There's a gift shop on the premises that features handmade Ozarks crafts. And the resort's tackle shop can supply you with all the fishing gear you need.

The resort puts out a newsletter several times yearly to keep former guests up-to-date on the latest fishing news.

OF INTEREST NEARBY: Bull Shoals State Park has day and evening activities for visitors, including occasional demonstrations by local artisans and performances by musicians.

FOR MORE INFORMATION: Write Gaston's White River Resort, #1 River Road, Lakeview, Arkansas 72642, or call (501) 431-5202.

GREAT SMOKY MOUNTAINS NATIONAL PARK
Gatlinburg, Tennessee

Great Smoky Mountains National Park is one of the most beloved parks in the national park system. Its location astride the border between Tennessee and North Carolina puts the park within two days' drive of nearly half the population of the United States.

The 520,003-acre park is one of the most biologically diverse areas in the country. This luxuriant region has more tree species than all of Europe, more black bears than any other national park, more than 200 species of birds, and 27 species of salamanders, some of which grow to more than two feet in length. For this reason, the United Nation's Man in Biosphere Program chose the park as a site for the collection of baseline data against which to measure the impact of humankind on the environment.

The park also has over 75 historic structures, many dating to the period of first settlement in this region. Costumed interpreters at some of these sites recreate the history of the hardy farmers and mountain folk who made a living in the narrow, wooded valleys of the Smokies.

ACCOMMODATIONS: $ Many visitors stay overnight at one of the park's 10 campgrounds, which altogether have more than 900 campsites. Three campgrounds are open all year: Cades Cove, Elkmont, and Smokemont. They require reservations between May 15 and October 31; call (800) 365-CAMP.

Backcountry camping at 116 designated sites is allowed with a permit.

The only lodging facility in the park is remote LeConte Lodge, at the summit of Mt. LeConte. It is only accessible by horseback or a half-day hike (five and a half miles and an ascent of 2,560 vertical feet). LeConte has no showers and no indoor plumbing. Rates include breakfast and dinner. Reservations are essential; call (615) 429-5704.

One of our very favorite family vacation places, the Nantahala Outdoor Center, in Bryson, North Carolina, offers a variety of lodgings from cozy log cabins with kitchens to motel-style rooms. Call (704) 488-2175.

DINING: The Nantahala Outdoor Center has three on-site restaurants, all fairly funky: Relia's Garden, a striking wooden birdcage of a structure; River's End, on the banks of the Nantahala River, and Slow Joe's.

The towns at the two main entrances to the Park, Gatlinburg

and Cherokee, have an abundance of restaurants and food stores. For campers, Cades Cove Campground has a store that stocks basic provisions. Picnic sites are located throughout the park.

ACTIVITIES

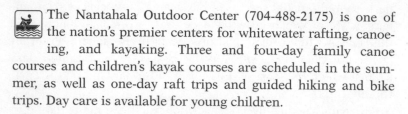

The Nantahala Outdoor Center (704-488-2175) is one of the nation's premier centers for whitewater rafting, canoeing, and kayaking. Three and four-day family canoe courses and children's kayak courses are scheduled in the summer, as well as one-day raft trips and guided hiking and bike trips. Day care is available for young children.

 735 miles of streams challenge trout and bass fishermen; Tennessee or North Carolina license required.

 Rental bikes are available from a concessioner at Cades Cove. The 11-mile loop through Cades Cove is great for family cycling.

The park's wild interior is crisscrossed by 900 miles of hiking and riding trails, among them a 72-mile stretch of the famed Appalachian Trail. Day hikes on the Appalachian Trail are possible from Davenport Gap, Fontana Dam, or Clingman's Dome.

 Guided rides from stables near several of the campgrounds. Hayrides from the Cades Cove stables.

 Ranger-led activities and campfire programs are scheduled daily during the summer months. Stop at either the Sugarlands Visitors Center near Gatlinburg, the Cades Cove Visitor Center near Townsend, or the Oconaluftee Visitor Center near Cherokee, North Carolina for a schedule.

The Smoky Mountain Field School, operated by the University of Tennessee, offers one- and two-day courses. Among the topics are wildlife, spiders, mountain wildflowers, geology, nature photography, and conservation issues. Call (800) 284-8885 or (615) 974-0150.

Wilderness Southeast, a not-for-profit outdoor education organization, conducts fully outfitted family camping trips several weekends each year in the Smokies. From a base camp, its groups explore the surrounding country on day hikes. The Wilderness Southeast guides impart a storehouse of information on the forest ecosystem, wildflowers, and animal tracks you discover on any walk. Call (912) 897-5108.

FOR CHILDREN: The six-mile-long valley of Cades Cove was a farming community in the 19th century. Today, it is a living history museum. Families can explore the handhewn barns and cabins and watch corn being ground into meal at the water-powered Cable Mill. Some members of the interpretive staff are descendants of the original settlers.

Oconaluftee Pioneer Farmstead, adjacent to the Visitor Center on Newfound Gap Road, is a restored 19th-century farmstead. Pioneer craft demonstrations are offered daily from mid-May through October.

The Great Smoky Mountains Institute at Tremont (615-448-6709) holds programs for families each July. Its three- to four-day long family camp features hiking, swimming, storytelling, and a special Appalachian music performance; the fee includes family-style meals, dormitory housing, and all activities. The institute also schedules a special summer Elderhostel program for grandparents and grandchildren.

OF INTEREST NEARBY: The Cherokee Indians are an integral part of the history of the Smoky Mountains. Worth a visit in any season is the Cherokee Oconaluftee Village and Qualla Crafts Shop south of the park in the town of Cherokee, North Carolina. An excellent museum tells the story of the Cherokee, and the gift shop sells high-quality Indian crafts.

FOR MORE INFORMATION: Write the Superintendent, Great Smoky Mountains National Park, 107 Park Headquarters Road, Gatlinburg, TN 37738, or call (615) 436-1200.

GUNFLINT LODGE
Gunflint Trail, Minnesota

The glacial shield that covered Canada and the northern United States in the Ice Age scoured out thousands and thousands of lakes. Today the area along the border between Minnesota and Canada is a recreational paradise. Boating, fishing, swimming, and hiking are activities common to all the lodges in the area, but few offer programs specifically designed for families. Gunflint Lodge is one that does.

Gunflint Lodge, 150 miles north of Duluth, has been a family business for more than 65 years. Its founder, Justine Kerfoot, was one of the pioneer resort operators along the Gunflint Trail in northern Minnesota. She transformed Gunflint Lodge from a few cabins with no indoor plumbing or electricity into a modern and comfortable resort. Her son Bruce and his wife, Sue, and their two sons carry on.

Gunflint Lake is a wonderful locale for a vacation. The United States-Canada border runs down the middle of the lake in front of the lodge. The legendary *voyageurs* traveled this lake in canoes to trade knives and axes and beads for furs. Today, the 1.2 million acre Boundary Waters Canoe Area Wilderness features 1,000 clear water lakes and some of the most pristine paddling opportunities anywhere.

ACCOMMODATIONS: $ to $$$ The 25 one- to four-bedroom cabins at Gunflint Lodge range from older cabins that are basic and comfortable to more recently built earth-sheltered units with wall-to-wall carpets, outside hot tubs, washer and dryer, queen and king-sized beds, and lazy boy recliners. All cabins have fireplaces, and most have a kitchen and sauna. Most of the cabins with kitchenettes have a coffee maker, popcorn popper, and a microwave.

The lodge offers a wide assortment of accommodation packages and plans. Many guests opt for one of the American Plan packages that include all meals, or the Modified Housekeeping Package that includes only dinners.

The Deluxe Family Package, offered from mid-June to mid-October, includes all meals, accommodations with a fireplace, a boat and motor with unlimited gas, two canoes, and the lodge's nature program. The package is available only for one-week stays. Children under 4 are free. A 12 percent service charge is added to the bill, in lieu of tipping.

If you want to do some of your own cooking, one of the housekeeping packages may be for you. Boats are not included in the cabin price, but may be rented.

DINING: The main lodge building was built in the early 1950s and refurbished in 1991. It is a year-round building with two massive stone fireplaces and big picture windows overlooking Gunflint Lake and the Canadian wilderness to the north. Justine Kerfoot, using an ax and saw, fashioned some of the original dining room furniture herself.

Breakfast service starts at 7 A.M., for those eager to start fishing, and lasts until 10 A.M., when the sleep-ins rouse themselves. It's an open menu at breakfast.

Lunch is served from noon to 2 P.M. The menu includes a homemade soup, which changes daily, plus a half-dozen hot and cold entrees. When the weather is nice, there's a cookout on the dining room porch. The kitchen prepares packed lunches for those who want to venture out for the day.

Dinners at Gunflint are special. The chef, who many say is the best in northern Minnesota, present four entrees each evening, usually including a fowl, a seafood, a red meat and a pasta. Homemade appetizers include walleye sausage and duck pate. A fresh soup is offered, as well as homemade bread and a tasty dessert. A children's menu is available. Children can be served ahead of adults, so they can adjourn to a movie in the lodge lounge.

A barbecue cookout, over Missouri hickory charcoal, is offered on Sunday evenings in the summer.

Cocktails, beer, and wine may be purchased with dinner.

ACTIVITIES

 The lodge's swimming season officially starts on July 1; the lake is usually ice-covered until April. Kids enjoy splashing and swimming from the small sand beach in front of the main lodge building. They can use a selection of small kayaks, tubes and fun bugs.

 Gunflint Lake is more than a mile wide and about eight miles long, with direct connections to several other lakes.
Sturdy, wide-beamed, 15-foot aluminum boats with 15-horsepower motors are available; canoes or kayaks must be used in the Boundary Waters Canoe Area Wilderness.

 The season runs from mid-May through late September for lake trout, walleye pike, and smallmouth bass. You can engage the services of a Gunflint Lodge fishing guide for a day or half-day. On daylong fishing trips your guide will prepare a shore lunch that includes some of the fish you catch. The lodge also has a fishing pro whose fishing productivity is astounding. The lodge can supply you with Minnesota fishing permits and arrange for Canadian documents as well. Live bait is available for purchase at the boat dock, and the lodge gift shop carries the essentials in tackle. If you forget your fishing rod and reel, the lodge will lend you equipment.

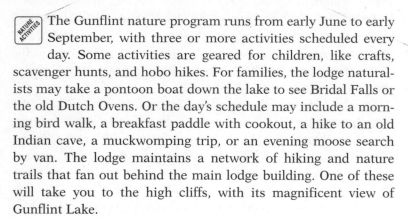 The Gunflint nature program runs from early June to early September, with three or more activities scheduled every day. Some activities are geared for children, like crafts, scavenger hunts, and hobo hikes. For families, the lodge naturalists may take a pontoon boat down the lake to see Bridal Falls or the old Dutch Ovens. Or the day's schedule may include a morning bird walk, a breakfast paddle with cookout, a hike to an old Indian cave, a muckwomping trip, or an evening moose search by van. The lodge maintains a network of hiking and nature trails that fan out behind the main lodge building. One of these will take you to the high cliffs, with its magnificent view of Gunflint Lake.

Gunflint Lodge is open in the winter for cross-country skiers. It offers over 100 kilometers of groomed, tracked trails that lace through the basin behind the lodge. About half the trails are double-tracked with a big Piston Bully groomer, while the other half are single-tracked.

Gunflint also features a dogsled program, with rides that vary from one hour to day long. Each team of up to 10 dogs takes two people at a time into the wilderness.

Gunflint Lodge is one of the leading outfitters serving the Boundary Waters Canoe Area Wilderness and Canada's Quetico Park. The lodge supplies all the food and equipment you need, including canoes and life jackets, tents with mosquito netting, sleeping bags, mats, and permits. You can choose from a self-guided trip, over any one of more than 50 routes, to one guided by a lodge employee. In the wilderness area, there are no homes or roads, no motorized vehicles, and no cans or bottles allowed. The lakes are crystal clear, with an abundance of fish. You're sure to see lots of waterfowl and maybe a moose or two.

FOR CHILDREN: Children aged 6 through 15 who are staying at the lodge for a week or more will be taken on a half-day guided fishing trip with other children at no extra charge.

The lodge's playground has horseshoes, swings, a sandbox and sandbox toys, and climbing equipment with a tree house. The swimming, boating, nature program, and overnight canoe trip are other activities that children will enjoy.

A large number of ducks consider Gunflint Lodge to be their summer home. Children are welcome to pick up a handful of their favorite food, cracked corn, from the shed at the boat dock. In the same shed, children will be fascinated by the fishing bait. The bathtub full of leeches holds a special appeal.

Baby-sitting can be arranged through the front desk.

NICETIES: The coffee pot is on in the lodge dining room from early morning until late at night. Tea and hot chocolate are also available, and there's a bottomless jar of homemade cookies at the front desk.

Thermoses filled with coffee, hot chocolate, tea, or lemonade are available for day trips.

Your fish catch is filleted, wrapped, and frozen at no additional charge.

The great room in the lodge lounge has games, books, and newspapers, including child-oriented materials. It also houses a large collection of Indian relics, objects the *voyageurs* lost when their canoes turned over in rapids, and articles from the fur trade.

OF INTEREST NEARBY: The town of Grand Marais on Lake Superior at the head of the Gunflint Trail is worth a visit. There you can tour a lumber mill, charter a sailing boat for a day on Lake Superior, patronize one of the local bakeries, visit the Coast Guard Station, go bowling, or tour the Cook County Historical Museum. Bears gather each evening to check out the bill of fare in the local dumpsters.

FOR MORE INFORMATION: Write Gunflint Lodge, 750 Gunflint Trail, 100GT, Grand Marais, MN 55604, or call (800) 328-3325; FAX: (218) 388-9429.

LUDLOW'S ISLAND LODGE
Lake Vermilion, Minnesota

An island is a special place, symbolizing a retreat, a haven, a place of tranquil isolation. Ludlow's Island, two hours north of Duluth and four from Minneapolis, is such a place.

Ludlow's Island is one of the 365 islands in 40-mile-long Lake Vermilion, one of northern Minnesota's glacial shield lakes. It is heavily forested with pines, aspen and birch. Every now and then, if you're lucky, you hear the cry of a loon. At night, the stars are incomparable.

Ludlow's Island Resort has the four-acre island to itself. Few island retreats are as conducive to a memorable family vacation as Ludlow's Island. The facilities and the ambience approach perfection.

Mark and Sally Ludlow and their four children are your hosts. The Ludlows have purposely limited the size of the resort so that they can know every guest on a first-name basis. You will probably find your children playing with their children. In a sense, you become part of their family during your stay.

ACCOMMODATIONS: $$ to $$$$ The 19 cabins at Ludlow's Island combine rusticity and comfort. They're the kind of cabins you might build for yourself, yet they're comfortable enough to earn 3 stars from the Mobil Guide. Each is close to the water and seems as though it's the only cabin on the island.

Mark's father handcrafted the oldest cabins in the 1930s (they've since been modernized). The newest were built in the late 1980s. All have pine or cedar walls, fireplaces, wall-to-wall carpeting and comfortable furnishings. Many have special touches like a vaulted ceiling, a loft bedroom, or a beautifully crafted built-in cabinet or bookcase. Each has a screened porch or a deck with a charcoal grill, and a kitchen equipped with a microwave, dishwasher, coffee maker, blender, toaster, popcorn popper and all the items you will need for cooking and eating (right down to wine glasses).

The cabins range in size from one to five bedrooms and can sleep 4 to 10 people. Some are single-level, others multilevel. Some have private saunas and washer-dryers. Some have built-in bunk beds, which children love! Each is individually named, not numbered—Northern Lights, Stardust, Night Owl and so on.

Eleven of the cabins are on the island, five are on the south shore (reachable by car), and three are on the north shore. Lake Vermilion is narrow here, so only 100 feet or so of water separate the island from either shore.

When you arrive at Ludlow's south shore dock, you'll find an old-fashioned telephone with a crank. A call to the lodge will bring the bell boat to the dock, which will transport you and your luggage to your cabin. If your cabin is on one of the shores, you will have your own boat for transportation to and from the island throughout your stay. If you prefer, a call will summon a lodge boat.

Families with young children should try to book a cabin on the island itself for easy access to the lodge and swimming area.

Ludlow's is open from early May to early October. From mid-June to mid-August, the lodge books cabins by the week, from Saturday to Saturday. Stays of less than a week in peak season may be possible, depending on cabin availability.

Daily maid service can be provided for an extra charge.

DINING: Ludlow's Island has no dining room. Your fully equipped cabin kitchen provides all the utensils for meal preparation.

Cook, Minnesota, 8 miles away, has two supermarkets, IGA and the Co-op, where you can buy fresh fruits, vegetables and staples. You can supplement these items at the lodge's Gourmet Pantry, a small room crammed with a wide assortment of essentials and delicacies. It's open 24 hours a day. If the pantry doesn't have what you need, ask the lodge staff to pick it up for you the next time they go to town.

The pantry also has an ice cream maker, waffle iron, woks, and a Cuisinart for borrowing. You can take whatever spices you need from the extensive selection on the spice rack behind the door.

The lodge supplies a list of restaurants within a reasonable drive or boat ride of the resort.

ACTIVITIES

 In a gently sloping, roped-off area of the lake.

 Vermilion Fairways, a five-minute drive from the lodge, has a nine-hole, par 36 course (3,400 yards).

 Two courts and a racquetball court (no charge) on the mainland; racquets available. The racquetball and tennis complex has showers and a fenced-in playground for young children.

 Sailboats, pontoon boats, fishing boats with motors, canoes, paddle boats, and speed boats suitable for pulling water skiers. Boats that don't require motors are free; motors are rented on a daily or weekly basis. Water skiing equipment is available at no charge.

 Lake Vermilion is a premier walleye, pike and bass lake. Ludlow's holds a weekly fishing clinic that provides information on equipment, fish habitat, and conservation. (The resort promotes a catch and release policy.) With every fishing boat, the lodge provides an anchor, net, minnow bucket and cushions. Live bait can be bought at the boat dock. Guide service is available. Ludlow's will clean, fillet, wrap and freeze your fish at no charge.

 Ludlow's has a combination nature and exercise trail on the north shore. Be alert for deer, and be sure to pick some blueberries in the rocky area near the end of the trail.

FOR CHILDREN: The island is a perfect place for children. It's a self-contained world.

The roped-off sand beach borders a safe swimming area, complete with a water slide and miniature kayaks. There are usually plenty of crawdads, minnows and tadpoles to chase. In the lodge, there's a game room with Ping-Pong, foosball and video games. The south shore has a playground with swings, treehouse, toys, and big wheel type tricycles.

Organized children's activities center on a "woods and water" theme. They're offered for an hour or two each weekday during the summer. Activities include tree-planting, eagle watching, paper making, a fishing derby, a marshmallow roast or hot dog cookout, a nature hike, wildlife-viewing cruises on a pontoon boat, and games.

Once each week the Ludlows take children for a ride in their amphibious car (adults have also been known to sneak aboard). Each evening, a movie is shown in the lodge.

A tent is always pitched on Camping Island, a few yards offshore of Ludlow's Island. Children can camp out there (younger ones will require adult supervision). Ludlow's provides sleeping bags, firewood, and marshmallow sticks.

Baby-sitting can be arranged with advance notice.

NICETIES: A community sauna and coin-operated washers and dryers are available for guests whose cabins don't have these amenities.

If you have young children, ask that a highchair be placed in your cabin before you arrive. Baby food grinders are among the items you can borrow from the Pantry.

A complimentary Sunday newspaper from Minneapolis is delivered to each cabin. The lodge reading room gets the Wall Street Journal and USA Today on weekdays.

A VCR can be checked out for use in your cabin. Tapes, including a wide selection of children's tapes, can be rented for a nominal fee.

OF INTEREST NEARBY: The Soudan iron mine is a 45-minute drive from the resort. For 80 years, the highest quality iron ore in Minnesota was mined here. The mine is now a state park where you can don hard hats and follow a guide on a tour 2,400 feet below the surface of the earth.

An excursion to a nearby lake makes a good day trip. Choose from Wolf Lake, where the lodge has a boat moored for your use, privately-owned Black Lake, or Trout Lake in the Boundary Waters Canoe Area. Check with the lodge for details.

FOR MORE INFORMATION: Write Ludlow's Island, P.O. Box 1146, Cook, Minnesota 55723 or phone (800) 537-5308 or (218) 666-5407.

SOUTHWEST AND MOUNTAIN STATES

YMCA OF THE ROCKIES
ESTES PARK CENTER
Estes Park, Colorado
SNOW MOUNTAIN RANCH
Winter Park, Colorado

Ringed by the rugged, snow-dusted peaks of Rocky Mountain National Park, and older than the park itself, the Estes Park Center combines a spectacular high-country setting with down-to-earth rates. Nothing fancy about the accommodations here, though the center offers a wide range of cabins and lodge rooms scattered through 860 acres. But the amenities include backdoor access to Rocky Mountain National Park, an ever-present, ever-changing mountain vista, and an extensive menu of activities. We always leave feeling doubly refreshed—first by the surroundings, and second by the knowledge that we enjoyed them at non-profit organization prices.

On the western side of the park—about 80 miles away by car if you go "over the top" on Trail Ridge Road—sits 4,950-acre Snow Mountain Ranch, at an elevation of 8,800 feet. This is also operated by the YMCA of the Rockies. Well-established as a ski center for many years, its mid-1980s face lift made it more attractive to summer visitors. Its cabins are wonderful. The one we occupied one fall week offered us a million-dollar view of a snow-covered peak on the Continental Divide.

Unique at Snow Mountain Ranch: the Vacation Kidney Center of the Rockies, a joint project of the YMCA of the Rockies, the National Kidney Foundation of Colorado, and University Hospital in Denver. It provides dialysis and post-transplant care for adults and children in a vacation setting.

Both the Estes Park Center and Snow Mountain Ranch are less than a two-hour drive from Denver. They are popular sites for family reunions: 600 on them in 1994 alone! In any given week, you'll find four generations gathered to enjoy the great outdoors.

ACCOMMODATIONS: $ to $$ Estes Park Center has more than 200 cabins and 11 lodges that can accommodate 4,000 guests. If your budget is a primary consideration, you can choose spartan accommodations at bargain basement prices. A family of five can easily be accommodated in a dormitory-style room in one of the Eastside Lodges (rooms include three sets of bunk beds, and a bath with a shower, but no tub). Each lodge has a comfortable lounge with a huge stone fireplace; after the children have gone to bed at night, many parents gather here for some adult talk and a cup of tea.

At the other extreme, but still inexpensive, the Estes Park Center offers three-bedroom cabins that sleep seven. Two-bedroom cabins are among the most sought-after accommodations. Each cabin includes a full kitchen, bathroom, and often a fireplace. There are also motel-style lodge rooms with two queen-size beds and a sofa bed or futon, a balcony, and full bath.

Rates at Estes Park Center are discounted in winter; it books up early for the prime months of July and August. Reservations from the general public are processed beginning in early April. To improve your chances of getting a reservation, you can pay a nominal yearly membership fee, which allows you to make reservations a month earlier than the general public. Family reunions can be booked through the group sales office, which is not part of the membership priority system.

Reservation procedures are similar at Snow Mountain Ranch, but here you're just as likely to run into a crowd during the ski season. Accommodations are in four lodges and more than 40 cabins nestled among the tall pines, with views of the Indian Peaks range to the east and Gore range to the west. The capacity is 1,700. Some lodge rooms include a double bed, bunk beds, and a full bath. The cabins are fabulous, with multiple bedrooms, well-equipped kitchens, and huge stone fireplaces.

DINING: Bowls of yogurt, trays of fresh fruit, rows of omelettes, bins of sausage and bacon, and an assortment of pastries thrown in for good measure—that's standard fare at the breakfast buffet every summer morning in the Pine Room at Estes Park Center.

If you manage to work up an appetite by lunch, you can

return to the Pine Room to order from a menu, or visit the snack bar in the General Store, which also stocks drinks and simple supplies for cabin cooking and lunches on the trail. Sack lunches may be ordered.

Dinner in the Pine Room is another smorgasbord, usually featuring several entrées and a wide assortment of salads and vegetables. For variety, try one of the restaurants in Estes Park, only a short ride by car or public trolley from the Estes Park Center.

At Snow Mountain Ranch, three meals a day are served in the Aspen Room. The resort also has a small store and a snack bar at which you can order buckets of spaghetti for consumption there or in your cabin. Within driving range for dinner are Winter Park, Granby and Grand Lake, which have a multitude of restaurants.

No alcoholic beverages are served or allowed in public areas at either site.

ACTIVITIES

 Outdoor courts at both facilities; no court fees.

 Heated indoor pools at both facilities.

 White-water raft trips can be arranged on nearby rivers.

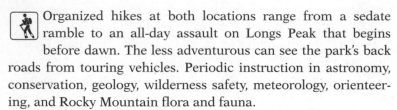 Organized hikes at both locations range from a sedate ramble to an all-day assault on Longs Peak that begins before dawn. The less adventurous can see the park's back roads from touring vehicles. Periodic instruction in astronomy, conservation, geology, wilderness safety, meteorology, orienteering, and Rocky Mountain flora and fauna.

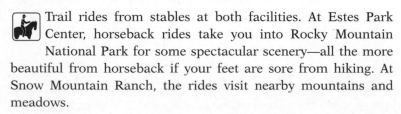 Trail rides from stables at both facilities. At Estes Park Center, horseback rides take you into Rocky Mountain National Park for some spectacular scenery—all the more beautiful from horseback if your feet are sore from hiking. At Snow Mountain Ranch, the rides visit nearby mountains and meadows.

 Crafts centers at both facilities; horseshoes, basketball, hayrides, volleyball, softball, family programs. Evening programs include campfires, movies, square dancing, classical and folk music, and an eclectic series of talks by guests.

While both facilities are open year-round, Snow Mountain Ranch is the center of winter action. Within a 15-mile drive are the Winter Park and SilverCreek downhill ski areas. The cross-country touring center at Snow Mountain Ranch is among the best in Colorado; rentals and instruction are offered. Ice-skating, winter-horseback rides, guided snowshoe hikes and sleigh rides are available. The program building houses a downhill ski rental shop.

FOR CHILDREN: In addition to all the regular programs, which are intended to include children, both facilities offer affordable day camps for children from age 3 through high school.

Estes Park Center's program is offered only during the summer, Mondays through Fridays. At Snow Mountain Ranch, the day camp is offered weekdays in the summer and seven days a week from September through May.

Activities include the standard day camp favorites, with heavy emphasis on the outdoors. Each center has a distinctive program, yet they share common goals aimed towards development of body, mind and spirit.

At the Estes Park Center, the Teen Barn is open from 8:30 A.M. to 10 P.M. Mondays through Fridays in the summer.

Younger members of your family are certain to become devotees of the Y's miniature golf courses.

NICETIES: A Y charge-card allows you to pay for all meals and activities when you check out.

On a rainy afternoon, seek solace in the libraries at either Estes Park or Snow Mountain.

At Estes Park Center, the Lula W. Dorsey Museum will show you what the turn-of-the-century tourist was likely to find. At Snow Mountain Ranch, be sure to peek into the Rowley Homestead Museum.

OF INTEREST NEARBY: Rocky Mountain National Park and the ranges that border it dominate both Estes Park Center and Snow Mountain Ranch. Touring the park by foot, horseback, or car, you can see deer, elk, and, if you're lucky, the elusive bighorn sheep. The simplest park trails, such as the paved walkway around Bear Lake, are as easy as a stroll around the block. But the rugged peaks can challenge the most experienced climber.

An unforgettable family outing is a drive up Trail Ridge Road, one of the highest stretches of highway in the world. Trees thin and finally give way to meadows of wildflowers in the Alpine tundra. A crisp breeze cuts even the warmest day. The thin air will leave you puffing.

Colorado's largest natural lake, Grand Lake, sits at the southwestern edge of the park, as well as man-made Lake Granby and Shadow Mountain Lake.

If you tire of the natural surroundings, you can find shopping, restaurants, and other tourist attractions in the cities of Estes Park and Winter Park.

FOR MORE INFORMATION: For Estes Park Center, call (303) 586-3341 or write Estes Park Center, 2515 Tunnel Road, Estes Park, CO 80511-2550. For Snow Mountain Ranch: Call (303) 887-2152 or write Snow Mountain Ranch, P.O. Box 169, Winter Park, CO 80482.

THE NATURE PLACE
COLORADO OUTDOOR EDUCATION CENTER
Florissant, Colorado

The full variety of Rocky Mountain scenery, ranging from the desert to Alpine tundra, comes into focus through the exciting natural history programs offered at The Nature Place. The classrooms for this family-owned retreat are the wildflower-bedecked meadows, trout ponds, aspen groves, rocky bluffs, and fragrant forests of pine, spruce and fir that fill its 6,000 acres.

Surrounded by national forest and within view of Pike's Peak, The Nature Place combines first-rate accommodations with in-depth study excursions designed to meet the varying needs and interests of both the young and old.

Owners Laura and Roger "Sandy" Sanborn have run separate camps for boys and girls on the site for more than four decades. In the late 1970s, the Sanborns opened The Nature Place as a kind of camp for families. A passage in a booklet that visitors find in their room sets the tone for a vacation experience here:

"In the outdoors we can be reminded that humans have evolved to wonder, that understanding is joy, and that the knowledge of the wholeness of the earth's systems is a prerequisite to survival."

Six weeks each summer and during the week between Christmas and New Year's, The Nature Place offers special six-night adventure programs for families. Each year, families come from all over the country to explore nature together.

During the summer adventure programs, guests go out on daily excursions with expert rock hounds, bird-watchers, and wildflower specialists. One day you will travel down the "shelf road" into Sonoran Desert country and find 500-million-year-old fish scales in some of the oldest sedimentary rock in the Rocky Mountains. At the Quick Homestead, a restored 1880s potato farm on the Sanborns' property, you may dip candles, bake biscuits, and make apple cider with an antique press.

The next day you may visit the Florissant Fossil Beds and see the remains of plants and insects preserved for 36 million years in volcanic ash and mud. Another day you will travel across Leavick Valley and ride up to Horseshoe Mountain to browse among the Alpine cushion plants at 11,500 feet. The young and fearless go "slickersliding" on the snow patches that remain into July and August. The hikers head for high country and a lake at the base of the glacial cirque, while those who simply want to relax enjoy a beautiful view of the valley below or inspect the wildflowers with greater care.

The winter week is crammed with outdoor activities, like cross-country skiing, broomball, tobogganing, ice-fishing, and skating on the South Platte River. Summer or winter, the days end with a lecture or slide presentation on nature history and socializing in front of a blazing fire.

ACCOMMODATIONS: $$$ Each of the 50 modern, spacious studio apartments has a full bath, fireplace, two twin or double beds, two easy chairs, and a vaulted ceiling loft with two studio couch beds. (The children will demand to sleep up there!) A small refrigerator, sink, and coffeemaker round out a kitchenette space. East-facing windows provide spectacular views of Pike's Peak.

A spacious lodge houses the dining room, meeting and play rooms, a lounge, and a library. Among the fixtures in the lounge are two telescopes for viewing Pike's Peak, the constellations, or an occasional deer. The downstairs game rooms house a Ping-Pong table, pool table, and television with a VCR.

Rates for a six-night stay vary slightly depending on the program; children under 5 are free, and between 5 and 15 they pay children's rates. Rates include accommodations, three meals per day, all recreation, instruction and guiding, transportation to sites on and off the ranch, and use of all facilities and equipment. Daily rates are also available.

DINING: Three excellent meals a day are served buffet-style at the lodge. There's usually a choice of two hearty entrées, and plenty of salad fixings.

In the summer, guests often take lunch out on the deck overlooking Pike's Peak, where the hummingbirds provide a constant source of entertainment. Sack lunches are provided for guests going on all-day outings.

During the week-long programs, one night will typically include a barbecue near the Tie Cabin, at which you'll be entertained by Duncan, the guitar-playing manager of the Sanborns' 125-year-old working cattle ranch. Often, Sandy can be persuaded to tell stories of the early settlers or the native peoples who preceded them.

Wine and cheese parties are held once or twice each week. Otherwise, no alcoholic beverages are available at The Nature Place; you may bring your own.

ACTIVITIES

 In glass-enclosed heated pool with view of Pike's Peak; adjacent hot tub and sauna.

 A highlight of the summer adventure weeks is tubing on the South Platte River.

 In several stocked trout ponds.

 The sports complex has an exercise room with weights, a Stairmaster, exercycles, a rowing machine, and a Nordic track; the gymnasium is equipped for basketball and volleyball.

Instruction in such creative arts as photography, pottery, lapidary, sketching, darkroom skills, and weaving. On clear evenings, the on-site observatory, which boasts the third largest telescope in Colorado, is often opened for star-gazing. Other evenings may include a slide show on beavers, geology, or the history of Cripple Creek.

Walk 20 minutes through the ponderosa pine forest and you will be at the Interbarn—an ecology center with exhibits on birds, plants, mammals, rocks, and fossils of the area, plus an inflatable planetarium and a seismograph.

With golden eagles, broadtailed hummingbirds, western tanagers, and olive-sided flycatchers among the over 50 species regularly seen around The Nature Place, bird-watching is a joy. Summer flowering plants vary greatly from the montane zone, where The Nature Place is located, to the subalpine zone on Horseshoe Mountain.

Cross-country skiing, toboganning, ice-skating, snow-tubing, sledding, hiking, and broomball. The Winter Family Week offers the option of a day of downhill skiing (extra charge). Watching the New Year's Eve fireworks over Pike's Peak is an unforgettable experience.

FOR CHILDREN: During many of the week-long programs, the age of participants ranges from infant to 80, and everyone has a good time. Parents with infants often carry them in snuglies or backpacks on hikes.

In general, children participate alongside their parents in all the activities, though special children's activities are scheduled through each of the special adventure weeks. On days when the featured field trip is especially strenuous, young children may stay behind with counselors for a day of games, swimming, nature explorations and videos.

Most of the educational displays at the Interbarn are especially designed for young learners. For example, a giant cell allows children and adults to get inside the life process.

The staff at The Nature Place is very attentive to the needs of children. One of the highlights of the winter week we spent there was the construction of a gingerbread Western town, which the kids dubbed "Candy County." Each evening, staff members helped the children add to the creation for hours, while parents went off to lectures or talked among themselves.

NICETIES: Bouillon, tea, hot chocolate, and coffee are provided in your room, and hot drinks are available in the lodge throughout the day. A plate of fresh-baked cookies usually greets guests returning from an all-day outing.

Both the library and the Interbarn have excellent collections of books on natural history. You're free to borrow them for the duration of your stay.

There's a stash of several dozen videotapes and a VCR in the lodge.

OF INTEREST NEARBY: If you come by car, plan a drive through Eleven Mile Canyon, just 30 minutes away. The trip to Sonoran Desert country will take you near the Royal Gorge. You may wish to drive or walk on the bridge across that well-known landmark, or take a funicular ride to the bottom or an aerial tram ride across the top.

In Colorado Springs you can visit the Air Force Academy or the magnificent rock formations at the Garden of the Gods. Pike's Peak is accessible either by car or by narrow-gauge railroad.

FOR MORE INFORMATION: Write The Nature Place, Colorado Outdoor Education Center, Florissant, CO 80816, or call (719) 748-3475.

YELLOWSTONE NATIONAL PARK
Yellowstone National Park, Wyoming

If anyone polled Americans on their favorite national park, the answer would probably be Yellowstone. For a family vacation experience, it beats a theme park hands down.

Yellowstone was designated a national park in 1872—the world's first—establishing the principle that certain natural features are national treasures. Although the most frequent image associated with Yellowstone is that of Old Faithful, Yellowstone actually encompasses several diverse ecosystems.

Besides harboring the most active and extensive thermal area in the world, it is the site of the Grand Canyon of the

Yellowstone River, a spectacular rift sliced through yellow rock walls; Yellowstone Lake, North America's largest mountain lake; many towering peaks, and the Yellowstone River, the longest free-flowing river in the United States. Surrounding these popular tourist stops are more than 1,000 miles of well-marked hiking trails, dozens of side-roads with spectacular views, innumerable fishing access points, and wildlife habitat that provides sustenance to bison, elk, deer, moose, eagles, coyotes, bears, and even wolves.

Most visitors to Yellowstone National Park see the park's sites from the comfort of their cars or a scenic overlook. Relatively few venture out onto the park's hiking trails. The lucky fewest— one out of 10,000—see the park in the most intimate way, under the auspices of the Yellowstone Institute, an organization devoted to making visitors fall in love with the park through participation in dozens of field seminars every year.

ACCOMMODATIONS: $ to $$$ TW Recreational Services Inc., the park's authorized concessioner, operates 10 separate lodging facilities at six locations, ranging from the old, dignified Mammoth Hot Springs and Lake Yellowstone hotels to the quirky, not-to-be-missed Old Faithful Inn to the strictly utilitarian Lake Yellowstone cabins. To best appreciate the park and minimize driving, it makes sense to stay a few days at several different places.

Only two lodgings are open in the winter—Old Faithful Snow Lodge and Cabins, in the heart of geyser country, and Mammoth Hot Springs Hotel, at the park's northern entrance.

The National Park Services operates 11 campgrounds in Yellowstone, with a 14-day limit during the summer. Campsites fill on a first-come, first-served basis, except for Bridge Bay, which accepts reservations up to eight weeks in advance through Ticketron (call 800-452-1111). Because of the huge numbers of visitors in the summer, campgrounds fill quickly.

TW Recreational Services operates a 300-slot RV Park at Fishing Bridge; call (307) 344-7311 for reservations.

DINING: Restaurants at each of the hotels and lodges offer varied menus at reasonable prices; in addition, Lake Lodge, Old Faithful Lodge, and Canyon Lodge have cafeterias. Lake Yellowstone Hotel has an elegant dining room with gorgeous views of the lake (make your dinner reservation in advance of your arrival). The dining room at the Old Faithful Inn has a lot of charm.

For a fun evening, sign up for one of the Old West Cookouts at Roosevelt Lodge, offered nearly every evening during the summer. Participants ride wagons or horses through gorgeous scenery to Yancey's Hole, the cookout site, where they're served cowboy coffee and charcoal-grilled steaks, corn on the cob, potato salad, corn muffins, Roosevelt beans, and dessert.

ACTIVITIES

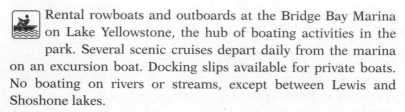 Rental rowboats and outboards at the Bridge Bay Marina on Lake Yellowstone, the hub of boating activities in the park. Several scenic cruises depart daily from the marina on an excursion boat. Docking slips available for private boats. No boating on rivers or streams, except between Lewis and Shoshone lakes.

Some of the best trout fishing in the West on the Yellowstone River and in Yellowstone Lake, where native cutthroats abound. Guided fishing boats available for charter. Permit required..

More than 1,100 miles of hiking trails crisscross Yellowstone. Park rangers will be happy to help you plan hikes ranging from a few hours to a few days (backcountry permits are required for overnight expeditions). Self-guided nature trails suitable for the inexperienced can be found at Mammoth Hot Springs, Grand Canyon of the Yellowstone, the Fountain Paint Pots, Firehole Lake Drive, the Upper Geyser Basin, Norris Geyser Basin, the Mud Volcano, and Calcite Springs Overlook/Tower Fall.

 Pick up a copy of "Discover Yellowstone" as soon as you arrive in the park. It lists all of the ranger-led activities that take place in the park during the summer.

The Yellowstone Institute offers several dozen different short courses on geysers, bears, birds, wildflowers, horsepacking, geology, and photography, with the park as its classroom. These are top-quality learning experiences; write the institute at Box 117, Yellowstone National Park, WY 82190 or call (307) 344-7381, ext. 2384 for a schedule.

Guided one- and two-hour rides at Mammoth Hot Springs Corral, Roosevelt Corral, and Canyon Corral between June and September. Thirty-minute stagecoach rides scheduled several times daily from Roosevelt Lodge across rolling, sage-covered hills.

Yellowstone is a wondrous experience in the winter. It's the best time to view elk and bison, which come down to the lowlands to graze. And the sight of geysers and fumaroles surrounded by snow is truly other-worldly. Winter activities include cross-country skiing (instruction and rentals available), snowmobiling, snowshoeing, snowcoach tours, wine-tasting parties, special theme dinner nights, and hiking.

Special activities, including slide shows, ranger talks, and storytellings, are scheduled almost every evening at the park amphitheaters.

FOR CHILDREN: Many of the ranger-led activities are aimed at children. And there are seven visitor centers with excellent interpretive exhibits about the park's natural and human history that will help put the scenery in perspective for children.

Each summer, the Yellowstone Institute offers several programs especially for children or families. Among the recent offerings: "Family Days in Sunlight," "Interpreting Yellowstone with Ranger Ted," "Three Days at the Buffalo Ranch" (for children between 8 and 12), and "Family Days with a Park Ranger Family." Early sign-up is essential.

NICETIES: There are laundromats at Grant Village Campground, Fishing Village RV Park, Canyon Village Campground, and Lake Lodge.

FOR MORE INFORMATION: For information about accommodations and concessioner-run activities, write TW Services, Inc., Yellowstone National Park, WY 82190 or phone (307) 344-7311. For general information about the park and ranger-led activities, call the National Park Service Headquarters at (307) 344- 7381.

PINE BUTTE GUEST RANCH
Choteau, Montana

Nestled in the foothills of the rugged East Front of the Rocky Mountain range in Montana is Pine Butte, a unique guest ranch. The ranch is part of an 18,000-acre nature preserve owned and operated by The Nature Conservancy, an international, non-profit conservation organization.

The heart of this preservation effort is Pine Butte Swamp Preserve, an area of lush wetlands, rolling prairies, brilliant wildflowers, and abundant animal life. The preserve is one of the most beautiful and biologically diverse places in Montana. The wildlife sheltered here include beaver, mink, cougar, elk, mountain goats, and bighorn sheep. And it's one of the few places in the lower 48 states where grizzly bears venture out of the mountains in search of food.

A few miles away lies Egg Mountain, also part of the preserve. Scientists from the Museum of the Rockies at Montana State University have been working here for several years on one of the most significant dinosaur fossil finds in North America.

ACCOMMODATIONS: $$$$ Pine Butte's rustic but comfortable cabins are set among the aspens, firs, and cottonwoods that line the South Fork of the Teton River. Built of native stone and wood, each spacious cabin is complete with fireplace, full bath and handmade furniture.

Between mid-June and early September the minimum stay is one week, from Sunday to Sunday. Transportation to and from Great Falls International Airport is provided on Sundays during the summer, at no additional charge. Reduced rates are available in May, early June, and mid-to late September, with a two-night minimum stay required.

DINING: All meals are served family-style in the central lodge dining room. The food is delicious, with exceptionally good homemade soups, breads, and pastries. The ranch's own garden supplies fresh vegetables and salads for mid-day and evening meals.

Sack lunches are packed for guests scheduled on daylong hikes or rides. Each week, breakfast and steakfry dinner rides are offered.

No alcohol is served, but guests are welcome to bring their

own. Ice and mixers are available during the social hour before dinner.

ACTIVITIES

 In a heated outdoor pool.

 Ranch guides will help anglers find the best spots along the Teton River. Beaver ponds and sub-alpine lakes are within easy hiking distance. Montana license required.

Morning and afternoon rides are scheduled each day, and an all-day ride is offered at least once. Many rides climb the trails to the surrounding foothills, with spectacular views of mountains and the plains.

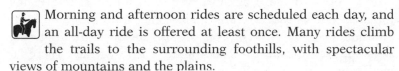 Ralph Waldt, the resident naturalist, has developed a trail map and brochure of the preserve and surrounding territory, which makes self-guided hikes easy. Guided hikes focus on the plants, animals and geology of the East Front. A favorite destination is Our Lake, a seven-mile hike with a 1,450-foot gain in elevation. The lake is nestled in a sub-alpine cirque at an elevation of 7,280 feet; bighorn sheep and mountain goats can frequently be seen here.

Information on the ecology of the preserve is woven into most of the activities of the ranch. An excursion to the Egg Mountain dinosaur dig is scheduled each week. Excursions to Freezeout Lake State Waterfowl Refuge are made in early summer when migratory birds are still in the area. An ancient seabed fossil-hunting tour, wildflower and birding expeditions, and paleontology tours of nearby tipi rings and a buffalo jump are also on the weekly program. For an extra fee, you can join an all-day excursion to Glacier National Park.

In the spring and fall, week-long natural history tours and workshops are scheduled on such topics as birdwatching, Montana grizzly bears, mammal tracking, nature photography, and paleontology.

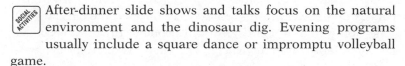 After-dinner slide shows and talks focus on the natural environment and the dinosaur dig. Evening programs usually include a square dance or impromptu volleyball game.

The ranch will organize five- to 10-day horseback trips into the beautiful Bob Marshall Wilderness Area.

FOR CHILDREN: Children are integrated into all of the ranch programs. Many horses in the stables are gentle and suitable for children who have little or no riding experience.

The Pine Butte Educational Center holds occasional workshops for children 7 to 18 years of age at the old Bellview School on the preserve. The workshops range from two to four days in length and emphasize hands-on learning. The teachers and naturalists who lead the program cover such topics as the Plains Indians, homesteaders, rare plants and animals, and local dinosaur discoveries. The program also includes group games, skits, nature walks, art projects, and creative writing. There's a moderate additional fee for the workshops.

NICETIES: The ranch's Natural History Center contains a collection of reference books, fossils, animal skulls and other bones, and a small, self-help gift shop with cards, books, T-shirts, and posters. All proceeds go to The Nature Conservancy.

Free laundry facilities are available.

Tea, lemonade, and cookies are served every afternoon in the dining room.

OF INTEREST NEARBY: The eastern entrance to Glacier National Park is 80 miles north of the ranch.

FOR MORE INFORMATION: Write Pine Butte Guest Ranch, HC58, Box 34C, Choteau, MT 59422, or phone (406) 466-2158.

WATERTON/GLACIER INTERNATIONAL PEACE PARK
West Glacier, Montana and Waterton, Alberta, Canada

The vast majority of visitors see Glacier National Park from their cars as they travel the only paved road through the park, the 50-mile Going To The Sun Highway. It is one of the most spectacular mountain drives anywhere. The roadway literally clings to the mountainside and crosses the Continental Divide at Logan Pass at an elevation of 6,664 feet.

But most of the 1.4 million acres of Glacier Park are inaccessible by car or van, and it is there that a vacationing family will find its most priceless treasures. The park's 10,000-foot mountain peaks hide 50 active glaciers, 200 sparkling clear lakes and fast-flowing streams, and an abundance of wildlife, including mountain lion, deer, bighorn sheep, and Rocky Mountain goats. In its remote wilderness, four threatened species—the bald eagle, gray wolf, peregrine falcon, and grizzly bear—have one of their last strong-holds.

Glacier is truly a hiker's park. More than 90 percent of its area is designated wilderness that can only be approached and appreciated by traveling on foot (there are more than 700 miles of trails). Walks can range from a 30 minute stroll to a two-week expedition.

Waterton Park, the Canadian contribution to Waterton-Glacier International Peace Park, adjoins Glacier, but you have to drive out of Glacier to get to it. It's worth the effort. Be sure to take the excursion boat ride on Waterton Lake. When you cross the international border by boat, you'll understand how insignificant political boundaries are to Mother Nature.

ACCOMMODATIONS: $ to $$ Major campgrounds, with hookups, are located near St. Mary, Rising Sun, Apgar, and Two Medicine. Primitive sites can be found at Kintla Lake, near the Canadian border, and just outside the park in Flathead National Forest and Lewis and Clark National Forest. Permits are required for backcountry camping.

Glacier Park accommodations include two grand old hotels—Lake McDonald and the Many Glacier Hotel—built by the Great Northern Railroad early in the 20th Century. There's also a modern lodge, Glacier Park Lodge, as well as several motels and cabin complexes. Book early, as all fill up well in advance. In general, the hotels are open from late May or early June through September.

In Waterton, the Canadian part of this international park, the 81-room Prince of Wales Hotel sits high on a bluff overlooking Waterton Lake. With the granite-faced peaks of the Canadian Rockies and the deep blue water of the lake stretching in front of it, this hotel seems to have been designed with a travel poster in mind. Inside, it's distinctively British in atmosphere and old-fashioned in decor.

DINING: Each of the hotels has its own restaurant, and the towns of West Glacier and Waterton have plenty of coffee shops and snackbars as well.

The dining room at Many Glacier Hotel is famed for its singing waiters and waitresses, college music majors who actually have to audition for the job of waiting tables. Several times each evening, service comes to a stop and the servers perform.

ACTIVITIES

 Nine-hole course at Glacier Park Lodge; 18-hole course in Waterton.

 Outdoor heated pool at Glacier Park Lodge.

 Rental rowboats and powerboats on Lake McDonald, the largest lake in the park. Excursion boats take guests across Swiftcurrent Lake, Lake McDonald, Two Medicine Lake, St. Mary Lake, and Josephine Lake in Glacier Park and Waterton Lake in Waterton Park.

 With a permit (no fee). The season extends from the third Saturday in May through November 30. The lakes and streams abound with native cutthroat, bull trout, Kokanee, and mackinaw.

 Guided trail rides ranging from two hours to all-day are offered by several outfitters in West Glacier. The Glacier Raft Co. (800-332-9995) offers longer trips that combine horseback riding with rafting.

 It's easy to take day hikes on your own. If you prefer a guided backpacking expedition, Glacier Wilderness Guides offers guided trips to remote mountain lakes and alpine meadows within the park. The outfitter has a wide selection of itineraries available on trips that range from a day hike to a six-day backpack. Call (406) 888-5333 or (406) 862-4802 from October to May.

The Glacier Raft Co. (800-332-9995) offers one- to five-day raft trips and raft/horseback expeditions in the Flathead wilderness area just to the south of the Park. The three forks of the Flathead River—North, Middle, and South Forks—together make up nearly 10 percent of the total mileage in the National Wild and Scenic River System. Children 5 and over are welcome on raft trips from early summer on, as long as the water is not too high (then the minimum age rises to 8).

FOR CHILDREN: The park's ranger programs are among the best in the national park system, with guided boat rides and hikes, evening campground programs and slide talks in the hotels among the offerings. There are special junior ranger programs each week. Each visitor center has displays about Glacier that will be interesting to children.

Many of the programs offered by the Glacier Institute are open to families with children 10 and older. Summer field seminars run from two to five days; "Explorations" courses are half and full-day educational experiences. The institute makes the park its classroom as you explore a glacier, raft a river, or hike a wilderness trail. Classes are fun, with the emphasis on being out-of-doors and participating in hands-on nature activities. Your family can learn to track wildlife, identify birds of prey, use a map and compass, sketch the natural environment, and appreciate a bit of Montana history.

The institute has limited cabin accommodations for participating families, with a shared kitchen and washrooms with showers. Write Glacier Institute, P.O. Box 1457A, Kalispell, MT 59903, or phone (406) 888-5215 from mid-June to mid-August or (406) 752-5222 at other times.

NICETIES: If driving over Going-To-The-Sun Road gives you the willies, do it the way the park's early visitors did: in one of the "Jammer" buses built by the White Motor Co. in the '30s. These bright red buses link all the lodges within the park, including Prince of Wales Hotel. They have roll-back canvas tops that allow for spectacular views. The drivers, or "jammers," point out scenic highlights. One-way or round-trip passage, and circle tours, are offered.

OF INTEREST NEARBY: The Northern Plains Indian Crafts Association has a trading center with Indian goods just outside Glacier, at St. Mary.

The Museum of the Plains Indian, 12 miles from East Glacier

Park at Browning, has exhibits on the customs of the Indians of the Great Plains.

The town of Waterton is charming, with a nice children's museum and many shops that sell imported British goods. In the summer, elk wander through the town's streets.

FOR MORE INFORMATION: For hotel reservations within the park, write Dial Tower, Phoenix, AZ 85077-0928, or call (406) 226-5551 mid-May to mid-September or (602) 207-6000 mid-September to mid-May. For general park information, write The Superintendent, Glacier National Park, West Glacier, MT 59936, or phone (406) 888-5441.

HIGH SIERRA FAMILY VACATION CAMP
Montecita-Sequoia Lodge
Sequoia National Forest, California

When's the last time you braided a lanyard? Whittled yourself a decorative walking stick? Jumped on a trampoline? Sang "Kumbaya" around a campfire? Probably when you were a child, having the time of your life at summer camp.

Educator Virginia Barnes believes it's important for adults to have a little camp in their lives, too. The High Sierra Family Vacation Camp she runs 10 weeks each summer at Montecita-Sequoia Lodge in the high Sierras is just what it sounds like: a camp to which families go together to escape the pressures of work, school, and domestic life.

Montecita-Sequoia Lodge occupies the site of an old girls' camp that Barnes ran from 1946 to 1987 at an elevation of 7,500 feet in California's spectacular Sequoia National Forest, about five hours from either Los Angeles or San Francisco and an hour and a half east of Fresno. Guests actually enter the property from Kings Canyon National Park.

Each six night family week is filled with opportunities: to make arts and crafts, explore a cave, ride horses, perfect your tennis stroke, learn to water ski, or try your hand at watercolors. In short, it's just like camp, but with much better food, a cocktail hour each evening, and attentive supervision for your children. For parents, Montecita-Sequoia provides the perfect mix of family time and adult time.

In the winter, Montecita-Sequoia becomes a cross-country ski center, providing unparalleled opportunities to ski through forests of sugar and loblolly pine and giant sequoia. Staff members meet guests' cars at the entrance to Kings Canyon National Park and escort them to the lodge, which is generally surrounded by snow from mid December through March.

ACCOMMODATIONS: $$ to $$$$ There's nothing fancy about the accommodations here. Guests are housed in eight rustic cabins, each equipped with a king-sized bed and two or three sets of bunk beds, or in 40 lodge rooms that can accommodate two to six persons. Cabin guests use a communal bath facility; the lodge rooms have private baths. Rooms are vacummed twice a week, but there's no regular maid service. During the family camp weeks, there are about 150 guests in residence.

There's no television anywhere on the premises. Two public telephones are available for guests' use. Smoking is permitted only in your room and on the far left side of the deck.

All meals and most activities are included in the weekly rate (daily rates are available on Saturday nights in the summer and during the spring, winter and fall). Guests are asked to leave a gratuity of 10 to 15 percent of their camp fee.

DINING: All of the meals are served buffet-style, which makes for easy eating with children. The food is tasty, wholesome, and, for the most part, organically grown. Vegetarians can be easily accommodated. Many guests take their plates out to the deck to enjoy the fabulous view of the Great Western Divide.

Breakfast, served from 7:30 to 9 a.m., features a choice of five cereals, made-to-order eggs or pancakes, fresh fruit and juices, and freshly ground coffee. Lunch, served from noon to 12:30 p.m. generally features a salad, sandwich and soup bar. If you're going on an all-day hike, you can request a trail lunch. Dinner, served from 5:30 to 7 p.m., features two or three entrees (one meatless) and a selection of salads.

Guests are expected to bus their own dishes and wipe down the tables.

The Pine Box Bar, in the Ponderosa Room, is open at noon, before dinner, and again from 9 to 11 p.m. An adults-only social hour precedes dinner.

Peanut butter and jelly is always available for finicky eaters. Highchairs and booster seats are readily available.

ACTIVITIES

 Two lighted hard-surface courts; instruction, equipment available.

In a heated outdoor pool or Lake Homavalo; hot tub adjacent to the pool. Guests must pass a swimming test before they can swim in the lake.

 Complimentary kayaks, canoes, sailboards, sailboats and paddleboats on Lake Homovalo; waterskiing instruction (extra charge).

 In Lake Homovalo or in the mountain streams and lakes in Sequoia National Park or Sequoia National Forest (license required).

About a dozen activities are offered during each of four activity periods daily. Options include art instruction with the "artist of the week," archery, arts and crafts, guitar lessons, volleyball, horsehoes, ping pong, basketball, fencing, riflery, waterskiing, and the trampoline. Each night, there's a special social activity, such as a mock casino, variety show or moonlit hike. Evening activities conclude with a campfire sing-along at 8:30 p.m.

Staff naturalists lead at least two hikes daily on trails in Sequoia National Forest or the national parks. Several go through groves of giant Sequoias, magnificent beyond belief. These 2,000-plus year-old trees are among the oldest and largest living things on earth.

The lodge has 20 horses for guests' use on guided rides. Instruction is required for guests without riding experience. Trail rides are offered twice daily (extra charge).

 Montecita-Sequoia operates its own Nordic ski shop, complete with plenty of child-size equipment, and maintains 35 kilometers of groomed trails (two diagonal stride tracks and a skating lane). Instruction and guided tours are offered. There's also easy access to about 85 kilometers of mapped trails in Sequoia National Forest; skiing through a grove of 250-foot tall giant Sequoias is an unforgettable experience. Telemarking is popular on the Starlight Trail.

 Ice-skating is offered on the lake through the winter; equipment available. Snowshoe rentals.

FOR CHILDREN: Owner Virginia Barnes taught education at San Jose State University for decades, so she takes the care and entertainment of children seriously. During the summer family weeks, Montecita-Sequoia offers supervised activities for children ages 2 and up for five hours a day, with a break for lunch with parents. Special activities are offered for several hours a day for younger children accompanied by a parent, grandparent or sitter.

Children are divided into groups according to their age. The "Guppies" (six through 23-month-olds) congregate in a playhouse called Guppy Getaway, complete with diaper-changing area and cribs. "Minnows," the 2-year-olds, also have their own cabin, called the Kiddie Corral, which is equipped with age-appropriate toys and a fenced-in playyard. They go on walks to the dock, make rudimentary arts and crafts, listen to stories, blow bubbles, play, and sing songs. "Tadpoles," ages 3 and 4, hang out in the Tadpole Pond (actually a toy-filled cabin) and go on insect safaris, nature hikes, motorboat rides, pony rides and fishing expeditions. "Chipmunks," ages 5 and 6, meet in the Chipmunk Den, and engage in the same sorts of activities as the Tadpoles.

Seven and eight-year-olds, called "Marmots," and 9- through 11-yaer-olds, called "Cougars," go on nature hikes, enjoy the trampoline, learn archery and riflery skills, make arts and crafts, and swim together. Teens play basketball or volleyball, improve their tennis game, go waterskiing, hike, shoot rifles, and make crafts.

Children from age 7 on up each go on an overnight outing with their group. The younger children sleep in a teepee across the lake from the lodge, while the teens go off to a campsite in the national forest.

For all the age groups, supervision is excellent. For preschool-aged children, the staff to child ratio is usually one to three. The regular counselors, all college students, are assisted by highly motivated high school students who have been chosen to participate in the lodge's KILT (Kids in Leadership Training) program. Off-duty counselors and "KILTs" will babysit during meals or other unsupervised periods for a fee.

Over the winter school holidays, a children's program for 7- to 11-year-olds combines ski lessons, supervised snow play and indoor recreation. Babysitting can be arranged for children 2 to 6.

NICETIES: For a nominal charge, the lodge staff will do guests' laundry on Wednesdays.

A nurse is on hand through each summer week.

The Ponderosa Room has a game cabinet stocked with plenty of jigsaw puzzles and board games.

OF INTEREST NEARBY: Montecita-Sequoia Lodge is right next to Kings Canyon National Park and just a few miles from Sequoia National Park. Here you can see the most impressive groves of giant Sequoias still standing in California (the only place in the world where they grow naturally). Besides these trees, the two parks are famous for their deep canyons and high peaks (Kings Canyon is deeper than the Grand Canyon). This is a hiker's paradise.

FOR MORE INFORMATION: Call (800) 227-9900 or (415) 967-8612 or write 1485 Redwood Drive, Los Altos, CA 94022.

YOSEMITE NATIONAL PARK
California

"No temple made with hands can compare with Yosemite. Every rock in its walls seems to glow with life. Some lean back in majestic repose; others, absolutely sheer or nearly so for thousands of feet, advance beyond their companions in thoughtful attitudes, giving welcome to storms and calms alike, seemingly conscious, yet heedless of everything going on about them." That was John Muir, the spiritual grandfather of Yosemite, writing in the 1860s. Though the words are almost 130 years old, it would be difficult to improve on them.

Yosemite holds a particular place in America's national consciousness, having inspired poets, photographers, painters and tourists ever since President Abraham Lincoln signed the proclamation that ensured its protection. It has something for everyone: awesome, glacier-carved canyons, spectacular waterfalls, groves of giant Sequoias, meadows full of subalpine wildflowers, and thousands of acres of untouched wilderness. Two of its natural features—giant rocks called Half Dome and El Capitan—will be instantly familiar to you.

You've heard, no doubt, about Yosemite's summer crowds. Don't worry about them. It's true that tourists converge on Yosemite Valley in July and August. But once you get 100 yards beyond the parking lots, you've pretty much got Yosemite to yourself. And don't neglect Yosemite as a winter destination. Despite its altitude, the weather is surprisingly mild. The average minimum temperature in February is 26 degrees, with average daily highs of 55 degrees. The winter light and the snow make Yosemite look entirely different than in the summer!

ACCOMMODATIONS: $ to $$$$ There are 1,785 guest rooms within the park, ranging from the rustic Housekeeping Camp, with its rental platform tents, to the "parlor rooms" at the famous Ahwahnee Hotel. All are operated by Yosemite Concession Services Corp. Reservations are taken up to a year in advance, though rooms can sometimes be snared at the last-minute. Call (800) 365-2267 or (209) 252-4848.

In Yosemite Valley, Housekeeping Camp is as close as you can come to camping without having to pitch your own tent. It offers 282 platform tents that sleep up to six persons each, with central restroom and shower facilities. Curry Village is slightly less rustic, with 628 units, including standard hotel rooms, cabins with private or shared baths, and canvas tent cabins (no cooking facilities). Yosemite Lodge, near the base of Yosemite Falls, is a modern 495-unit facility with motel rooms and cabins. The Ahwahnee, in a class by itself, is one of the most celebrated hotels in all the national parks. It has 123 guest rooms and four "parlor rooms," or suites.

Just inside the southern entrance, the Victorian era Wawona Hotel has 104 hotel rooms, half with private baths. Because it's off the valley floor, the atmosphere here is less hectic.

In the high Sierra near the park's eastern entrance, Tuolumne Meadows Lodge, open only in the summer, has 69 canvas tent cabin units, with shared shower and toilet facilities. White Wolf Lodge, also open only in the summer, offers 24 canvas tent cabins, with a shared bath, and four cabins with private baths.

For the adventuresome, Yosemite's five High Sierra Camps offer dormitory-style, sex-segregated accommodations, reachable only by foot; breakfast and dinner are served daily. Each camp is 5.7 to 10 miles from the next one along a scenic loop trail, which facilitates camp-to-camp hiking. These accommodations are so popular that they are assigned by lottery in mid-December. The minimum age for children is 7. Inquire about naturalist-led seven-day hikes that stop at the camps.

Yosemite has thousands of campsites, but they fill up early. Reservations are required year-round for Yosemite Valley's auto-accessible campgrounds and for several others from spring through fall. Reservations should be made exactly eight weeks in advance. For campground reservations, all (800) 365-2267; from abroad, call (813) 572-7527.

A new resort option just two miles outside the park's southern entrance is Marriott's Tenaya Lodge, a AAA four-diamond facility. Elegant and extremely comfortable, this is a family-friendly all-seasons resort, featuring supervised children's activities, spacious guest rooms, a fitness center, bicycle rentals, on-site horseback riding, and both indoor and outdoor pools. Call (800) 635-5807.

DINING: Each of the park's major hotels offers both casual and formal dining options. The Ahwahnee is famed both for its kitchen and its ambience. Groceries can be purchased at six locations within the park.

The dining rooms at Marriott's Tenaya Lodge are run by executive chef Jeff Zelkin, who was first in his class at the Culinary Institute of America. That means you can expect more than ordinary hotel fare here.

ACTIVITIES

 Nine-hole course at Wawona.

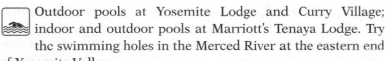 Outdoor pools at Yosemite Lodge and Curry Village; indoor and outdoor pools at Marriott's Tenaya Lodge. Try the swimming holes in the Merced River at the eastern end of Yosemite Valley.

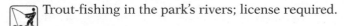 Whitewater rafting on the Merced River, just outside the park. Inquire at Curry Village.

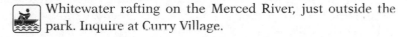 Trout-fishing in the park's rivers; license required.

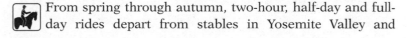 Rentals available at Yosemite Lodge (year-round), Curry Village (summer only), and the Marriott. Eight miles of marked and paved bicycle paths adjoin the main roads through the valley.

From spring through autumn, two-hour, half-day and full-day rides depart from stables in Yosemite Valley and

Wawona; the stable at Tuolumne Meadows offers rides in the summer. Call (209) 372-1248. One- and two-hour and half-day rides through Sierra National Forest and to Mariposa Grove leave from Yosemite Trails Pack Station, next to Marriott's Tenaya Lodge. Call (209) 683-7611.

Yosemite is ideal for both serious and casual hikers. Options range from an short 1/2 mile round-trip stroll from a parking lot to spectacular Bridalveil Fall (the highest waterfall in North America, and the fifth highest in the world) to a 17-mile hike, with an elevation gain of 4,800 feet, to the top of Half Dome, to multi-day hikes that require backpacking experience. For family hikers, there are many other options in between. Park rangers can recommend hikes suitable for your family. Don't miss a walk through the giant Sequoias at Mariposa Grove.

The park's ranger-led programs range from guided walks to storytelling sessions around a campfire to talks on rock-climbing to photography workshops to stargazing. In the reconstructed Miwok-Paiute Village behind the Yosemite Valley Visitor Center, you can attend daily programs about Yosemite's first residents.

In the summer, the Yosemite Theater features theatrical productions six night a week that teach the history of Yosemite through song and dance. In one, "Sarah Hawkins Contemplates a Fourth Marriage: the Story of a Pioneer Lady," you'll learn about the rigors of pioneer life, from a mother's point of view. In "Conversations with a Tramp," an actor portraying John Muir gives you insights into this visionary's life and his 25-year battle to save Yosemite's Hetch Hetchy Valley. From spring through fall, the Art Activity Center offers free art classes every day.

Badger Pass Ski Area, California's oldest operating ski area, offers downhill skiing in the winter. Five lifts (one triple, three double and one surface) and nine runs with mostly beginner and intermediate terrain; 8,000 foot summit, ski schoool, day lodge.

With 350 miles of skiable trails and roads, Yosemite is an incomparable place to cross-country ski. The center of Nordic activity is Badger Pass, with 90 miles of marked trails, including 23 miles of machined-groomed track and skating lanes to Glacier Point and the Clark Range Vista. Overnight cross-country skiing treks are offered to the Glacier Point Hut. Call (209) 372-1244.

 Curry Village has an outdoor ice-skating rink; snowcat tours and snowshoe walks depart from the Badger Pass Day Lodge. At Crane Flat Campground, there's a designated sledding, tobogganing and inner-tubing hill.

The Yosemite Mountaineering School and Guide Services offers beginner through advanced rock climbing classes from spring through fall. Call (209) 372-1335.

FOR CHILDREN: Within Yosemite, the Happy Isles Nature Center and the Sierra Club's LeConte Memorial feature exhibits and hands-on activities that help children appreciate Yosemite. Each is reachable on the park's shuttle bus.

Each week, park rangers offer special hikes for familes from Happy Isles and White Wolf Lodge. Check the Yosemite Guide for the current schedule. Children 8 through 12 will enjoy participating in the Junior Ranger Program, which meets at Yosemite Valley and Tuolumne Meadows a few mornings a week. Children will also enjoy the role-playing and historical demonstrations at the Pioneer Yosemite History Center at Wawona. In the summer, stage-coach rides are offered daily except Mondays and Tuesdays.

Marriott's Tenaya Lodge operates Camp Tenaya for 5- to 12-year-olds on weekends through the year and daily in the summer. It runs from 9 A.M. to 4 P.M., with an evening session from 6 to 10 P.M. Children should be signed up by 9 P.M. the night before; the camp may be cancelled if fewer than four children are signed up. The fee includes lunch or dinner, and a t-shirt. Children meet in a playroom on the hotel's lower level, but spend much of the time outdoors. They make arts and crafts, square dance, take nature walks in Sierra National Forest, and go on scavenger hunts. In a teepee on the hotel's grounds, they picnic and learn Indian lore. Babysitting can be arranged for younger children.

Near Fish Camp, children will enjoy a ride on The Logger steam train, which travels through Sierra National Forest. Call (209) 683-7273.

NICETIES: To reduce traffic congestion, the park operates free shuttle buses in Yosemite Valley and the Wawona area in the summer.

At both Happy Isles and the Tuolumne Meadows Visitor Center, families can check out an "Explorer Pack," a day pack filled with guide books and suggestions for enhancing their exploration of the park.

Many of the stores in the park rent binoculars for a nominal fee.

FOR MORE INFORMATION: For recorded park information, call (209) 372-0200.

NATIONAL WILDLIFE FEDERATION CONSERVATION SUMMITS
Bellingham, Washington (and other locations)

The National Wildlife Federation Conservation Summits set a standard for family nature vacation/education programs that is close to perfection. The locations are wonderful. The programs are great. And there is something for every member of the family. What more could you ask?

Four summits are scheduled every summer. Each summit is located in an area of great natural beauty, within a distinctive ecosystem. The federation strives for geographical and ecological diversity in its choice of locations. Among the recent summit locations have been the Blue Ridge Mountains in North Carolina; the Rocky Mountains in Colorado; the White Mountains in New Hampshire; the Big Island in Hawaii, and the area around Zion National Park.

These week-long nature retreats offer programs for all age levels—adults, teens, 5- through 12-year-olds, and preschoolers, and even child care for infants through 2. The emphasis in all these programs (except for the youngest) is on discovering nature through outdoor, hands-on, experiential activity. The participants in these programs run the gamut from parents and children, to intergenerational family groupings, to single-parent families, to older couples without children.

Each summit program is built around the ecology of the area in which it's held. Staff members are environmental educators who have expertise in the flora and fauna of that region.

We have taken part in numerous summits. Our observations here are based mainly on our participation in the Northwest Summit in Bellingham, Washington. The basic format of a summit is the same from one location to another.

ACCOMMODATIONS: $$ to $$$$ The National Wildlife Federation uses the facilities of other organizations to house its summits—conference centers, lodges, colleges, or resorts. Therefore, accommodations vary from summit to summit. At all, access to the out-of-doors, basic human comforts, and good value are common denominators. While some are not luxurious, all are well-suited to a week-long family nature adventure. Many have recreational amenities—swimming pools, tennis courts, and even golf courses—that summit participants are free to use in their spare time.

The Northwest Summit used the facilities of Western Washington University, where summit participants were housed in dormitories. In contrast, the White Mountains Summit used the facilities of the grand old Mt. Washington Hotel. A Southeast Summit was held one year at Kiawah Island Resort. A Blue Ridge Mountains Summit was held at the YMCA of the Smokies.

Rates for a National Wildlife Federation Summit are divided into program fees and accommodation fees. Program fees are paid to the National Wildlife Federation. Accommodation fees are paid to the host institution and include meals (children's rates are available). Each family must also buy a family membership in the National Wildlife Federation for a nominal fee.

DINING: Summits use the dining facilities of the host institution. Food is served either buffet-style, cafeteria-style or family style.

Every summit participant, from the youngest to the oldest, receives a brightly colored National Wildlife Federation neckerchief at registration, which serves as the dining room ID card. As the week progresses, participants find ingenious ways to wear their neckerchiefs—as belts, as arm or leg bands, and as headbands.

Box lunches are provided for groups going on daylong field trips.

Often, a special dinner is held on one night. A salmon bake was the highlight of the Northwest Summit.

ACTIVITIES

Each age group has its own summit program. The daily program starts at 8:30 A.M. and ends at 3:15 P.M. Adults design their own program from a catalogue they receive several months before the summit begins.

 Adult activities include lectures, workshops, and outdoor experiences. Among the options at the Northwest Summit were explorations of beach, tide pools, woodlands, both long and short nature hikes in the Cascade Mountains, whale-watching cruises, bird-watching trips, and instruction in nature photography, ecological landscaping, and sharing nature with children.

Late-afternoon and evening programs round out the summit day. Lectures for adults and crafts for all fill the period from 3:30 to 5:30 P.M. At Bellingham, topics included the Northwest coast, whale biology, acid rain, wilderness survival techniques, and the seafood industry.

The entire summit group gathers at 8 P.M. for an evening program—a square dance, a sing-along, and slide programs by nature photographers.

FOR CHILDREN: Children's programs are organized and led by teachers, naturalists, and outdoor educators. All have extensive experience in environmental education for young people.

"Your Big Backyard" is a morning program for 3- and 4-year-olds. Preschoolers develop an appreciation for the natural world through activities that include touch and feel expeditions, short hikes, storytelling, nature crafts, dramatic play, and creative cooking. In a week's time, the program's topics include baby animals and their homes, insects, trees, flowers, mammals, and birds. "Your Big Backyard" ends at noon, when parents pick up their children for lunch. Child care is available from 1 to 5 P.M. for a nominal additional charge.

Five- to 12-year-olds take part in the all-day "Junior Naturalist" program. The group is broken into four clusters by age: 5 and 6, 7 and 8, 9 and 10, and 11- and 12-year-olds. Crafts, games, short discovery hikes, and films are all utilized in the learning experience. But the heart of the "Junior Naturalist" program is field trips. At the Northwest Summit, the "Junior Naturalist" group went on four full-day field trips to nearby state parks and museums—two to beaches and tide pools, one to forests and mountains, and one to a shipyard and fish hatchery. The group studied woodland, beach, tide pool, river, bay, and marsh ecologies. At the end of the day, parents got briefings on crabs, whales, seaweed, rocks, clouds, fishing boats and eagle nests from tired but happy children.

The "Teen Adventure Program" for ages 13 through 17 emphasizes outdoor leadership, group problem solving, and interpersonal skills. Activities may include hiking, photography, orienteering, a ropes course, and nighttime astronomy sessions. Participants are expected to attend all sessions from 8:30 A.M. to 3 P.M. throughout the week. At the Northwest Summit, teens hiked in the mountains, visited the beach and tide pools, and went on a whale-watching cruise.

Children in the "Junior Naturalist" and "Teen Adventure" programs generally eat lunch with their parents, unless the parents are off on their own field trips. After-program care is available for the 5- to 12-year- olds from 3 to 5:30 P.M., which allows parents to participate in all-day programs and afternoon field trips. During the afternoon, children swam, crafted with clay, and learned ballads of the sea.

A baby-sitting service for infants through 2 is available from 8 A.M. to noon and from 1 to 5 P.M. for a nominal fee. Parents provide any supplies—diapers, bottles, snacks—that a child may need.

FOR MORE INFORMATION: Write the National Wildlife Federation, Conservation Summits, 1400 Sixteenth St. N.W., Washington, DC 20036-2266, or call (800) 245-5484.

STRATHCONA PARK LODGE AND OUTDOOR EDUCATION CENTRE
Vancouver Island, British Columbia, Canada

Located deep in the heart of Vancouver Island, this secluded mountain resort is hard to top as a destination for a nature-oriented family vacation. Strathcona Lodge is surrounded by some of the most spectacular recreational land in North America and is just a few miles from the half-million-acre Strathcona Provincial Park, which serves as the venue for many of the lodge's nature activities.

Strathcona Park is largely untouched by humanity, with magnificent snow-capped mountain peaks dominated by the Golden Hinde, the highest point on Vancouver Island at 7,219 feet. The park's valleys are filled with forests of Douglas fir, cedar, and hemlock—trees that were already old in 1778 when Captain James Cook landed at nearby Nootka Sound. Floral displays paint the park from spring through fall, and wildlife abounds. Blue grouse, ruffed grouse, and the rare Vancouver Island white-tailed ptarmigan are found here. Wolves, cougar, and black bear are abundant, but not often seen. The park also has unique mammals like the coastal black-tailed deer, Roosevelt elk, and endangered Vancouver Island marmot.

Staff members at the lodge view themselves as interpreters of the natural world and welcome families as participants in a discovery process. No age limits for participation are set, and single-parent families and large extended families are especially welcome. The programs offer something for everyone who enjoys natural beauty and the excitement of the great outdoors.

ACCOMMODATIONS: $ to $$ The cottages, chalets, rooms, and apartments at Strathcona Park Lodge are beautifully situated on the shore of the 30-mile-long Upper Campbell-Buttle Lake chain. All rooms are modestly, but comfortably furnished, with sweeping views of the lake and mountains. Extended families should inquire about the Seale House, a large chalet that can accommodate up to 20 people; it has eight bedrooms, three decks, a loft, and a kitchen.

Daily or weekly rates are available. Units with kitchens require a two-night minimum stay. Reduced rates are available for children under 12.

Families can book accommodations alone or an all-inclusive package that provides for meals, equipment, participation in outdoor programs, and instruction in outdoor activities.

DINING: Guests from all over the world converge at mealtimes in The Whale Room. The atmosphere is friendly, casual, and informal. Delicious home-cooked meals are served buffet-style. Nutrition is emphasized, and vegetarian entrées are available, often featuring fresh vegetables and herbs from the lodge's own gardens.

For adults, intimate dining with personal service and "Heart Smart" cooking is available in the Hi-Bracer Lounge during the summer.

ACTIVITIES

 In a protected area in the sparkling lake.

 The canoes, kayaks, sailboats, and motorboats at the lodge can be rented by the hour or day.

 Rainbow and cutthroat trout fishing in the lodge's lakes from mid-April until mid-October; guides available. Steelhead fishing year-round in the nearby Gold and Campbell rivers, summer salmon fishing in the Pacific Ocean.

 Families can participate in outdoor, nature and adventure programs as part of a pre-arranged package, or simply sign up on a daily basis. Activities include kayaking, canoeing, sailing, rockclimbing, ropes course initiatives and nature walks.

The six-day "Family Adventure" package, offered twice each summer, allows parents and young children to share outdoor experiences together. Canoeing, sailing, nature hikes, and a ropes course provide the active moments, and nightly campfires provide the quiet times.

The "Best of Adventure" program includes daily introductions to outdoor adventure activities, such as kayaking, rockclimbing, and the ropes courses, throughout the summer, with sailing each evening.

The "Grandparent-Grandchild" program is immensely popular. This inventive program includes shared activities like canoeing, hiking, and nature studies, as well as an optional overnight camping experience.

The "Explore Central Vancouver Island and Nootka Sound" package, beginning each Sunday in July and August, is suitable for families.

Outstanding slide and video presentations are offered on summer evenings.

FOR CHILDREN: Children from about age 8 and up can join with their parents in all program activities, according to their interests and abilities. Younger children will enjoy playing and swimming at the beach, or taking nature walks or canoe trips with their parents.

Older children can be enrolled, for a fee, in a Wilderness Youth Leadership Development (WYLD) summer program. Youth Camps are divided by ages—Adventure Camp for 10- and

11-year-olds, Youth Leadership Camp for 12- and 13-year-olds, WYLD Expeditions for 14- to 16-year-olds, and Senior Youth Advanced Skills Training for 16- to 18-year-olds. Special rock-climbing, sailing, kayaking and mountain travel camps are also offered. You must book your children in a youth camp in advance.

Baby-sitting can be arranged at the office the evening before it is needed.

NICETIES: Coffee and tea pots are on in the dining room throughout the day.

Camping equipment and some other outdoor gear can be rented at the lodge.

OF INTEREST NEARBY: Young children will enjoy a visit to the adventure playground and sand beach at nearby Buttle Lake Campground in Strathcona Park.

The town of Campbell River is renowned for its salmon and trout fishing. Families can book a boat and guide for a day's fishing or fish off the new Discovery Pier. The 600-foot-long pier is open 24 hours a day and has built-in rod holders, bait stands, fish-cleaning tables, and benches. You can rent all the equipment you need for a day of family fishing; be sure to sample the pier's famous ice cream cones.

The Campbell River Museum and Archives moved into a new building in the spring of 1994. High-caliber traveling exhibits are being presented while the permanent collection is developed. The foyer area offers panoramic views of Discovery Passage and Quadra Island.

Quinsam River Salmon Hatchery is near Campbell River. Take its self-guided tour and explore its nature trails. Picnic facilities are available here.

The Kwakiutl Museum in the Cape Mudge Indian Village on Quadra Island, a 30-minute ferry ride from Campbell River, has a fine collection of Native American artifacts. Potlatch regalia, tribal masks, and costumes recently returned to the Kwakiutl people after 55 years in the National Museum of Man in Ottawa.

The small community of Gold River, west of Strathcona Park, is in a popular caving area and is the point of embarkation for day cruises to the rugged west coast of Vancouver Island aboard the *m.v. Uchuck III*. The boats visits Friendly Cove, a native village site with a standing totem pole and polished pebble beaches.

FOR MORE INFORMATION: Write Strathcona Park Lodge, Box 2160, Campbell River, BC, Canada V9W 5C9, or call (604) 286-8206; FAX: (604) 286-6010.

OLYMPIC NATIONAL PARK
Port Angeles, Washington

You don't have to go all the way to Central America to teach your children about rain forests. Olympic National Park protects the continental United States' largest and finest temperate rain forest. Because of its uniqueness, the park has been designated a Biosphere Reserve and World Heritage Site. A vacation here is a wonderful way to introduce children to an environment unlike any they've ever experienced before.

Walking along a moss-carpeted path through a forest of towering 700-year-old Douglas firs as a fine mist moistens your face is an experience you'll never forget. You'll see Sitka spruce and western hemlock trees that reach nearly 300 feet in height and 23 feet in circumference, as well as hundreds of fallen giants that serve as "nurseries" for new seedlings. The carpeting of moss and lichen and the epiphytes that seem to hang from every branch give the forest an eerie feeling. The 145 inches of rain each year ensure that everything stays green.

But Olympic National Park offers more than just rain forest. It actually includes three distinctive ecosystems: the rainforest, the scenic ocean strip (the longest stretch of wilderness beach in the continental United States), and the rugged, glacier-clad mountainous core, dominated by Mt. Olympus, with a peak nearly 8,000 feet above sea level. Each of its sections is a wonderful place for exploration and learning.

ACCOMMODATIONS: $ to $$$ The park has about 900 campsites in 18 campgrounds; all sites are available on a first-come, first-served basis (groups may make reservations at the Kalaloch and Mora sites). Toilets, fresh water, picnic tables, and grills are provided at all campgrounds, but none has showers, laundries, or utility connections. Backcountry camping is allowed with a permit.

Olympic also has two wonderful hotel/cabin resorts—Lake Crescent Lodge and Kalaloch Lodge, and two motels—Log Cabin Resort, on the northeast end of Lake Crescent, and Sol

Duc Hot Springs Resort, in the Sol Duc River Valley 40 miles west of Port Angeles. In addition, there's another grand old lodge, Lake Quinault Lodge, just a few hundred yards outside the park's southern boundary in the Olympic National Forest.

Lake Crescent Lodge (206-928-3211), open from late April through late October, has 42 motel and cottage units and lodge rooms, some with fireplaces, along the beautiful shore of Lake Crescent at the foot of Storm King Mountain. The main building was built in 1916 and retains the charm of yesteryear, with its lobby furnished with mission oak furniture and dominated by a huge stone fireplace.

Sol Duc Hot Springs Resort (206-327-3583), open from mid May through early October, offers campsites and lodgings in 32 cabins, some with kitchens. The main lures here are the three large hot mineral pools and the heated outdoor swiming pool.

Log Cabin Resort (206-928-3325), open late May through early October, has 28 motel units, cabins, chalets, and camping log cabins (you supply our own linens) secluded among old firs and cedars on the sunny side of Lake Crescent.

Kalaloch Lodge (206-962-2271), the only lodging that's open year-round, occupies a spectacular site on a bluff overlooking the Pacific. The beach below is littered with pieces of driftwood that look like beached whales. At low tide, hundreds of shore-birds come to feed in the intertidal zone. The lodge offers accommodations in the main building, motel rooms in the detached Sea Crest House, and cozy log cabins with one or two bedrooms (with brass beds), woodburning stoves, and complete kitchens.

Lake Quinault Lodge (206-228-2571) is a charming old-fash-ioned lodge (augmented by a new wing) in a beautiful lakefront setting next to a rainforest. It is well-situated for exploring the park's southern end.

DINING: Lake Crescent, Kalaloch, Lake Quinault, Sol Duc Hot Springs, and the Log Cabin Resort have lovely dining rooms that emphasize regional cooking. Kalaloch has a separate coffee shop as well, and Sol Duc Hot Springs has a poolside deli.

General stores near each of the resorts sell groceries and housekeeping supplies.

ACTIVITIES

 Heated outdoor pool at Sol Duc Hot Springs Resort; heated indoor pool at Lake Quinault Lodge. Swimming in the Pacific Ocean at Kalaloch and Ruby beaches, north of Queets (watch for dangerous riptides and drifting logs) and in Lake Crescent and Lake Quinault.

 Rental fishing boats, paddleboats, and canoes at the lake resorts and Fairholm Visitor Service Area.

 For salmon, trout, and char, in season. No license required, but a state punchcard must be obtained to fish for steelhead and salmon. Clamming at Kalaloch Lodge; rental shovels available.

 The park offers naturalist programs from July to September at several locations around the park; Kalaloch, Hurricane Ridge and Hoh have the most. Among the offerings: guided beach or coastal walks, meadow explorations, walks through the rain forest, and campfire programs. In addition, the park has many self-guided nature trails. Pick up maps at the Port Angeles Olympic Park Visitor Center, 3002 Mt. Angeles Rd., on the south side of Port Angeles; the center features an interesting slide show, museum displays, a small nature trail, and a discovery room for children.

The Hoh Visitor Center also has informative displays and is the starting-off point for several self-guided trails. The Hurricane Ridge Visitors Center offers sweeping views of Mt. Olympus and the Strait of Juan de Fuca; there's a slide show every 30 minutes and informative exhibits. Among the things you'll learn is that the park provides shelter for about 5,000 Roosevelt elk and smaller mammals including blacktail deer, cougars, river otters, and jumping mice.

For visitors who want more depth to their experience, the Olympic Park Institute (206-938-3720) offers several dozen seminars, multi-day family outings and Elderhostels each year. Among the topics: the aquatic ecology of the Olympics, ecology of the ancient forest, whale watching hikes, the world of salmon, cedar bark basketry, sharing the joy of nature, and the myths and legends of the Northwest.

FOR CHILDREN: Older children will enjoy the evening programs at the larger campgrounds. Typical topics are "The Coastal Forest from a Slug's Eye" and "Tidepools: Holding on Tight." The daily tidepool walks at Mora and Kalaloch are a big hit with kids of any age. Special children's activities are offered throughout the summer.

Children can qualify as Junior Rangers by completing the activity sections in the park's activities guide, collecting and turning in a bag of litter, going for a nature walk with their families, and attending a ranger program.

The Olympic Park Institute offers some field seminars in which families are welcome. "Peter Puget Voyage" is a five-day voyage of south Puget Sound on replica longboats, with camping at night. "Puget Sound Discovery" is a weekend trip on a long-boat replica. Seashore Safari" is a weekend-long exploration of the shore, using games, crafts, dramatics, and creative activities to teach children about life at water's edge. "Making Sense of the Night Sky," offered three times each summer, teaches families about the phenomena and lore of the night sky.

FOR MORE INFORMATION: Write the Superintendent, Olympic National Park, 600 East Park Ave., Port Angeles, WA 98362 or call (206) 452-0330. Request general travel information from Olympic Peninsula Travel Association, P.O. Box 625, Port Angeles, WA 98362.

HAWAII VOLCANOES NATIONAL PARK
Volcano Village, Hawaii

On Super Bowl Sunday a few years ago, one of us found ourselves driving up Hawaii Highway 11 in the company of a very unhappy 9-year-old boy. "I can't believe I have a mother who was dumb enough to book us into a hotel without televisions on Super Bowl Sunday," he said as he twirled the tuner on the car radio in an unsuccessful attempt to find a broadcast of the game.

The complaining continued the whole 30 miles up the road to Hawaii Volcanoes National Park—until we pulled into a parking lot at the edge of the Kilauea Crater. "Awesome," he said, as he gazed out over the world's most active volcano, with a caldera 10 miles in circumference and, in some places, a depth of 1,300 feet.

He never said another word about the Super Bowl. Such is the power of a volcano to engage the imagination of a child.

Even in a state renowned for its diverse natural attributes and a country with a distinguished national park system, Hawaii Volcanoes National Park stands out. This is not just some stuffy, outdated museum with exhibits on what causes volcanoes. This is the real thing.

ACCOMMODATIONS: $ to $$ The Volcano House may be the only hotel in the world perched on the rim of a volcanic crater. The absence of TVs in the guest rooms isn't the only thing that makes it seem part of a bygone era. As they did in the previous century when the current lodge's predecessor still stood, guests gather each evening in the parlow in front of the massive lava-stoned fireplace to talk about what they did that day. It's the kind of place where you expect to run into Graham Greene.

Rooms are comfortable, but not in the least luxurious. The main building offers some crater views; the Ohia Wing is funkier and less expensive. We liked the Ohia Wing because it had its own library and sitting room, furnished with chairs and couches made out of highly polished koa wood.

The hotel also manages some barebones cabins in a koa and eucalyptus forest at the Namakani Paio Campground, three miles away. For all accommodations, call Volcano House at (808) 967-7321.

Just down the road from Volcano House is a charming smaller inn, Kilauea Lodge and Restaurant, which is suitable for families with older (and quieter) children. The moderate rate includes breakfast. Call (808) 967-7366.

Families with an active, reserve or retired military person among their members can book inexpensive accommodations at the Kilauea Military Camp, one mile from the park. Guests have golfing privileges at the Volcano Golf & Country Club. Call (808) 967-8333.

DINING: At Volcano House, three meals a day are served in the lovely Ka Ohelo dining room, with tables overlooking the crater. The Hawaiian dishes are the highlights on the menu. At breakfast, the 'ohelo berry-topped pancakes are a must. At any meal, you can have all the Kona coffee you can drink.

The nearby Kilauea Lodge and Restaurant serves superb meals in front of a fireplace.

ACTIVITIES

 Over 150 miles of trails that take you through both rain forests and across rock-hard lava beds that resemble moonscapes. A mile-long trail leads from Chain of Craters Road to Pu'u Loa, which, with 15,000 carvings, constitutes the largest concentration of prehistoric petroglyphs in Hawaii. Well into the 19th Century, Hawaiians carved cup-like holes in the lava flows to serve as repositories for the umbilical cords of new-born babies. The one-fifth-mile long trail to the edge of Halemaumau Crater takes you to the legendary home of Pele, Goddess of Hawaiian volcanies. Pilgrims still leave gifts of ti leaves, flowers and vegetables on the rim to assure their good fortune.

Ranger-led hikes and slide presentations. The park Visitor Center has exhibits, models and maps, and shows color films of recent eruptions. At the Hawaiian Volcano Observatory, there are exhibits on volcano monitoring.

For an update on eruptions (no kidding), call (808) 967-7977. A recent message said, "Aloha. Kilaue continues to erupt, and lava is entering the ocean at the end of Chain of Craters Road. A steam cloud blasts skyward where lava enters the sea 200 yards from the road's end. The steam cloud may obscure the view of lava entering the ocean. At night, the steam cloud blows off-shore, often revealing spectacular visions of the lava entering the sea."

At Volcano House, the bar is a lively place in the late after-noon and early evening.

With proper provisions and conditioning, you can climb Mauna Loa, the second highest active volcano in the world. The trail starts in a parking lot at 6,600 feet eleva-tion, and climbs eight miles—and 7,000 feet—to the Moku'aweoweo Crater. There are cabins at 10,000 feet and the summit, which sleep 9 and 11 respectively, and have water catchment devices and pit toilets. Allow three or four days for the whole trip.

FOR CHILDREN: Volcanoes National Park is totally captivating for children. Even if your child is the type of child who demands a ride to a friend's house a block and a half away, he'll look forward to hiking here. Somehow a hike seems more appealing if the terrain is volcanic rock and there are signs warning you that "cliff edges and temporary platforms created by flowing lava may collapse at any time."

Children will especially like the short walk through the cool, subterranean Thurston Lava Tube, formed when an outer crust of lava hardened and the hot magna continued to rush through. And the walk from the end of 25-mile-long Chain of Craters Road, where the Wiha'ula Visitor Center stood until the 1989 eruption of Kilauea knocked it off its foundation, is certain to be a child-pleaser. You cross hundreds of acres of lava beds. Along the way you pass the ruins of Waha'ula Heiau, the Temple of the Red Mouth, which dates from about 1250 A.D. Take along a picnic lunch to eat on the volcanic cliffs overlooking the Pacific, where you can watch the surf crash on to black sand beaches.

OF INTEREST NEARBY: The island of Hawaii—or the Big Island, as it is sometimes called—may be the most ecologically diverse of the Hawaiian islands. You could happily spend a week here and not see it all.

The island is dominated by five volcanic mountains (two of them still active). And its beaches—particularly those at Kailua-Kona and along the Kohala coast—are superb. In recent years, numerous luxury hotels have risen up on them.

Waimea is ranch country, headquarters of the famed Parker Ranch, which has a visitor center in Kamuela.

The Waipio Valley is a fascininating site for a day trip. You can ride a four-wheel drive vehicle down a treacherous mountain road to the six-mile-long valley, one of the last outposts of Hawaii's taro farmers. It's an interesting slice of Hawaiian life.

Between Waipio Valley and Hilo, Akaka Falls State Park is worth a visit. It's the site of the longest unbroken waterfall in the state.

FOR MORE INFORMATION: Write the Superintendent, Hawaii Volcanoes National Park, Box 52, Hawaii 96718 or call (808) 967-7311.

CAMP DENALI
NORTH FACE LODGE
Denali National Park, Alaska

For families visiting the 49th state, Denali National Park demands a stop. Not only is it the site of Mt. McKinley, the highest mountain peak in North America, but it is also the wilderness home of over 35 species of mammals, including grizzly bears, moose, caribou, white mountain sheep, and wolves. Bird life and wildflowers abound in the summer months. The park is as big as Massachusetts, but only one major road penetrates its heart.

Most Denali National Park visitors stay for one or two nights at one of the major hotels near the park entrance. But McKinley cannot be seen from the park entrance, and private vehicle use of the Denali road is limited. Visitors who want more than a short taste of this unique national park will want to stay at Camp Denali or North Face Lodge, a family-operated vacation retreat in the heart of the Denali wilderness.

Camp Denali and North Face Lodge are Denali National Park's best-kept secrets. In the center of the park with spectacular views of majestic Mt. McKinley and surrounding peaks, they specialize in naturalist-led hikes to learn about the park's natural history. The Cole family began Camp Denali as a rustic tent camp in 1951, and acquired nearby North Face Lodge, a former motel, in the late '80s.

Camp Denali staff meet guests at the Alaska Railroad depot at the Park entrance for the start of an unforgettable five-hour, 180-mile journey by bus into the center of one of America's great wilderness preserves. The gravel road passes over wooded glacial stream valleys and mountain passes of Alpine tundra. The driver-naturalist gives pointers on spotting animals in the spruce forest and on the tundra slope.

The excitement mounts with each discovery: a cow moose and her newborn calf, half hidden in a dense willow thicket; a group of five bull caribou with this season's antlers partly grown, grazing on a tundra ridge; a band of 20 white mountain ewes and frolicking lambs on a precipitous rocky outcropping; a blond grizzly bear digging for roots on a gravel bar. Your own camera and binoculars are put to use continually. The driver stops frequently to set up a 20-power spotting scope on a tripod for more distant sightings.

Those who seek in-depth nature experiences in the company of kindred souls will not be disappointed here.

ACCOMMODATIONS: $$$$ At Camp Denali, accommodations are comfortable, but basic. Individual log and frame cabins each have a private view of the Alaska Range and Mt. McKinley. Cabins have propane lights, small wood stoves, and a private outhouse; handmade calico quilts make them feel cozy. The main buildings, which include the lodge living room, the dining room, and the central shower and toilet facility, are a three- to seven-minute walk away.

North Face Lodge is about a mile away from Camp Denali on a tundra meadow at 1,700 feet above sea level. It has its own living room, kitchen and dining room, and its own program of activities. Accommodations are in 15 modern, twin-bedded guest rooms, with private baths and central heating.

All meals, transportation, and activities are included in the rates. The minimum stay is three nights; children's rates are available. Families receive a 10 percent discount if three or more family members occupy the same cabin.

If you prefer to cook your own meals, you can reserve one or two of the Hawk's Nest cabins, at much lower rates than Camp Denali or North Face Lodge. But you must bring your own provisions, and the staff prefers that you bring your own car. Guided activities and recreational equipment are not included in the rate.

The short season at Camp Denali, early June to early September, necessitates fixed arrival and departure dates.

DINING: Breakfast follows a 7 A.M. wake-up call sounded by a triangle at the corner of the Potlatch Dining Room. The day starts right with Camp Denali's seven-grain hot cereal, sourdough hotcakes with lingonberry syrup, sausage quiche, or croissants and rhubarb jam.

With the wide variety of outdoor activities at Denali, lunches are usually taken on the trail. After breakfast each guest constructs his or her own sack lunch from the smorgasbord of homemade baked breads and sweets, sandwich fillings, fresh fruit, greenhouse-grown lettuce, and trail mix.

Dinner is served family style with guests and staff intermingled at tables of 12. Dinner menus include Alaskan halibut, chicken filo, and such energy-replenishing desserts as home-baked pies and cakes and chocolate mousse.

ACTIVITIES

 Canoeing at two and a half mile-long Wonder Lake nearby. After a rainy day, nearby Moose Creek may be high enough for a guided raft trip.

The camp's mountain bikes can be put atop one of the buses. Your family's endurance determines the distance traveled before the staff drops you at the start of your bike trip back to the lodge. The roads are largely empty of traffic, with only the park's shuttle buses to dodge. You're more likely to see a caribou on the road than a car.

Organized walks. Each day's schedule offers new opportunities to explore nature on hikes of varying difficulty. For instance, one of the naturalist-guides might lead a hike up the 1,500-foot, wildflower-carpeted alpine ridge line behind the lodge. Mt. McKinley and its snow-clad neighbors dominate the view during the entire hike. A half-day outing toward Wonder Lake by bus and foot is designed for those keen to see mammals and birds.

After dinner each evening, the camp staff presides over slide shows, films, and discussions. The topics range from mountaineering on Mt. McKinley, to loons, to the reminiscences of a staff couple about a winter in the Alaskan bush. On the final evening of your stay, Wally Cole, the co-owner, sums it all up with his slide show, "Moods of Denali."

The highlight of your stay may be a one and a half hour flight around Mt. McKinley in a light plane. The Coles arrange flights from the nearby Kantishna airstrip with local bush pilots. Another world is visible from the windows of these planes—a world of jagged peaks, highways of glacial ice, perhaps a group of climbers attempting to scale North America's highest mountain.

FOR CHILDREN: There are no specific programs for younger children, and no baby-sitting services are available. But children over 8 with the stamina for moderate hiking, an interest in nature, and the capability to share a wilderness learning experience are welcome here.

Panning for gold is a favorite activity with children. Patient staff members instruct in the methods the old-time miners used, and guests invariably find flakes of gold in the cold mountain streams.

NICETIES: The Coles and their staff treat you and your family as welcome houseguests, not paying guests. At the end of a one-week stay you'll find that you've become as attached to the people and meaning of this place as you were to the summer camp you attended as a child. The kitchen crew fills cards with recipes, and staff and guests exchange addresses and farewell hugs.

There's a storeroom full of things you may have forgotten, like day packs, rainwear, waterproof boots, boot grease, and fishing tackle.

The living room/library is a retreat for reading and relaxing.

FOR MORE INFORMATION: From late May to early September write Camp Denali/North Face Lodge, P.O. Box 67, Denali National Park, AK 99755, or call (907) 683-2290. From early September to late May write Camp Denali, Box 216, Cornish, NH 03740 or call (603) 675-2248.

VIRGIN ISLANDS NATIONAL PARK
St. John, U.S. Virgin Islands

St. John is unique among Carribean islands in that more than half its 45-square-mile land mass and most of its shoreline waters are protected by a national park. The island's natural resources are without peer in the Caribbean.

The climb to any ridgetop is rewarded with a vista of green islands and blue waters. Along the way you are certain to see many of the island's 100-plus species of birds, and even some feral cats, mongoose, wild donkeys, or goats.

Some hiking trails follow numerous old Danish plantation roads past the ruins of sugar cane factories, whose cane presses were powered by windmills when the colonial Danes made sugar here in the 18th century. Others lead you to an area where you can see old petroglyphs.

Superb beaches, many of them deserted and pristine, are the major attraction for families. Trunk Bay has one of the world's best beaches and offers an underwater nature trail just off shore for snorkelers.

ACCOMMODATIONS: $** to **$$$ Maho Bay Camps (phone 800-392-9004), our favorite destination on St. John, sits in glorious isolation in the northwest quadrant of the island, surrounded on three sides by national park land. It has been called "a resort with an ethic" because of its owner's determination to show that it is possible to live in a fragile environment without spoiling it.

At Maho Bay, guests stay in 116 tent-cottages set on a lush tropical hillside overlooking the bay. The tent-cottages are built on stilts, surrounded by trees and within sight of only a few other cottages. Each tent-cottage is linked to the registration desk, store, dining pavilion, and toilet blocks by raised board-walks.

The tent-cottage floor plan is simple but functional—a sleeping alcove with twin beds, a small combination kitchen-dining area with a trundle-couch suitable for two children, and a private deck. Each tent-cottage has electricity and is outfitted with cooking and eating equipment; cooking is on propane stoves, and food is kept cool in ice chests. Water is stored in a five-gallon plastic container. Toilet blocks have flush toilets and lukewarm showers.

Two newer resorts operated by Mahor Bay offer more luxurious accommodations, though they're still environmentally friendly. Harmony offers eight spacious dwelling units that feature the latest techniques in conservation and site restoration; electricity is generated solely by sun and wind power. The "lumber" from which the units were crafted is actually made from discarded plastic and tile.

Estate Concordia, 25 minutes from Maho Bay, is a 10-unit lodge that looks out on Salt Pond Bay and Ram Head. The island's best snorkeling, shelling and hiking are found here, and there's a hillside swimming pool.

Cinnamon Bay Campground, operated within the national park by a concessioner, offers bare sites for tent campers, sites with tents already erected, and very basic beach cottages. Call (800) 223-7637 for reservations.

The most family-friendly luxury hotel on the island is the Hyatt Regency St. John Resort. Its 285 air-conditioned rooms, suites and townhouses look out over a 1,200-foot white sand beach and Great Cruz Bay. It has a quarter-acre fresh-water swimming pool, six lighted tennis courts, and four restaurants set amidst 34 acres of tropical gardens. Call (800) 233-1234 or (809) 693-8000.

DINING: At Maho Bay, the open-air restaurant serves buffet breakfasts and dinners, but no lunches. Dinners feature two main entrees, one of which is almost always vegetarian. The food here is ample, delicious, and healthful. You can eat lunch in your cottage or take a picnic to the beach.

At Cinnamon Bay, a cafeteria offers dining on an outdoor terrace.

The camp stores at Maho Bay and Cinnamon Bay stock cooking essentials—staples, canned and dried foods, dairy products, bread, frozen meats, some fresh vegetables, juice, soda, beer, and wine. Almost all food is imported from the mainland, which is reflected in its price.

At the Hyatt Regency St. John, Ciao Mein specializes in oriental and Italian specialties. The casual Cafe Grand, overlooking the beach, serves breakfast and dinner, as well as some themed dinner buffets.

The town of Cruz Bay has a wide selection of restaurants specializing in seafood and West Indian cooking.

ACTIVITIES

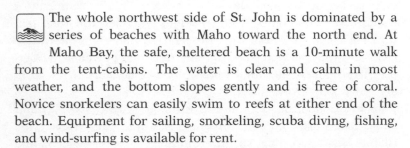

The whole northwest side of St. John is dominated by a series of beaches with Maho toward the north end. At Maho Bay, the safe, sheltered beach is a 10-minute walk from the tent-cabins. The water is clear and calm in most weather, and the bottom slopes gently and is free of coral. Novice snorkelers can easily swim to reefs at either end of the beach. Equipment for sailing, snorkeling, scuba diving, fishing, and wind-surfing is available for rent.

Maho Bay rents sunfish, sea kayaks, wind surfers and snorkeling equipment. The Maho Bay staff can arrange a variety of boat trips, scuba diving expeditions, and snorkeling adventures. There's a complete watersports program at the Hyatt, as well.

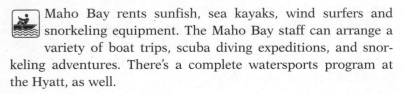

At Maho Bay, Hamilton Eugene does an excellent job of relating the island's history and folklore and introducing you to its natural beauty. His island tour is scheduled several times a week.

The national park offers tours and lecture programs on the flora, fauna, and history of St. John. Park rangers also lead snorkel trips along the underwater trail in Cinnamon Bay and organize several adventure hikes each week. Other park programs focus on the ecology and history of the island.

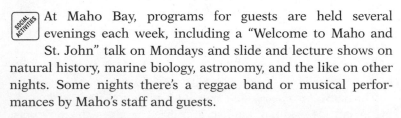

At Maho Bay, programs for guests are held several evenings each week, including a "Welcome to Maho and St. John" talk on Mondays and slide and lecture shows on natural history, marine biology, astronomy, and the like on other nights. Some nights there's a reggae band or musical performances by Maho's staff and guests.

FOR CHILDREN: Maho Bay has no special programs for children, and children under 4 are discouraged. But for older children, staying here is a terrific adventure. Birds continually swoop through the branches and land just a few yards away. Hermit crabs and lizards skitter through the leaf litter on the forest floor.

At the Hyatt, Camp Hyatt, a supervised program for 3- to 11-year-olds, is offered year-round for a nominal charge, as is Rock Hyatt, an adventure, sports and social program for teens.

Children will enjoy many of the ranger programs at the national park.

NICETIES: At Maho Bay, departing guests leave leftover food in the "Help Yourself Center," which makes it easy for arriving guests to get a start on provisioning their cottages. The "Help Yourself Center" also has books and games for borrowing.

OF INTEREST NEARBY: Hawksnest Bay is a good place to introduce children to snorkeling. Zillions of colorful fish dart in and out of the elkhorn coral in water shallow enough to be non-threatening.

The Annaberg Sugar Refinery makes an interesting excursion. Children can learn about how sugar can is processed and watch islanders demonstrate local basket-making, cooking, and gardening techniques.

FOR MORE INFORMATION: Write the Superintendent, Virgin Islands National Park, P.O. Box 7789, St. Thomas, U.S. Virgin Islands 00801.

INDEX

GEOGRAPHICAL INDEX